M000158816

The Politics of Knowledge in Premodern Islam

Islamic Civilization and Muslim Networks

Carl W. Ernst and Bruce B. Lawrence, editors

The Politics of Knowledge in Premodern Islam

Negotiating Ideology and Religious Inquiry

by

Omid Safi

The University of North Carolina Press

Chapel Hill

Set in Monotype Garamond
by Tseng Information Systems, Inc.
Manufactured in the United States of America

The publication of this book was supported by a subvention
from the Colgate University Research Council.

The paper in this book meets the guidelines for permanence
and durability of the Committee on Production Guidelines for
Book Longevity of the Council on Library Resources.

Library of Congress Cataloging-in-Publication Data

Safi, Omid, 1970–
The politics of knowledge in premodern Islam : negotiating ideology
and religious inquiry / by Omid Safi.
p. cm. — (Islamic civilization and Muslim networks)
Includes bibliographical references and index.
ISBN 0-8078-2993-5 (cloth : alk. paper)
ISBN 0-8078-5657-6 (pbk. : alk. paper)
1. Seljuks—History. 2. Islamic Empire—Politics and government.
I. Title. II. Islamic civilization & Muslim networks.
DS27.S25 2006
956.1'014—dc22 2005052886
10 09 08 07 06 5 4 3 2 1

ʿishq ast dar āsmān parīdan

"Look! This is love . . .
to leap towards the heavens."

*Dedicated to my mother and father,
who taught me to leap heavenward,*

to my wife, who was there waiting for me,

to my children, who carried me.

Contents

Map and Illustrations

Foreword

The Politics of Knowledge in Premodern Islam: Negotiating Ideology and Religious Inquiry is the fourth volume to be published in our series, Islamic Civilization and Muslim Networks.

Why make Islamic civilization and Muslim networks the theme of a new series? The study of Islam and Muslim societies is often marred by an overly fractured approach that frames Islam as the polar opposite of what "Westerners" are supposed to represent and advocate. Islam has been objectified as the obverse of the Euro-American societies that self-identify as "the West." Political and economic trends have reinforced a habit of localizing Islam in the "volatile" Middle Eastern region. Marked as dangerous foreigners, Muslims are also demonized as regressive outsiders who reject modernity. The negative accent in media headlines about Islam creates a common tendency to refer to Islam and Muslims as being somewhere "over there," in another space and another mind-set from the so-called rational, progressive, democratic West.

Ground-level facts tell another story. The social reality of Muslim cultures extends beyond the Middle East. It includes South and Southeast Asia, Africa, and China. It also includes the millennial presence of Islam in Europe and the increasingly significant American Muslim community. In different places and eras, it is Islam that has been the pioneer of reason, Muslims who have been the standard-bearers of progress. Muslims remain integral to "our" world; they are inseparable from the issues and conflicts of transregional, panoptic world history.

By itself, the concept of Islamic civilization serves as a useful counterweight to that of Western civilization, undermining the triumphalist framing of history that was reinforced first by colonial empires and then by the Cold War. Yet when the study of Islamic civilization is combined with that of Muslim networks, their very conjunction breaks the mold of both classical Orientalism and Cold War area studies. The combined rubric allows no discipline to stand by itself; all disciplines converge to make possible a refashioning of the Muslim past and a reimagining of the Muslim future. Islam escapes the timeless warp of textual norms; the additional perspectives of social sciences and modern technology forge a new hermeneutical strategy that marks ruptures as well as continuities, local influences as well as cosmopolitan accents. The twin goals of the publication series in which this volume of essays appears are (1) to locate Islam in multiple pasts across several geo-linguistic, sociocultural frontiers, and (2) to open up a new kind of interaction between humanists and social scientists who engage contemporary Muslim societies. Networking between disciplines and breaking down discredited stereotypes will foster fresh interpretations of Islam that make possible research into uncharted subjects, including discrete regions, issues, and collectivities.

Because Muslim networks have been understudied, they have also been undervalued. Our accent is on the value to the study of Islamic civilization of understanding Muslim networks. Muslim networks inform both the span and the function of Islamic civilization, while Islamic civilization provides the frame that makes Muslim networks more than mere ethnic and linguistic subgroups of competing political and commercial empires. Through this broad-gauged book series, we propose to explore the dynamic past, but also to imagine an elusive future, both of them marked by Muslim networks. Muslim networks are like other networks: they count across time and place because they sustain all the mechanisms—economic and social, religious and political—that characterize civilization. Yet insofar as they are Muslim networks, they project and illumine the distinctive nature of Islamic civilization.

We want to make Muslim networks as visible as they are influential for the shaping and reshaping of Islamic civilization.

Carl W. Ernst
Bruce B. Lawrence
Series editors

Acknowledgments

After the ten years of research it has taken to bring this project to fruition, these are a few lines that I have looked forward to writing.

The last few years of this project have overlapped with the birth of my precious girl, Roya, and my adorable son, Amir. It should not come as a total surprise that many of the metaphors that come to my mind about this project involve the painful yet joyous process of giving birth.

This project has benefited from three "midwives," who have each contributed something unique to its delivery. I am grateful to Dr. Vincent Cornell, who has been for me something that was once thought to be extinct: an everyday mentor. Without his guidance, I would not have been in this field in the first place, nor would I have survived the long and treacherous journey. I am indebted to Dr. Bruce Lawrence, whose brilliant insights have inspired me at every turn. He has challenged me to rise to my full potential, and without that presence this project would have been much more conventional, and far less daring. In Dr. Carl Ernst I have been fortunate to find a gentle scholar of impeccable scholarship. His close attention to the nuance of texts and theoretical frameworks for the study of religion continues to serve as a model for me.

I am also thankful to other scholars from Duke who have provided me with the tools I have needed to complete this project. Rkia Cornell has shown the patience of a saint in training me to read through Arabic Sufi texts. Kathy Ewing has aided me in incorporating anthropological insights. Bill Hart has cured my critical-theory phobia.

I have benefited from my association with scholars from a number of other institutions, who have also offered me support. The support of Ahmet Karamustafa, Jamal Elias, E. Sara Wolper, Alan Godlas, Shahzad Bashir, Ebrahim Moosa, Frank Lewis, Shahab Ahmed, Anna Gade, Qamar ul-Huda, and Carolyn Fleur-Lobban has allowed me to get through many a dark night. Hamid Algar shared with me his insightful comments on Saljūq intellectual figures and opened my eyes to the necessity of situating ʿulamāʾ and Sufis in their historical context. His close attention to primary sources has motivated me in a way that perhaps is best reflected in the more than one thousand footnotes in this project. Michael Sells continues to encourage me in believing that it is indeed possible to teach in an intimate liberal arts college (with heavy teaching demands) and still produce meticulous scholarship. His friendship and mentorship are deeply treasured. Nasrollah Pourjavady has reached back through the centuries and re-embodied Aḥmad Ghazālī for me. How I have marveled at his command of Sufi texts and his *dhawq*.

One of the most cherished aspects of my training has been the opportunity to share a sense of fellowship with other students in the Islam Studies program at Duke. These friends are more than merely colleagues, they are companions of the heart: Scott Kugle, Zia Inayat Khan, Rick Colby, Rick Collier, Robert Rozehnal, Seemi Ghazi, John Lamoreaux, Kecia Ali, Hugh Talat Halman, and Jamillah Karim.

I am grateful to my students over the years. I had the great privilege of teaching at Meredith College and Duke University, before taking my current position as an associate professor of philosophy and religion at Colgate University. The opportunity of sharing my ongoing research with them has been perpetually rewarding. Teaching at a liberal arts college allows one the great joy of working closely with students in relationships that transcend the conventional professor-student hierarchy. I am particularly indebted to Nicole Baker, Matthew Hotham, Khatera Abdulwali, Brianne Goodman, Tushar Irani, Alexis Gewertz, Natalie Jarudi, Ilyse Morgenstein, and Ali Mitnick. Matt and Khatera proved their ultimate loyalty by reading through various drafts of this manuscript and making invaluable suggestions. Blessed is the teacher who is surrounded by such luminous souls.

My research on this project has been dependent on a whole host of primary sources, most of them unavailable at the libraries of Duke University and Colgate University. Without the almost daily assistance of the interlibrary loan staff of both universities, this project would simply not have materialized. When I call them my "ILL angels," they may not realize how heartfelt those words truly are. Ellie Bolland and Ann Ackerson, thank you so much!

It is a great challenge to establish one's teaching at a new institution when one is finishing a massive project such as this. I have been blessed with tremendous support from the folks at Colgate University. Without the encouragement of the kind souls at Colgate, this process would have taken much longer. I am indebted here to John Ross Carter, who embodies a faithful colleague and mentor. The conversations with a dear friend, Georgia Frank, have been treasured even more than I might have let on. Lesleigh Cushing has brought rigor in reading sacred texts and humor back into our department, and I am deeply grateful for the blessing of her friendship. Ms. Jeanie Getchonis, thank you for the delightful spirit you bring into our lives. I am also thankful to Jim Wetzel, Nancy Ries, Chris Vecsey, Karen Harpp, Noor Khan, Bruce Rutherford, David Dudrick, and Rebecca S. Chopp for their friendship.

While academics usually lament the loss of their time, I have also become mindful of the importance of space. I am thankful to "Ms. Judy" of the ever-welcoming Barge Canal Café for providing me my own permanently occupied section of this local haven, ready with its eternal supply of great coffee and even better conversation.

I am deeply grateful to Elaine Maisner of University of North Carolina Press, the ever-thoughtful editor who has patiently worked with me in bringing this volume to fruition. I am also grateful to David Hines for his help and to Paul Betz, especially for his patience in readying the manuscript for the production process. Special thanks go to Eric Combest, who copyedited the manuscript very carefully, making tremendously helpful suggestions. I owe thanks as well to Johanna Woll, the Islamic Image Collection specialist at the Massachusetts Institute of Technology. She has been amazingly helpful in guiding me toward the images from the Aga Khan Visual Archives that are used in this book.

I am delighted to see this volume in the series on Islamic Civilization and Muslim Networks, and I hope that my own study of the importance of negotiated and contested networks in Saljūq society of premodern Islamdom will make a valuable contribution to that series.

I am thankful to Matthew Gordon and Carole Hillenbrand for their helpful suggestions. They had offered their services as readers for this manuscript in its various incarnations. I would be remiss if I did not thank another reader particularly. Many Muslim mystics hold that the true saints of God are bound to remain hidden. That is how I felt about this reader of the manuscript, before his identity was at long last revealed to me. I am particularly grateful to that true unruly friend of God, Ahmet Karamustafa. The one commodity that we academics possess in a mortally finite amount is time, and I am humbled beyond belief that Ahmet would take the time to go through this manuscript with a careful eye. It is conventional *adab* to state that no reader is responsible for one's errors and shortcomings, and I am happy to oblige with that recognition. Yet nothing short of the commitment to truth demands that I acknowledge how this work would have been replete with embarrassing errors were it not for Ahmet.

Apart from all of the above, my greatest source of support in the many good times and the few bad ones has been my family. This project has taken me away from them on far too many occasions. To my father and mother, I remain eternally grateful for allowing me to dare to dream my dreams. No one has ever been blessed with more loving and sacrificing parents. To my brothers and sister, may the next fifteen years give us many more chances to enjoy each other's company than the last fifteen.

I am grateful for my beautiful wife, Holly, and for her sacrifices on a daily level. For so many nights she has taken care of our children while I have retreated to my study. She is the rock of our family. Her patience and compassion are the two wings that have allowed this project to soar. For our son Jacob, this project has meant a few too many nights of not having Bābā Jān there to tuck him into bed. This brings me back to our daughter, Roya, and our son Amir. My precious little girl with the big brown eyes and my adorable boy of the loveable curls, may you someday know how you have replenished my heart and soul when I have needed it the most.

This project is dedicated to my beautiful children, my luminous wife, and my loving family.

Transliteration Systems and Chronologies

There is an old joke, frequently told by Persian and Turkish Sufis, regarding the famous wise fool, Mullā Naṣr al-Dīn [Turkish = Hoca]. He was asked to give a sermon in front of hundreds at a mosque. He ascended to the top of the pulpit, and said, "Who knows what I am going to talk about?" The crowd, no doubt baffled, sat in silence. Mullā Naṣr al-Dīn said, "Well, if you don't know what I am talking about, then I will not waste my time on you." He got up and left.

The next day, he came back to the same mosque and repeated his question. The crowd, trying to learn their lesson from the previous day, raised their hands in unison. Mullā Naṣr al-Dīn said, "Well, if you know what I am going to talk about, then there is no point in me wasting my breath." He got up and left.

On the third day, he returned to the mosque for a third time and repeated the same question. The crowd had prepared for this. Half of them raised their hands, while the other half remained silent. Mullā Naṣr al-Dīn turned to the crowd and said: "Since half of you know what I am going to say, I ask them to tell the other half that do not." He got up and left.

A long-standing and virtually glorious tradition requires scholars of Islamic studies to bemoan the limitation of transliteration systems. The problem is real, particularly for a project like this that makes a point of incorporating Arabic, Persian, and Turkish sources. Is it clear to the audience that al-Djuwaynī of *Encyclopaedia of Islam* is the same person a Persianist might refer to as Joveyni? Much have I anguished over calling the famed theologian Ghazālī or al-Ghazālī. The choice is indeed political: does one favor the Arabic transliteration system over its *ʿajamī* counterparts? In doing so, how does one come to privilege or contest the old Arabist bias of Islamic studies? What does one do when the sources themselves are not in agreement, now referring to him as al-Ghazālī, now as Ghazālī?

I have attempted to strive for consistency. Without being entirely satisfied, I have adopted the IJMES transliteration system for Arabic to transliterate all the terms. I have made very minor changes to the Arabic system of IJMES, such as using "īy" instead of "iyy" when the final "ī" form is doubled (for example, Niẓamīya, al-Shāfiʿīya, etc.). I am well aware that many Persian and Turkish names end up being transliterated in a way that does not accurately reflect their pronunciation. For example, the figure who sparked my interest in this project will always be Eynol-Qozāt Hamedānī to me, not ʿAyn al-Quḍāt al-Hamadhānī. Yet my goal has been to ensure that the interested parties can reproduce the orthography of the names in the original languages.

It is my sense that some of the readers of this work may not care about the choice of the transliteration system, while the most advanced scholars will be able to easily deduce the original from any system. Perhaps the best that we can do is to recall Mullā Naṣr al-Dīn's example and ask those who know to inform those who do not.

The manuscript was initially typed using the Macintosh font Jaghbub. Being unable to convert that font into a format usable for typesetting, we underwent the arduous process of converting the diacritical marks into a new font. Now I know why the great Persian bard Hafez said: "The pain of this love I have tasted—don't ask . . . !"

The documenting of dates provides another challenge. Whenever possible, I have used a double notation system of the *hijrī* calendar followed by the Gregorian (Christian) one. As such, a notation such as 505/1111 indicates an event that took place in the 505th lunar year after the *hijra* of Prophet Muḥammad from Mecca to Medina, coinciding with the solar year 1111 C.E. In the beginning stages of this project, I relied upon the tried and true resource, Ferdinand Wüstenfeld's *Vergleichungs-Tabellen der Muhammedanischen und Christlichen Zeitrechnung* (Leipzig, 1854). Praise be to God who provides us with more convenient Internet sources. I have been delighted to use the services of the "Conversion of Islamic and Christian dates" web page, provided by Orientalisches Seminar der Universität Zürich. This reliable site is accessible at <http://www.unizh.ch/ori/hegira.html>.

A double-notation system is a bit cumbersome, but I hold it necessary. It is an essential reminder that people around the world conceive of time and space differently. It is the most basic level of *not* projecting our own Western worldview on premodern Nile-to-Oxus subjects. The double-notation system is my attempt at representing my own approach to the material: giving a voice to the concerns and worldviews of my premodern friends while acknowledging my own situatedness in a largely (though not exclusively) Western worldview. The tension between the two recapitulates much of the intellectual, aesthetic, and spiritual tensions of my own life. I have deemed it best to preserve the tensions, and not bury them.

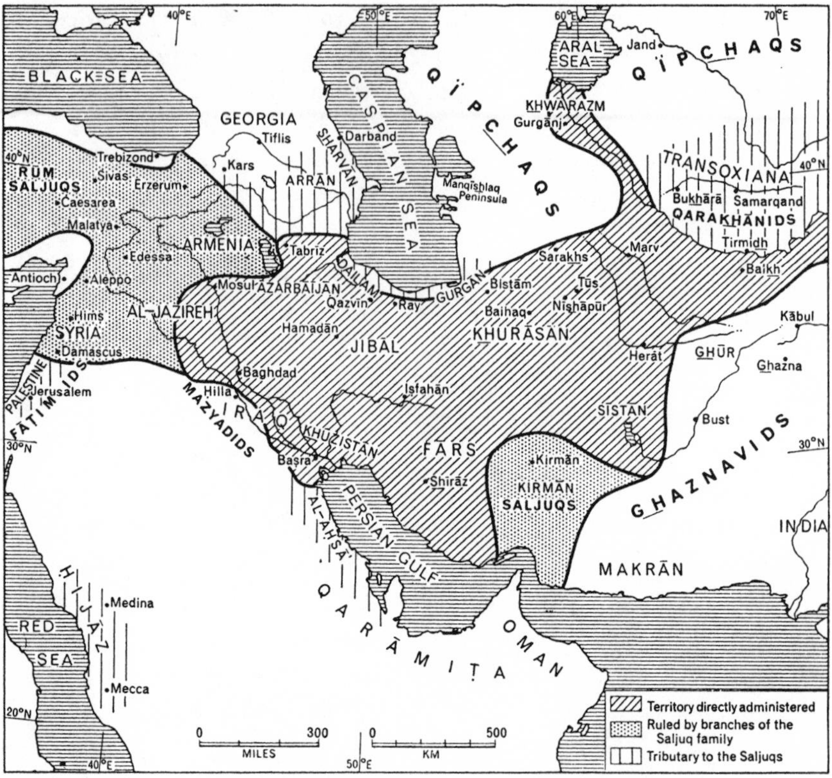

Map of the Saljūq Empire at the death of Malik-Shāh (485/1092)
(Reprinted with the permission of Cambridge University Press)

Introduction

In an appealing and deceivingly simple article tracing the connections between ideology and the study of religion, Bruce Lincoln states that it is difficult to understand the systems of ideology that operate in one's own society for two reasons: first, that one's own consciousness is itself a product of the very system that one is seeking to analyze. Second, and more importantly for our present purposes, "[T]he system's very *success renders its operations invisible*, since one is so consistently immersed in and bombarded by its products that one comes to mistake them (and the apparatus through which they are produced and disseminated) for nothing other than 'nature.'"[1]

This project is about making the political ideology of the ruling class of one particular Islamic society *un-invisible*. The premodern Islamic world of Iran in the eleventh and twelfth centuries C.E., the era of the Great Saljūqs, would seem to be distant enough from my own experience to allow for an in-depth, critical exploration of the way in which ideology can mediate between the realms of religious thought and politics.[2] How I got to the Great Saljūqs, however, was not so much by design as by learning from disaster.

After the 1979 Iranian revolution my family left Iran to move back to the States, where I had been born. The main reasons were twofold: to avoid my conscription into the military (*niẓām vaẓīfa*) and to allow me to pursue a career in medicine. Somewhere along the way, after a few classes on Persian poetry and Islamic mysticism, the idea of spending years in medical school seemed less attractive than reading up on these mystics, who (at the time) seemed to offer me a nostalgic glimpse of the less complicated world before 1979.

In graduate school, I tried my best to immerse myself in Rumi or another one of the Persian mystics whom I had hoped would help me recover the fluid religiosity of my childhood. Like many other expatriate Iranians, I sought to—and perhaps needed to—identify a de-politicized (and preferably de-historicized) realm of spiritual poetry out of which I could resurrect a worldview that was at once spiritual and rational, tolerant and modern. As naïve as that process sounds even to my own ears now, it was precisely through studying one such mystic that I came back full circle and was forced to confront the same questions of religious ideology that had led my family to leave Iran in the first place. Years later, I came to see the wisdom of the words of another soul who had spent the majority of his life in exile, Edward Said. Without minimizing the sense of loss, Said rightly points out the constructive elements of being in exile, in the sense of enabling, even forcing, one to incorporate multiple viewpoints and parameters.[3]

It would be tempting for me to fabricate a tale about how I set out with great purpose and deliberation choosing a period of Islamic history to study. That would be a wonderful narrative, but it would not be my story. The truth of my own experience with this project which by now has consumed almost fifteen years of my life, is that it is not one that I could have imagined writing a few years ago. It, like so many scholarly projects, grew out of a complete failure: a fiercely and pathetically ahistorical paper on the Indian Chishtī Sufi Masʿūd Bakk (d. 790/1387). The paper had two consequences: earning the merciful wrath of my mentors and introducing me to a figure whom Masʿūd Bakk had emulated, ʿAyn al-Quḍāt Hamadānī (d. 525/1131).

I had grown up with Sufi poetry and had read my share of Islamic philosophy and mysticism in graduate school. But nothing could have prepared me for what I was about to find in ʿAyn al-Quḍāt: a passionate and fiery mystic whose rhetoric would soar to the highest discourse on lover and beloved, and in the next paragraph unleash a scathing critique of unjust sultans and administrators of his time period. He was for me Rumi and Ibn ʿArabī, poet and social critic, lover and philosopher, all wrapped up in one. My first reading through his masterpiece, the *Tamhīdāt*, was both inspiring and frustrating. It was the great novel that one never wants to end, turning each page more and more slowly when nearing the end. The end for this brilliant intellectual, sadly, was a tragic execution at the hands of the Saljūq regime.

The accounts of his death are fantastic, and I will return to them in the sixth chapter of this study. He is said to have been condemned in court, hung from the gallows, and burnt in front of the madrasa in which he taught. Especially considering his execution at the young age of thirty-three, the number, range, and depth of the writings left behind by ʿAyn al-Quḍāt astonished me. On so many occasions I wondered how the history of Persian Sufism, indeed the landscape of religiosity in the Persianate world, would have looked had he been allowed to live to a ripe age. That sense of loss for what could have been led me to what had been; I had to find out why he was killed, why he had to be killed, why the narratives state over and over again that he was killed so violently, and why all this was done in front of his madrasa. The overlap between religion and politics, mysticism and heresy, punishment and protest, was here in full effect. To figure out something about why he was killed, I had to know something about his followers, those whom he criticized, and those who issued the death sentence against him and executed him.

What had started out for me as a very conventional study of one individual mystic in the rather unimaginative genre of "life, times, and works" began to expand to a study of the social history of eleventh-and twelfth-century Islamdom. It had been natural enough for me to be interested in Sufis like ʿAyn al-Quḍāt. The "zooming back" process started to include other communities that I had hitherto not thought much about: the communities of the Sufis' disciples and hagiographers, the communities of competing *ʿulamāʾ* (religious scholars), the court administrators, the ʿAbbāsid caliphs and their court, the Saljūq sultans and their court, poets and historians, soldiers and viziers. Somehow I found myself with copies of ʿAyn al-Quḍāt's wondrous texts along with remarkably dull Saljūq chronicles side by side on my cluttered desk. I would soon need a bigger desk and a much wider framework.

The same theorist cited above, Bruce Lincoln, goes on to state that for the "would-be student of ideology" it might be more fruitful to examine the "ideological products and operations of other societies."[4] The "other" society that I would study was still Islamic Iran, but safely removed 900 years from the turmoil of the 1979 revolution. My project would consist of making the ideological operations of the Saljūqs *visible*. The ideological operation with which I have been particularly concerned is the negotiation between power and the politics of knowledge. I have sought here to examine the interconnectedness of Saljūq political ideology and religious inquiry in premodern eleventh- and twelfth-century Iran and Iraq. A corollary goal is that of reading the apparatuses through which this ideology was produced and disseminated. In other words, it is to identify the discourse of religious legitimacy not as "natural", but as one that is contextual, constructed, situated, and contested. If the events of 1979 (and the subsequent exile/migration) had proven too traumatic to allow for a critical study, I sought to study some of the same dynamics in the distant world of the Saljūqs.

Politics and Legitimization through Claims of Orthodoxy (*nīkū iʿtiqād*)

From the tenth century onward, successive waves of Central Asian Turkic tribes entered the Iranian plateau.[5] Many of these tribes held considerable military power, and were able to overpower existing regimes. The earliest tribe to be armed not only with raw force (*shawka*) but also with an ideological claim as the upholders of allegedly normative Sunni Islam was the Saljūq tribe. In 429/1038 the Saljūq warlord Ṭughril entered Nīshāpūr and made the sermon (*khuṭba*) in his own name. It was here that he adopted the honorific *al-sulṭān al-muʿaẓẓam* ("Exalted Ruler"). The Saljūq forces triumphantly entered the caliphal capital of Baghdad in 447/1055, supposedly to rescue the Caliph al-Qāʾim from an Ismāʿīlī uprising. Unlike the conveniently distant Sunni Ghaznavids, the powerful Saljūq presence and power had to be both acknowledged and legitimized. This project is concerned with intertwined issues of power and knowledge that arose as a result of the Saljūq presence and the ramifications of Saljūq state ideology for political loyalty and religious inquiry. Our primary concern is to document how Saljūq political culture informed the parameters in which intellectual inquiry could be undertaken, and in return, the ways in which this same intellectual process was used to legitimize Saljūq state ideology.

The Saljūqs are repeatedly described in the historical sources as possessing *nīkū iʿtiqād*, quite literally "good-doctrine," that is, orthodoxy. Every construction of orthodox doctrine needs to be defined against a heretical opposite. In the case of the Saljūqs, this opponent was Ismāʿīlism.[6] The Ismāʿīlī threat was conceived of as both doctrinal and political. To combat Ismāʿīlism, the construction of Saljūq orthodoxy required a process of manufacturing heresy. The raison d'être of the Saljūqs was defending Sunni Islam. This required a response to the epistemological *and* military threats that were assumed to endanger the safety, integrity, and unity of the Islamic *umma* (community). The military response of the Saljūqs against the Ismāʿīlīs was accompanied by a state-sponsored systematization of the various Islamic intellectual disciplines and the propagation of that state-approved interpretation of Islam through the madrasa system. This process of validating certain branches of knowledge implied the invalidation of realms of thought which were deemed heretical. We are also concerned here with the political and intellectual process of validation/invalidation undertaken by the Saljūqs and the ʿulamāʾ who supported them. I will argue that Saljūq ideology involved a dual process of legitimizing irresistible power by empowering orthodox knowledge.

The first element of Saljūq ideology was the legitimization of irresistible power. Ruling over a region that now featured Persian, Arab, and Turkish Muslim (as well as significant non-Muslim) populations, the Saljūqs sought to legitimize themselves based not only on Islamic principles, but also on Turkic and pre-Islamic Iranian Sāsānian ideals. A number of significant legal scholars and viziers deployed the above modes of legitimization, arguing that in every age God bestows power and force (*shawka*) on a single group. In this age, that single group was held to be the Saljūq Turks. The task of defining the problematical and perpetually changing relationship between the Saljūq Sultanate (holders of power) and the ʿAbbāsid Caliphate (symbol of religious authority) fell most directly on the capable shoulders of Niẓām al-Mulk and scholars such as Abū Ḥāmid al-Ghazālī. At the same time, religious figures (ʿulamāʾ and Sufis) in the Saljūq state were called upon to bless the Saljūqs, conferring on their otherwise brute power an aura of sacrosanct authority. While certain Sufis (Aḥmad-i Jām, Abū Saʿīd-i Abī ʾl-Khayr) were successfully appropriated by the Saljūqs, some such as Aḥmad-i Ghazālī remained neutral. The Sufis (such as ʿAyn al-Quḍāt) who opposed the Saljūq state ideology and questioned the basis of its legitimacy were forcefully silenced. Both the theoretical justification of the sultanate on Islamic and Sāsānian grounds as well as the seeking of saintly baraka (transferable power-grace) are processes of acknowledging and legitimizing irresistible power.

For the Saljūqs to legitimize themselves as the upholders and guardians of Sunni Islam, they needed to draw clear distinctions between orthodox and heretical thought. The Saljūqs' military struggle against the allegedly heretical Ismāʿīlī forces was mirrored by the ideological battle the Saljūq-patronized religious scholars waged against what they deemed heretical thought. The need to identify, demarcate, and defend orthodoxy was part and parcel of Saljūq ideology. This brings us to the second element of Saljūq ideology, that of defining, regulating, and enforcing orthodoxy.

Empowering orthodox knowledge involved a collaborative effort between the Saljūq Sultans and the supreme administrator, Niẓām al-Mulk, who established madrasas for the propagation of state-approved Islamic thought. The foremost proponents and symbols of this state-sponsored orthodoxy were Abū ʾl-Maʿālī al-Juwaynī and his student, Abū Ḥāmid al-Ghazālī. While previous scholars, such as al-Qushayrī and Abū Nuʿaym al-Iṣfahānī, had been involved in the systematization of Islamic thought, that movement had not been coupled to the madrasa as the site of the production of knowledge. From this point on the *madrasa* would produce religious scholars who produced and propagated the Saljūq-sponsored ideology, as well as civil administrators who would carry on the task of running the bureaucracy of the empire.

A further dimension of the Saljūq attempt to empower orthodox knowledge was their patronage of those Sufi saints who were depicted as bestowing their baraka on the Saljūqs, thus legitimizing them. The Saljūqs often contributed to the establishment of Sufi lodges (*khānaqāh*s) for these Sufis and their descendants. The khānaqāh and the madrasa were the two institutions of knowledge sponsored by the Saljūqs, and many religious scholars of this time period moved with great fluidity between the two. I will argue that what the Saljūqs were primarily interested in was not the mystical teachings of Sufi masters per se, but rather the power of sainthood as a social phenomenon, the power to legitimize.

The Saljūqs and Ideological State Apparatuses

The French theorist Louis Althusser differentiated between what he termed repressive State Apparatus and coercive Ideological State Apparatuses in an influential essay titled "Ideology and Ideological State Apparatuses (Notes towards an Investigation)."[7] The repressive State Apparatus includes the police, government, administration, courts, army, and prison system.[8] While there would be one Repressive State Apparatus, there could be a plurality of what Althusser termed coercive Ideological State Apparatuses. The different facets of the coercive Ideological State Apparatuses could be manifested in a wide variety of institutions, including but not limited to religious, educational, family, trade-union, etc.[9] One important distinction between the two is that while the Repressive State Apparatus operates by violence, the coercive state apparatuses function by ideology. Althusser states that no class can hold state power for a long period of time unless it can exercise hegemony over the coercive Ideological State Apparatuses.[10]

The Great Saljūqs held power for over a century, a long time by the standards of the turbulent world of premodern Islamdom. This project is partially concerned with identifying their Repressive State Apparatus, which operated through violence and brought them to a position of power. However, it is even more interested in their multifaceted usage of various coercive Ideological State Apparatuses. As Althusser predicted, these apparatuses are multiple, and can operate through a number of different formats. To see all the various ways that Saljūq ideology operated in society, we must look beyond just political history, or even a study of the Saljūq government.

In this study, I will look at a number of different institutions that fit the parameters of what Althusser identified as coercive Ideological State Apparatuses. These will include the madrasa, the khānaqāh, surveillance and reconnaissance, and the land-grant (*iqṭāʿ*) system. In order to account for these multifaceted apparatuses, we will have to examine a wide range of sources and communities. In a section following this introduction, I will identify the key individuals and primary sources consulted in this project.

Time Period of the Study

One of the more challenging aspects of this study is setting chronological boundaries that can be justified with respect to the available data. Most studies of the Great Saljūqs point to their ruling period, namely 429/1038 to 552/1157, as the bookends of their study. However, my own discussion of the Saljūqs will start earlier, in the aftermath of the bitter defeat they suffered at the hands of the Ghaznavid Sultan Maḥmūd in 420/1029. It was at this time that the Saljūqs distinguished themselves from other Central Asian Turkic tribes migrating to the Iranian plateau by ideologically presenting themselves as champions of Sunni Islam. By 431/1040, the Saljūqs had recovered to the point of being able to infiltrate Khurāsān. I will be most concerned with the activities of the Great Saljūqs in the Iranian Plateau and Iraq up to 552/1157. However, it is perhaps misleading to suggest that 552/1157 is the end period for this study, as almost all the available data about this period comes from historical sources composed during the two centuries after this date.

This revised chronology highlights the importance of three significant mystics whose hagiographies are important sources for the study of how the Saljūqs come to be legitimized and contested; two are examples of successful cooperation between the political and mystical powers. The first, Abū Saʿīd-i Abī ʾl-Khayr (d. 440/1049), is associated with the first two Saljūq warlords, Ṭughril (d. 455/1063) and Chaghrī Beg (d. 452/1060), as well as the architect of the whole Saljūq regime, the vizier Niẓām al-Mulk (d. 485/1092). The second saintly figure, Aḥmad-i Jām (d. 536/1141), is associated with the last ruler of the Great Saljūqs, Sultan Sanjar (d. 552/1157). The relationships between these men of power—some whose power was through raw force, and some through authoritative sanctity (*wilāya*)—mark the beginning and end of our study. The third figure, the already alluded to ʿAyn al-Quḍāt, comes in the middle, marking the most vigorous challenge to the dominant Saljūq state ideology.

Muslim Networks in the Saljūq Era: Culture of Negotiations and Contestations

In a thought-provoking essay on the ramifications of ideology for religious studies, Gary Lease has argued that all societies are perpetually involved in producing systems of ideologies. Furthermore, "In order to sustain such sets, or systems of ideologies, authority is needed to impose them on those segments of society which may have constructed quite different, or variant catalogs of definitions."[11] In applying this thesis to the Saljūqs, we are confronted with segments of society that did have alternate definitions, or alternate sets of ideologies. The success of the Saljūq regime as a military, administrative, religious, and intellectual system depended on its ability to come to terms with these various competing systems of ideology, embedded in distinct though interconnected Muslim networks.

One of the key ambitions of this project is that of expanding our scope beyond the conventional genre of dynastic history. Instead, I propose that a social history of the premodern period in Muslim societies needs to account for the various networks of contestation and negotiation among the multiple social, political, religious, and mystical clusters. Saljūq culture, both political and intellectual, was primarily characterized by an ongoing and shifting network of *negotiations* among these various networks: between the Saljūqs and the ʿAbbāsid Caliphs, the Saljūqs and their military core of Türkmen tribesmen, the Turkic Saljūqs and their Persian administrators, the various Saljūq princes, the competing aspirants to the vizierate and the intellectuals they patronized, the various intellectuals seeking teaching posts at prestigious madrasas, the saints bestowing their baraka on the Saljūqs in exchange for promises of justice and compassion for the people, and between the disciples of the Sufis and the Saljūq notables. Even in those cases where a coalition of forces was able to establish dominance, it did not go unchallenged. No less a figure than the premier theologian of the age, Abū Ḥāmid al-Ghazālī, was charged with heresy. Niẓām al-Mulk, the principal vizier of the age and the architect of the Saljūq state, was constantly dealing with political maneuverings against him by his antagonists. The foremost Saljūq warlord, Sanjar, spent forty years putting down uprisings from within his own family. Any in-depth study of Saljūq politics and society will have to be framed against this background of contention.

In order to be able to document these networks of contestation among the many different systems of ideologies, it is important not to limit our approach to any one genre of primary sources, be they historical chronicles, works of theology, or Sufi hagiographies. To get a sense of the contested world of Saljūq ideologies, it is imperative to juxtapose many different types of sources. One of the distinguishing features of this project is that it juxtaposes some seventy thousand pages of primary sources from a wide range of genres to document the negotiations among these various Muslim networks. I have discussed the key figures and genres of primary sources analyzed throughout this project in a section that will follow this introduction.

Outline of This Project

Beyond the introduction, this project will proceed through six chapters. The first two, by identifying the social and political background of Iran in the aftermath of the Saljūq invasion, attempt to make their ideological claims *un-invisible*. The last two chapters deal with Sufis who have either legitimized the Saljūqs (and been patronized by them), or alternatively contested Saljūq state ideology. The middle two chapters act as a bridge. Chapter 3 identifies the interest that the Saljūqs displayed in intellectual institutions, particularly the madrasa and the khānaqāh, along with other institutions such as the land grant and surveillance. Chapter 4 will look at the role of political treatises written by madrasa scholars in legitimizing the Saljūqs' religious ideology.

The first chapter, "Deconstructing the Great Saljūq Myth," discusses the rise of the Saljūqs from a nomadic confederation of tribes in the Central Asian steppes to the would-be defenders of normative Islam. In doing so, I will begin with their alleged (and well publicized) rescue of the ʿAbbāsid Caliphate when the latter was confronted with an Ismāʿīlī revolt. I will seek to make visible the elements of Saljūq ideology that have been accepted uncritically by virtually all later scholars. Saljūq ideology has been so successful that it has been accepted as natural.[12]

I will begin by identifying the central narratives cited by later historians in which the ideological justifications of the Saljūq regime are first introduced: their obedience to Sunni Islam, their loyalty to the ʿAbbāsid Caliphate, their promotion of social order, their patronage of ʿulamāʾ and Sufis, and their putting down of heretical movements. I will then undermine such idealized legitimizing narratives by bringing to light underexplored sources and narratives. I will demonstrate that contrary to these ideological claims, the Saljūqs were in reality yet another pillaging Central Asian tribe marching onto the Iranian plateau. What set them apart was that the caliph viewed them as the most cooperative of these groups. During the subsequent two generations, Niẓām al-Mulk provided the Saljūqs with a complete image makeover, representing them as the defenders of normative Islam and Islamdom.

Central to the conclusion of this chapter will be a deconstruction of the key concept of Saljūq state ideology, the myth of Saljūq loyalty to the ʿAbbāsid Caliphate. While the Saljūqs paid lip service to their support of the ʿAbbāsid Caliphate, this chapter documents tensions and hostilities between the two, even leading to Saljūq attempts to do away with the caliphate altogether. Once we have de-privileged the Saljūqs as the idealized defenders of Sunni Islam, we are better situated to undertake a closer study of the actual relations between the holders of power and holders of knowledge. By focusing on the hostilities between the Saljūq Sultanate and the ʿAbbāsid Caliphate, as well as by documenting the social strife created by the Saljūqs, I aim to render their ideology visible.

The second chapter focuses on the life and career of the man that many sources came to identify as the personification of the Saljūq regime: Niẓām al-Mulk. This chapter, titled "The Niẓām's Realm, the Orderly Realm," will present Niẓām al-Mulk as the linchpin connecting together the Saljūq Turks, the ʿulamāʾ, the Sufis, and the ʿAbbāsid Caliphate. Many of the coercive state apparatuses, such as the patronage of madrasas and the systems of surveillance and reconnaissance, were orchestrated by Niẓām al-Mulk to support the Saljūq state ideology.

It is one of the tenets of this project that the rise of various schools of thought in this period was directly linked with the fate of their political patrons, and the case of Niẓām al-Mulk provides us with a great example. The early period of Niẓām al-Mulk's career coincided with that of the vizier ʿAmīd al-Mulk Kundurī (d. 456/1064). Kundurī used his position of prominence to exile the Ashʿarī (and by extension, Shāfiʿī) scholars from Khurāsān. When Niẓām al-Mulk brought about the fall of ʿAmīd al-Mulk, he was also able to secure the return of the Ashʿarī-Shāfiʿī clan, for whom he established the Niẓāmīya madrasa. Clearly, any study of the intellectual trends in this time period would have to account for such political competitions. Likewise, a political history of the Saljūqs should keep an eye on the ramifications of political upheaval for various schools of thought patronized by different political notables. I will also focus on the contrasting advice offered by Niẓām al-Mulk and Kundurī with respect to dealing with the caliphate.

This chapter will also deal with the challenges to the authority of Niẓām al-Mulk toward the end of his illustrious career from both a rival vizier, Tāj al-Mulk, and the most powerful female political figure of the day, Tarkān Khātūn. I will demonstrate that the assassination of Niẓām al-Mulk was not due to an Ismāʿīlī conspiracy but to the plotting of these two characters. Not even the great Niẓām al-Mulk's authority would go uncontested.

Chapter 3, entitled "Saljūq State Apparatuses," identifies the main coercive ideological state apparatuses deployed by Niẓām al-Mulk, including the iqṭāʿ system, surveillance and reconnaissance, the establishment of madrasas, and the patronage of khānaqāhs. In discussing these institutions, I will also discuss how they each managed to contribute to the larger process of legitimizing and maintaining Saljūq rule and legitimacy. I will also note how these apparatuses came to be contested from both within and outside of the Saljūq state.

Chapter 4 is titled "The Shifting Politics of al-Ghazālī." This chapter will focus on *the* madrasa intellectual of the Saljūq era, the notable al-Ghazālī. Rather than presenting his philosophical or theological views, I will trace how he continuously changed his political treatises to account for the changing political times. As the Saljūqs rose to positions of greater and greater prominence vis-à-vis the ʿAbbāsid Caliphs, al-Ghazālī turned gradually from a model focused on the caliphate to one envisioning cooperation between the caliphate and sultanate before finally writing his last two political treatises completely focused on the Saljūq Sultanate. The writing of these political treatises that deployed both an Islamic and an Iranian Sāsānian model of legitimization served to reinforce Saljūq state ideology.

The fifth chapter, "Bargaining with *Baraka*," deals with a theme central to my project: the legitimization of the Saljūqs through Sufi hagiographies. I identify three individual Sufis who are frequently depicted in both historical works and Sufi hagiographies as having lent their baraka to legitimize the Saljūqs. I will offer close readings of these narratives to discern patterns of negotiation between communities of Sufis and communities of politicians.

A key argument of this chapter will be that the Sufis must be understood as men and women of power, a quality well known to the Saljūqs. I begin by problematizing the application of nineteenth- and early twentieth-century Protestant notions of the imagined category of mysticism to the lives of premodern Muslim Sufis. It is my contention that if our understanding of mysticism is based on a private experience of the Divine held in isolation from a social life, then we are bound to misconstrue the social significance of premodern Muslim mystics. I will also challenge positivist readings of hagiographies that have tended to dismiss these works as fanciful and hyperbolic narratives designed to appeal to ignorant masses. While this approach has characterized much of European and Iranian scholarship dealing with Saljūq hagiographies, I will argue the contrary, namely, that hagiographies are mythic texts—not meaning that they are somehow untrue, but in the sense that they are sacred stories believed to be true by a community, which thus acts based on paradigmatic notions identified in these narratives. Rather than looking at them as "legends appealing to primitive masses" (the evaluation of a prominent European scholar of Sufism),[13] I will analyze them as carefully crafted texts connecting two elite communities—one political and one saintly.

To do so, I will emphasize the crucial role of hagiographies written by the disciples of the Sufi teachers in constructing legitimizing relations between Sufis and Saljūq notables. In the case of Abū Saʿīd-i Abī ʾl-Khayr, we have not one but two contemporary hagiographies written by his descendants which attempt to outdo one another in depicting the affinity of their saintly ancestor and the Saljūq powers, specifically Niẓām al-Mulk. The hagiography about Aḥmad-i Jām depicts the saint as repeatedly saving the life of Sultan Sanjar, from Ismāʿīlī threats. This is significant because the Ismāʿīlīs are the ultimate anti-Saljūq trope in the historical sources. By presenting themselves as anti-Ismāʿīlī, the descendants of the Sufis are identifying themselves fully with the constructed memory of the Saljūqs as protectors of orthodoxy.

The disciples of these saints were able to use the legacy of the Sufi teachers as spiritual capital to offer a retrospective blessing of the sheer force that had brought the Saljūqs into power. In exchange for this service, they often received Saljūq patronage in form of khānaqāhs built for them. The saints themselves are often depicted as extending their baraka to the Saljūqs in exchange for a promise that the people who lived under the saints' *wilāya* ("authoritative sanctity") would be treated justly.

The last chapter deals precisely with attempts to construct different ideologies to the dominant ideology of the Saljūqs: while some Sufis such as Abū Saʿīd-i Abī ʾl-Khayr and Aḥmad-i Jām aligned themselves with the Saljūqs, such was not the case with all Sufis. Chapter 6, entitled "An Oppositional Sufi," centers around a powerful figure, ʿAyn al-Quḍāt Hamadānī, who rose against the Saljūqs, and contested their state ideology at the price of his life.

This chapter will also include extended critiques of the way in which the legacy of premodern Persian Sufism has tended to be studied in recent scholarly works. In the works of some scholars, ʿAyn al-Quḍāt is represented as a timeless martyr, à la Manṣūr Ḥallāj (d. 309/922). I will argue that in doing so, these scholars have robbed ʿAyn al-Quḍāt of his *timely* challenge to the ruling state ideology which led to his death in the first place. In reading him as timeless, they have made him irrelevant to his own time. To counter that, I will contextualize ʿAyn al-Quḍāt's life and teachings in the troubled milieu of the Saljūqs. I will also demonstrate how he challenged all the dominant discourses of his time period, whether kalām and falsafa, or even conventional Sufism. He was also the first critic of the arch-Saljūq intellectual, al-Ghazālī. Far from seeking to legitimize Saljūq ideology, ʿAyn al-Quḍāt called into question the basis of their rule, the association of religious scholars with them, and the economic underpinning of their system. In doing so, he presented the most thorough contestation of the Saljūq state ideology in this period.

In the conclusion, I will review the main thesis, followed by a brief discussion of the ramifications of this project for Islamic studies, Sufi studies, Middle Eastern studies, and religious studies.

Historiographic Contributions of This Study

The Saljūqs clearly played a crucial role in the premodern history of the Nile-to-Oxus region. Many of their administrative, intellectual, and political legacies were utilized by the subsequent Turkic dynasties that were to rule the region from Bengal to Cairo for the next five hundred years.[14] Several of their institutions even survived well into the Ottoman and Safavid periods. In spite of their great importance, scholarship on the Saljūqs is still at a rudimentary stage. For example, we lack even a single reputable monograph in a European language devoted solely to Saljūq history. As Claude Cahen has lamented, "No comprehensive scholarly history of the Selchukids exists; the pages devoted to them in the general histories of Islam or of the Turks are inadequate."[15] Furthermore, Stephen Humphreys has also noted that there are no general studies of the different aspects of Saljūq ideology.[16]

One of the historiographic emphases of this study is the necessity of incorporating insights from Arabic, Persian, Turkish, and even Syriac sources. The social history of premodern Islam in the eleventh and twelfth centuries cannot be told singularly from the perspective of Arabs, or Persians, or Turks. Our approach to this bygone world cannot be tainted by the anachronistic modern nationalism and absurd linguistic chauvinism that have prevented even accomplished scholars from exploring sources in different languages. Closely linked with the linguistic issue is that of civilizational frameworks. The premodern Islamic world that this study examines was a multiethnic one. It was composed of the contributions of and tensions among different groups of Arabs, Persians, Turks, and others. Nor can the full story be told exclusively through sources in any one of those languages. Our approach needs to mirror the complexity and the pluralism of the multiethnic, multilingual society that we seek to study.

Let me offer some examples of how the above tendencies have impoverished Saljūq scholarship. Even contemporary works of Western scholarship often reflect the old Arabcentric bias of Islamic studies, neglecting many or all of the available Persian and Turkish sources. In doing so, they clearly miss out on most of the important political nuances of the period.[17] Works of intellectual history are often unaware of the non-Arabic writings of some well-known figures, even of the famed al-Ghazālī.[18] Similar problems can be detected in some contemporary studies of the Saljūq era undertaken by Arab scholars who do not have access to Persian sources.

By the eleventh century Arabic was still the dominant language of Islamdom, but that dominance was no longer uncontested. Some contemporary Iranian studies of the period—steeped in notions of Persian nationalism—have imagined Sufism as an Iranian response to "Arab" Islam.[19] They ignore the fact that Persian scholars like al-Ghazālī and Juwaynī wrote the bulk of their works in Arabic and also overlook that the rulers of Iran up until the twentieth century have mainly been from Turkish backgrounds. While the region of Iran and the Persian language are overlapping discourses, they are not equivalent and should not be collapsed into one and the same.

Similarly, Turkish scholars often acknowledge the Great Saljūqs (Turkish: *büyük selçuklular*) as the precursors to the "Turkish" Anatolian Saljūqs. In doing so, they characterize the Saljūq era as a "Turco-Islamic" history, thus neglecting the importance of Persianate Sāsānian symbols and institutions.[20] The three approaches above are singularly deficient as frameworks through which one can recreate the social history of this wonderfully complex society.

Another important historiographic emphasis of this study is to recover Sufi hagiographies as an important source for the social history of premodern Islamdom. For too long these texts have been read either in a pietistic fashion, searching for spiritual edification, or through the dismissive attitudes of positivistic historicism. The hagiographies allow us to gain insights into segments of society that do not show up in the courtly chronicles focused on sultans, viziers, and caliphs. Even some of the very learned scholarly works which do seek to integrate the role of the ʿulamāʾ in Islamic societies include almost no references to Sufis.[21] It is hoped that this project offers a way for us to expand our reconstruction of the premodern Islamic period beyond the conventional circles of sultans and ʿulamāʾ to include Sufis. Conversely, it is also intended to move the academic study of Sufism in the direction of studying the social impact of Sufis.

Above all, we need to find more subtle ways of reading tārīkh texts. We begin by acknowledging that all historical texts are ideological in nature, presenting particular constructions of their subjects. When matters of religion and politics appear most natural is precisely where the ideologies have been most successful. Our persistent goal is to get beyond positivistic readings of historical narratives and to understand this contextual complexity.

The challenges that prevent scholars from incorporating these historiographic insights are as much institutional as personal. The academic study of Islam in the United States has tended to be undertaken through two main umbrella organizations that have become sites for the production and dissimulation of knowledge in this field. The first, patterned after the area studies model, is the Middle East Studies Association (MESA). MESA is well known for its strong emphasis on political, economic, and historical aspects of the Nile-to-Oxus region. The second, the American Academy of Religion (AAR), is composed of various scholars and students of different religious traditions who approach the material under the rubric of religious studies.

It is perhaps a telling sign of the state of Islamic studies that the dates for these organizations' conferences conflict with each other virtually every single year, thus forcing the interested parties to choose one or the other. As a result, the Islamicists at the AAR tend to remain somewhat more distant from some of the current research on historical and political developments in the Nile-to-Oxus region. Conversely, a frequent complaint cast against MESA's format is that amidst all the political and economic discussions, religion, as a serious category of analysis, is left behind; Islam as shifting reference gets lost. Both groups, in short, suffer from missing out on the creative opportunity to explore the material they are already familiar with from other perspectives.

I have spent the better part of the past few years trying to research the interconnected and overlapping discourses of political authority, religious inquiry, and saintly *wilāya*. As a scholar in the field, I have also had the privilege—and frustration—of participating in both conferences. I was recently asked to participate in a conference on Sufism, where I presented a paper on the love theory of ʿAyn al-Quḍāt Hamadānī. At the end of the talk, a senior member who knew me from MESA came up, thanked me for the talk, and stood there with a perplexed look on his face. He finally got up the courage to say: "That was *great* . . . *but* I thought you were a Saljūq historian."

The largest historiographic ambition of this project is for us to move away from such convenient bifurcations. I urge historians to take the social role of Sufis and ʿulamāʾ more seriously, and for the scholars of Islamic thought to be more engaged in exploring the worlds inhabited by the figures and texts they study. It sounds like a simple and obvious plan, yet one that has not been fully implemented in the study of premodern Islamdom. This project is a humble step towards achieving that greater goal. And so it goes . . .

Chronology of the Great Saljūqs and ʿAbbāsids

Reign of the Saljūq Sultans

Ṭughril Beg	447/1055 to 455/1063 (military campaign from 431/1040)
Alp Arslān	455/1063 to 465/1072
Malik-Shāh	465/1072 to 485/1092
Maḥmūd b. Malik-Shāh	485/1092 to 487/1094
Bark Yāruq	487/1094 to 498/1105
Malik-Shāh II	498/1105
Muḥammad b. Malik-Shāh	498/1105 to 511/1118
Sanjar	511/1118 to 552/1157 (also ruled in eastern Iran from 490/1097)

ʿAbbāsid Caliphate during the Great Saljūqs Era

Al-Qāʾim	Died 467/1075
Al-Muqtadī	Died 487/1094
Al-Mustaẓhir	Died 512/1118
Al-Mustarshid	Died 529/1135

Key Figures and Primary Sources

Up until the present work, there has not been a single study in English devoted solely to the Great Saljūqs. The most thorough available source is the fifth volume of the *Cambridge History of Iran*, which focuses on the Saljūq and Mongol periods. The first three articles in this volume deal with the Saljūq period, and they are indicative of the way in which studies of the Saljūqs suffer from a certain "split personality." Each article focuses on a different segment of the society (political *or* intellectual), without much of an attempt to situate the subjects in a wider social context. C. E. Bosworth's "The Political and Dynastic History of the Iranian World (A.D. 1000–1217)"[1] is more or less a straightforward political history, focusing on the rise and fall of sultans from various dynasties. The second essay, A. K. S. Lambton's "The Internal Structure of the Saljuq Empire"[2] focuses on the vizierate institution and the multifaceted structures introduced by Niẓām al-Mulk. The third essay, A. Bausani's "Religion in the Saljuq Period,"[3] treats religious trends under the rubrics of "Sunnism," "Shīʿism," and "Sufism."

What is most problematic about the above three articles is that they treat sultans, viziers, ʿulamāʾ, and Sufis in isolation from one another, as if they had little to do with one another. In Bosworth's discussion of political history, there is little indication that the rise and fall of the various sultans had intellectual ramifications, or that these Sultans were involved in the patronage of madrasas and khānaqāhs. Likewise, Bausani's treatment of the Sunni, Shīʿī, and Sufi scholars includes little discussion of the political involvement of these religious intellectuals.

This project aims to reconstruct the relations between the disciplines of power and knowledge in premodern Islam by reconstructing a world in which political and religious figures interact, negotiate, and contest each other's authorities. As such, the key figures of this project will include sultans and caliphs, viziers and court administrators, ʿulamāʾ and Sufis.

The Saljūq Sultans

Ṭughril Beg, Muḥammad ibn Mīkāʾīl b. Saljūq. (reigned 447/1055 to 455/1063) and Chaghrī Beg, Dāwūd b. Mīkāʾīl b. Saljūq (d. 452/1060). Both of these men rose on the scene as supreme military leaders around 431/1040, although their status as sultan was not confirmed until 447/1055. Given their proximity to the unknown, questionable, and probably non-Muslim background of the Saljūq tribe, they had to be legitimized through being associated with Muslim sources of saintly authority. As a result, they are connected with two saintly figures (Bābā Ṭāhir and Abū Saʿīd-i Abī ʾl-Khayr), who are depicted as lending their *baraka* to legitimize them.

Alp Arslān b. Chaghrī Beg (reigned 455/1063 to 465/1072). It was during the rule of this figure that Niẓām al-Mulk rose to power and established the first Niẓāmīya madrasa.

Malik-Shāh b. Alp Arslān (reigned 465/1072 to 485/1092). The rule of Malik-Shāh is held up by many as the apogee of the Great Saljūqs. Much of this, of course, would have to be attributed to his capable vizier, Niẓām al-Mulk.

Maḥmūd b. Malik-Shāh (reigned 485/1092 to 487/1094).

Bark Yāruq b. Malik-Shāh (reigned 487/1094 to 498/1105).

Malik-Shāh II b. Bark Yāruq (brief reign, 498/1105).

Muḥammad b. Malik-Shāh (reigned 498/1105 to 511/1118).

Sanjar b. Malik-Shāh b. Alp Arslān (reigned 511/1118 to 552/1157). His death in 552/1157 marks the end of the Great Saljūq period. He is associated with the last Saljūq Sufi of note, Aḥmad-i Jām.

The Relevant ʿAbbāsid Caliphs

al-Qāʾim, ʿAbd Allāh b. al-Qādir (d. 467/1075). This caliph is depicted in the sources as having asked for the military assistance of the Saljūqs.

al-Muqtadī, ʿAbd Allāh b. Muḥammad al-Qāʾim (d. 487/1094). The death of this caliph, two years after that of Niẓām al-Mulk and Malik-Shāh, contributed to the instability that arose after the period of glory under these figures.

al-Mustaẓhir, Aḥmad b. al-Muqtadī (d. 512/1118). This caliph was connected to al-Ghazālī, who named a political treatise identifying the rights of the imamate after him.

al-Mustarshid, al-Faḍl b. al-Mustaẓhir (529/1135).

The Relevant Viziers

While all of the figures below are significant in their own right, I will focus to a large extent on Niẓām al-Mulk as the architect of the Saljūq regime. Some historical sources even went so far as to dub the whole era *al-dawla al-niẓāmīya*, a pun implying both "the systematized state" as well as "the Niẓām's government." I will analyze Niẓām al-Mulk's mediating role between the two generations of Saljūq sultans and caliphs, as well as his interactions with the Sufi master Abū Saʿīd-i Abī ʾl-Khayr. In addition, I will also discuss his crucial role in bringing the Ashʿarī-Shāfiʿī scholars back from exile and establishing the Niẓāmīya madrasas for them.

ʿAmīd al-Mulk Kundurī (d. 456/1064). The first vizier of the Saljūqs, and the figure responsible for exiling the Ashʿarī-Shāfiʿī from Khurāsān. He mediated the first meetings between the Saljūqs and the Sufis (Bābā Ṭāhir), as well as their first meeting with the ʿAbbāsid caliph. In these latter meetings, he translated—both literally and in terms of protocol—the discourse for the non-Arabic speaking Saljūq sultan.

Niẓām al-Mulk (d. 485/1092). The mastermind of the whole Saljūq regime. While his power should not be underestimated, I will also document opposition to him, both from figures such as Kundurī (above), as well as from later rivals such as Tāj al-Mulk and Tarkān Khātūn. Niẓām al-Mulk is responsible for deploying many of the multiple coercive ideological state apparatuses used in legitimizing the Saljūqs, such as iqṭāʿ, the establishment of the madrasas, and negotiations with the Sufis.

ʿAzīz al-Dīn Mustawfī (d. 525/1130). The patron of ʿAyn al-Quḍāt, and the uncle of the later historian al-Kātib al-Iṣfahānī, more famed as Saladin's scribe. It is through this personal connection that we come to know a great deal about the tensions between ʿAyn al-Quḍāt and the Saljūq court.

Qawwām al-Dīn Dargazīnī (527–8/1132–3). The vizier generally held accountable for the martyrdom of ʿAyn al-Quḍāt. I will attempt to modify the traditional understanding of this controversial figure by documenting his connections to other Sufi figures, such as Ḥakīm Sanāʾī (d. 1131), to demonstrate that his opposition to ʿAyn al-Quḍāt was not due to a hatred of Sufi teachings, but for more specific political reasons having to do with ʿAzīz al-Dīn Mustawfī.

The Relevant ʿUlamāʾ and Sufis

A key component of this project is the role of both ʿulamāʾ and Sufis in legitimizing the Saljūqs. In fact, it is a bit misleading to speak of ʿulamāʾ *and* Sufis, since Saljūq intellectual thought was characterized by a great deal of fluidity between the khānaqāh and the madrasa. Many of the leading religious scholars of this period were deeply immersed in Sufism, and many Sufis were also among the most respected members of the ʿulamāʾ.

The focus here will not be on their juridical, theological, or mystical teachings in abstract, but on the various and subtle ways in which they lent their legitimizing power to the newly (and nominally) converted Saljūq Turks. In the case of the Sufis, I will focus on the contested process of bargaining with baraka, where sources portray the Sufis as legitimizing the rulers in exchange for promises of justice and patronage. In the case of the madrasa intellectuals, such as al-Ghazālī, I will focus on their successive political treatises, each of which mirrored the changing social realities: the more dominant the Saljūqs became, the more strongly al-Ghazālī moved to legitimize them, even addressing them as the "God's caliph" and "shadow of God on Earth." The writing of such political treatises and the baraka of the Sufis provided the Saljūqs with desperately needed legitimization.

To borrow a vivid metaphor from another religious tradition, the Sufis of the Saljūq era are almost Krishna-like, manifesting themselves whenever social order decayed and unrest was seen as threatening the fabric of society. Even if one holds that their message is timeless, their manifestation in the sources is most *timely*. They show up in the narratives when Ṭughril is about to conquer Baghdad (beginning of the Great Saljūqs), and when the Ghuzz confederation of tribes had overtaken Khurāsān in the 1150s (end of the Great Saljūqs). On the contrary, there are almost no hagiographic narratives connecting Sufis to the Saljūq rulers, such as Malik-Shāh, who were at the zenith of Saljūq power. This should not come as a great surprise. As Edward Shils reminded us long ago, "Ideologies arise in conditions of crisis."[4]

Ibn Sīnā (d. 1037). Persian philosopher and vizier, who came to be represented as the archetype of the Faylasūf, the Islamicate philosopher steeped in and extending the legacy of Greek philosophy, in this time period.

Abū Saʿīd-i Abī ʾl-Khayr (d. 440/1049). Persian Sufi master, accredited with many of the institutional elements of the khānaqāh. He is portrayed as interacting with and lending legitimacy to both the first two Saljūq warlords, Ṭughril and Chaghrī Beg, and perhaps more importantly, Niẓām al-Mulk.

Bābā Ṭāhir (d. after 446/1055). Persian poet and Sufi. The narrative of his interaction with Ṭughril before the latter's conquest of Baghdad is the classic articulation of bargaining with baraka. The fact that his interaction with the Saljūqs is prominently featured not in a Sufi hagiography but in a work of dynastic history (*tārīkh*) points to the pervasive nature of the legitimizing discourse of the Sufis.

Imām al-Ḥaramayn al-Juwaynī (d. 478/1085). The leader of the Shāfiʿī-Ashʿarīs, and the teacher of al-Ghazālī. Ironically, the exile imposed on him by the vizier Kundurī—due to Juwaynī's Ashʿarī-Shāfiʿī beliefs—ended up earning Juwaynī his greatest honorific. Through his teachings in both Mecca and Medina, he came to be known as the imām of the two sanctuaries, *Imām al-ḥaramayn*. He too was already deeply connected to Niẓām al-Mulk, who brought Juwaynī back to teach in the Nīshāpūr Niẓāmīya. Juwaynī was the model of a madrasa intellectual before there was al-Ghazālī.

Al-Qushayrī (d. 465/1072). A prominent example of a Sufi incorporating Ashʿarī theology. He is an important contributor towards the systematization of Sufi thought. He suffered more than Juwaynī during the persecution of the Ashʿarī-Shāfiʿīs, even being dragged out of his home and temporarily imprisoned.

Abū Ḥāmid Al-Ghazālī (d. 505/1111). The most successful example of a madrasa intellectual in this time period. I will focus not on his well-known philosophical and theological views, which have already received a great deal of scholarly attention, but on his political treatises, such as the *al-Mustaẓhirī*, the *Naṣīḥat al-mulūk*, and the dubious *Tuḥfat al-mulūk*.

ʿAyn al-Quḍāt Hamadānī (d. 525/1131). The best example of a voice of dissent against the dominant religious ideology of the Saljūqs. He presented the most thorough challenge to the legitimacy of the Saljūqs, calling into question their ideological claim to justice, the basis of their economic system, and their association with the ʿulamāʾ. He advised his disciples at the court to leave the Saljūqs altogether and devote themselves instead to the authority of the Sufi masters. His was not a call to dispense with authority altogether, but rather an alternate vision of reality that contested the dominant Saljūq state ideology.

Aḥmad-i Jām (d. 536/1141). The prominent Sufi who presents another example of successful cooperation between communities of Sufis and political forces. He is portrayed as having saved Sultan Sanjar, the last of the Great Saljūqs, from assassination at the hands of the Ismāʿīlīs. Aḥmad-i Jām's descendants and disciples were able to call on the above cooperation/connection to ask rulers of subsequent dynasties to offer them patronage.

Genres of Primary Texts Analyzed

There is no shortage of scholarly works that deal with intellectuals who flourished in the Saljūq age. Many of these works, some quite excellent in their stated parameters, follow the standard "life, times, and works" genre.[5] On the economic and administrative side, there are only short and ultimately insufficient chapters in works that are devoted to emphasizing later periods.[6] When scholars discuss the politics of knowledge, they all too often content themselves with quoting the same excerpts from Saljūq chronicles that detail the interactions between a particular Saljūq sultan and a Sufi. A typical case is the ubiquitous reference to the meeting between Ṭughril Beg and Bābā Ṭāhir.[7] However, these passing references almost never include a deeper analysis of how these negotiated meetings fit into larger processes of legitimization. It is precisely such questions that will concern us in the second half of the present study in which I examine the contested interactions between Sufis and Saljūqs. The first half will document the rise of the dominant Saljūq state ideology and the multiplicity of state ideological apparatuses.

While this study will present an overview of Saljūq history, it is not primarily a work of dynastic history. Nor is it my intention to write a conventional intellectual history of the Saljūq era. Rather, my aim is to investigate the nexus of political loyalty and intellectual inquiry: how does Saljūq political culture inform the parameters in which intellectual inquiry might be undertaken? How might such an inquiry be used to reflect, deflect, or affect the political culture in which it is framed? To answer these questions, I have analyzed a wide range of primary sources, which might broadly be categorized into the following eight groups:

Historical Annals These texts are arranged in a chronological fashion, listing the major political and social events of that year, strange oddities, and the passing away of significant leaders and intellectuals. They are exclusively in Arabic.

ʿImād al-Dīn al-Kātib al-Iṣfahānī, *Nuṣrat al-fatra wa ʿuṣrat al-fiṭra* (abridged by al-Bundārī as *Zubdat al-nuṣra*). ʿImād al-Dīn (d. 597/1201) is the famous historian who rose to the rank of Saladin's personal scribe (*kātib*). This has led many of the sources to refer to him simply as al-Kātib al-Iṣfahānī. The *Zubdat al-nuṣra* is an invaluable source, as it was the first written history of the Great Saljūqs. It had the benefit of being based on an earlier, no longer extant, source, the memoirs of the vizier Anushīrwān b. Khālid (d. 738/1137).[8] Iṣfahānī's text was abridged by another scholar from Isfahan, al-Bundārī. Al-Bundārī dedicated his abridgement to the Ayyūbid ruler al-Muʿaẓẓam in 623/1226.[9]

Ibn al-Athīr, *al-Kāmil fī 'l-tārīkh*. Ibn al-Athīr's "comprehensive" history (*al-Kāmil*) is an essential source for the study of the impact of the Saljūqs on ʿIrāq and their relations with the caliphate. Ibn al-Athīr died in 630/1232.

Ibn Kathīr, *al-Bidāya wa 'l-nihāya*. Ibn Kathīr (d. 774/1373) was a noted Mamlūk scholar and historian. His text provides us with interesting information about the social and intellectual unrest during the Saljūq era. His *al-Bidāya* is indebted to many earlier historians, ranging from Ṭabarī and Ibn al-Jawzī, Ibn al-Athīr, and Sibṭ ibn al-Jawzī.[10]

Works of Dynastic History There are no extant works of this genre which were composed during the period of the Great Saljūqs themselves. However, historians of many of the offshoots of the Great Saljūqs (such as the Anatolian Saljūq dynasty) as well as some of the later Turkic dynasties devote significant sections to the Great Saljūqs. It is precisely these works (although they were edited over seventy years ago) that have yet to receive a thorough critical reading. The works of this genre came to be written increasingly in Persian, part of an ongoing trend in the eastern lands of Islamdom to compose works of history (*tārīkh*) in Persian. All of the works below, with the exception of the *Zubdat al-tawārīkh*, are Persian texts. For closer historiographic analysis of these sources, refer to Julie Meisami's masterful study, *Persian Historiography*, which offers a thorough analysis of the relationship among these texts.

Ẓahīr al-Dīn Nīshāpūrī, *Saljūq-nāma*. One of the earlier Persian texts on the Great Saljūqs. Nīshāpūrī died circa 582/1186. Narratives from this text come up frequently in later sources, often quoted verbatim.

Rāwandī, *Rāḥat al-ṣudūr*. Muḥammad b. ʿAlī Rāwandī dedicated his famous text, probably the best-known source for the study of the Great Saljūqs, to an Anatolian Saljūq ruler around 600/1204. His work is dependent on the *Saljūq-nāma* of Nīshāpūrī, listed above.[11]

Mustawfī Qazwīnī, *Tārīkh-i guzīda*. Mustawfī Qazwīnī (d. after 740/1339–40) was a historian and a geographer, who is perhaps better known for his geographic text *Nuzhat al-qulūb*. His *Tārīkh* relied upon Ṭabarī, Ibn al-Athīr,

Juwaynī, and Rashīd al-Dīn Ṭabīb, while adding some new material for the Il-khānid period.[12]

Ṣadr al-Dīn Ḥusaynī, *Zubdat al-tawārīkh*. This work is also known as *Akhbār al-dawla al-saljūqīya*. The editor of this text, the famed Muḥammad Iqbāl, goes through an extensive discussion dealing with the authorship and composition of this text. Given that the text refers to the *Zubdat al-nuṣra*, which is none other than Bundārī's abridgement of ʿImād al-Dīn al-Kātib al-Iṣfahānī's *Nuṣrat al-fatra* (discussed in the previous section), it cannot date any earlier than the seventh/thirteenth century. That it refers to the ʿAbbāsid caliph, al-Nāṣir li-Dīn Allāh (d. 622/1225), as "our master" (*mawlānā*) would seem to confirm a composition date around the first quarter of the seventh/thirteenth century.[13] Juwaynī's *Tārīkh-i jahān-gushāy* cites from this text. Iqbāl argues that the *Zubdat al-tawārīkh* is particularly important for documenting the history of the Saljūq family before its arrival on the Iranian plateau, and for later events at the end of the Great Saljūq period, from 550/1155 to 590/1193. In this project, I have relied upon this text to document the Saljūq family's background before its rise to prominence and in making visible the mythmaking process which is involved in the narrative of their conversion.

Gregory Abū ʾl-Faraj (known as Bar Hebraeus), *Chronography of Bar Hebraeus*. This Syriac text, written before 1286, is a remarkable universal history which provides us with an interesting outsider's perspective—one which is neither Arab, nor Persian, nor Turkish. For our purposes, it was his access to the no longer extant *Malik-nāma* which is of particular interest, as it provides us with intriguing details on the impact of the Saljūq invasion upon the Iranian plateau. It is also an important historiographic reminder of the necessity of including non-Muslim sources when they shed new light on a subject.

ʿAlāʾ al-Dīn ʿAṭā Malik b. Muḥammad Juwaynī, *Tārīkh-i jahān-gushāy*. Juwaynī (d. 681/1283) is one of the more noted premodern historians, frequently admired for his rigorous approach to historical material. His main relevance for our purposes is in providing valuable firsthand accounts of the conquest of the Ismāʿīlī stronghold, the castle of Alamūt. He had accompanied the Mongol warlord Hülegü on this conquest, culminating in the sack of Baghdad.[14] He was the teacher of Rashīd al-Dīn Ṭabīb, listed below.

Rashīd al-Dīn Faḍl Allāh Ṭabīb, *Jāmiʿ al-tawārīkh*. Rashīd al-Dīn (d. 718/1318) is generally considered the greatest historian of the Il-Khanid period. Rashīd al-Dīn's interests ranged widely, from history, medicine, theology, and administration to agriculture. Many scholars consider the *Jāmiʿ* to be the most important source for the history of the Mongols.[15] His representations of the Saljūqs are important in documenting later perceptions. His work is indebted to Juwaynī's *Tārīkh-i jahān-gushāy*.

Biographical Dictionaries These sources provide biographical information about various notables (political and intellectual) of the Saljūq era. Al-Subkī's work focuses on the Shāfiʿī ʿulamāʾ, Ibn Rajab's on their Ḥanbalī counterparts. Ibn Khallikān's frequently cited *Wafāyāt* deals with both political and intellectual notables. Since these works provide little information on philosophers, I will discuss the biographical works dealing with that group later on.

Ibn Khallikān, *Wafāyāt al-aʿyān*. Ibn Khallikān (d. 681/1282) represented the synthesis of the Mamlūk scholar/historian/judge. He had briefly studied with Ibn al-Athīr. His *Wafāyāt*, one of the most important premodern biographies of scholars and political figures, provides us with information about many figures of this time period. While Ibn Khallikān is most useful for the Mamlūk period, many of his anecdotes regarding Saljūq-era figures are from sources that are no longer extant. He is said to have finished the *Wafāyāt* in 672/1274.[16]

Tāj al-Dīn al-Subkī, *Ṭabaqāt al-shāfiʿīya*. An indispensable source for the intellectual life of this period. As the title suggests, it focuses exclusively on Shāfiʿī scholars. Subkī died in 771/1369.[17] Subkī goes to great lengths to suggest that Ashʿarī thought and Shāfiʿīsm have always been linked inseparably. Scholars, such as Makdisi, have interpreted such adamant insistence as a sign that even by the eighth/fourteenth century such linkages were met with frequent challenges. For our purposes, there are valuable insights about Ghazālī, Niẓām al-Mulk, and ʿAyn al-Quḍāt provided here. The over one hundred pages of information on Ghazālī provide our most detailed source about this famous intellectual. It also serves as a great reminder of the importance of Ghazālī in later works, enshrining him as *the* Shāfiʿī scholar. The inclusion and prominence of Niẓām al-Mulk's entry is also significant since it demonstrates the fluidity of the boundary between the religious scholars and court administrators.

Qāḍī Abū ʾl-Ḥasan Muḥammad ibn Abī Yaʿla, *Ṭabaqāt al-ḥanābila* and its continuation by Ibn Rajab, *Dhayl ʿalā ṭabaqāt al-ḥanābila*. The latter work was completed before 795/1392. These two are our most important sources for the lives of key Ḥanbalī scholars of the Saljūq period, such as Khwāja ʿAbd Allāh Anṣārī. Among other information, they provide ample proof that many Ḥanbalīs in this time period were Sufis, again demonstrating the fluidity of the categories ʿulamāʾ and Sufis.[18]

Histories of Viziers A recurring intent of this project is to document the ways in which the vizierate mediated negotiations between political and intellectual figures. I use the following histories of viziers, as well as the competing clusters of individuals who were attempting to rise to the highest ranks of administrative supremacy, to document this process. The rise of an individual to a significant administrative post often implied that the intellectuals he patronized would also receive appointments at prestigious madrasas. Conversely, the fall of a vizier and the intellectuals he patronized were also linked. The Saljūq vizierate was most effectively embodied (though still contested) in the person of Niẓām al-Mulk, who played a crucial role in the ordering and systematizing of the realm. The chronicler Ibn al-Athīr dubbed the whole Saljūq era *al-dawla al-niẓāmīya*.

Najm al-Dīn Qummī, *Tārīkh al-wuzarāʾ*. This text was composed sometime around 584/1188 and is an important source of information on Saljūq viziers for the fifty years prior to its composition. The early date of its composition (fifteen years before Rāwandī's *Rāḥat al-ṣudūr*) also adds to its value. It is particularly important since it starts with the vizierate of Qawwām al-Dīn Dargazīnī (d. 527/1133), the controversial figure held accountable for the execution of ʿAyn al-Quḍāt. Through this source, one can arrive at a radically different depiction of Dargazīnī than what is available through Sufi hagiographies focused on ʿAyn al-Quḍāt's passion. According to this source, Dargazīnī was a complex figure capable of both incredible kindness and quick wrath. More importantly, it demonstrates that the vizier was not opposed to Sufism and in fact had a publicly known relationship with the famous Sufi poet Ḥakīm Sanāʾī (d. 1131). As such, one cannot attribute the execution of ʿAyn al-Quḍāt to a simple anti-Sufi tendency on Dargazīnī's part.

Hindū Shāh ibn Sanjar Nakhjavānī, *Tajārib al-salaf*. Another work of the same genre, composed in 724/1323. Texts such as the *Tajārib* are an important indication of the prominence accorded to Niẓām al-Mulk in later histories of premodern Islamic administration. While most viziers are discussed in a few paragraphs that take up a page or so of the current printed text, Niẓām al-Mulk's section takes up fifteen pages. In addition, this source lists all of Niẓām al-Mulk's progeny who ascended to the vizierate, thus demonstrating that the Niẓām al-Mulk phenomenon was indeed a multigenerational one.

Sayf al-Dīn ʿAqīlī, *Āthār al-wuzarāʾ*. This source seems to have been composed around 875/1470. ʿAqīlī's patron in Herat was the vizier Khwāja Qawwām al-Dīn b. Niẓām al-Mulk Khwāfī, who operated in the court of Sultan Ḥusayn Bayqarā.

Khwānd Mīr, *Dastūr al-wuzarā'*. This work was composed in the year 914/1508. In terms of scope, it offers a history of major viziers starting with the Umayyads and ʿAbbāsids, going through Barmakids, Samanids, Daylamis, Ghaznavids, Saljūqs, Khwārazmshāhīs, and culminating with the Timurids.

ʿAbbās Iqbāl, *Vizārat dar ʿahd-i saljūqān-i buzurg*. A twentieth-century Iranian scholar of premodern Islamic administrative history, ʿAbbās Iqbāl [Āshtīyānī] published this monumental study in 1959, which brought to light many previously unknown details about the institutions of the Saljūq vizierate. All subsequent modern studies of the Persian vizierate are indebted to him. Iqbāl's *magnum opus* is particularly valuable in enabling us to reconstruct the impact that Niẓām al-Mulk had on the later history of premodern political administration. The vizier's impact extended beyond his own work and the institutions he orchestrated. It persisted through the many generations of his descendants who continued to be called upon by the Saljūqs to serve as viziers.

Political Treatises These were often written to legitimize the institution of the sultanate, or to provide administrative guidelines for it. Both Niẓām al-Mulk's *Siyāsat-nāma* and al-Ghazālī's *Naṣīḥat al-mulūk* have been edited and translated, yet they have not been sufficiently analyzed in terms of how they managed to subtly (but not always harmoniously) legitimize the Saljūqs on both Islamic and pre-Islamic Sāsānian grounds. It is perhaps an indication of the incomplete nature of Saljūq studies that one of the most important political treatises of al-Ghazālī, *Tuḥfat al-mulūk*, has received no attention in Western sources. I will offer an analysis of this text, which if proven to be an authentic work of al-Ghazālī would force us to radically re-evaluate our estimation of al-Ghazālī as a political thinker.

Niẓām al-Mulk, *Siyāsat-nāma*. This is quite simply the most important Persian premodern political treatise. The work was clearly composed by Niẓām al-Mulk toward the later stages of his life, between the years 479/1086 and 484/1091. The text foreshadows growing tensions between Niẓām al-Mulk and Malik-Shāh and anticipates the developments in the Saljūq court that led to the capable vizier's demise. It is also our most important source for documenting Niẓām al-Mulk's vision of a centralized Perso-Islamic state, demonstrating his attempts at instituting ideological state apparatuses, such as systems of surveillance and reconnaissance.

Abū Ḥāmid al-Ghazālī, *Naṣīḥat al-mulūk, Tuḥfat al-mulūk*, and other political writings. The first two are among the more important treatises attributed to Ghazālī. The *Naṣīḥat* was translated into English by F. R. C. Bagley.[19] There has been a healthy debate over whether this text was dedicated to Sultan Muḥammad ibn Malik-Shāh or Sultan Sanjar. Jalāl al-Dīn Humāʾī, who edited the Persian text, stated that the text was probably written in 502–3/1108–9, although he conceded that it could have been a bit earlier, circa 499/1105.[20] There is some controversy over the authenticity of the second part of the *Naṣīḥat*, as well as the *Tuḥfat*, and I will discuss those matters in chapter 4. If these works are to be taken as authentic, it would be particularly important for this study, as it establishes how al-Ghazālī moved even further away from the caliphate and closer to the Saljūq sultans toward the end of his life. This coincides, conveniently, with the rise of Saljūq power. The *Tuḥfat*'s contents have yet to be analyzed closely. The text is designed to legitimize the Saljūqs as just emperors (*pādshāh*s) who support *nīkū iʿtiqād* ("right doctrine," "orthodoxy") and are the closest people to God in the whole world.[21] Even if these texts are ultimately deemed to be spurious, the attribution of such Saljūq-friendly sources to al-Ghazālī so soon after the famed theologian's death is significant in documenting how later scholars wished to trace their own ideas back to al-Ghazālī. This is particularly the case for the *Naṣīḥat*, which was widely translated into Arabic.

Works of Individual Religious Scholars At times the term *ʿulamāʾ* can be a broad category that tends to blur distinctions without revealing a great deal. Sufis living in the Saljūq era could be (and often were) religious scholars, and religious scholars could (and often did) pursue the spiritual path (*ṭarīqa*). A recurring feature of the Saljūq intellectual milieu was the fluidity of these categories and indeed their mutual impact on one another. It would clearly be a mistake to perceive those who occupy these categories or their worldviews as being diametrically opposed to one another.

As part of this genre, I will examine the works of the two most important madrasa scholars of this period, Abū ʾl-Maʿālī al-Juwaynī and Abū Ḥāmid al-Ghazālī. Rather than identifying al-Juwaynī and al-Ghazālī primarily as jurists *or* theologians (or any other single pigeonhole), I will categorize them in terms of their institutional role as teachers in the madrasa system and propagators of the Saljūq-sponsored articulation of Islam. This heavily ideological formulation consisted of a synthesis of Ashʿarī theology, the Shāfiʿī madhhab, and a rigorously Sharʿī interpretation of Sufism. As Marshall Hodgson has recognized, by participating in Saljūq-patronized institutions, these members of the ʿulamāʾ were in fact giving up their role as oppositional figures in political life.[22] Far from being oppositional figures, they had been fully appropriated as the legitimizers of the Saljūqs and participated in their coercive state apparatuses.

If the madrasa ʿulamāʾ had come to dilute their oppositional role, the Sufis preserved a full range of responses to the dominant Saljūq ideology. Some Sufis (Aḥmad-i Jām, Abū Saʿīd-i Abī ʾl-Khayr) came to be fully identified with the Saljūq system, others remained mostly neutral in the political domains (Aḥmad-i Ghazālī), while a minority took up a defiant oppositional role (ʿAyn al-Quḍāt Hamadānī). It is a testimony to the success of the dominant Saljūq ideology that ʿAyn al-Quḍāt is the only figure from among the ʿulamāʾ and Sufis whom we can document as contesting the very basis of Saljūq legitimacy.

Abū Ḥāmid al-Ghazālī (d. 505/1111). This is the Saljūq intellectual most easily identifiable with a Saljūq-patronized institution, the Niẓāmīya madrasa. His many writings, including *al-Munqidh min al-ḍalāl, Fayṣal al-tafriqa bayn al-islām wa ʾl-zandaqa*, and *Faḍāʾiḥ al-bāṭinīya wa faḍāʾil al-mustaẓhirīya*, all support the Saljūq ideological interpretation of Islamic thought. In these writings, al-Ghazālī polemically dismisses Ismāʿīlī teachings, and severely restricts the usefulness of philosophers. I have already mentioned his political treatises, the *Naṣīḥat al-mulūk* and the dubious *Tuḥfat al-mulūk*. Also useful are his letters (*Faḍāʾil al-anām min rasāʾil ḥujjat al-islām*) written to significant Saljūq figures. These letters document his close relations with the Saljūq political leaders as well as that, like every other Saljūq figure, al-Ghazālī did not go uncontested: he too was accused of heresy by his detractors.

ʿAyn al-Quḍāt Hamadānī (d. 525/1131). This is the sole figure from the Saljūq era whom we can document as a major and consistent opponent to the dominant Saljūq ideology. His *Tamhīdāt* contains cryptic challenges to the economic basis of the Saljūq regime and to the association of the ʿulamāʾ with them. All of these points are articulated fully and explicitly in the letters which he wrote to his disciples at the Saljūq court. These letters are preserved in the *Nāma-hā-yi ʿAyn al-Quḍāt-i Hamadānī*. These letters represent a powerful voice of dissent, challenging the dominant state ideology, just as his last composition, the *Shakwa al-gharīb*, attests to the fatal consequences faced by those who tried to contest the dominant Saljūq state ideology.

Aḥmad-i Jām (d. 536/1141). Aḥmad-i Jām was another of the significant Saljūq Sufis from the end of the period of the Great Saljūqs. I will examine two of his compositions, *Rawḍat al-mudhnibīn*, and *Miftāḥ al-najāt*. It is significant to note that apart from the hagiographic tradition that associates him with the Saljūqs, he also dedicates these texts to the Saljūq Sultan Sanjar. His texts represent a clear example of a Sufi working to legitimize the Saljūqs.

Hagiographies In this work I will analyze the hagiographies written about two significant Saljūq era Sufis, Abū Saʿīd-i Abī ʾl-Khayr and Aḥmad-i Jām. In doing so, I will document how the genealogical and spiritual descendants of Sufi masters would retrospectively come to depict the Sufi teachers as having blessed or otherwise legitimized the rule of certain Saljūq notables. My interest in these sources will be to decipher patterns in these narratives, which on one hand portray the saints as legitimizing the rulers and on the other hand as demanding patronage from them.

One of the historiographic goals of this project will be demonstrated in chapter 5, where I will argue for the importance of incorporating hagiographic material into our construction of the social history of premodern Islam. I aim to demonstrate that, contrary to the readings of positivist scholars of Sufism, these hagiographies are not trivial texts written for the mindless and the easily amused, but rather carefully crafted narratives connecting two communities of power, one political and one saintly.

The *Asrār al-tawḥīd*, the best known hagiography of Abū Saʿīd, was composed by one of his descendants, Muḥammad ibn Munawwar ibn Abī Saʿd ibn Abī Ṭāhir ibn Abī Saʿīd. To the best of our estimation, this text was composed around 574/1178–9. It was presented before the year 599/1202–3 to the Ghurīd Sultan, Muḥammad ibn Sām.[23] In addition, it was extensively circulated among the descendants and disciples of Abū Saʿīd in Khurāsān and Herat.

A cousin of the above author, another third generation descendant of Abū Saʿīd, composed the second hagiography related to the famous saint from Mayhana. This hagiographer, Jamāl al-Dīn Abū Rūḥ Luṭf Allāh ibn Abī Saʿīd, authored the lesser-known *Ḥālāt wa sukhanān-i Abū Saʿīd-i Abū ʾl-Khayr,* which was utilized by Ibn Munawwar. Jamāl al-Dīn died in the year 541/1147.[24]

A third significant hagiography that will be consulted in this project is the one dedicated to Aḥmad-i Jām (536/1141). This text, the *Maqāmāt-i zhanda pīl*, was composed by Sadīd al-Dīn Ghaznavī around 552/1152. This text is an example of successful relations between communities organized around a saint and political figures. There are many narratives in which Aḥmad-i Jām is depicted as having saved Sultan Sanjar from the Ismāʿīlīs, receiving patronage in return.

Histories of Philosophers The histories of philosophers from this period often trace the sages (*ḥukamāʾ*) back to the Greek philosophers. They give us an important insight into the difficulty of classifying a figure like ʿAyn al-Quḍāt as purely a Sufi, since he is also included in these works.

ʿAlī ibn Zayd Bayhaqī, *Tārīkh ḥukamāʾ al-islām*. Bayhaqī perished during the Ghuzz onslaught, sometime between the years 548/1153 and 565/1169. This source provides us with interesting material on Ibn Sīnā as well as ʿAyn al-Quḍāt, who is claimed as a philosopher. This text presents ʿAyn al-Quḍāt as one who "mixed the words of Sufis and philosophers." It is also a crucial source for documenting that in less than one generation after ʿAyn al-Quḍāt's martyrdom, the vizier Dargazīnī was held personally responsible for his execution. ʿAyn al-Quḍāt's inclusion in this philosophical *ṭabaqāt* work predates his inclusion in any Sufi *tadhkira*. Bayhaqī also authored the *Tatimma ṣiwān al-ḥikma* as a sequel to Abū Sulaymān Manṭiqī Sijistānī's *Ṣiwān al-ḥikma*. This important text was translated into Persian in the fourteenth century.

Shahrazūrī, *Nuzhat al-arwāḥ*. Shahrazūrī was a seventh-/thirteenth-century illuminationist (*ishrāqī*) philosopher, who followed in the footsteps of Shaykh al-Ishrāq, Shihāb al-Dīn Yaḥyā Suhrawardī (d. 587/1191). His biographical work, the *Nuzhat al-arwāḥ*, is our main source for the life of Suhrawardī. In addition, it provides 122 biographical entries on a number of Greek and Islamic philosophers.[25]

Nāṣir al-Dīn b. ʿUmdat al-Mulk Munshī Yazdī, *Durrat al-akhbār wa lamaʿat al-anwār*. Yazdī's work was essentially a partial Persian translation of Bayhaqī's *Tatimma ṣiwān al-ḥikma*. Yazdī's text was composed under the patronage of Ghiyāth al-Dīn Muḥammad, the son of the famous vizier and historian, Rashīd al-Dīn Faḍl Allāh Ṭabīb. As such, it was probably composed sometime between 725/1325 and 736/1336.

Having introduced and identified the key figures and texts, we are now well situated to move to a historiographic analysis of the Great Saljūqs.

The Politics of Knowledge in Premodern Islam

Chapter One

Deconstructing the Great Saljūq Myth

This urgent plea was sent from the ʿAbbāsid Caliph al-Qāʾim Bi Amr Allāh to the Turkish warlord Ṭughril Beg of the Saljūq tribe in 450/1058:

Allāh, Allāh!
musalmānī rā daryāb,
ki dushman mustaulī shud, wa shuʿār-i qarmaṭiyān ẓāhir gasht.

(By God, by God!
Save Islām [*musalmānī*].[1]
The cursed enemy has overcome us, and the
Qarmaṭī[2] propaganda is widespread.)

The text of this letter is featured prominently in many historical chronicles, and its tone has shaped much of the contemporary scholarship on the late ʿAbbāsid period and the rise of the Saljūq dynasty.[3] Recent scholarship holds that the Sunni Caliphate had been weakened for a century (dubbed the "Shīʿī century") during which it was manipulated by Shīʿī Buwayhid amīrs. Furthermore, the caliphate is held to have been undermined by the establishment of the Fāṭimī Ismāʿīlī Caliphate-Imamate in Cairo in 969 C.E.[4] The Qarmaṭīs in the caliphal letter refer to the Fāṭimīd-backed forces led by a Turkish military leader, Basāsīrī, who had captured Baghdad, proclaimed the Shīʿī call to prayer and inserted the name of the Fāṭimī Caliph al-Mustanṣir in the *khuṭba* in 450/1058. Furthermore, Basāsīrī had exiled the ʿAbbāsid Caliph to ʿĀna and killed some of his administrators, including the vizier Abū ʾl-Qāsim ʿAlī b. al-Ḥasan b. Maslama, in a most gruesome manner.[5] Al-Kātib al-Iṣfahānī summarizes the anxieties of this age in a pun-filled, poetic statement: "The example (*sunna*) of Basāsīrī was a hideous one, and almost extinguished the Divine Light. This was because he insisted on calling people to follow the bastard in Egypt (*fa-annahu daʿa ilā ʾl-daʿī bi-miṣr muṣirr^{an}*)."[6] According to these accounts, the caliph repeatedly begged for Ṭughril's help. The sources credit Ṭughril with heeding the caliph's cry for help by quoting this Qur'anic verse in his response letter: "*Go back to them. We shall soon come with our armies which they will not be able to face. We shall drive them out of (the land) with ignominy, and they will be humbled.*"[7]

The historical chronicles go on to record Ṭughril's march to Baghdad and defeat of Basāsīrī. They detail, in a grand style, his restoring of the caliph to the caliphate.[8] The chronicles credit the Saljūqs not only with rescuing the caliphate, but also with reestablishing social order and propagating a normative interpretation of Islam, that is, the same "saving of Islam" that is alluded to in the caliphal letter. Much of contemporary scholarship has naively come to accept this depiction of the Saljūqs. Even the usually astute historian of premodern Muslim Iran, C. E. Bosworth, does not problematize this construction: "Ṭoghrïl's march to Baghdad has often been viewed as a Sunni crusade to rescue the Caliph from his Shīʿī oppressors . . . We can only guess at Ṭoghrïl's inner motives, but it is surely relevant to note that his Iranian advisers included many officials from Khurāsān, the most strongly Sunnī part of Iran."[9] Likewise, a recent survey of Islamic history, written by the prominent social historian Francis Robinson, reiterates this notion by further emphasizing the connections between the Saljūqs, ʿAbbāsids, and religious orthodoxy: "The Caliphate was given another lease of life as the Turks freed the Abbasids from their Buyid thralldom and created a new institution, the universal Sultanate. Henceforth the Caliph bestowed legitimacy on the effective holders of power as he did when he crowned the first Saljūq Sultan in 1058, while it was now the Sultan's duty to impose his authority on the Islamic community, defending it against attacks from outside and denials of God's word within."[10]

Nor has this type of a characterization been limited to works originating in the field of Islamic studies. Even post-Kemalist works of Turkish scholarship, steeped in modernist nationalism, have perpetuated such a depiction of the Saljūqs and their relationship with the ʿAbbāsid Caliphate. The Turkish scholar Ibrahim Kafesoğlu states:

> When the Seljuks appeared on the scene in the eleventh century, they found a Muslim world in complete political disarray . . . Moreover, to the great consternation of Sunnī Muslims, the Caliph in Cairo was a Shīʿī and bent on imposing his authority and version of Islam on them all. In Baghdad, the legitimate successor to Muḥammad was little more than a puppet in the hands of another Shīʿī dynasty. It seemed to many

> Sunnīs that true, orthodox Islam would soon be displaced by heresy. In addition to political and religious disunity, Islamic culture had begun to decline . . . As Sunnīs, the Seljuks came on the scene as liberators, rescuing the ʿAbbāsid Caliph from his Shīʿī masters, and crushing heresy wherever they found it.[11]

The themes here are as familiar as they are recurrent: "freeing" the ʿAbbāsid Caliphate, defending Islamdom from external attacks, and purging Islamic thought from internal heresies. For the most part, contemporary scholarship on the Saljūqs, whether it comes from the perspective of Islamic studies, Iranian history, or Turkish studies, has come to accept the depiction of the Saljūqs in the historical chronicles as historical fact rather than *a construction* which has been deliberately manufactured and propagated by successive generations of historians and administrators intent on justifying and legitimizing the Saljūqs. Our starting point in this venture is the deconstruction of this carefully crafted ideological presentation of the Saljūqs, what I shall refer to as the Great Saljūq Myth. As Julie Meisami has stated, "The medieval historian's primary interest lay less in recording the 'facts' of history than in the construction of meaningful narratives."[12] Likewise, we will be concerned here with uncovering the various layers of meaning in these constructed Saljūq narratives.

State (*dawla*), Order (*niẓām*), and Religion (*dīn*)

To recognize the construction of the Saljūq image and its function as propaganda in legitimizing the Saljūqs, it is useful to recall the concept of ideology.[13] The sources that sought to legitimize the Saljūq presence took part in an ideological process of justifying the Saljūqs. Saljūq ideology was not inimical toward religion but should not be collapsed to religion either.[14] I am here uninterested in whether the Saljūqs were pious Muslims in their personal lives. I am, however, greatly concerned with *how* the depiction of Saljūqs as pious Muslims is used in sources to legitimize them. I aim to investigate the various ways in which the Saljūqs and their accomplices appropriated religious symbols to legitimize themselves. This new and powerful ruling dynasty that hailed from regions outside the heartland of Islamdom did not have access to the genealogical modes of religious legitimization that appealed to descent from the Prophet (as in the case of the ʿAbbāsids). However, Saljūq ideology could not, and indeed did not, ignore other means of appealing to rich religious symbols to justify their rule. The narratives that were designed to legitimize the Saljūq rule appealed to five modes of legitimization by claiming that the Saljūqs

1. were obedient to (Sunni) Islamic principles
2. were loyal to the ʿAbbāsid Caliphs
3. promoted social order throughout the realm and protected Muslim lives and properties
4. patronized (Sunni "orthodox") religious scholarship
5. put down heretics/social deviants.

These five elements are not listed per se in the sources; rather, depending on the situation, the narratives appeal to one or more of these modes of legitimization. Our concern is first to recognize each of the above assertions as a key element of Saljūq ideology in the narratives we are to encounter. I intend to read the historical sources and political narratives, even poetry and hagiography, of the Saljūq era as part of a massive process to legitimize the Saljūq rule. Having pointed out the constructed nature of the Great Saljūq Myth, my secondary aim in this chapter is to document historical evidence that undermines these modes of justification. For example, whereas the sources are interested in depicting the Saljūqs as promoting social order, I will marshal evidence to document the social discord brought on by the Turkish warlords. Whereas the sources strive to depict a harmonious relationship between the Saljūqs and the caliphs, I will document a contested, often tense negotiation for power and authority. We will come back to these five domains of justification repeatedly in rereading the historical narratives dealing with the rise of the Saljūqs. I do not aim to provide a positivistic historical narrative of the Saljūq rise to power or an exhaustive overview of Saljūq history.[15] Rather, I intend to analyze the ways in which these historical narratives function as ideological propaganda in justifying a Saljūq regime that had little recourse to conventional models of religious legitimacy.

The political treatises and historical chronicles of this period posit a direct connection between social order (*niẓām*) and orthodoxy in matters of religion (*dīn*). The movements that were deemed heretical (an identification which naturally depended on the perspective of the defining group) were almost always accused of upsetting social order. One example of this linkage is the depiction in al-Iṣfahānī's *Nuṣrat al-fatra* (now available only in al-Bundārī's abridgment, *Zubdat al-nuṣra*) of the above-mentioned Fāṭimīd-backed revolt of al-Basāsīrī in 450/1058: "The order of Islām became disordered (*ukhtalla niẓām al-islām*). The Abode of Peace (*Dār al-salām*)[16] became weakened."[17] Much along the same lines, the able Saljūq administrator, Niẓām al-Mulk, stated, "The most important thing which a king needs is sound religion (*dīn-i durust*), because kingship and religion are like two brothers; whenever disturbance (*idṭirāb*) breaks out in the country religion suffers too; heretics (*bad-dīnān*) and evil-doers (*mufsidān*) appear; and whenever religious affairs are in disorder (*bā-khalal*), there is confusion (*shūrīda*) in the country; evil-doers gain power and render the king impotent and despondent; heresy grows rife and rebels make themselves felt."[18]

In his eulogy on Niẓām al-Mulk, al-Kātib al-Iṣfahānī again returns to the above association of *Niẓām* and *Dīn*, stating, "Niẓām al-Mulk restored order (*niẓām*) to the state,[19] and stability and correctness to religion (*fa-ʿāda ʾl-mulk ilā ʾl-niẓām wa ʾl-dīn ilā ʾl-qawām*)."[20] What is of interest to us here is the manner in which the two semantic fields of state (*mulk*) and religion (*dīn*) were made to interpenetrate one another in Saljūq ideology: the religion's strength and stability (*qawām*) were ideologically connected to the order (*niẓām*) of the realm (*mulk*). Furthermore, religion had to be ordered, to protect it from heretical attacks. The Saljūq state was also religiously sanctioned, meaning that the Saljūq ideology of social order and justice would appropriate symbols of religious legitimacy. The interplay between *niẓām* and *dīn* underscores the tension (and the relationship) between religion and ideology in the case of the Saljūqs; these are clearly related categories that should nonetheless not be collapsed onto one another. Saljūq ideology made full use of religious symbols, and conversely the religious system patronized by the Saljūqs had a great role in legitimizing their existence.

Saljūq ideology was a multifaceted phenomenon and by necessity had to acknowledge the ʿAbbāsid Caliphs, the symbols of religiously legitimized political rule. We shall later on examine the *actual* relationship between the sultans and the caliphs, a relationship that was far from harmonious. At this time, it is the depiction of this relationship in Saljūq-legitimizing sources that is of concern to us. We have already identified the assertion of a close relationship between the Saljūqs and the ʿAbbāsids as the second component of Saljūq ideology. The Saljūqs moved in a span of one generation from identifying themselves as humble clients (*mawālī*)[21] of the caliph to being his "right hand" (*yamīn*). In his official letters written in 454/1062, Ṭughril is heralded as "the exalted Emperor of Emperors, King of the East and West, Reviver of Islam, Lieutenant of the Imām, and Right Hand of the Caliph of God, the Commander of the Faithful."[22] While the term *yamīn amīr al-muʾminīn* still implies subordination to the caliph, it was also a strong reminder to the caliph that without the powerful Saljūq military presence, the caliph would be rendered politically powerless.

The Saljūqs' alleged obedience should not be separated from their claim of following a "right-belief" (quite literally, *ortho-dox*) interpretation of Islam, which is identical with the first component of Saljūq ideology. The chronicler Qazwīnī, one of the historians (along with Rāwandī, Nīshāpūrī, and Rashīd al-Dīn Faḍl Allāh) who participated fully in the legitimizing of the Saljūqs, states that while many of the previous Muslim regimes were *mulawwath*, "beset by defilement and pollution" (of thought, i.e., heresy),[23] the Saljūq kings were pure and clean (*pāk*) of this defilement. They were Sunni, *pāk-dīn* (of pure religion), *nīkū iʿtiqād* (orthodox), and beneficent to their flock. It was due to the *baraka* of these factors, Qazwīnī alleges, that no one rebelled against them, causing them distress.[24] We have identified the putting down of heretical movements as a key component of Saljūq ideology. Historians of premodern Islamdom would surely recognize the great number of rebels who did in fact revolt against the Saljūqs. Surely had there been no heretics in their midst, Niẓām al-Mulk would not have spent chapter after chapter in the *Siyāsat-nāma* bemoaning their influence. What Qazwīnī's claim conveys is not so much a *historical depiction* as an ideological claim of orthodoxy that is used to justify the Saljūqs. We are in a real sense dealing here with a political genre that mirrors saintly hagiographies.

Qazwīnī was neither the first nor the last chronicler to ascribe religious orthodoxy to the Saljūqs. The chronicles vie with one another in depicting the Saljūqs' obedience to Islam by offering a parade of exotic adjectives: *miṭwāʿ wa munqād-i farāʾiḍ wa sunan*[25] (obedient and submissive to the religious duties and prophetic paradigm), supporters of and obedient to the *ḥaḍrat-i muqaddas-i nabawī*[26] (the sanctified Prophetic presence), and *mitwāʿ wa muʿāḍid-i islām wa farāʾiḍ* (obedient to and helpers of Islam and religious duties).[27] This exaggerated emphasis surely begs the question and deserves further examination, which we shall undertake shortly.

The Saljūqid historian Rāwandī most clearly articulates the alleged connection between upholding normative Islam and the success of an empire. In the introduction to his *Rāḥat al-ṣudūr*, written for the Anatolian Saljūqid ruler Kay-Khusrau ibn Arslān, Rāwandī underscores this point by comparing the Saljūq enterprise to a tree: "The root of this tree is edification and promoting religion (*taqwiyat wa tarbiyat-i dīn*). The fruit of this tree is establishing good institutions such as madrasas, khānaqāhs, mosques, hospices, bridges, water-stations for the pilgrimage road, the training of scholars, associating with ascetics and saints, donating money, renewal of the creed of justice, and maintaining of the traditions of government."[28]

Rāwandī further claims that the baraka (transferable and powerful blessing) of the Saljūq state was due to their patronizing of scholars, a feature which we have identified as the fourth element of Saljūq ideology. According to Rāwandī, these religious scholars came forth from diverse regions of the world, in particular the "two ʿIrāqs"[29] and Khurāsān. Furthermore, the Saljūq chronicler stated that the scholars

> composed books of jurisprudence, and gathered prophetic traditions. They brought forth so many books on the definite and allegorical verses of the Qurʾan, exegesis, and authentic prophetic traditions that the root of the faith was firmly established in the hearts. This resulted in the heretics (*bad-dīnān*) losing all hope [of gaining supremacy] . . . The realm of the Saljūq Sultans was established through the *baraka* of the pen [used] in writing juridical opinions, and the piety of [the great scholars]. When the *pādshāh*, vassal, military commander, vizier, and all the military would operate their possessions and land-grants according to the Islamic law and the juridical opinions of the Imams of the faith, the land was cultivated, and the provinces were inhabited.[30]

The composite nature of Saljūq ideology can be seen by noting that in the above example, the Saljūq patronage of scholars—the fourth component—reinforces the first component (obedience to *nīkū iʿtiqād* Islam) as well as the fifth component, which involved putting down heretics.[31] These, in turn, strengthen the overall security and well-being of the whole realm—the third component of Saljūq ideology. As previously stated, the narratives that sought to legitimize the Saljūqs not only emphasized one mode of justification, they also moved rather freely among several modes. At this point, I will demonstrate how the Saljūq-legitimizing chronicles incorporated all five components of Saljūq ideology in constructing the Great Saljūq Myth.

The Great Saljūq Myth as Articulation of Saljūq Ideology

There are no extant historical chronicles from the early years of the Great Saljūq era (1055–1157). Almost all of our available data about the Saljūqs comes from later sources that were in one way or another engaged in the retrospective process that I call pious and urgent mythmaking. In using the concept of myth, I do not mean to suggest that it is simply untrue in a positivist historical fashion. Rather, I am using this term to imply a type of sacrosanct history, particularly concerned with origins, which is believed to be true by those who ascribe to the myth and propagate it.[32] The Great Saljūq myth was a pious myth, as it seems to have been sorely needed and perhaps sincerely believed by its constructors and transmitters. Its construction was also urgent: it was fully elaborated in times that also suffered from social unrest and had a need for appealing to ordered-orthodox earlier times.[33] Thus, I propose to read the chroniclers' depiction of the Saljūqs as being the result of a pious and urgent mythmaking process designed to legitimize the new and powerful rulers of Islamdom. I aim to demonstrate that the early Saljūqid historical narratives were in reality ideological propaganda that were carefully and deliberately constructed to legitimize the Saljūq rule and to conceal any information which did not fit the modes of justification.

Myths are usually concerned with origins, and in this first chapter I will deliberately focus on the depiction of the origins of the Saljūq family in the chronicles, the emergence of the Saljūq clan as a distinct family within the Oghuz tribe, their appearance on the Iranian plateau, and their eventual transformation from a nomadic family into a ruling dynasty. Initially, it might seem perplexing to focus on the origins of the dynasty and its rise to power, especially when it is universally acknowledged that the apogee of its power was not achieved until the third Great Saljūq Sultan, Malik-Shāh, who ruled from 1072 to 1092.[34] My choice of this earlier period is deliberate and tied to historiographic issues. We do not possess any extant sources that were written during the life of the first three Great Saljūq Sultans themselves. All the historical chronicles were written well after the rise and break-up of the Saljūq dynasty and retrospectively attempt to justify the Saljūqs as upholders of Sunni Islam and as humble servants of the caliphate. They often portray the Saljūqs as pious forerunners of the later Turkic dynasties. In order to challenge this retrospective construction and de-privilege it, I will utilize two types of sources: first, I will pay significant attention to the only source on Saljūq history written before the appearance of Niẓām al-Mulk (and thus the first ideological articulation of the Great Saljūq Myth), a treatise titled *Malik-nāma*, which is itself no longer extant but which has been partially preserved by certain later authors. The image of the Saljūqs that emerges from the *Malik-nāma* stands in a sharp contrast to the later ideological constructions of the Great Saljūq Myth. Second, there are some allusions and fragmentary reports in the later chronicles that do not fit the image of the Saljūqs as rescuers of the caliph and upholders of normative Islam and social order. I will also highlight these fragments, further challenging the accepted depiction of the Saljūqs that was intended to legitimize them.

The later chapters explore the implications of "saving" Islam. In order to rescue Islam, the Saljūqs and the intellectuals affiliated with them had to systematize, control, define, and propagate their construction of Islamic thought. It is not my contention that their construction of Islam was somehow wrong, even as I do not take their definition of orthodoxy as somehow normative and proscriptive. Rather, I am concerned with the very process of claiming and constructing orthodoxy. Every construction has to include certain elements even as it excludes (explicitly and implicitly) many others. The Saljūq construction of religious orthodoxy was neither random nor uncontested. A major part of this project is concerned with tracing the elements that were appropriated for the Saljūq construction of Islam and documenting the ones that were marginalized. However, before we get to a discussion of the construction of the Islam that was being saved, we should take a closer look at the group who was being asked to save Islam, as in the caliphal plea *Musalmānī rā daryāb*. The irony is inescapable: a nomadic Turkish family from Central Asia, which as recently as three generations before had been non-Muslim, was asked by the religious and symbolic figurehead of Islamdom to save Islam itself. Who were the Saljūqs, and how did they arrive at the position of power that led the caliph to approach them? How were the Saljūqs transformed from one family within one clan of a large confederation of Turkish tribes to the effective rulers of premodern Islamdom in its heartland (Iran and Iraq)? These are the questions that I will explore initially, before moving on to the articulation and deconstruction of the Great Saljūq Myth.

Saljūqs and Oghuz

The Oghuz were a confederation of tribes who migrated from inner Asia toward the Iranian plateau well before the rise of the Saljūqs to power. Already by the eighth century, the Oghuz had moved from the Orkhon and Selenga valleys of Mongolia toward the areas of Irtysh and Syr Darya.[35] In discussing the Oghuz tribesmen from Balkh who captured the Saljūq Sultan Sanjar in 548/1153, Ibn al-Athīr remarks, "Some Khurāsānī historians have mentioned that these Oghuz came over to Transoxiana from the regions of the marches which are in the remotest Turkish lands during the reign of the Caliph al-Mahdī (775–85 C.E.)."[36] By 309–10/921–22, the Arab traveler Ibn Faḍlān had noted the presence of the Oghuz in the steppes between the Volga and Khwārazm.[37] He mentioned a band of the Oghuz who were living in extreme poverty and wandered "like straying wild asses."[38] It is also significant to document that Ibn Faḍlān recorded the military-political-tribal titles given to the Oghuz leaders, which one encounters repeatedly in later Ghaznavid and Saljūq history: *Yabghū* (chief), *sū-bāshī* (also called *ṣāḥib al-jaysh*, military commander), and *Īnāl* (a lesser commander).[39] The Oghuz were not a homogenous ethnic group, and they tended to assimilate different tribes as they moved out of Mongolia. The Turkish encyclopedist Maḥmūd Kāshgharī lists twenty-two tribes of the Oghuz, some of which may even have been non-Turkish.[40] Kāshgharī states, "The Oghuz are a tribe of the Turks, the Türkman. They consist of twenty-two branches, each of which has a distinctive brand (*ʿalāma*) on its animals by which it is known from the others. The chief of them is the Qïnïq, to which our present Sultans belong."[41]

Kāshgharī adds that each of the above twenty-two divisions of the Oghuz were a subtribe, and each subtribe in turn was made up of several subbranches. It is at the level of subbranches that the "the names of the sub-tribes are the name of their ancestors . . . just as among the Arabs one says 'Banū Salīm'."[42] This would seem to imply that the Great Saljūqs started out as simply one family within the subbranch of one of the twenty-two subtribes comprising the Oghuz.

In presenting the impact of the Oghuz-Saljūq migration into the regions of the Iranian plateau and Iraq, and in documenting their disastrous impact on the citied cultures, one may be tempted to classify this as yet a further chapter in the dichotomy of "city-culture" (presumably Persian, and fully Islamic) and "nomadic-culture" (primarily Turkish, always suspected of paganism, or at best superficial Islamization).[43] Even the distinguished historian of premodern Iran, C. E. Bosworth, does not problematize this depiction and passes this judgment on the Saljūqs: "The Seljuqs were all unfamiliar with the ways and usages of civilised life."[44] But one should be careful about seeing these categories ("refined-citied-Persian" vs. "ruffian-nomadic-Turkish") as absolute reflections of the social reality. For instance, the learned Turkish scholars of this time, who valued the preservation of the riches of Turkish language and culture, already bemoaned the "slurring" in the speech of Turks. This slurring (*rikka*) was presumed to be the result of Turks mixing with Persians, settling in their lands, or having become bilingual.[45] If we accept the correlation proposed by Kāshgharī, linking Persianate citied cultures[46] with a slurring and decline of "elegant Turkish," it is quite significant that the Oghuz were singled out from all the Turkish groups as having had the "lightest of the dialects," implying that they had the greatest level of contact with Persianate citied cultures.[47] Another example that points to the vast network of connections between the Persians and the Turks is the Turkish proverb quoted by Kāshgharī: *Tātsïz türk bolmās, bāšsïz börk bolmās* (A Turk is never without a Persian [just as] a cap is never without a head.)[48] Even if some of the sources (e.g., *Siyāsat-nāma*) at times fall back on essentializing the "Persian" versus the "Turk," we must recognize that the historical reality was a far more nuanced one, with various levels of cooperation, conflict, and assimilation.[49]

While the Islamization of the Turkish tribes had begun a few centuries earlier, the process was far from having been completed, or of even resulting in a majority of Turks accepting Islam. There were ongoing battles between recently converted Turkish tribes and pagan ones. Ibn al-Athīr reports that in the year 435/1043–44, ten thousand "tent-dwellers" from Balā-Sāghūn and Kāshghar in Transoxiana embraced Islam. Ibn al-Athīr's sigh of relief ("God thus eliminated their evil from being directed towards Muslims"[50]) surely resonated in the citied cultures of Khurāsān and Transoxiana which had been subjected to periodic raids of the pagan, nomadic Turkic tribes. The great number of converts at this occasion, even if exaggerated, suggests that the conversion of Turks to Islam was far from complete even in the mid-eleventh century, at the time of the Saljūqs' rise to power. The possible pagan origin of the Turkish intruders, and of the Saljūq tribe in particular, posed a significant problem for the later chroniclers to deal with—and also to cover up.

We are fortunate to possess an account in the anonymous tenth-century geographical treatise *Ḥudūd al-ʿālam*[51] that describes the early Oghuz confederacy. This rather unflattering account was written after the Oghuz had entered lands bordering *Dār al-islām* but well before the Saljūq rise to power. It helps to offset some of the glowing descriptions of the early Saljūqs by chroniclers who were all too eager to please their patrons:[52]

> The Ghūz[53] have arrogant faces (*shūkh-rūy*) and are quarrelsome (*sitīza-kār*), malicious (*badh-rag*), and malevolent (*ḥasūd*). Both in summer and winter they wander along the pasture-lands and grazing-grounds (*charāgāh-va-giyā-khwār*). Their wealth is in horses, cows, sheep, arms, and game in small quantities. Among them merchants are very numerous. And whatever the Ghūz, or the merchants, possess of good or wonderful is the object of veneration by the Ghūz. [The Ghūz] greatly esteem the physicians (*ṭabībān*) and, whenever they see them, venerate them (*namāz barand*), and these doctors (*pijishkān*) have command over their lives (*khūn*) and property (*khwāsta*). The Ghūz have no towns,[54] but the people owning felt-huts are very numerous. They possess arms and implements (*silāḥ va ālāt*) and are courageous and daring (*shūkh*) in war. They continually make inroads (*ghazw*) into the lands of Islam (*nawāḥī-yi islām*), whatever place be on the way (*ba har jāʾī uftadh*), and [then] strike (*bar-kūband*), plunder, and retreat as quickly as possible. Each of their

tribes has a [separate] chief on account of their discords (*nā-sāzandagī*) with each other.[55]

The dominant characteristics of the Oghuz confederation that emerge from this account are their nomadic lifestyle, the customary raiding into the sedentary Islamic lands,[56] and a fierce temperament. The reverence for the physicians and doctors might very well be an allusion to the prominence of shamanic figures.

Again, it is tempting to conclude from the above account that the Oghuz confederation was nothing more significant than a wandering, nomadic bunch of ruffians. It is important to point out that contrary to the claim of the above account and certain other chroniclers, sedentary culture was not completely unknown to them.[57] Both Masʿūdī and Ibn Ḥawqal report that the Turks lived in an *al-qarya al-ḥadītha* (Persian: *dih-i nau*, Turkish: Yengi-Kent, English: new town) on the lower Syr Darya. Many of these urban Turks were from the Oghuz confederation and included both *bawādī* (nomads) and *ḥaḍar* (sedentaries).[58] Kāshgharī produced a map in which he identified the lower Syr Darya as "land of the Oghuz towns."[59] In light of the political shrewdness of the later Saljūqs in dealing with political and intellectual notables (*aʿyān*),[60] it should not come as a surprise that they already had some measure of familiarity with citied Islamic cultures, and in particular in dealing with the merchants and the ʿulamāʾ of these sedentary regions. The merchants among the Oghuz, mentioned in the *Ḥudūd al-ʿālam*, were no doubt responsible for bringing their products to the cities, thus negotiating sedentary and nomadic cultures. This negotiation was intensified and became more complex with the entry of the Saljūqs into the heartland of Islamdom in the eleventh century.

A recurrent term pertaining to both the Saljūqs and the larger Oghuz is that of the *Türkmen* [Persian= Turkamān/Turkaman]. This term came into use in the latter part of the tenth century. For some historians, such as Bayhaqī, it is a convenient term to refer to all the Oghuz who were harassing the frontiers of the Ghaznavid empire.[61] The Saljūq vizier Niẓām al-Mulk also uses this term to refer to the tribal following of the Saljūq Sultans. In the *Siyāsat-nāma*, the able vizier impresses on the sultan that the *Turkamānān* are the sultan's kin and had served the realm faithfully in the beginning.[62] The great encyclopedist and lexicographer Maḥmūd Kāshgharī provides an amusing legend in which the title Türkmen is given to certain tribesmen of the Oghuz by none other than Dhū ʾl-Qarnayn! In this account, the mysterious "two-horned" figure (often identified in Muslim literature with Alexander the Great[63]) comments that a certain group of tribesmen are *Turk-mānand* (i.e., they look like

Turks).[64] In another section, Kāshgharī specifically identifies the Türkmen as the Oghuz.[65] For our purposes here, it is the future role the Turkmen would play as a social force in Saljūq society that is of primary interest.

The Saljūq Family

There has been considerable scholarly debate over the correct transliteration of the eponym of the Saljūqs. V. Barthold held that in accordance with Turkish sources, such as the *Dīwān lughāt al-turk* of Maḥmūd Kāshgharī, the proper spelling should be Seljük.[66] Furthermore, the noted Russian Orientalist also pointed out that the common European spelling of *Seljuq* violates the rules of vowel harmony in Turkish.[67] In fact many of these Turkish sources specifically spell the name as Sin-lām-jīm-kāf. Kāshgharī was well known for his attention to phonetic differences and includes the name in the class of palatalised words (i.e., those with front vowels).[68] However, almost all the Persian and Arabic sources distinctly record the name of the tribe as sīn-lām-jīm-wāw-qāf—Saljūq. The connections between this name and derivations such as *salmak* (attack, charge) and *salchuq* (dashing, charging) are not yet clear. These etymologies are derived from the root of *sal*, which means "to move (something), to put into motion with some implication of violent motion."[69] In the present work, I shall adopt the transliteration Saljūq to honor the Persian and Arabic sources, while acknowledging that the original Turkish pronunciation might in fact have been closer to that suggested by Kāshgharī and favored by Barthold.

There are some significant disagreements among the sources regarding the rank and nobility of the Saljūq family within the wider Oghuz confederation. On one hand, Kāshgharī records the narrative from the *Tārīkh* of Abū ʾl-ʿAlāʾ [ibn] Ḥassūl (d. 450/1058),[70] which claimed that the Saljūqs' ancestry was traceable (through thirty-four generations) to the mythic Tūrānī king Afrāsiyāb.[71] In the later accounts, these claims to royal ancestry are even ascribed to the early Saljūq figures themselves. The *Saljūq-nāma* of Nīshāpūrī and the *Jāmiʿ al-tawārīkh* by Rashīd al-Dīn Faḍl Allāh depict the Saljūqs as having refused to pay taxes to the Ghaznavid Sultan Masʿūd by replying, "We are from the race of kings (*niẓhād-i pādshāhān*)."[72] This remark, conspicuously absent from the earlier chronicles, clearly stands at the end of a long historiographic transformation of the origins of the early Saljūqs. While one is tempted to dismiss these accounts from a positivistic historical perspective, they are an important indication of the attempt of the later Saljūq chronicles to retrospectively bestow nobility upon the Saljūqs in order to cover their rather humble origins. It should be recalled that the very same Ibn Ḥassūl, an official in Ṭughril's court who was possibly the head of his chancery, was commissioned to write a work titled *Tafḍīl al-atrāk* (The Preeminence of the Turks). That this work was written in Arabic, a language of which the Saljūq warlords themselves were ignorant,[73] is indicative of the fact that such works were written for the benefits of others (i.e., to legitimize the Saljūqs in the eyes of the established Arab and Persian Muslim notables who were suspicious of the newly powerful ruling dynasty). These works represent the earliest attempts at a process of legitimization, a process that would become progressively more sophisticated and systematic in the subsequent generations.

On the other hand, we can find other accounts that contradict the regal origins theory of the above chroniclers and suggest instead a rather humble beginnings for the family of the future sultans. These sources state that the Saljūqid clan members carved out poles for the nomadic tent-huts (*khargāh-tarāsh*) and were in the service of the Turkish *pādshāh*s.[74] It is interesting to note how vehemently some modern Turkish scholars have rejected the association of the Saljūqs with this craft, which would have been essential to a nomadic tribe. Some Turkish scholars have even attempted to cover up the manifestation of this account in earlier sources and dismissed it as "groundless."[75] Khwānd-Mīr, who had access to the no longer extant *Malik-nāma*, offers a middle-ground position, and states that the Saljūqs were "from the reputable commanders" (*az jumla umarā'-i muʿtabar*) in the service of the *Yabghū* who ruled the Khazar plains in the lower Volga and southern Russia.[76]

The Prehistory of the Saljūq Clan: Duqāq and Saljūq

There is little in the early history of the Saljūq family to have predicted their transformation into a successful dynasty. In tracing the prehistory of the Saljūq clan, we are faced with yet another historiographical problem. The most useful text on the early history of the Saljūqs is the no longer extant *Malik-nāma*.[77] While this work has not reached us, two premodern authors who had access to the *Malik-nāma* quote extensively from it. The first of the two premodern authors was the Persian historian Ghiyāth al-Dīn ibn Humām al-Dīn, better known as Khwānd-Mīr.[78] The second was the Syriac author Bar Hebraeus, who also had access to the Persian *Malik-nāma*, and is perhaps the most important non-Muslim source for the early history of the Saljūqs.[79] Claude Cahen has emphatically argued for the necessity of incorporating Syriac chronicles, and in particular Bar Hebraeus's *Chronography*,[80] into a study of the early Saljūqs.[81] The insights provided by the two authors quoting from the *Malik-nāma* are necessary to offset the mythmaking endeavors of later sources on the Saljūqs. As I shall demonstrate, some of the later sources omitted specific details about the founders of the Saljūq dynasty that did not fit into the ideological construction designed to legitimize the Saljūq state.

As is the case with other rare Turkish names which passed on to Persian and Arabic chronicles, there is considerable disagreement over the correct spelling of the name of the head of the Saljūq family. Khwānd-Mīr records his name as either Duqāq[82] or Wuqāq.[83] The other source going back to the *Malik-nāma*, Bar Hebraeus, preferred Tuqāq.[84] The later Muslim sources echo this ambivalence.[85] What can be established with certainty about Duqāq was that his strength and bravery earned him the honorific *Timūr-Yāligh*, "iron-bow."[86] He is believed to have been in the service of the *Yabghū*, the ruler of the Khazar Turks.[87] The later Saljūq mythology portrays Duqāq as having prevented the *Yabghū* from attacking the Abode of Islam (*Dār al-islām*).[88] Ibn al-Athīr records an account in which the *Yabghū* had gathered up his army in order to attack Muslim lands. Duqāq argued with him and tried to persuade the *Yabghū* to spare the Muslims. The discussion boiled over, and Duqāq hit the Yabghū over the head (with a stick?), causing some injury. Duqāq was in great personal danger, until there was a rapprochement between the two at a later point.[89] Neither of our two earliest sources directly citing the *Malik-nāma* (Khwānd-Mīr and Bar Hebraeus) mentions this alleged struggle between Duqāq and the *Yabghū*. Our task is more than to simply dismiss this later account as somehow spurious and mythical. We need to examine *how* this account fits into a larger pattern of legitimizing the Saljūqs. This later tradition is no doubt a retrospective attempt to already identify the ancestor of the tribe as having "saved" Muslims from the infidels. As we have seen, claims of protecting Muslims and Islamdom against internal and external threats and injustice were an important component of Saljūq ideology. This narrative deploys the third component of Saljūq ideology, that of promoting social order and protecting Muslim lives and properties.

Duqāq's son, Saljūq, is significant for the later history of the clan which bears his name for his shrewd adoption of Islam. He is stated to have been the first among his people to have accepted Islam and to have lived among Muslims (*saʿāda bi ʾl-īmān wa mujāwarat al-muslimīn*).[90] Ḥusaynī describes Saljūq as having accepted the "pure, primordial religion" (*al-dīn al-ḥanīfī*).[91] The statement describing the Saljūq faith as pure from its origin belongs to the same discourse of legitimization that will attempt to depict the Saljūqs as purifying Islamic thought later. The account of Saljūq's conversion can be verified through the *Malik-nāma*, where it is asserted that "the opening of his heart was illuminated through the lights of *tawḥīd*, and Saljūq along with his kin and servants became Muslims. They occupied themselves with learning the Qurʾan and the injunctions of Islamic law."[92] There is no reason to dismiss the sincerity of this conversion altogether, especially given some of the monotheistic inclinations already present among the Oghuz.[93] On the other hand, the emphasis on learning the Qurʾan and sharīʿa by anything more than a small minority of the decidedly non-Arabic speaking (and overwhelmingly illiterate) tribes seems farfetched. Furthermore, the earliest sources suggest an equally pragmatic reason: Saljūq told his clan that unless they embraced the religion of the land in which they now resided, they would not be able to persist there. The Syriac historian Bar Hebraeus records Saljūq as having told his progeny, "If we do not enter the faith of the people of the country in which we desire [to live] and make a pact with them (or conform to their customs), no man will cleave to us, and we shall be a small and solitary people."[94] Having agreed on this, the Saljūqs sent an envoy to the Khwārazm city of Zandāk and asked for some religious scholars to be sent out to them. The people of the town sent them a missionary (*mubashshir*), plus gifts for the new converts.[95]

Hijra, Ghazw, and Orthodoxy: Islamic Modes of Legitimizing the Saljūqs

The later chronicles make an explicit connection between Saljūq's adoption of Islam and the relocation to the "Abode of Islam" (*Dār al-islām*). Saljūq is credited with having moved his family from *Dār al-ḥarb* to *Dār al-islām*, specifically to the region of Jand (in the lower Syr Darya) around the year 960 C.E.[96] Jand was a city well-known to the Oghuz. The author of *Ḥudūd al-ʿālam* mentions that Jand (=Kh.vāra) was the place in which the ruler of the Oghuz would spend winters.[97] There are also other explanations given for this move. A very reasonable explanation has Saljūq moving his tribe from the Khazar plains to Turkistān due to some enmity between him and the ruler. Initially, Saljūq was a favorite of the *Yabghū*, even rising to the rank of *Sū-bāshī* (Arabic: *qāʾid al-jaysh*). Many of the sources bring up this title,[98] and even the encyclopedist Maḥmūd Kāshgharī (ca. 969/1077) introduces *Sälčük* (i.e., Saljūq) as "the grandfather of the present Sultans. He was called *Sū Bāšī*."[99] The sources are also unanimous in asserting that the wife of the Turkish *Yabghū* was responsible for the rift between the young commander and the *Yabghū*. In one account she is described as having become alarmed at the increasing power of the young commander. In another account, easily reconcilable with the first, she is depicted as having been offended when Saljūq attempted to assume a more prominent seat in the royal court than the king's own family.[100] She incited her husband to kill the young commander, but Saljūq left just before falling prey to this trap.[101] One can also not dismiss the possibility that the perpetual search for pasture lands might have led Saljūq to seek out new grounds.

There are two later ideological meanings that are ascribed to this act of migration to Jand. Certain Muslim sources seek to interpret this move as a *hijra*, a movement from the Abode of Infidelity to the Abode of Islam.[102] On the other hand, some Turkish nationalist historians such as Kafesoğlu have interpreted this movement of Saljūq, his family and servants, 1,500 camels, and 50,000 sheep[103] as "the great Oghuz migration."[104] The scholars who wish to see some manifest destiny in this migration would do well to recall the difference between migration and conquest.[105] While these two modes of interpretation differ vastly in their orientation, they are both attempts to impose an ideological interpretation on an act that was simply part of the perennial nomadic concern to find new grazing lands for the flock. Perhaps all such skirmishes and migrations contain their own ideological components. The key here is that upon conversion, these skirmishes are framed in an Islamic discourse. In other words, the attempts to place the migration into a hijra framework deploy the first component of Saljūq ideology, which emphasizes Saljūq obedience to Islam.

The sources are in agreement that after arriving in Jand and having embraced Islam, Saljūq prevented the agents of the pagan *Yabghū* from collecting the *kharāj* tax from the Muslim population of that town. However, there are significant disagreements among the sources going back to the *Malik-nāma* and later sources in terms of how this story is interpreted. Ibn al-Athīr interpreted these battles as *ghazwa*,[106] while another source ascribed the honorific *al-Malik al-ghāzī* to Saljūq as a result of these confrontations.[107] This account can be seen as a further elaboration of the topos of Saljūqs as *ghāzī* warriors that we have already seen with Duqāq. This mode of interpretation deploys the third component of Saljūq ideology, promoting social order and protecting Muslim lives and properties. The earliest version of this narrative is found in Khwānd-Mīr. Here, the gist of the conflict is tied not to an ideological defense of Muslims, but simply to the recapture of a flock of camels that had been stolen by the forces of the pagan kings.[108] A simple skirmish over a flock of sheep between two Turkish tribal forces had come to be reinterpreted in later chronicles and recast in the context of the defense of Muslims against attacks from outside threats. The ideological meaning ascribed to the skirmish is recognizable as one of the core elements in the main ideological legitimization of the Saljūqs, that of promoting social order. Saljūq is said to have died at a very advanced age, perhaps 107.[109] As impressive as the longevity of the eponym of the Saljūqs is, it might also indicate an attempt to bridge the gap between the (pagan) prehistory of the family and their (ideologically justified) presence.

The tension between the Saljūq family and the *Yabghū* would not wane. The Ghaznavid historian Bayhaqī informs us that there was still "an ancient group-prejudice, a strong dislike, and blood[-shed]" (*taʿaṣṣub-i qadīm wa kīna-yi ṣaʿab wa khūn*) between the descendants of Saljūq and Shāh-Malik, the son and successor of the same *Yabghū*.[110] Shāh-Malik ambushed the Saljūq family in the year 425/1033–34, killing between seven and eight thousand of the Saljūqid tribesmen. By the year 433/1041–42, the Saljūqs had regrouped and defeated Shāh-Malik.[111] From this point on, they were able to assert themselves as the paramount force in the Qïnïq tribe and thus the Oghuz as a whole. While most of our historical chronicles are interested in placing the rise of the Saljūq dynasty within the narratives of Islamic or Perso-Islamic history, it is also essential to locate the Saljūq success as an important chapter in the intratribal (and intertribal) Turkish competition for supremacy in western and central Asia. These are not mutually exclusive; as I will demonstrate later, the early Saljūqs themselves were interested in the Perso-Islamic history narrative, but that narrative should not lead us to exclude the intratribal competition.[112]

The future destiny of the Saljūq clan is retrospectively predicted in a rather strange dream attributed to Saljūq. In this dream, he is said to have urinated fire, the sparks of which spread to the east and the west (*inna-hu yabūlū nār^an yatalaẓẓa sharāri-hā fi ʾl-mashāriqi al-arḍ wa maghāribi-hā*).[113] The dream-interpreter (*muʿabbir*) consulted by Saljūq offered an interpretation which no doubt proved pleasing to the warlord: his descendants were destined to rule over the whole Earth. I here disagree with Bosworth's dismissal of the *muʿabbir* as being merely a "Turkish shaman."[114] As much as urination might strike our contemporary sensitivities as being an odd symbol for conveying universal dominion, it was a common symbol in premodern Muslim dream manuals, frequently tied to virility and power.[115] One could also see urine as being a symbol of "seed."

The same type of reinterpretive process is evident in recasting the events of the subsequent generation: Ibn al-Athīr records Saljūq's son, Mīkāʾīl (the father of both Ṭughril and Chaghrī), as partaking in a *ghazwa* against the pagan Turks and attaining to martyrdom in the path of God (*fa astashhada fī sabīl Allāh*).[116] By now it is almost redundant to remark that this narrative is also not found in the earlier source, *Malik-nāma*. Given the connotations of *ghāzī* not merely as a warrior, but as a warrior of faith, one already sees in this narrative the seeds of legitimization that were fully articulated for the Saljūq Sultans of three generations later. The topos of the Saljūqid ruler as the *ghāzī* taps into two modes already mentioned in the ideological justification of the Saljūqs: the obedience to Islam as well as the desire to offer protection for Muslim lives. The sources provide no other details regarding Mīkāʾīl other than his alleged martyrdom. This account (combined with Saljūq's remarkable longevity) fills in the gap, bringing the narrative right up to Ṭughril himself: the pagan background, or at best recent conversions of the Saljūq clan, is covered by claiming the Saljūqs as multigenerational fighting champions for the faith and protectors of Muslim lives and properties.

Having thus portrayed the founders of the Saljūq clan as *ghāzīs* intent on protecting Muslims from external threats, historians such as Rāwandī can then legitimize the Saljūqs' rule by describing the entire Saljūq family as "possessing religion (*dīn-dār*), avoiding heedlessness [of God], . . . desirous of visiting the house [of God] Kaʿba, and [seeking] intimacy with the Imams of the faith." Rāwandī goes on to praise the "pure belief and the purity of creed" (*iʿtiqād-i pāk wa ṣafā-yi ʿaqīdat*) of Suljūq Sultans like Ṭughril, claiming that no one possessed more "Muhammadan religion" than this sultan.[117] Qazwīnī lays an even greater emphasis on the "Ortho-doxy" of the Saljūqs; he describes them as having been "pure and clean" (*pāk*), namely, of the defilement of heresy. According to Qazwīnī, the Saljūqs were Sunni, "of pure religion" (*pāk-dīn*), quite literally "ortho-dox" (*nīkū iʿtiqād*), and beneficent toward their flock.[118] The later Anatolian Saljūq chronicler, Āqsarāʾī, credited the Great Saljūqs with having possessed *ṭahārat-i iʿtiqād*, literally "[ritual] purity of belief."[119] This term, along with *nīkū iʿtiqād*, are perhaps the most direct Persian/Arabic equivalents to the English "orthodoxy," meaning "correct belief" or "right doctrine."[120] As part of the ideological language of legitimization, belief was something that could be ritually pure or defiled. As with material sources of impurity like urine and blood, beliefs are now described as being alternatively pure or impure, even contaminable when they come into contact with suspect elements. The Saljūqs were claimed as possessing the correct belief; their non-Muslim tracks had been sufficiently covered. They could then be depicted as purifying the other elements that were held to defile the pure religion. It is imperative to recognize that all these accounts deploy that element of Saljūq ideology which emphasizes their obedience to an orthodox interpretation of Islam. This appeal to a normative view of Islam is used to justify the new and powerful ruling Saljūqs in absence of genealogical modes of religious legitimacy.

The Weakened Saljūqs as Clients of the Caliph

In the subsequent decades, the Saljūqs became involved in the petty rivalries of Transoxiana and Khwārazm, lending their fighting services to Qarakhānid (also called Īlik-Khānid) and Ghaznavid forces.[121] The Saljūqs had been weakened by two successive events: first, the Saljūq bands had split up, some moving to Khurāsān under the leadership of Arslān Isrā'īl.[122] This splintering was a natural event in the life of a nomadic confederation perpetually in need of new grazing lands, yet it significantly weakened their military solidarity. The second event was Sulṭān Maḥmūd's imprisoning of the Saljūqid leader, Arslān Isrā'īl. According to Nīshāpūrī, Sulṭān Maḥmūd had made peace with the Īlik-khān kings of Turkistān.[123] The Īlik-khān ruler had been wary of the size of the Saljūq clan, and he sent an alarming message to Maḥmūd in which he stated that the Saljūqs were a group with "complete power and organized force." He managed to convince Maḥmūd that while the Ghaznavid king was busy with raiding India, the Saljūqs might create "strife (*fitna*) and corruption (*fasād*)."[124] Already in the Īlik-Khānid warning there is a link between *fitna* and *fasād*, a foreshadowing of later Saljūq themes. While this connection is found in earlier periods of Islamic history, it becomes a constant refrain in the historical annals of this time period. As Meisami has pointed out, *fitna* (civil strife) and *fatra* (slackening) are constantly juxtaposed against *dawla* (prosperous rule, period of rule, dynasty) in this time period.[125]

Maḥmūd set out to Bukhārā to inspect the Saljūqs personally in 416/1025.[126] Isrā'īl attended Maḥmūd's camp with his son Abū 'l-Fawāris Qutulmush ("The Sanctified"). Maḥmūd asked Isrā'īl whether he could count on the Saljūq leader should a foe attack Khurāsān while the Ghaznavid king was preoccupied with conquests in India. The young (and naïve) Saljūqid commander, Isrā'īl, pledged his loyalty to the Ghaznavid ruler. Maḥmūd, no doubt attempting to gauge the size of the Saljūqid forces, asked how many fighters Isrā'īl would be able to summon. Isrā'īl presented the sulṭān with two arrows and a bow that could be used to summon the forces. Isrā'īl boasted that the first arrow would bring 100,000 men, the second 50,000, and the bow 200,000. It is worth noting that Nīshāpūrī (and following him, Rashīd al-Dīn Faḍl Allāh) comments that Isrā'īl's response arose out of "pride resulting from intoxication, and youthful boasting."[127] Ironically, it seems that Isrā'īl's boast cost him his life; following the obligatory wine-drinking session, Maḥmūd, who was no doubt alarmed by the sheer number of forces claimed by Isrā'īl, imprisoned the Saljūqid warlord at the fortress in Kālanjar for seven years.[128] Ultimately, Isrā'īl perished there.[129] After the two above events that weakened the Saljūqs, they suffered successive defeats—first at the hands of Sultan Maḥmūd in 419/1028,[130] followed by their defeat in 425/1034 at the hands of Shāh-Malik of Jand.[131]

Once again the later chronicles attempt to reinterpret the account of Maḥmūd's imprisoning of Isrāʾīl and cast it in a framework which would prove favorable to the Saljūqs. They depict the imprisoned Isrāʾīl as having sent a dying wish to his kinfolk, pleading, "Exert yourself in seeking kingship. If they defeat you ten times, do not become dismayed and do not turn back. This king [Maḥmūd] is born from a slave (*mawlā-zāda*),[132] he does not have a [noble] genealogy, and is a traitor. Kingship will not remain with him, but will pass on to you."[133] At this time, the Saljūqs were obviously in no position to seek kingship, even within their own Qïnïq tribe, much less the wider Perso-Islamic world. This plea is yet another retrospective interjection. At the same time, the contrasting of Sultan Maḥmūd as *mawlā-zāda* with the Saljūqs' alleged "noble" heritage fits into the discourse of legitimizing the Saljūqs.

Even with all the above troubles, the Saljūqs successfully petitioned the Ghaznavids to allow them to cross the Jayḥūn (Oxus) river in 1025. However, there were already concerned voices within the Ghaznavid camp: Arslān the Ḥājib[134] beseeched the sultan to deny them this access, stating that their number was too great, they were massively armed, and this could all lead to strife (*fitna*).[135] Arslān's concerns not withstanding, the sultan did grant them permission, and the Saljūqs crossed the Oxus and set up camp near Nasā and Bāward circa 1025. That the Saljūqs carried with them a sizable flock of animals is suggested by the size of the gift (seven hundred camels, three hundred Turkish sheep) they made to the governor of Khurāsān.[136] Rāwandī reports that as long as Sultan Maḥmūd was alive, the Saljūqs did not advance any further.[137]

The Ghaznavid Sultan Maḥmūd died in the year 421/1030, and his two sons Muḥammad and Masʿūd fought among themselves, until Masʿūd became the sultan.[138] The death of the able Maḥmūd seems to have provided the Saljūqs with an opportunity to fortify their hold on Khurāsān. In 426/1035, they wrote an exceedingly humble letter to the Ghaznavid vizier, Abū ʾl-Faḍl. This letter, recorded in Bayhaqī's *Tārīkh*, starts out with the revealing statement: "From the slaves Bayghū [i.e. *Yabghū*],[139] Ṭughril, and Dāwūd [i.e., Chaghrī Beg], the clients (*mawālī*) of the Commander of the Believers."[140] The Saljūqs pleaded that they had been on good terms with the previous Qarakhānid ruler, ʿAlī-Tegīn. However, since that ruler's death, his son had oppressed the Saljūqs. They further stated that the Ghaznavid general Āltūn-Tāsh had permitted them to use his lands as a grazing area for their flock.

The Saljūqs humbly asked the Ghaznavids to be permitted to use the plains of Nasā and Farāva for their flock. They vowed, in return, to put down *mufsids* (evil-doers) from Khwāraz, Jayḥūn, and Dihistān, and to keep the "'Irāqī Türkmen" under control. This letter, which appears in a Ghaznavid source not connected to the legitimizing of the Saljūqs (and in fact at times hostile to them), already contains the seeds of Saljūq ideology, which would be fully articulated in the subsequent generations. The labeling of the Saljūqs as "clients" of the 'Abbāsid Caliph has been identified as a key component of Saljūq ideology. The claim of putting down *fasād* (corruption, perverse unruliness), often associated with heretical movements, is none other than another component of Saljūq ideology.

Here we come across one of the central historiographic contributions of the present study. This letter is an important document in demonstrating that the legitimization of the Saljūqs was not entirely a product of the later chronicles, but a fuller articulation and reinterpretation of modes of justification already begun by the Saljūqs themselves much earlier. It should not be assumed that the ideological justification of the Saljūqs was a process in which they themselves had no interest or participation.[141] While the construction and articulation of the Saljūq ideology was undertaken by their able administrators, affiliated scholars, and chroniclers, they themselves had begun to deploy some of these modes of legitimization. We cannot simply present the Great Saljūq Myth as a product of later generations of historians; we have to account for the Saljūqs' own agency in the construction of this discourse.

The deeper penetration of the Saljūqs into Khurāsān resulted in the deep distress of many locals. This was to prove a recurrent pattern in the next fifty years all across the Iranian plateau and Iraq, as we shall document. Furthermore, it would be hard to exaggerate the significance of the Saljūq-legitimizing sources covering up these social commotions in order to perpetuate the myth of the Saljūqs as upholders of social order. Even as Saljūq-legitimizing historians such as Qazwīnī claim that the Saljūqs won over the hearts of the people of Khurāsān and acted as intermediaries in their disputes,[142] other historical narratives undermine this depiction by documenting that toward the end of 418/1027–28, the citizens of Nasā and Bāward went to the Ghaznavid court (in Ghazna) to complain of the *fasād-i turkamanān*, that is, the "perverseness caused by the Türkmen."[143] The evidence of these sources (which were not involved in the process of legitimization of the Saljūqs) tends to suggest that far from protecting Muslim cities, the Saljūqs had a devastating impact on the cities of Khurāsān.

There is a curious silence in many of the Saljūq chronicles regarding the exact whereabouts of the Saljūq leaders and their activities in the early 1030s. Most of the later Muslim sources provide little information about the Saljūqs between the above complaints in 1027–28 and the later battles with Sultan Masʿūd in 1040. There are only scant suggestions in most Muslim sources that when the Saljūqs lost hope of the Ghaznavid Sultan releasing their imprisoned uncle, they changed their policy from one of "geniality" to one of "terror" against the people in the frontier areas (*abdalū īnās al-nās bi-īḥāsh al-ḥāshiya*).[144] None of the Muslim sources dared to elaborate on this campaign of terror. It is the Syriac historian, Bar Hebraeus, who provides details of Saljūq activities which contradict all later mythologization of Saljūqs as upholders of social order: Ṭughril and Chaghrī are described as having crossed the Jayḥūn (Oxus) and "utterly destroying the city of Dāmghān."[145] They are also depicted as having committed the same atrocity in Rayy.[146] On this point we have a later confirmation through Āqsarāʾī, who states that Ṭughril personally was responsible for the plunder and murders in Rayy.[147] This frank admission (from a source written under Saljūq patronage, nonetheless!) confirms that one cannot draw a neat division between "wild" Oghuz and a "city/Muslim-protecting" Ṭughril. The leaders themselves were intricately involved in these *fitna*s. Bar Hebraeus further blames the whole "Ghūzzāye" (i.e., Oghuz) for slaughtering Arabs and Kurds in Armenia and talking spoils, and also for killing Kurds in Urmiya in Ādharbāījān. Perhaps the most shocking allegation is that they entered the city of Marāgha, took prisoners, and burned the main mosque.[148] In all likelihood, these actions were led by Chaghrī Beg, who was leading the expedition to Ādharbāijān.[149]

The silence of the Muslim sources can best be explained as part of an attempt to cover up or sanitize the actions of the Saljūqs that did not fit the paradigm of upholders of social order. As we have seen, this theme was a crucial part of the process of legitimizing the Saljūqs, as the second component of Saljūq ideology. As such, narratives that did not fit this ideological model were marginalized. The Saljūq legitimizing chronicles are not interested in giving a complete account of what the Saljūqs did. Rather, they emphasized those aspects that could be used to legitimize and justify the Saljūqs and distanced themselves from the narratives that problematized the Great Saljūq Myth.

The Demise of the Ghaznavids in Iran

In 429/1037–38, the Saljūqs took full advantage of the disarrayed state of the Ghaznavids who were still reeling after Maḥmūd's demise. Under Ṭughril's leadership, they took over the strategic and rich area of Khurāsān. In 430/1038, Masʿūd personally came to Khurāsān from Ghazna and deported the Saljūqs from Khurāsān.[150] However, by this point the Saljūqs knew all too well how to defeat the technologically superior Ghaznavid army: Masʿūd's army was more equipped for heavy, direct confrontations where their famed elephants could inflict great damage. The Saljūqs, on the other hand, used their maneuverability and evasive skills to exhaust Masʿūd and his army during a series of widely spread-out skirmishes. After a series of battles ranging from Khurāsān to Ghazna and Harāt, the Saljūqs gradually gained the upper hand.[151] Masʿūd had attempted to delegate the task of controlling the Saljūqs to his deputy, the governor of Khurāsān. The *ʿamīd* saw himself as no match for the increasingly powerful Saljūqs, yet Masʿūd forced him to engage the Saljūqs in a direct battle at Sarakhs in 429/(May) 1038.[152] The governor's forces were decimated, and this victory gave the Saljūqs confidence to take over the rest of Khurāsān.

The final defeat of the Ghaznavid forces came at the crucial battle of Dandānqān[153] in 431/1040.[154] The Ghaznavid ruler Masʿūd returned to Khurāsān with his elephant army to defeat the Saljūqs once and for all. He attempted unsuccessfully to keep Ṭughril and Chaghrī from joining forces. The result was a glorious victory for the Saljūqs and a devastating defeat for the Ghaznavids. The Saljūq-friendly sources depict Masʿūd as having abandoned all hope of regaining Khurāsān and falling into a drunken stupor after his defeat at Dandānqān.[155] This depiction cannot be accurate, since Masʿūd attempted (unsuccessfully) to raise another army to fight the Saljūqs. The historian Bayhaqī mentions the presence of 16,000 Oghuz in Dandānqān. Based on this number, some scholars have speculated that after Dandānqān, some 64,000 Oghuz Turkmen—including women and children—moved into Khurāsān.[156] This battle was so significant for the Saljūqs that Ṭughril Beg ordered a throne to be erected on the battlefield and mounted it. He demanded the attendance of all the nobles and ordered them to acknowledge him as the *amīr* of Khurāsān.[157] It is significant that at this early date, the title *sulṭān* was not yet used for the Saljūqs. Ṭughril is merely designated as a commander. He then dispatched a letter to the rulers and nobles of Turkistān.[158] This act symbolized the Saljūq's warning to the rival Turkish tribe, forcing them to back off from Khurāsān. It is also an important indication of the policy of the Saljūqs to seek acknowledgment by the *aʿyān* (nobles) even in these early stages.

What followed the glorious Saljūq victory in Dandānqān was a typical demonstration of tribal solidarity, one using the symbols of Central Asian warriors. All the Saljūq leaders[159] convened and made a pact to support one another. Ṭughril gave an arrow to his brother (Chaghrī) and asked him to break it. He heeded the command and broke the arrow. Ṭughril put the two pieces on top of each other and asked Chaghrī to break them again, which he did. When the arrow was broken three-fold, he could only break them with great difficulty. When the arrow was broken four-fold, he was no longer able to break them. Tughril Beg said, "This is a parable for our condition. [When we stand alone], every minuscule force will intend to break us. If we are united, none shall conquer us. If a division comes between us . . . the enemy shall prevail and kingship will depart from us."[160] From a historiographic perspective, it is intriguing to note that Rashīd al-Dīn Faḍl Allāh's account,[161] which is for the most part verbatim as Rāwandī's, omits the breaking of the bows narrative. That trope, which derives from Central Asian symbols of authority, was perhaps too Turkish for later historians attempting to fit the Saljūqs into a more conventional narrative of Perso-Islamic history.[162]

The defeated Masᶜūd turned to his brother, Muḥammad, for help to gather up support for one last battle against the Saljūqs. Muḥammad, whose eyes had been removed on Masᶜūd's order, sarcastically reminded the Ghaznavid Sultan that if he were not blind,[163] he might have been able to be of some help. Masᶜūd's son, Mawdūd, did wage a battle against the Saljūqs—he was defeated as his father had been before him. The two sons of Muḥammad, meanwhile, avenged their father's blindness by killing their uncle Masᶜūd in an ignoble fashion.[164] With Masᶜūd's death, the last significant obstacle in the way of the Saljūq march on Khurāsān (and the rest of the Iranian plateau) was removed. The Saljūqs reached an effective agreement with the subsequent Ghaznavid rulers: the Saljūqs would keep Khurāsān and the rest of the Iranian plateau; the Ghaznavids would reign over Sīstān, Ghazna, and India.[165]

The *Fitna* Brought on by the Saljūqs in Khurāsān

According to Nīshāpūrī, after defeating the last remnants of the Ghaznavids in Khurāsān, the Saljūqs spread "like the locust" over the rest of Khurāsān. Nīshāpūrī adds, "They began to show arrogance (*taṭāwul*), engaged in highway-robbery (*rāh-zadan*), [incited] tumult (*shūr*), strife (*fitna*) and disturbance (*āshūb*). They disturbed the whole realm of Khurāsān, bringing disorder (*mukhbaṭ*)."[166] The Saljūqs proceeded to the two main cities in Khurāsān, Ṭūs and Nīshāpūr. Al-Kātib al-Iṣfahānī records that the Saljūqs entered Ṭūs after defeating the *shaḥna* of that town. They proceeded to "enter and search the homes" and committed other atrocities.[167] Even if the account from the *Malik-nāma*, cited in Bar Hebraeus, which depicts the Saljūqs as having killed one hundred thousand souls in Ṭūs, is an exaggeration, it does hint at a large-scale massacre which no later Muslim source would mention.[168] These acts of urban unruliness, which undermined the core component of Saljūq ideology (that of protecting Muslim lives and properties), are omitted from all sources that seek to legitimize the Saljūqs.

The Saljūq forces, led by Ṭughril Beg, entered Nīshāpūr in Ramaḍān of 429/1038. To officially mark his conquest, Ṭughril had his name inserted into the *khuṭba*, and assumed the titles of *pādshāh*[169] and *al-sulṭān al-muʿaẓẓam* (the exalted sultan).[170] The sources are unanimous in documenting the great level of distressed agitation (*iḍṭirāb*) and uprising (*inqilāb*) among the citizens of Nīshāpūr. This tension was only relieved when Ṭughril's herald announced that the Saljūqs had no qualms with the inhabitants of the towns and would not harm a living soul.[171] These accounts function to emphasize Ṭughril's magnanimity. When placed within the actual historical context, however, the massive distress of the citizens of Khurāsān appears fully justified. They were faced not with the upholders of social justice, but with a plundering, pillaging, and murdering mass of nomads whose power was no longer held in check. It is important to point out that while some of the later sources, such as Ibn al-Athīr, do admit that the Oghuz committed many perverse atrocities, brought on destruction, and stole (*afsadū wa nahabū wa kharrabū 'l-balād wa sabū*), they attempt to remove the agency from Ṭughril. Instead, they depict Ṭughril's entry into Nīshāpūr as an attempt to *stop* the Oghuz from these acts of *fasād*.[172] This dichotomy between Ṭughril and the Oghuz is not reflected in the earlier sources and is a retrospective attempt to exonerate the first Saljūq Sultan Ṭughril from atrocities by attributing them instead to his followers.

The Saljūq tribesmen had desired to plunder (*ghārat*) the whole town immediately, but Ṭughril prevented them from doing so, asking them to uphold the sanctity of Ramaḍān.[173] He went on to state that nothing would be gained by pillage, and would only cause them to lose respect in the sight of others. Even al-Iṣfahānī states that many of the tribesmen mockingly said that Ṭughril seemed to think himself worthy of issuing religious injunctions and that he had perhaps lost his mind! The compromise reached was to postpone the plunder until after the ʿĪd; according to al-Iṣfahānī, Ṭughril said, "Grant them respite for the rest of this month, after the [ʿĪd of] al-Fiṭr, do what you will (*aʿmalū mā shiʾtum baʿd al-fiṭr*)."[174] Again, the respect allegedly shown by Ṭughril for Islamic symbols functions to affirm the first component of Saljūq ideology, obedience to Islam. It also taps into the third component, that of protecting Muslim lives and properties, a theme we have repeatedly encountered in the early Saljūqid narratives.

It was during this interim that the letter from the ʿAbbāsid Caliph al-Qāʾim Bi Amr Allāh arrived. It is important to note that the actual content of this letter is not stated in any of the extant Muslim sources, which no doubt desired to cover any tensions between the caliph and the Saljūqs. The late Saljūq source Āqsarāʾī admits that the caliph's letter contained "advice and threats."[175] In al-Iṣfahānī's account, all that is recorded of the letter is that the caliph warned the Saljūqs, reminded them of God, asked them to respect the rights of God's servants, and to restore God's cities.[176] Rashīd al-Dīn Faḍl Allāh makes it clear that this advice was meant to "put fear in" the Saljūqs (*bi-takhwīf naṣīḥat karda*).[177] The letter was no doubt intended to reprimand the nomadic Saljūqs' plundering of cities in Khurāsān and to prevent them from creating further social strife and economic instability. Once again, it is the Syriac source by Bar Hebraeus, which relies on the *Malik-nāma*, that provides us with the stipulations of the caliph:

> I. . . . The countries which you have taken are sufficient for you. You will not hanker after the countries of the rest of the governors of the Arabs; and you will not harm them.
> II. You should hold yourself in strict subjection, inasmuch as you are our vassal. And you will swear unto us legal oaths concerning the divorce of your wives, and the freeing of your slaves, and undertake to give dues of all thy possessions, if you resist our command.
> III. And you will act righteously, and not deceitfully, and will not set men of error (i.e., unbelievers) over the members of the flock [of the faithful].
> IV. You will send each year the tribute of the counties which you have taken, according to the customs of your predecessors. If you will do these things, you will be decorated with robes [of honor], and will be addressed with the honorific titles which [men] may legally apply to your kingship. And you will not be a tyrant.[178]

It is interesting to note that Ṭughril did not comply with the demands of this letter. He objected that he had no control over the actions of his men, that he did need further pasture lands for their animals, and that he did not fully comprehend the oaths he was being asked to abide by and would only promise to pay the tributes if he was able to. Bar Hebraeus summarizes his response as such: "What is certain is this—that Ṭughril Beg did not accept even one of the [four] stipulations."[179] So much for the myth of the obedient Saljūq Sultans, always subservient to the ʿAbbāsid Caliph.

The omission of the contents of this letter from all the Muslim sources after the *Malik-nāma* is crucial. Its inclusion would have jeopardized two of the ideological tropes used to legitimize the Saljūqs: the second, which emphasizes their unwavering obedience to the caliph, and the third, which depicts them as promoting social order.

Upon the advent of ʿĪd al-Fiṭr, the Saljūqs gathered to begin the *yaghmā*, "plunder." Ṭughril mounted his horse, seeking to stop the Saljūq tribe from entering Nīshāpūr. His brother, Chaghrī Beg, insisted on plundering the town, even threatening (with a dagger) that he would take his own life if he were not permitted to plunder the town![180] Al-Kātib al-Iṣfahānī records that Ṭughril offered 40,000 dinārs to Chaghrī to forgo the plunder. Most of this sum was paid by the town's people, even though the later sources (Nīshāpūrī and Rashīd al-Dīn Faḍl Allāh) attempt to credit Ṭughril personally with this act of generosity.[181] This should again be seen as an attempt in the historical chronicles to bolster the status of Ṭughril as the protector of Muslim lives and properties, fulfilling the third component of Saljūq ideology. On the other hand, one would not expect that all of Ṭughril's actions were of the disorderly nature documented above. Al-Kātib al-Iṣfahānī relates that Ṭughril "forbade, gave orders, made grants, levied taxes, administrated efficiently, abolished things, ordered affairs correctly, entrusted matters," and presided every Sunday and Wednesday over *maẓālim* (para-sharīʿa juridical) sessions.[182]

There are some charming anecdotes in the chronicles that attest to the lack of the familiarity of the Turkish warlords with the luxurious commodities available in citied Islamicate cultures. It is reported that Ṭughril was presented with a *lauzīnaj*, an almond-based delicacy.[183] The Turkish warlord ate the sweet and commented that it would be good, if only some garlic was added to it.[184] Certain members of the Oghuz are also reported to have seen some camphor and mistaken it for salt. Upon eating it,[185] they remarked that it was the most bitter salt they had seen.[186] Ibn al-Athīr quietly remarks "and many more tales have been told of them like these . . ." All these anecdotes are meant to suggest the lack of familiarity of the Oghuz with the niceties of citied Perso-Islamicate culture, and they also imply the shock (and perhaps amusement) the Oghuz brought to the civilized class of Khurāsān.

The Saljūqs also used the interim of Ramaḍān to begin one of their most important tasks, responding to the caliph's letter. We have seen that many of the elements that go back to the prehistory of the Saljūqs all contribute to the Great Saljūq Myth and feed into a larger discourse of legitimizing the Saljūqs. The letter written to the Caliph al-Qāʾim Bi-Amr Allāh represents one of the most fully developed articulations of Saljūq ideology. It is crucial to point out that the text of this letter is featured prominently in all the sources that attempt to justify the Saljūqs and is significantly missing in both of the sources going back to the earlier *Malik-nāma*. One can even question whether such a letter was ever written. What is significant for our purposes is not whether this letter was actually written or not, but how this text perpetuates Saljūq ideology in the sources which seek to legitimize the Saljūqs. The text of this letter, allegedly written in 432/1040, deserves to be quoted in full:[187]

> We, the servants from the family of Saljūq, have been a perpetually obedient group, supporters of the state (*dawlat*) and obedient to Islam and helping it (*miṭwāʿ wa muʿāḍid-i islām*).[188] We have always striven in waging war against the enemy and jihād, and have been assiduous in visiting the exalted Kaʿba. We had an uncle who was honored and respected amongst us, [by the name of] Isrāʾīl b. Saljūq. Yamīn al-Dawla Maḥmūd b. Sabuktagīn seized him, even though he had performed no crime or iniquity. Maḥmūd imprisoned him in a castle named Kālanjar in India for seven years, until he passed away there. [Maḥmūd] also imprisoned many of our kin and folk in [other] citadels. When Maḥmūd died, and his son Masʿūd succeeded him, he did not attend [properly] to the affairs of the realm, and instead preoccupied himself with ludicrous amusements and pleasure.
>
> The folk of heretical innovation (*ahl-i bidʿat*) found an opportunity to engage in corruption and perverse unruliness (*fasād*).[189]
>
> Whoever chooses amusements loses his flock.[190]
> Whoever pursues drinking ruins his judgment.[191]
>
> The notables and the renowned folk of Khurāsān asked us to rise up in their defense and protection. Masʿūd's army attacked us. There were attacks and retreats, defeats and victories for both of us, until at last, we encountered good fortune. The last time that Masʿūd himself attacked us—with a huge army—with the help of Almighty God, we got the upper hand. Under the attention of the Sacred and Purified Prophetic Presence [which supported us], Masʿūd was defeated and humiliated. With his [battle] standard overturned, he turned his back and fled, leaving to us victory and the dominion.
>
> He who obeys God becomes a king (gains power).
> He who obeys his passions is annihilated.[192]
>
> In gratitude for this gift, and thanks for this victory, we spread justice and equity [through the whole realm], and distanced ourselves from

the path of injustice and tyranny. We desire for our task to be based on the path of religion and the order of the Commander of the Believers.

> Whoever makes kingship subservient to the religion,
> all Sultans will become obedient to him.
> Whoever makes the religion subservient to kingship,
> everyone will covet [his rank].[193]

This letter is a rich source of Saljūq ideology. It contains frequent appeals to religious symbols to fortify its authors' claim. The letter both begins and finishes with an emphatic acknowledgment of caliphal authority. This claim is intended to distinguish the Saljūqs from the Buwayhids, who were allegedly holding the caliph hostage, as well as from the Fāṭimī presence, which directly undermined the ʿAbbāsid Caliphal claim to authority. The piety of the Saljūqs is emphasized through their desire to visit the Kaʿba and differentiates them from the Qarmaṭīs. It is appropriate to recall here that none of the first three Saljūq Sultans did visit the Kaʿba, and neither had their forefathers. The Saljūqs claim to have initiated their actions in Khurāsān only as a response to the *aʿyān* (nobles) of that region. In reality, we have seen how the Saljūq conquest was a cause of great concern and distress for the local notables. The Saljūqs again emphasize their care for the *raʿyat* (flock, i.e., people), a claim that was to be repeatedly undermined by their actions. Again, what is of concern to us is not so much the authenticity of these claims, but how these claims deploy key components of Saljūq ideology. Of particular relevance for our study of the relationship between power and the politics of knowledge is the emphatic association between *bidʿa* and *fasād*: heretical innovations in the realm of thought had to be identified and circumscribed as they were believed to lead almost inevitably to social unruliness. This tendency to identify heresy would prove to be of great importance in how the discourses of Islamic thought were articulated under Saljūq patronage.

While the Saljūqs went out of their way to emphasize their obedience to the caliph, their actions betrayed other motivations. Rather than waiting for a caliphal response, they proceeded on to the realpolitik task of dividing up and ruling their new kingdom. (In their defense, it might be said that they did not have the luxury of awaiting a response.) According to Rāwandī, the Saljūq leaders divided up the rule (*wilāyat*) of the realm, and each one of the leaders was appointed to one end of the realm.[194] Chaghrī Beg, the elder brother, made Marv his *Dār al-Mulk* (Abode of the government) and focused more on Khurāsān.[195] His name was mentioned in the *khuṭba* there, and he assumed the title of *Malik al-mulūk*, "the King of kings."[196] One cannot entirely dismiss the idea that his reason for having chosen the more eastern lands was to distance himself from the caliphate (as early as their conquest of Nīshāpūr, Chaghrī had refused to sign on to the conciliatory letter the Saljūqs had written to the caliph).[197] Certain numismatic evidence suggests that Chaghrī's relationship with Ṭughril was far more nuanced than being either a subordinate brother or simply a coruler of the empire.[198]

Other senior leaders of the Saljūq clan would also receive significant areas to rule: Mūsā, the Great Yabghū,[199] was appointed to the rule of Bust, Harāt, Sīstān, and those regions which he could conquer.[200] Qāwurd, the elder son of Chaghrī Beg ruled Ṭabas and some regions of Kirmān.[201] Ṭughril Beg came towards ʿIrāq.[202] Ibrāhīm Īnāl[203] along with the nephew of Amīr Yāqūtī (the son of Chaghrī Beg Dāwūd) and his cousin Qutulmush remained in Ṭughril's service as they collectively moved to Rayy and established another Dār al-Mulk there. The establishment of various Dār al-Mulks in Marv and Rayy (and, later on, in Iṣfahān) demonstrates that the idea of a centralized monarchy was not indigenous to the Turkish rulers. Their ruling model can perhaps be best described as "collective sovereignty," or "family confederation,"[204] and was far from the centralized Perso-Islamic monarchy Niẓām al-Mulk would so eagerly attempt to establish.

Contrary to the claims of the letter sent to the caliph, the Oghuz as a whole and their venerable leaders (Ibrāhīm Īnāl, Chaghrī, and not least of all, Ṭughril) continued their wide-scale massacre and pillage, even though many of the later Muslim sources attempted to minimize the extent of these actions or to deny them altogether. As we have seen, Nīshāpūrī recorded some evidence of these *fitna*s, detailing the atrocities of the Oghuz in Khurāsān, the people's anxiety in Nīshāpūr, and the tension between Ṭughril and Chaghrī over whether or not to plunder Nīshāpūr.[205] Qazwīnī, for his part, avoids discussing any social commotion tied to Ṭughril himself, although, as we shall see, he does mention the tyranny of Ibrāhīm Īnāl.[206] Rāwandī, who has a more detailed account of Ṭughril's conquests, likewise omits any mention of murders, plunders, or social commotion.[207] Rāwandī took most of his accounts from earlier sources, specifically Nīshāpūrī's *Saljūq-nāma*.[208] And so his omission of the problematic accounts (from a perspective committed to legitimizing the Saljūqs) that appear in Nīshāpūrī is surely not accidental. The details presented in the earlier texts were suppressed and omitted from the later Saljūq constructions of the origins of the Saljūqs because these accounts did not fit the ideological construction of Saljūqs. These narratives are as much propaganda as they are history. The concern of these historical chronicles is not simply to provide information on the Saljūqs but rather to construct a paradigm for their presence that would account for their brute force while legitimizing it by relating it to established symbols of religious authority.

A specific outcome of the feelings of distressed agitation in Nīshāpūr was a popular revolt against Ṭughril's appointee, Ibrāhīm Īnāl, who had been appointed as the *shaḥna* in Nīshāpūr. Ibrāhīm had proven to be an oppressive tyrant, and the citizens of Nīshāpūr cried out against him. In a letter written to him, they said, "O Commander, abandon tyranny and adopt justice, because there is a world to come after this. Nīshāpūr has seen (in the past) and will see (in the future) many commanders such as you . . . The weapon of the people of Nīshāpūr is their dawn-time prayer, and the One who hears our complaints is All-Knowing. Even if our Sultan is away, our God is near: He is Alive and never dead, Awake and never slumbering, Aware and never heedless."[209] While Ibrāhīm Īnāl finally did cease his tyranny, it must be reemphasized that the reports of this revolt as well as the general uprising is eliminated from Rāwandī.

The overall impact of the Saljūq conquest on economic and commercial life in Khurāsān was devastating. The eighth-/fifteenth-century historian Mīr-Khwānd described the impact on Nīshāpūr in the following terms: "That region became ruinous, like the disheveled tresses of the fair ones or the eyes of the loved ones, and it became devastated by the pasturing of [the Türkmen] flocks."[210] It was in the midst of all these conquests and plunders that a caliphal envoy, Abū Isḥāq Fuqāʾī carried a letter back to Baghdad, stating that "when the Saljūqs found the son of Yamīn al-Dawla [i.e., Sultan Masʿūd] going astray from the path of righteousness and falling into corruption and discord, they began to plunder Muslims, and sack cities. *In spite of all this*, they remain servants of the Amīr al-muʾminīn, and protect the towns and God's servants. This group has established the principles of justice . . . They have abandoned the signs of tyranny."[211] (emphasis mine)

An exhaustive reading of all the Muslim and non-Muslim sources would seem to suggest that the content of this letter, if not its ideological claim, was more representative of the actual impact of the Saljūqs upon caliphal politics; far from being the upholders of justice and Islamic principles that Niẓām al-Mulk and the later chroniclers would have one believe, they were simply one looting and pillaging power among others. The difference was in the attitude of the caliph toward them: they were viewed as the most likely group holding military force to be willing to cooperate with the caliph and show acknowledgment of caliphal authority. While the Saljūqs claimed to be the clients of the caliph as early as the 1030s, the actual relationship with the caliph was far more complex than that. To document this, we shall have to retrace the Saljūq conquest and migration from Khurāsān to ʿIrāq. Upon the arrival of Saljūqs in ʿIrāq, they engaged in an ongoing negotiation of power and authority with the caliph.

Saljūq *Fitna* from Khurāsān to ʿIrāq

It was after having secured Khurāsān that Ṭughril finally turned to ʿIrāq. The Saljūq-friendly sources, such as Qazwīnī's *Tārīkh-i guzīda*, merely provide an impressive list of Ṭughril's conquests across the Iranian plateau. Ṭughril stumbled onto some good fortune in Rayy, which undoubtedly helped him in his future conquests. While staying at the residence of ʿAlī Kāma (the Daylamī),Ṭughril found and confiscated his host's hidden treasure. The same happened at the residence of Majd al-Dawla Rustam. He distributed this unexpected wealth among his troops. Newly invigorated, Ṭughril and his troops set out toward ʿIrāq, Ādharbāījān, Kurdistān, and Fārs.[212] In the year 433/1041–42, Ṭughril proceeded to conquer Gurgān and Ṭabaristān, thus bringing to an effective end the Āl-i Ziyār rule there. The ruler there agreed to pay thirty thousand dinārs a year to Ṭughril, who had virtual control there in any case. Between 434 and 436/1042 and 1045, Ṭughril led various military conquests at Khwārazm,[213] Qazwīn,[214] Abhar, Zanjān, and Hamadān, fighting the remnants of the Daylamī and Ghaznavid forces.[215] The citizens of Qazwīn, long known for their political independence, initially blocked Ṭughril's path until finally they were subdued by a rainstorm "of arrows and stones." The Daylamī king, Abū Kālijār, successfully prevented Ṭughril from capturing Iṣfahān in 436/1044–45, and it became a tributary state of the Saljūqs. Perhaps what is more intriguing in the above narratives is what has not been included, specifically, mentions of continued plunder and pillage of these towns.

The *Malik-nāma* depicts a vastly different picture of the Saljūq activities. Bar Hebraeus reports that two years after the above letter (438/1046), the Oghuz entered Ḥūlwān (close to the present Kirmān-shāh) and burnt it. They tortured the men of this town until they revealed their hidden treasures, they raped the women and "deflowered their virgins."[216] Ibn al-Athīr records similar atrocities in Daskara by a Saljūq commander, Ibrāhīm ibn Isḥāq. In addition to the usual plundering and extortion, this commander is also reported to have beaten "women and children."[217] Al-Kātib al-Iṣfahānī depicts the Saljūq army as having been like a "thundering flood," and his poetic description of the atrocities committed by Ṭughril's army during their march toward Iraq deserves to be quoted at length: "Every beauty they came across, they disfigured. Every fire they passed, they extinguished. Every house they passed, they dismantled. How many dams they broke, how much shame they left behind . . . Many kings escaped from their path, fearing the Turks . . . Every town they entered they subjugated the people. They ruled the towns through fear and terror."[218]

This same feeling of "fear and terror" (*ruʿb*) is described as overcoming the people of Baghdad when Ṭughril marched into town with his army to wed the caliph's daughter.[219] Even though the Saljūq chronicles lavish praise after praise upon the Great Saljūqs and extol their establishment of a peaceful order, the historical reality of the time was vastly different. The people of Baghdad, Nīshāpūr, Ṭūs, Marāgha, and many others indeed had a great deal to worry about from the nomadic forces descending upon them. Contrary to what is reported in Saljūq chronicles, the people of these towns had not asked for the Saljūqs to rescue them. What awaited them was not a peaceful social order but all too real prospects of pillage, plunder, rape, and even wide-scale massacre. With respect to the Saljūq impact on Iraq, we have the independent confirmation of Bar Hebraeus, who relied on the *Malik-nāma*: "In every place where his troops meet together they plunder, and destroy and kill. And no one district (or, quarter) is able to support them for more than one week because of their vast number. And from sheer necessity they are compelled to depart to another quarter in order to find food for themselves and their beasts."[220]

When Ṭughril himself appeared in the vicinity of Baghdad, the people's reaction was far from embracing a hero. Overcome with fear, they ran for their lives and took shelter in the western portions of Baghdad.[221] Significantly, the Turks of Baghdad removed their tents to the outskirts of town.[222] Even prior to Ṭughril's arrival, the Iraqi Turks had pleaded with the caliph not to let "this enemy" (*hadhā ʾl-khuṣm*) come near them. The caliph had allegedly promised to keep Ṭughril away from the Turks, a promise he did not keep.[223] The apprehension of the Turks was fully justified; upon arrival in Baghdad, Ṭughril set upon a systematic massacre of two groups, the Daylamīs and the Turks. Bar Hebraeus offers a gruesome account of many of the nomadic Turks (from Iraq) being drowned in the Tigris.[224] Far from seeing other Turks as potential allies, the Oghuz tribe first had to deal with those who were the most like them and thus presented the most likely source of contention. The Iraqi Turks had been assimilated into city life, assuming professions far beyond the conventional mercenary soldier. There are reports of them having been bakers, vegetable sellers, and bathhouse staff.[225] Ṭughril ordered the confiscation of all the possessions belonging to the Baghdad Turks.[226] One of the first statements uttered by Ṭughril to the caliph was "If I did not honor you, I would have destroyed all Baghdad with the edge of the sword."[227] This episode is yet another demonstration of the fact that the Saljūq rise to power needs to be seen in the context of an intra-Turkish tribal conflict in addition to that of Perso-Islamicate dynastic history.

Many of the commoners, dissatisfied with Ṭughril's treatment, left town. Ṭughril's army ambushed and killed many civilians. This episode also led to an "increase in people's distress and an escalation in fear" (*wa ishtadda 'l-balāʾ ʿala al-nās, wa ʿaẓima al-khawf*).[228] The caliph is reported as having complained to Ṭughril, "This was not my expectation at all, for I imagined that my glory would be increased by your coming, and that religion would be triumphant through your nearness to me. Although I have suffered the very reverse of these things, my trust is in God."[229] Ṭughril responded, "I am subject to thy command. And as to these things that have taken place, thou knowest full well that they have happened because of the evil Turks who were in thy service. I am myself not blameworthy."[230] Only after the above assurance did the caliph proceed to mint coins in Ṭughril's name.

Problematizing the Myth of Saljūq Obedience to the Caliph

Contrary to the ideological claims on the behalf of the Saljūqs in the chronicles, the dominant paradigm of interactions between the caliph and the sultan was not one of obedience, but rather of negotiation and contestation of power. The caliphate and the sultanate clearly needed each other, yet this does not mean that either was willing to concede supremacy in the political realm. Unsubstantiated claims that the sultan governed the realm while "the Caliph helplessly stood by" can no longer be accepted.[231] A careful examination of the interactions between the first Saljūq Sultan, Ṭughril Beg, and the ʿAbbāsid Caliph elucidates this point. The caliphs and the sultans routinely interfered with the appointing of administrators by the other. When the caliph al-Qāʾim bi Amr Allāh sought to appoint Ibn Dārist as his own vizier in 453/1061, Ṭughril wrote a letter (through ʿAmīd al-Mulk Kundurī) to the caliph, stating that the appointment "would not please him [i.e., Ṭughril]."[232] The reciprocal situation was also known to happen. When the Sultan Alp Arslān moved to appoint Īt-gīn Sulaymānī as the *shaḥna* of Baghdad in 464/1071–72, the caliph opposed the move since one of Sulaymānī's sons had killed a slave of the caliph. The sultan was forced to appoint another candidate.[233] Each of these episodes became a negotiating battle for the sultan and the caliph. It clearly demonstrates that the ʿAbbāsid Caliph was not simply willing to hand over all temporal control to the Saljūqs.

We are now finally positioned to view the plea from the caliph to Ṭughril Beg to come to Baghdad in order to "save Islam" as an important component of the attempt to justify the Saljūq conquest. According to our earliest source, the *Malik-nāma*, the caliph had actually been unwilling to have Ṭughril in Baghdad, yet through sheer necessity was forced to urge Ṭughril to come there.[234] While all the later chronicles focus on the caliphal gifts showered on Ṭughril and the Turkish warlord's respect toward the caliph, none of them wished to bring up this tension. Saljūq obedience to the caliph was a crucial component of Saljūq ideology, so much so that any evidence to the contrary (such as depicting caliphal angst at the arrival of the alleged rescuers) was eliminated from most of the later sources.

The sources committed to legitimizing the Saljūqs (Nīshāpūrī, Rāwandī, Rashīd al-Dīn Faḍl Allāh, etc.) focus on Ṭughril's defeat of al-Basāsīrī, his restoration of the caliph to *dār al-khilāfa*, and his performance of the Ḥajj. All three claims deploy key components of Saljūq ideology: putting down heretical movements, obedience to the caliph, and following normative Islamic practices. Qazwīnī states that Ṭughril arrived at Mahrawān (Nahrawān?) in the Ramaḍān of 447/1055 and overthrew the Buwayhids. In the same year,[235] the caliph ordered the *khuṭba* to be said in Ṭughril Beg's name and for his name to be minted on the coins.[236] He was also given an honorific name: *al-Sulṭān Rukn al-Dawla* (pillar of the state) *Abū Ṭālib Ṭughril Beg Muḥammad ibn Mīkāʾīl Yamīn Amīr al-Muʾminīn* (right hand of the Commander of the Faithful). Ṭughril allegedly excused himself to leave for Ḥijāz, in order to perform the Ḥajj, and at last came to Baghdad.[237] Likewise, Rāwandī also records that when Ṭughril arrived in ʿIrāq, he first undertook a journey to the Kaʿba and Medina. Only then did he return to a state-tent (in Baghdad), where the caliph paid him a great deal of respect and praised him immensely. The sultan was given a crown and a throne there, and the caliph did not withhold any favors from that world conqueror (*jahān-gīr*). The Saljūq chronicles also emphasize that after this move, the people (*raʿyat*) were able to rest in peace, and they sent prayers upon Ṭughril. When the sultan and the caliph arrived at the gate of Baghdad, Ṭughril descended from his steed and walked on his own toward the caliph. The caliph told him, "O Pillar of the Faith (*yā rukn al-dīn*), mount [your steed]!" His honorific was thus changed from (Rukn) al-Dawla to (Rukn) al-Dīn,[238] further signifying the incorporation of religious symbols into Saljūq ideology.

Many of the significant elements of the above narrative—Ṭughril's obedience to Islamic injunctions, the reestablishment of social order, and even the exact circumstances surrounding the bestowal of the honorific *Rukn al-Dīn*—are contradicted by sources going back to the original *Malik-nāma*. Mīr-Khwānd doubted whether Ṭughril ever performed the Ḥajj, instead stating that the pretense of going to Mecca might have been simply a ruse.[239] Bar Hebraeus also provides ample evidence to document that Ṭughril's arrival in Baghdad was not a cause of celebration and did not lead to "people resting in peace." The Syriac historian records that upon entering Baghdad, Ṭughril's forces proceeded to capture many of the nomads and kill "the Daylamis, the Turks, and the pagans." They proceeded to drown the nomads in the Tigris and confiscated many houses for themselves. The sources relying on the *Malik-nāma* depict the situation surrounding the caliphal bestowal of the honorific *Rukn al-Dīn* in a vastly different form from its depiction in later sources. According to the *Chronography* of Bar Hebraeus, Ṭughril had seized the city of Isfahan in order to pressure the caliph to bestow on him titles "with names (i.e., titles) which befitted his kingship."[240] This demonstrates that the bestowal of this title might not have had to do with the defeat of Basāsīrī, but was achieved through Ṭughril's forceful pressure on the caliph to grant him titles which not only acknowledged his military and political prowess (thus the title *Rukn al-Dawla*) but also tapped into symbols of religious legitimacy (hence the title *Rukn al-Dīn*).

Perhaps most revealing of the realpolitik nature of contestations of power and authority between the Saljūq warlord and the caliph was the tense situation that occurred immediately after the Basāsīrī episode. The conflict dealt with negotiations with the caliph over sustenance for Ṭughril's army. The sultan, through the advice of his vizier, ʿAmīd al-Mulk[241] Abū Naṣr Kundurī, was able to take over the bread rations of Baghdad. The excuse was that he needed to insure that the army would receive their necessary lot. Ṭughril was even able to determine the amount allotted for the caliph.[242] This negotiation marked the importance of the vizier in negotiating between the sultan and the caliph, but it also underscored the political savvy of the Saljūq regime at a relatively early state of their political rule.

An even more serious case of negotiating political authority involved the intermarriages between the Saljūq clan and the ʿAbbasids during this time period. In the year 448/1056–57, the caliph wed Arslān Khātūn bint Chaghrī, the niece of Ṭughril.[243] This marriage seems to have cemented the relations between the Saljūqs and the caliphate. Al-Kātib al-Iṣfahānī stated, "After this marriage, the two realms [the caliphate and the sultanate] were mixed together. *Dīn* and *Dawlat* were reciprocally matched."[244] While the ʿAbbasid Caliphs seemed pleased to marry the Turkish Saljūq women, they were much more hesitant to give their own daughters in marriage to the upstart Turkish Saljūqs. This double standard, rooted in ʿAbbasid and Arab anxieties over genealogy, created a very tense situation of political conflict between Ṭughril and the caliph. In Dhu ʾl-qaʿda of the year 452/1060–61, Ṭughril's wife passed away in Zanjān. In the next year, the Turkish warlord requested to marry the daughter (or possibly the sister) of the Caliph al-Qāʾim.[245] The sultan went to Ādharbāījān and settled in Tabrīz. He left ʿAmīd al-Mulk behind in Baghdad to act as his agent (*wakīl*) in asking for the hand of Sayyida al-Nisāʾ.[246] The caliph resisted this, which aroused the anger of the aged warlord. He remarked, "Is this my reward from the Caliph al-Qāʾim? I have killed my own brother in obedience to him (*hadhā jazāʾī min al-imām al-qāiʾm? wa qad qataltu akhī fi ṭāʿatihi*).[247] I have spent my whole life so he may have an hour of rest, and have spent my money, so that he might be rich. What do you think?"[248] He even took off the honorary black robes given to him by the ʿAbbāsid Caliph, donning white apparel instead.[249] Before being invested with the black caliphal *khilʿat*, Ṭughril's favorite color for regal attire had been white. This changing of apparel symbolizes a willingness to overthrow caliphal recognition and revert back to his own mode of authority. The situation escalated to the point of Ṭughril ordering ʿAmīd al-Mulk to confiscate all the caliphal land grants, leaving for the caliph only the villages and lands which had been in ʿAbbāsid hands before al-Qādir Billāh.[250] This was no short-lived controversy: a year passed before the caliph was forced to consent to this marriage. One cannot entirely dismiss racial and age factors in the caliph's hesitation in consenting to this arrangement. Again, it is intriguing to note that later sources attribute the confiscation not to Ṭughril but to ʿAmīd al-Mulk. Furthermore, it is the lands of the *Nawwāb*, and not the caliph himself, which are described as having been confiscated.[251] This, once again, demonstrates the attempt in later sources to cover up tensions between the sultanate and the caliphate.

If one may read between the lines, it is significant that in receiving the would-be bride, Ṭughril brought his entire army to Baghdad. This might be taken as a precaution, should the caliph renege on his consent. The sources describe the citizens as having been "frightened and alarmed" (*wa artāʿat al-raʿya*).[252] The caliph reluctantly agreed and sent the *Qāḍī al-quḍāt* with the Sayyida to Tabrīz to perform the marriage ceremony. They authorized a *mahr* of four hundred silver dirhams and one gold dīnar.[253] Ṭughril wished to move to his Dār al-Mulk in Rayy for the ceremony of bringing the bride to the groom's house. However, Ṭughril died in the course of this journey, on the 8th of Ramaḍān in the year 455/1063.[254] According to Qazwīnī, Ṭughril had suffered a sudden death,[255] and one should at least entertain the possibility that he might have been poisoned. One cannot entirely dismiss the idea that the suspicious circumstances were somehow related to the caliph not wishing his daughter to consummate her marriage with the aged (and non-Arab) warlord. The Sayyida, still with her dowry, was escorted back to Baghdad.[256] The marriage, from all accounts, does not appear to have been consummated.[257] George Makdisi rightly suspects that this whole episode might have been part of a plan on behalf of the Saljūqs to produce an offspring who could be simultaneously a Saljūq and an ʿAbbāsid and thus claim full religious legitimacy while holding military power.[258] As we shall see in the next chapter (in the situation orchestrated by Tarkān Khātūn), such an offspring became the source of much tension between the Saljūq Sultan and the ʿAbbāsid Caliph. On this occasion, however, Ṭughril's passing marked the end of a remarkable career, one that had witnessed the transformation of the Saljūqs from a nomadic family to the political backbone of the ʿAbbasid realm. Ṭughril's tomb stands today in Rayy, South of Tehran (see illustration 1.1).

The tensions between the ʿAbbāsids and the Saljūqs naturally did not end with Ṭughril. Perhaps the most serious conflict occurred towards the end of Malik-Shāh's reign. The sources hint at an "estrangement" (*waḥsha*) between the powerful sultan and the caliph. Malik-Shāḥ "suggested" to al-Muqtadī that the ʿAbbāsid Caliph might consider moving from Baghdad to any city he chose in "Damascus or Ḥijāz."[259] The sources do not dwell on the ramifications of this *waḥsha*, yet it is hard to interpret it as anything other than the Saljūq Sultan wishing to assert a monopoly of authority over Baghdad without the presence of the caliph. It is imperative to read this account in line with what Niẓām al-Mulk reveals about advice given to the sultan by certain viziers (probably Tāj al-Mulk) to remove the caliph altogether.[260] It is greatly suspicious that the chroniclers bring up this event immediately after the account of Malik-Shāh's poisoning, as if to suggest the possible role of the ʿAbbāsid Caliph.

From a historiographic perspective, most sources seem to downplay conflicts between the Saljūqs and the ʿAbbāsids, and so one has to examine all the available sources with a keen eye to uncover evidence of these tensions. We can draw significant inferences especially from the numismatic evidence. We know from the above sources that the caliph had Ṭughril's name minted on the coins issued in Baghdad after the Basāsīrī incident. However, after Ṭughril the subsequent Saljūq Sultans were not allowed to add the title *sul-*

1.1. The tomb of Sultan Ṭughril in Rayy (Melanie Michailidis, 2003, Courtesy of the Aga Khan Visual Archive, M.I.T.)

ṭān after their names on coins issued in Baghdad. The coins issued to Sultan Ṭughril Beg in Nīshāpūr bear the caliph's name and after the year 439 include Ṭughril's title of *al-sulṭān al-muʿaẓẓam* and *Shāhānshāh*. Alp Arslān also included the same honorific in coins issued in Nīshāpūr, but we do not possess coins minted in Baghdad that bear his name. During the reign of Malik-Shāh, the Baghdad coins issued in the year 485/1092 mention the caliph's name, whereas the sultan's name is mentioned without the honorifics of *al-sulṭān*.[261] The honorifics of *al-sulṭān al-muʿaẓẓam* and *Shāhānshāh* are indeed mentioned in the coins minted in Iṣfahān during Malik-Shāh's reign.[262] The coins issued to Bark-yāruq in Baghdad in 487/1094 and 489/1096 do not include any of the usual honorifics.[263] In the subsequent generation, coins issued to Sultan Muḥammad do not bear the title of al-sulṭān when they were issued in Baghdad (year 500/1106–7), but do so when they were minted in other regions, such as Lūrdijān and Isfahan.[264] It seems that while the sultans were free to claim grandiose titles of political authority for themselves in coins issued outside of Baghdad, the caliph specifically kept the honorifics associated with the Saljūq warlords to a minimum on the coins issued in Baghdad. Numismatic evidence thus becomes crucial to trace political propaganda (by including grandiose titles) and confirm political maneuvering (by suppression of these titles on Baghdad coins).

One other historiographic clue which allows us to ascertain the strained relationship between the caliph and the sultan is the inclusion (or omission) of the Sultan's name in the all-important Friday sermon (*khuṭba*). The Saljūq Sultans always desired that their names be mentioned in the Baghdad khuṭba, and the caliphs refused this honor when they were able.[265] According to Ibn al-Athīr, the mention of Sultan Masʿūd was dropped from the Baghdad khuṭba, while Sanjar's name was omitted from the khuṭbas in all of Iraq in 526/1131.[266]

These tensions grew until they reached alarming heights in the twelfth century. After the death of Sultan Muḥammad in 1118, when much of the Saljūq structure had disintegrated, the Caliph Muktafī exerted his own political authority and, according to Ibn al-Athīr, ruled "without a Sultan" for some time. The extent of Saljūq impact upon caliphal authority is all the more clear when the rule of a caliph "without a Sultan" is so emphasized by the prominent historian. The chronicler Rāwandī reports that the late Saljūq Ṭughril (not to be confused with the sultan of the same name discussed above) was persuaded by a Turkish Atabeg, Muḥammad Pahlawān-jahān, to remove the caliph from temporal power. The followers of the sultan and the Atabeg addressed a crowd in this manner: "If the Caliph is the imam, then his constant occupation must be the performance of prayer (*namāz*), as prayer is the foundation of the faith and the best of deeds; his pre-eminence in this respect and the fact that he serves as an example is sufficient for him. This is true sovereignty; the interference of the Caliph in the affairs of temporal rule is senseless; they must be entrusted to the Sultans."[267]

My purpose in bringing up these narratives has been to deconstruct the myth of Saljūq obedience to the caliphate and instead recognize it as a key component of Saljūq ideology. It has not been my intention to write a straightforward political history of the Saljūqs. Rather, I have aimed to point out the deft construction of the Saljūq paradigm vis-à-vis religious and political symbols of authority. As should be clear by now, the relationship between the Saljūqids and the ʿAbbāsids was never one of straightforward obedience, but rather a tense negotiation for power and authority. Negotiation, in fact, characterizes all elements of Saljūq culture: political, social, and intellectual. In the next chapters we will consider how these political negotiations affected the institutions of knowledge in the Saljūq era, and how political ideology and the religious construction of orthodoxy ratified each other. In order to do so, we will turn to a study of the man who is singularly accredited with establishing the main institutions of the Saljūq polity: the able administrator, Niẓām al-Mulk (d. 1092), whose honorific literally meant the "Order of the Realm."

Chapter Two

The Niẓām's Realm, the Orderly Realm

The vizierate was a dominant institution of Saljūq political and intellectual culture. The viziers had fulfilled significant administrative functions from an early period of Islamic history.[1] They had previously reached significant heights of power during the time of a family of viziers known as the Barmakids, who served the ʿAbbāsid Caliphs al-Mahdī (r. 775–85 C.E.) and Harūn al-Rashīd (r. 786–809 C.E.).[2] However, it was under the Saljūq regime that the institution of the vizierate reached a new apogee of power by becoming responsible for mediating negotiations between political and intellectual figures as well as between the sultanate and the caliphate. The service provided by the viziers to the Saljūqs was all the more important given the Saljūq warlords' lack of political experience in the complex and nuanced universe of the Perso-Islamic world. While the historical chronicles are filled with the descriptions of the battles of Saljūq Sultans from Ṭughril to Sanjar, the viziers were the linchpins that held together the entire Muslim networks of various sultans and caliphs, intellectuals and soldiers, Sufis and jurists. The Saljūq vizierate was most effectively embodied (though not without contention) in the person of Niẓām al-Mulk, who played a crucial role in the ordering and systematizing of the realm. There is no shortage of panegyric praise devoted to him, such as that offered by the poet Muʿizzī (d. circa 519–21/1125–27), who was known as the "prince of poets" (*Amīr al-shuʿarāʾ*):[3] "You are that blessed vizier through whose competence the Saljūq realm reached the Heavenly heights of *ʿIlliyīn*."[4] (*ʿIlliyīn* is part of the celestial cosmology of Paradise, where according to Qurʾan 83:17 the Record of the Righteous is kept.)

Panegyrics aside, Niẓām al-Mulk held more power, distributed throughout more social sectors, than any of his contemporary Saljūq Sultans or ʿAbbāsid Caliphs. At least, this is how some of the biographers of the time period remember him. The Shāfiʿī hagiographer al-Subkī, who might well be suspected of sympathy towards the vizier because he patronized so many Shāfiʿī scholars, stated, "His vizierate was for thirty years. But his vizierate was not a vizierate: it exceeded the Sultanate!" (*wa lam takun wizāratuhu wizāratan, bal fawq al-salṭana.*)[5]

It is no great exaggeration to state that Niẓām al-Mulk, the epitome of the vizierate, simply *was* Saljūq administration in the eyes of many of the later historians and the masses. Historical sources state that the masses mourned Niẓām al-Mulk's passing much more than that of any caliph or sultan.[6] One of the chroniclers, Hindū-Shāh Nakhjawānī, states that after the passing of Niẓām al-Mulk, there was not much for the people to mourn about when the sultan passed away a month later (*vafāt-i sulṭān ba'd az vafāt-i khwāja dar naẓar-i khalq-i jahān aẓmī ziyāda nadāsht*).[7] If we are to take these accounts seriously, to his contemporaries Niẓām al-Mulk was not a government official; he simply *was* the government. He had come to represent the continuity and stability, the structuring and ordering (*niẓām*) of the realm (*mulk*). It was both the case of a man becoming identified with a set of institutions as well as the institutions becoming personified through him.

Oriental Institutions *Not* at Random Strung: Naẓm, Niẓām, and "Stringing" along Saljūq Institutions

It was under Sultan Alp Arslān that Abū 'Alī Ḥasan from Ṭūs *became* Niẓām al-Mulk.[8] Contrary to what is often assumed, the famous Abū 'Alī Ḥasan ibn 'Alī al-Ṭūsī was neither the first nor the last vizier honored by the famous honorific of *Niẓām al-Mulk*. The title had been previously awarded to Abū Muḥammad Ḥasan ibn Muḥammad Dahistānī,[9] and some of Ḥasan Ṭūsī's own descendants also bore that weighty honorific. Yet, the general honorific became something of a proper noun: there is no mistaking the identity of the person the sources refer to as Niẓām al-Mulk.

The etymology of this ubiquitous title reveals a great deal about his actual function in the realm. *Niẓām* is derived from *naẓm*, which is often associated with lending systematization, structure, and ordering; as a secondary connotation it refers to the whole genre of poetry. The original meaning of *naẓm*, however, came from stringing together pearls: "Joining (pearls) in a row; composing (verses); order, arrangement; a string (of pearls); poetry, verse (opp. to *naṣr* [Arabic: *nathr*], 'prose composition') . . ."[10] This etymology has led scholars to suggest that poetry "strings" along verses (i.e., pearls) along the "thread" of rhyme. The ordering-stringing is contrasted with the "scattering" (literal meaning) of *nathr*, or prose.[11] This idea of ordering-stringing has been discussed at length by some of the prominent scholars of Persian literature such as A. J. Arberry and Annemarie Schimmel.[12] It is perhaps surprising that the same discussion of "ordering" has not been applied to *naẓm*'s cognate, *niẓām*. The *Persian-English Dictionary* of Steingass defines *niẓām* as "joining in a row, stringing (pearls); arranging, governing, regulating; adorning, making verses . . ."[13] This poetic image is a most fitting description for understanding the significance of Ḥasan ibn ʿAlī al-Ṭūsī, Niẓām al-Mulk. He embodies the order and arrangement of the realm. He is the *niẓām* of the *mulk*: the "thread" that "strings" together various Saljūq institutions to achieve a harmonious operation. To use metaphors of literature and music, Niẓām al-Mulk composed and orchestrated Saljūq administration. He did not *create* these various components, any more than one who strings pearls together in a necklace creates the pearls. The various Saljūq institutions such as the land-grant system, the *madrasa*, and the surveillance system, predated Niẓām al-Mulk. Yet he "strung" them together to achieve the larger goal of operating the Saljūq realm and legitimizing it as never before. It is perhaps for this reason that so many sources—albeit erroneously—credit him with having founded these institutions.

The historical sources have also seized upon the pun on Niẓām al-Mulk's name in subtle and clever ways. The historian Khwānd-Mīr stated that it was due to the serenity of the Khwāja during Alp Arslān's reign that the affairs of the "realm (*mulk*) and people assumed the attribute of order (*niẓām*) and the reign of government and religion headed in the right direction."[14] This task was to be accomplished in a number of ways: the amelioration of the relationship with the caliph, the quenching (or at least controlling) of strife (*fitna*) among the Sunni schools of law (sing, *madhhab*; pl., *madhāhib*), the establishing of *madrasa*s which bore his name, and the restructuring of the land-grant (*iqṭāʿ*) system. We shall examine these policies in greater depth later on.

The History of the Vizierate and Recent Sources

There is no shortage of debate about the origin of the vizierate institution, as various scholars have advanced theories regarding its origin.[15] For our purposes it is not so much the origins of the vizierate which are of interest, but the way in which it functioned to connect Saljūq politicians, caliphs, soldiers, Sufis, and jurists. I will first identify some of the important sources which have become available in the past few decades—sources which remain underutilized in many Western academic studies of this time period. In the past few decades, a number of key primary sources dealing with the institution of the vizierate in premodern Islam have been edited and published. Among them, one can point to Khwānd Mīr's *Dastūr al-wuzarā'*, Sayf al-Dīn Ḥājī ibn Niẓām ʿAqīlī's *Āthār al-wuzarā'*,[16] and Najm al-Dīn Abū 'l-Rajā' Qummī's *Tārīkh al-wuzarā'*.[17] In addition, two significant secondary studies on the Saljūq vizierate deserve special mention: Carla Klausner's *The Seljuk Vizierate: A Study of Civil Administration 1055–1194*[18] and ʿAbbās Iqbāl Āshtiyānī's *Vizārat dar ʿahd-i salāṭīn-i buzurg-i saljūqī*.[19] Klausner's study, which draws heavily upon Āshtiyānī's magnum opus, provides invaluable data regarding administrative details of the Saljūq vizierate. She is not, however, greatly interested in the intellectual ramifications of the vizierate system. Nor does she treat the *madrasa* patronage of viziers in any detail. Āshtiyānī's *Vizārat*, though a masterpiece of premodern Iranian political history, pays scant attention to the interaction between viziers and religious figures. It is the role of the viziers in orchestrating these clusters of Muslim networks that frames our inquiry here: the interactions of viziers with intellectuals and the ramifications of institutions established by viziers for the frameworks of intellectual inquiry.

The viziers acted as a linchpin between Saljūq leaders (the patrons) and the competing groups of intellectuals who held the power/knowledge to legitimize the patrons. Any study of the political history of the Saljūqs would be incomplete without incorporating the role of various viziers and the competition between the aspirants to these posts. Likewise, any study of the various discourses of religious inquiry under the Saljūqs has to account for the participation of these viziers and the religious institutions they founded (e.g., *madrasa*s, *khānaqāh*s, etc.). The rise of an individual to the post of the vizier often implied that the intellectuals he patronized would also receive appointments at prestigious madrasas. Conversely, the fall of a vizier and the intellectuals he patronized was also linked. The prominence of certain legal, theological, and mystical schools of thought under the Saljūqs—the Ashʿarī theological school, the Shāfiʿī legal school, and a Sharʿī-oriented *Uṣūlized* Sufism—can be at least partially attributed to the sponsorship of Niẓām al-Mulk and the institutions he patronized. All of these strands existed prior to the rise of the Saljūqs. However, the vast network of madrasas founded by Niẓām al-Mulk constituted a site where these modes of knowledge would be replicated and perpetuated.

The Rank of the Vizierate in the *Saljūq Dīvān*

Āshtiyānī's *Vizārat dar ʿahd-i salāṭīn-i buzurg-i saljūqī* identifies the components of the five *divāns* which together composed the Saljūq court. In decreasing order of influence, they were:

1. *Ṣadārat* or *Vizārat*, the highest office.
2. *Istīfā'*—the one who attained to this post was the *Mustawfī*
3. *Ṭughrā*—the commander of this dīvān was called the *Ṭughrā'ī*; he was in charge of composing regal commands.
4. *Ishrāf*, headed by the *Mushrif*.
5. *'Arḍ al-jayūsh*, whose head was the *'Āriḍ*.[20]

Of the five *dīvān*s, it was the vizierate which had the highest rank. The vizierate was personified most effectively in the person who virtually came to be synonymous with the institution: Niẓām al-Mulk. Both the archetype and the most perfect manifestation of a Perso-Islamic vizier, he became to Perso-Islamic politics what Buzurgmihr had been to the Sasanian polity. The chronicler Ibn al-Athīr dubbed the whole Saljūq era *al-dawla al-niẓāmīya*,[21] a pun implying both "the Niẓām's realm" as well as "the systematized state." While one could devote a whole study to his political and administrative prowess,[22] we are concerned here with his function as the nexus linking the processes of the systematization of the state and the construction of Islamic orthodoxy undertaken by scholars at madrasa. In this chapter, I will analyze the rise of Niẓām al-Mulk to power before proceeding in the next chapter to study the madrasa as the key institution with the greatest impact on the pursuit of religious knowledge.

The Early Religious Training of Niẓām al-Mulk

The sources record his full name as Abū 'Alī Ḥasan ibn 'Alī ibn Isḥāq al-Ṭūsī, although the historical chronicles unanimously refer to him by his honorific, Niẓām al-Mulk, or even simply as *Khwāja* (Master). Niẓām al-Mulk was descended from an aristocratic background, that of the *dihqāns* (landowners),[23] from the region of Sabzawār, near Ankū. Niẓām al-Mulk's father joined the service of the Ghaznavids, and was a financial officer responsible for the region of Ṭūs.[24] Ibn Khallikān states that the young Ḥasan was born in the region of Nawqān near Ṭūs on the twenty-first of Dhu 'l-Qa'da, 408 (10–11 April 1018).[25]

Given his later political accomplishments, it would be easy to overlook the young boy's thorough religious training; he is said to have received much of his early religious training from his father. By the age of eleven, he had impressed many of his teachers by his acumen and sharp memory, having already memorized the whole of the Qur'an, according to Khwānd-Mīr.[26] He had also displayed a particular interest in learning prophetic traditions.[27] Like his father, he too followed the Shāfiʿī *madhhab*, which no doubt is reflected in the emphasis that the approving sources put on his mastery of the two foundational sources of Islam.[28] As we shall see in the next chapter, which deals with the madrasas Niẓām al-Mulk founded, this Shāfiʿī orientation had very important consequences for the later history of Islamic learning.

Many of the sources which detail his early training emphasize that, both in earlier stages of life as well as his more advanced years, the vizier spent a great deal of time with various religious scholars and jurists.[29] He would move on to receive more advanced training in various disciplines of the Islamic sciences; he had studied with Muḥammad ibn Mihrayuzd the *adīb* and Abū Manṣūr Shujāʿ ibn ʿAlī ibn Shujāʿ in Isfahan. He received further training in the *ḥadīth* sciences under the famous Sufi Abū ʾl-Qāsim al-Qushayrī (d. 465/1072) in Nīshāpūr.[30] He later studied the same subject in Baghdad with Abū ʾl-Khaṭṭāb ibn al-Baṭir.[31] Subsequently, he received further religious training in Balkh, where he studied with another *muḥaddith* named Abū ʿAlī Ḥasan ibn ʿAlī ibn Aḥmad ibn Jaʿfar Balkhī Wakhshī.[32] This study of ḥadīth made a deep impression on him. In his later days, the vizier is reported to have attended the Niẓāmīya madrasa he had established and narrated prophetic traditions for the other scholars.[33] Ibn Khallikān and Ibn Kathīr both report that Niẓām al-Mulk both learned and taught hadīths, and was fond of stating, "I am conscious of not deserving that honor, but I hope to link myself with the chain of those who have transmitted the ḥadīth of the Messenger of God, Peace and Blessings of God be upon Him."[34]

Al-Subkī, the Shafiʿī biographer even offers a list of scholars who have transmitted ḥadīths from Niẓām al-Mulk: Naṣr ibn Naṣr ʿUkbarī, Abū Muḥammad al-Ḥasan ibn Manṣūr al-Samʿānī, and others.[35] The contemporary Persian scholar Kasāʾī adds to the above list the following scholars: Abū ʾl-Fatḥ Muḥammad ibn Abī ʾl-Ḥusayn Muḥammad ibn ʿAbd Allāh Bisṭāmi and Dhū ʾl-faqār ibn Muḥammad, known as Ḥamīdān Ḥasanī ʿAlawī Marwazī. Of course it needs to be acknowledged that the reporting of this account in a Shāfiʿī hagiographic source might be intended by al-Subkī to flaunt the deep connection between the followers of his *madhhab* and the two foundational sources of Islamic thought, Qurʾan and ḥadīth. It is one thing to expect a *madrasa*-educated *ʿālim* to be fluent in these disciplines, but somehow more impressive to hear that a career politician like Niẓām al-Mulk was also a master of them.

In addition to the link with the already mentioned al-Qushayrī (author of the famous Sufi treatise *al-Risāla*), it has also been asserted that as a young child Niẓām al-Mulk met the famous Sufi sage Abū Saʿīd ibn Abī ʾl-Khayr in

Mayhana.[36] This narrative is featured prominently in hagiographic accounts which posit links between Niẓām al-Mulk and certain Sufis. I will undertake a thorough analysis of these accounts in chapter 5. Niẓām al-Mulk's connections with the Sufis are frequently recalled in the later sources: Ibn Khallikān records that "the court of the vizier Nizām al-Mulk was greatly frequented by doctors of the law and Sufis, towards the latter of whom he was very beneficent."[37] Not being content to merely record this link, Ibn Khallikān proceeds to provide a narrative explaining the origin of this connection:

> Being asked the reason of the favor which he [Niẓām al-Mulk] showed them [the Sufis], he answered: "I was in the service of a certain *amīr*, when a Sufi came to me and made me a pious exhortation. He said: 'Serve Him whose service will be useful to you, and be not taken up with one whom dogs will eat to-morrow.'
>
> I did not understand his meaning at that time. However, the *amīr* used to drink from morning to evening. He also had some dogs which were ferocious like beasts of prey, and devoured strangers at night. Now it happened that once when he was overcome with intoxication, this *amīr* went out alone, and was torn to pieces by the dogs, which did not recognize him. I then knew that this Sufi had received a revelation on the subject. Ever since, I treat these people with respect, in hopes that I may obtain a similar grace."[38]

Distinct from the narratives involving Abū Saʿīd's relationship with Niẓām al-Mulk, which strive to document the names of all the relevant disciples and descendants of the famed saint, the narrative here is virtually untraceable. The point here is not to lend legitimacy to any one particular Sufi or to a specific group of descendants. The vizier describes himself as having been in the service of "a certain *amīr*" when "a Sufi" came to him.[39] The main point of this passage, naturally, is not to link the vizier to the *baraka* of any specific Sufi master, but to document him having turned from the service of worldly rulers to that of Sufis. The tragic fate met by the *amīr* is of course intended to heap upon him all the infamies possible in the mythic world of premodern Islam: drunkard behavior and being torn to pieces by animals. The animal chosen in this mythic narrative are the ritually impure dogs. The worldliness of the *amīr*, his immoral drunkenness, and the impurity of the dogs are all connected to document his *fasād* (corruptness, perverse unruliness). The counterpoint is the piety and insight of the Sufis and the pious devotion of the vizier to them.

In any case, Niẓām al-Mulk's long-term devotion to Sufis came to be accepted by historians and Sufis, premodern hagiographers and contemporary Western scholars. Ibn Kathīr's introduction to the same narrative of the Sufi (who enjoined Niẓām al-Mulk to devote himself to the service of One whose service would contain benefits) states, "He [Niẓām al-Mulk] was in the habit of respecting Sufis tremendously (*wa kāna yuʿaẓẓimu al-ṣūfiyya taʿẓīman zāʾidan*)."[40] ʿAqīlī's *Āthār al-wuzarā* states that the vizier had "companionship with ascetics, scholars, and great saints."[41] This relationship is further established by Niẓāmī-yi ʿArūḍī, who in critiquing Niẓām al-Mulk for not having paid sufficient attention to poetry and poets offers the following intriguing evidence: "Nor did he pay any attention to any one except religious leaders and mystics."[42] Sufi sources, such as Ibn Munawwar's famous biography of Shaykh Abū Saʿīd, identified Niẓām al-Mulk as the disciple of "all the Sufis, on the account of our Shaykh."[43] What is significant for our purposes is that Sufi hagiographies and historical chronicles alike depict Niẓām al-Mulk as a patron and a disciple of the Sufis. Again, this is important evidence of Sufism not being a marginal social and intellectual phenomenon, but rather as appropriating (and as being appropriated by) the most important political figure of the Saljūq era. Contrary to some anthropologically-based studies of Sufism, it is clearly a mistake to identify Sufism as a rural/illiterate movement to the detriment of the connection that Sufis have to metropolitan centers of power.[44]

The Administrative Training and Early Political Career of Niẓām al-Mulk

After the completion of his religious training, Niẓām al-Mulk dedicated himself to mastering administrative skills. One of his distinguishing marks was his attention to courtly writing and composition in both Persian and Arabic, the two necessary languages for Perso-Islamic administration. Al-Subkī claims that he was unsurpassed in the crafts of accounting, composition, and mastery of both Arabic and Persian.[45] He was very committed to mastering the craft of composing courtly documents in an elegant style. When his son Fakhr al-Mulk was appointed by Malik-Shāh to the vizierate of Fārs, Niẓām al-Mulk wrote him, urging him to gain mastery of Arabic prior to starting this prestigious post: "This is the province of Fārs, and everyone there is learned. If someone who is appointed to the chief administrative tasks does not know Arabic, cannot speak it [properly], cannot write letters in Arabic, and does not possess good calligraphic skills, he will be faulted and ridiculed."[46]

He again demonstrated his interest in fine composition, this time in Persian, in his *Siyāsat-nāma*. The learned British scholar E. G. Browne attests to the value of the work as both a literary masterpiece as well as an important historical document: "The *Siyāsat-nāma* is, in my opinion, one of the most valuable and interesting prose works which exist in Persian, both because of the quantity of historical anecdotes which it contains and because it embodies the views on government of one of the greatest Prime Ministers whom the East has produced."[47]

After having completed his religious training and gained a mastery of composition skills, the young Ḥasan of Ṭūs was ready to embark on his political career. After the defeat of the Ghaznavids in Dandānqān in 429/1037, the central Khurāsānian plateau was deemed to be too unstable due to the Saljūq migration, conquest, and plunder. Therefore, Ḥasan's father's left Ṭūs for Ghazna, which offered a more stable political life. It was at the Ghaznavid court that Ḥasan learned courtly administration for the first time in the regal *dīvān*.[48] The centralized model of government utilized by the Ghaznavids would leave a huge impression on the rising administrator. In many of his later writings, he would repeatedly call back on paradigms established under the Ghaznavids as a model to be emulated by the Saljūqs. For example, Niẓām al-Mulk praises Sultan Maḥmūd Ghaznavī for having an army composed of various races, which the vizier deemed less likely to lead to disorder.[49] He also praises the Ghaznavīs for their proper observances of ancient Persian court etiquette, a subject that he did not seem to have as much success persuading the recently detribalized Saljūqs to observe and respect.[50]

In his next stage of administrative training, Ḥasan served an Abū ʿAlī ibn Shādhān as a *dabīr*. This ruler apparently mistreated the able vizier, made fun of him for being overweight, and also confiscated his possessions.[51] Ḥasan left his services and sometime around 444/1052 contacted for the first time a Saljūq figure: Chaghrī Beg Dawūd in Marv. This marked the beginning of his service to the Saljūq family, a symbiotic and multigenerational relationship that continued till the end of *Khwāja*'s life and beyond through many of his descendants. Historical sources such as Ibn al-Athīr depict that aged Turkish warlord Chaghrī Beg receiving Ḥasan warmly, literally entrusting his affairs to Hasan's capable hands. Chaghrī put Ḥasan's hands in the hands of his son and successor, Alp Arslān, and told him, "This is Ḥasan, from Ṭūs. Respect him, as you would a father, and do not act against his judgment."[52] The narrative specifically states that on his journey to Marv, Ḥasan took with him his two young sons, who would later come to be known as Fakhr al-Mulk and Mu'ayyid al-Mulk. These two sons would be completely raised within the Saljūq administrative system, and would follow their father as viziers. However, before Ḥasan could rise to the position of prominence, he had to overcome a significant obstacle: his first serious political adversary, the very capable ʿAmīd al-Mulk Kundurī.

Competition between Niẓām al-Mulk and ʿAmīd al-Mulk

Abū Manṣūr Muḥammad ibn Manṣūr Kundurī, better known as ʿAmīd al-Mulk, "the Support of the Realm," served Ṭughril faithfully for over twenty years, starting in 446/1054.[53] Later historians portray him as having possessed a keen intellect and perception and a mastery of composition.[54] According to Ibn Khallikān, he was "one of the most eminent men of the age for beneficence, liberality, acuteness of mind, and abilities as a *kâtib* [scribe]."[55] Given the status of the Saljūqs as outsiders to the Perso-Islamic universe, it is understandable that these composition skills would be emphasized for both Niẓām al-Mulk and ʿAmīd al-Mulk.

Many historical narratives emphasize the close relations between Ṭughril and ʿAmīd al-Mulk. It has already been mentioned that it was Kundurī who was left behind in Baghdad to secure the hand of the caliph's daughter (or sister) in marriage for Ṭughril.[56] That Kundurī was chosen to handle this most contentious situation is a testimony to Ṭughril's trust in his judgment and negotiation skills. Al-Kātib al-Iṣfahānī further reiterates ʿAmīd al-Mulk's rank in Ṭughril's court by stating that the sultan "saw and heard through Kundurī's eyes and ears."[57] It was ʿAmīd al-Mulk who mediated Ṭughril's meetings with all significant political, religious, and saintly figures. He was the sole companion of the Turkish warlord when they went to meet the famous saint Bābā Ṭāhir outside of Hamadān.[58]

ʿAmīd al-Mulk also mediated the interactions of the Saljūq Sultan with the ʿAbbāsid Caliph: Al-Kātib al-Iṣfahānī records an account of Ṭughril's appearance before the Caliph al-Qāʾim bi Amr Allāh. In this instance, Kundurī acted as the translator for the Turkish warlord, who did not speak Arabic. He is described as having been not only a "translator" (*mutarjim*), but also an "elucidator" (*mufassir*).[59] This might be taken as a literal and metaphorical example of the vizier "translating" Perso-Islamic manners and courtly rituals for the Turkish warlord and is an important indication of the necessity of the vizierate as a mediating institution between the sultanate and the caliphate. The later activities of Niẓām al-Mulk would simply elaborate on this mediation role.

With the death of Ṭughril, his nephew Alp Arslān—assisted by the able vizier, Ḥasan—rose to power. The sultan seems fully steeped in the Turkish warlord tradition. The great Turkish lexicographer, Kāshgharī, states that Alp meant "brave"[60] and Arslān, "lion," a name used for kings.[61] However, the first task was to decide the fate of the two capable viziers who were the prominent statesmen of this time period. There was both a personal and an ideological conflict between Ḥasan and ʿAmīd al-Mulk. Khwānd-Mīr states that Niẓām al-Mulk was "afraid of the perfection of the sagacious cunning and vision of ʿAmīd al-Mulk."[62] This rift was at least partially over the competition of seeking the post of vizierate to the young Sultan Alp Arslān. Ḥasan had been serving the young warlord before he became sultan and expected to continue to do so. ʿAmīd al-Mulk, who had served Ṭughril for twenty years, would have represented continuity in the administration. It is also possible that ʿAmīd al-Mulk might have initially favored Ālp Arslān's brother, Sulaymān, and in fact might have attempted to have him recognized as the next sultan.[63] If this account is to be trusted, it would provide one more reason that Ālp Arslān would have favored Niẓām al-Mulk over ʿAmīd al-Mulk. However, this tension was more than just a matter of petty jealousies and political ambitions. There was a substantial ideological difference between the two aspirants to the vizierate in terms of their intellectual orientations as well as in their approaches to the caliphate, as we shall see. There were many theological and legal conflicts between Ismāʿīlīs and Sunnis, Karrāmīya and Sunnis, and also between various Sunni interpretations (most prominently Ḥanafīs versus Shāfiʿīs and Ashʿarīs versus Ḥanbalīs). The historical chronicles of the time period, which are often arranged in a year-by-year fashion, usually discuss all such *fitna*s (social strife) under each year's listing. These were much more than civil intellectual debates and often involved social unrest, fires, and fighting on a massive scale that resulted in the murder of hundreds if not thousands of individuals. Any intellectual and political figure had to pick sides and attempt to navigate these contested waters. The existence of these theological and legal polemics also meant that any politician who would attempt to walk a middle ground would be leaving himself open to charges of treason by one side or another or both. As a result, various historical sources depict Niẓām al-Mulk and al-Kundurī's theological and legal preferences in vastly different and contradictory ways, which have to be analyzed closely and sorted through.

The majority of sources depict Kundurī's outlook as having been characterized by his *taʿaṣṣub*, "fanaticism," in favor of the Ḥanafī *madhhab*. According to Ibn al-Athīr, Kundurī was exceedingly biased against the Shāfiʿīs (*kāna shadīd al-taʿaṣṣub ʿalā al-shāfiʿīya*).[64] He had asked Ṭughril for permission to have the Shīʿa (*rawāfiḍ*) cursed from the pulpits (*manābir*) of Khurāsān. To the above, he added—seemingly based on his own authority—a curse to be directed against the Ashʿarīs (*fa amara bi laʿnihim wa aḍāfa ilayhim al-ashʿarīya*).[65] Given the close association between the Ashʿarī theological orientation and the Shāfiʿī *madhhab*, in practice this translated to a vendetta against the Shāfiʿīs as well as the Ashʿarīs. As a consequence, many of the Shafiʿī leaders were exiled from Khurāsān or left it voluntarily. Perhaps the most famous among them, Abū ʾl-Maʿālī Juwaynī, had to flee Nīshāpūr and live in Mecca and Medina for four years. Ironically, it was due to this exile and the subsequent opportunity to teach at both the Sacred Precinct of Mecca and the Prophetic Mosque in Medina that he earned the honorific *Imām al-ḥaramayn*, meaning, "Imām of the two Noble Sanctuaries" (Mecca and Madina).[66] This led to another episode of strife and discord (*fitna*) between the Shāfiʿīs (who tended to be Ashʿarīs) and the Ḥanafīs (who tended to be more oriented—although not exclusively—to the Māturīdī theological school).[67]

As an example of how difficult it is to come up with a definitive assessment of the theological orientations of Kundurī and Niẓām al-Mulk, it is interesting to note that other sources attempt to paint a more conciliatory depiction of Kundurī. Al-Kātib al-Iṣfahānī confirms the above *taʿaṣṣub*, but also adds that he eventually abandoned his fanaticism and came to recognize the virtue of both (i.e., Shāfiʿī and Ḥanafī) schools.[68] Ibn Khallikān reports the contradiction between Ibn al-Athīr's report and Samʿānī's *Kitāb al-ansāb*, where Juwaynī—who in other sources is reported as having been *exiled* by Kundurī—is here reported as having been a "companion" of Kundurī. The author of *Wafāyāt al-aʿyān* goes so far as to state that Kundurī "had no other merit but that of his intimacy" with Juwaynī![69] Ibn Khallikān's apologetic remarks aside, most scholars have tended to side with Ibn al-Athīr on this account and have held Kundurī responsible for exiling the Shāfiʿī-Ashʿarī scholars from Khurāsān. The best informed opinion remains that of Richard Bulliet, who, in his masterful and still unsurpassed study of the politics of Nīshāpūr, states that Kundurī's reason for singling out the Ashʿarīs (primarily, and Shāfiʿīs by association) had less to do with theological reasons and more with "divide and conquer" policies designed to gain control of Nīshāpūr.[70] In Bulliet's opinion, "Never since the early days of the ʿAbbāsid Caliphate had such a theological persecution been set in motion."[71]

There are similar difficulties in coming to an accurate assessment of Niẓām al-Mulk's policies. Whereas some sources praise Niẓām al-Mulk's ability to act conciliatory toward Ḥanafī and Shāfiʿī *madhhab*s, other sources (probably more favorable toward the Ḥanafīs) accuse him of being fanatical in support of the Shāfiʿīs. For now, it seems best to state that Niẓām al-Mulk was a committed Shāfiʿī-Ashʿarī who was given to pragmatic cooperation between the Ḥanafī and Shāfiʿī *madhhab*s. His attitude toward the two *madhhab*s (Ḥanafī and Shāfiʿī) seems to have been guided by realpolitik as much as anything else, as all the Saljūq rulers, like the majority of Turks, were followers of the

Ḥanafī *madhhab*.[72] As such, it would not have been prudent for Niẓām al-Mulk to advocate the Shāfiʿī *madhhab* to the detriment of the Ḥanafīs. This sense comes out clearly in his *Siyāsat-nāma*, where he diplomatically states, "In all the world there are only two doctrines which are good and on the right path; one is that of Abu Hanifa and the other that of ash-Shafiʿi (Allah's mercy be upon them both) and all the rest are vanity and heresy."[73] As it can be seen, he did not follow the "divide and conquer" policies of Kundurī, but seems to have aimed more for maintaining balance and harmony between the competing factions.[74]

Kundurī and Niẓām al-Mulk: Alternate Models of Dealing with the Caliphate

There was another important difference in the political strategies of Kundurī and Niẓām al-Mulk, which has gone unnoticed by most Western scholars: the relationship between the Saljūq rulers and the ʿAbbāsid Caliphate. One of the most important theoretical challenges faced by the Saljūq legitimizers—in this case the viziers—was that of coming to terms with the religious authority of the caliphate while maintaining the Saljūqs' claim to political power. ʿAmīd al-Mulk's approach consisted of advising the Saljūq Sultans to strong-arm the caliphs into submission, exemplified in the episode involving securing Ṭughril's bride, the caliph's daughter (or sister). In some sources, ʿAmīd al-Mulk is personally blamed for having confiscated the caliph's lands until he agreed to the marriage.[75]

Niẓām al-Mulk, on the other hand, seems to have preferred a more congenial and cooperative relationship between the Saljūq Sultanate and the ʿAbbāsid Caliphate. This strategy eventually earned him the praise of not only the Saljūq Sultans but also the ʿAbbāsid Caliphs. Al-Subkī records a touching narrative of the interaction between the Caliph al-Muqtadī and Niẓām al-Mulk. Whenever the vizier would enter into the presence of the caliph, al-Muqtadī would have Niẓām al-Mulk sit before him (*bayna yadayhi*) and would say to the vizier, "O Ḥasan, son of ʿAlī, God is pleased with you as the Commander of Believers is pleased with you." Niẓām al-Mulk is said to have been joyous at hearing this, adding the pious remark, "I hope that God Almighty grants his prayer."[76] This episode earned Niẓām al-Mulk the hitherto unprecedented title of *Raḍī amīr al-muʾminīn*, "One who receives the satisfaction of the Commander of the Believers."[77] This honorific is cited in most of the sources which are favorable toward Niẓām al-Mulk, such as ʿImād al-Dīn Iṣfahānī/Bundārī's *Zubdat al-nuṣra* and others. In many such sources, Niẓām al-Mulk's respectful obedience (*taʿẓīm*) to the caliph is counted as one of the vizier's key virtues (*maḥāsin*).[78]

The differing strategies for dealing with the ʿAbbāsid Caliphate represent more than the personal preferences of Niẓām al-Mulk and ʿAmīd al-Mulk. The Saljūq Sultans were confronted with conflicting advice in dealing with the caliphate. One faction, represented at this early time period by ʿAmīd al-Mulk (and later by Tāj al-Mulk) gravitated toward displacing the caliphate altogether. Their advice tended to encourage the Saljūq Sultan to pressure the politically weak ʿAbbāsid Caliphs into submission. This strategy was vigorously rejected by Niẓām al-Mulk, who favored cooperation with the caliphate. In a slightly later period, when Niẓām al-Mulk was composing the *Siyāsat-nāma*, he warned the sultan against listening to the advice of certain administrators who "hold privileged positions in this empire," noting, "They try to persuade the Master of the World of overthrow the house of the ʿAbbasids, and if I were to lift the lid from the top of that pot—Oh! The disgraceful things that would be revealed."[79]

The above attitude is surely due to no sentimental attachment to the ʿAbbāsid Caliphate. Rather, as with most of his institutional and theoretical endeavors, there is a practical agenda. Niẓām al-Mulk seems to have grasped that without the legitimization that came from being seen as the military arm of the ʿAbbāsids, the Saljūqs would be perceived as little more than yet another horde of warring tribesmen marching onto the Iranian plateau from Central Asia. By cooperating—however uneasily—with the ʿAbbāsid Caliphate, they could lay claim to being protectors of the caliphate, the champions of "right-doctrine" Islam, and indeed rescuers of Islamdom.

ʿAmīd al-Mulk's Death

Ultimately, Niẓām al-Mulk and ʿAmīd al-Mulk represented divergent paths for the Saljūq regime. Even though they were both competent, brilliant, and dedicated viziers, there would have been no way for both of them to serve Alp Arslān in the same rank. As he would repeatedly during his illustrious career, Niẓām al-Mulk emerged victorious in this political wrestling match. In the year 456/1064, he had ʿAmīd al-Mulk deposed and ultimately killed. As the timing indicates, he waited for the ascension of the young Sultan Alp Arslān before instigating this plan. The sources detail the circumstances surrounding this act and show a surprising obsession with the fate of the deposed vizier's sexual organ: according to one account, Kundurī's unpleasant fate included having his scrotum stuffed with straw![80] Other Muslim sources were quick to propose alternative theories: Ibn al-Athīr states that al-Kundurī had been castrated much earlier, under Ṭughril's rule. In this version, the sultan had sent out the vizier to arrange for a marriage. Kundurī instead wed the woman himself, thus earning the wrath of the sultan. Ṭughril did retain Kundurī's services as vizier after (of course) castrating him.[81] This episode even inspired a poet, ʿAlī b. al-Ḥasan al-Bākharzī, to compose a poem: "They said: 'The Sultan, in his glory, effaced his [Kundurī's] sign of manhood (*simat al-faḥūl*)'. I said: 'Quiet! His manhood is now increased, since he is freed from both testicles.'"[82]

Regardless of the above details and the dispute regarding a celebrity's "manhood," the sort that a medieval chronicler reports with great enthusiasm, that ʿAmīd al-Mulk did die of a gruesome fate instigated by Niẓām al-Mulk is attested to in a number of sources, including Ibn Athīr's *al-Kāmil fi 'l-tārīkh* and the *Mujmal al-tawārīkh wa 'l-qiṣaṣ*.[83] Other sources add a prophetic and poignant touch to this story by recording that the dying ʿAmīd al-Mulk conveyed a letter to Niẓām al-Mulk in which he stated, "Tell the Vizier that by killing viziers, you have brought a hideous practice (*sunnat*) and heretical innovation (*bidʿat*) into this world. It won't be long before this practice (*sunnat*) will befall you and your descendants."[84]

The above theme is recorded in many of the other sources dealing with this time period. While no doubt an exaggeration, Nīshāpūrī states that "since then, not a single vizier has died of natural causes."[85] Many of these sources also record Kundurī's poignant letter to Alp Arslān, which stated, "It was due to the grace of your uncle Ṭughril Beg that I reached the top level of government in this world, and the rule of the ephemeral realm. Now, due to your lack of mercy, I have attained to martyrdom, and the blessing of eternal paradise. So, due to you two I have attained to worldly felicity and heavenly salvation. I have attained to what there is to be desired from things material and spiritual."[86]

With ʿAmīd al-Mulk removed from the picture, Abū ʿAlī Ḥasan al-Ṭūsī was finally in a position to implement his remarkable political vision for Saljūq administration.

Niẓām al-Mulk's Career under Alp Arslān

The young Saljūq Sultan was no expert in dealing with the sophisticated politics of the Perso-Islamic civilization. Niẓām al-Mulk records Alp Arslān as addressing the Saljūq elite, "I have told you once, I have told you twice, I have told you a hundred times. You Turks are the army of Khurāsān and Transoxiana. You are strangers in this land, and we have taken this realm by the word, and by force (*qahr*)."[87] This quotation is useful in demonstrating the Saljūqs' own understanding of *force* in their legitimization. Furthermore, it paints an image of the Saljūqs, even after having attained to power, as still mostly outsiders in this Perso-Islamic civilization. In dealing with the nuances of this complex society, Alp Arslān wisely entrusted many of the administrative duties of the realm to the capable vizier Niẓām al-Mulk. This he did for both the present state of the realm and its clear future. Alp Arslān entrusted his ten-year-old son and eventual successor, Malik-Shāh, directly to Niẓām al-Mulk for instruction in management of armies and governmental administration. Furthermore, the sultan divorced one of his own wives, the daughter of the Ibkhāz ruler, Buqrāṭ IV, and married her to Niẓām al-Mulk. This signaled the very close relationship between the two.[88]

One of the first tasks of Niẓām al-Mulk under Alp Arslān was to ameliorate relations with the caliph. As with many other time periods of Islamic and Iranian history, political, mercantile, and intellectual ties were cemented by marriage ties, and Niẓām al-Mulk fully understood this. Many of his first decisive actions involved cementing the relationship between the Saljūqs and the ʿAbbāsids through some strategic wedding bonds. The unhappy caliph's daughter, who was supposed to have been married to Ṭughril, was returned to Baghdad.[89] No doubt acting on his father's directions, the vizier's son, ʿAmīd al-Dawla Abū Manṣūr, acted as the *wakīl* (agent) in wedding Alp Arslān's daughter, Khātūn al-Safrīya, to the Caliph al-Muqtadī in 463/1070.[90] Niẓām al-Mulk personally acted as the sultan's *wakīl* during this ceremony.[91] Furthermore, the vizier arranged for the marriage of his own daughter, Safrā Khātūn, to the caliph's son, Amīr ʿIddat al-Dīn. Niẓām al-Mulk orchestrated more strategic marriages during the reign of the subsequent Saljūq Sultan, Malik-Shāh, as well.

Unlike his uncle Ṭughril, Alp Arslān never visited Baghdad. Instead, he devoted himself to military conquests. No doubt his absence from Baghdad allowed the caliph to assert his own authority. This relative autonomy helped in soothing the tensions between the Saljūqs and the ʿAbbāsids. As for the Saljūqs, Alp Arslān seems to have heeded Niẓām al-Mulk's advice in ameliorating the relationships with the ʿAbbasid Caliphs. The sultan developed a policy of sending one of his viziers to the caliph when he felt that there was a problem which needed redress. In one such example, the vizier Abū ʾl-Aʿlāʾ Muḥammad ibn Ḥusayn was sent to Baghdad to "strengthen the relationship with the caliph, and turn it to love."[92] This is another example of the viziers mediating the interactions between the Saljūqs and the ʿAbbāsids.

In contrast to his successor, Malik-shāh, Alp Arslān seems to have implicitly trusted Niẓām al-Mulk's loyalty even when confronted with contradicting propaganda. On one occasion, a spy[93] presented Alp Arslān with a letter informing the sultan of Niẓām al-Mulk's suspiciously excessive number of belongings. When the sultan read the letter, he simply handed it over to Niẓām al-Mulk, stating, "Take this letter. If what they say is true, then correct your behavior, and refine your actions. If what they say is false, forgive them, and give them some further tasks so that may be too busy as to occupy themselves with speaking ill of people."[94] No doubt it was this trust that Alp Arslān demonstrated in his capable vizier that allowed Niẓām al-Mulk to move forward with the implementation of his vision of "stringing" together Saljūq institutions.

The Vizier's Political Savvy

Niẓām al-Mulk's savvy was perhaps never clearer (and more appreciated by Alp Arslān) than during the blunder in which Alp Arslān was captured by Ārmānūs, the Christian *qayṣar* (caesar). Alp Arslān had been captured along with a hundred of his servants while he was on a hunting expedition. Fortunately for him, his captors had not recognized him. When Niẓām al-Mulk was given news of this potential disaster, he orchestrated an elaborate ruse in which he pretended the sultan was still in his camp and merely sick. The vizier then attended a peace settlement with the caesar. After having agreed to a peace, the shrewd vizier casually asked that the hundred "servants" be released as a demonstration of good faith by Ārmānūs. It was not until much later that the caesar's forces learned of their blunder and became "awed and perplexed" at the vizier's savvy.[95] Needless to say, this episode further endeared Niẓām al-Mulk to Alp Arslān and impressed upon the young sultan that sheer military prowess needs to be complemented with the political sagacity of a vizier.

Niẓām al-Mulk: The *Atabeg* Vizier

Niẓām al-Mulk's services to the state extended far beyond mere administrative duties. Ibn al-Athīr reports that in the year 464/1071, Niẓām al-Mulk was sent on behalf of Alp Arslān to put down the rebellion of a certain Faḍlūn, who had taken hold of a fortress in Fārs.[96] This is a clear testimony to his true rank as an *atabeg*, that is, not merely an administrator for the sultan, but also a military commander.[97] This was not an isolated event; Niẓām al-Mulk would frequently dress in full military attire and lead half of Alp Arslān's army into battle.[98] Nor were his military expeditions limited to his services to Alp Arslān; under Malik-Shāh, Niẓām al-Mulk again aided in the campaigns against the sultan's uncle, Qāwurt, in the year 465/1072.[99]

Even the Shāfiʿī hagiographer al-Subkī, who is usually more concerned with the intellectual accomplishments of figures, states that Niẓām al-Mulk took part in military campaigns in Rūm (Anatolia), Aleppo, Khurāsān, and Transoxiana.[100] It would seem reasonable to conclude that part of Niẓām al-Mulk's success in running the affairs of this "army with a state" (to recall C. E. Bosworth's thought-provoking description of the Saljūqs) was precisely due to this military background and his ability to negotiate with the various Saljūq military commanders. All too often he is characterized in secondary sources as an administrative genius, that is, the ultimate "man of the pen" in contradistinction to the "men of the sword." However, when he advises the sultan in the *Siyāsat-nāma* in how to deal with the Turkmen tribesmen and military soldiers, he speaks from a personal military experience which was taken seriously even by the relatively unsophisticated Saljūq warlord.

The Fate of Ashʿarī-Shāfiʿī Scholars under Niẓām al-Mulk

One of Niẓām al-Mulk's first tasks under Alp Arslān was to end the strife between the Shafiʿīs and Ḥanafīs. He attempted to bring back the Shafiʿī scholars who had fled Khurāsān or been exiled in the wake of the persecution brought by ʿAmīd al-Mulk. The most significant of these returning scholars, of course, was Imām al-Ḥaramayn al-Juwaynī, who was put in charge of the newly established Niẓāmīya *madrasa*. Al-Juwaynī's close relationship with Niẓām al-Mulk is already apparent in the title of his treatise *Al-ʿaqīdat al-niẓāmīya*, meaning both "the systematized creed" and "the Niẓām-i creed." I will treat the role of madrasa scholars in more detail in the next two chapters.

Alp Arslān's Death and the Rise of Malik-Shāh to Power

Alp Arslān met an unexpected, tragic, and unnecessary fate. In the year 465/1072 he captured a certain porter of a castle by the name of Barzamī[101] (alternatively, Yūsūf Khwārazmī[102]), who had some information about one of the sultan's adversaries near the Oxus region. Yūsūf did not cooperate in revealing the information, and the sultan ordered his execution. Yūsūf, in a last act of desperation, pulled out a knife and attacked the sultan. Rather than relying on his servants and attendants to deal with the vastly outnumbered fool, the sultan decided to make a show of his own military skills by relying on a bow and arrow to kill Yūsūf. He missed, and to the surprise of all who were present, Yūsūf succeeded in reaching Alp Arslān, dealing him a fatal wound.[103] In his dying moments, Alp Arslān met with Niẓām al-Mulk and offered his *waṣīya* to the vizier who had served him so faithfully.[104] In death, as in life, Alp Arslān is depicted as trusting the vizier in whose capable hands the administration of the realm had been all along.

Niẓām al-Mulk's Reign under Malik-Shāh

After Alp Arslān's murder, the leadership of the Saljūq clan fell on the young shoulders of a seventeen-year-old prince, Malik-Shāh. In the beginning years of Malik-Shāḥ's reign, the young sultan handed over control of all affairs to his capable vizier. This policy, which might be seen as a continuation of his father's, is depicted in the sources as having resulted in both the "realm" (*mulk*) and "religion" (*dīn*) returning to "order" (*niẓām*).[105] Again, it is important to note the typical Saljūq themes of order (the opposite of *fitna*, discord) and the overlapping discourses of *mulk* and *dīn*. It also marks another pun on the vizier's honorific, linking together *Niẓām* and *Mulk*. In Saljūq ideology, *Mulk* and *Dīn* were in turn seen as twins. As Niẓām al-Mulk was fond of stating, "Kingship and religion are like two brothers."[106]

Niẓām al-Mulk extended his responsibilities to include leading the army on an even more regular basis than he had done under Alp Arslān. He personally led an army from Transoxiana back to Khurāsan and from there to Rayy. He also led an army against Malik-Shāh's uncle (and rival) Qāwurt, defeating him near Hamadān.[107] In gratitude for these invaluable services, Malik-Shāḥ bestowed the title of *Atābeg* upon Niẓām al-Mulk, an honor which had never been given to a vizier before.[108] The *atābeg* system was one of the distinctive features of Saljūq administration, although it is possible that its origins are to be located in the Türkmen custom. The *atābeg* served both a social and a political function: to train the young Saljūq prince and to control the domain of the various rulers, preventing military rebellion.[109]

The recent discovery of certain administrative texts from the Saljūq court provides a clear demonstration of the intimate connection between Niẓām al-Mulk and Malik-Shāh during their period of cooperation. The following letter, a rare extant document from the Saljūq court, details Malik-Shāh's decree to extend Niẓām al-Mulk's position as his vizier:

> When the Exalted and Almighty [Divine] Presence chose me from all of humanity for being a *pādshāh*, and made me a vicegerent (*khalīfa*) in

> ruling over the world . . . He [likewise chose] him [Niẓām al-Mulk], who is the best of the Persians (*tājīkān*). In this epoch, none has seen or heard of a distinguished master (*khwāja*) like him. I have considered him to be like a father, and have entrusted the realm, myself, and the army to him.
>
> Now I have wanted the folk of the worlds to know what my relationship to him is like. It is for the sake of the people that I have prepared these honors [for Niẓām al-Mulk], and I have declared your rule flow over all, so that what you say it is as if I have said, and what you do is as if I have done. I have trusted the responsibility of both worlds unto you, so that in this world you can ensure peace for [God's] creation, and prevent tyranny and suffering, and provide the army's pay and stipend on time. Then you will make the world all over cultivated, so that [the memory] of my kingship and your vizierate will remain until the Resurrection Day.
>
> There is no *pādshāh* greater than me, and no vizier or councilor worthier than you. In that world [i.e., the Hereafter] where God hears the cries, you will deal with all questions and answers [dealing with how we have treated our subjects]. I will have peace, since you have been invested with authority. I have not, out of my own selfishness, overridden you, and have made your command absolute over all. I have ordered that you annihilate all those who would wish evil on you. Now, if there is any shortcoming, it is out of your own negligence.[110]

There are a number of points in the above decree that deserve closer analysis. In Malik-Shāh's use of the title of a divinely appointed *khalīfa* to refer to himself, there is already the seed of a direct challenge to the legitimacy of the ʿAbbāsid Caliph. When he had achieved political maturity, Malik-Shāh entertained thoughts of removing the caliph from power altogether, exiling him from Baghdad, and appointing his own grandson as the next caliph-king. Details of this will be provided below. When seen in this context, Malik-Shāh's deliberate usage of the title *khalīfa* in referring to his own rule is certainly not accidental and is heavily impregnated with suggestive allusions. These ambitions went directly against Niẓām al-Mulk's long-standing policy of seeking a mutually beneficial relationship with the ʿAbbāsid Caliphate.

The second point that emerges from the above document is Malik-Shāh's trust and confidence in Niẓām al-Mulk. This trust, which can be verified through a myriad of other narratives, was expressed in no uncertain terms as that of a "son" toward a "father." The paternal relationship between the able vizier and Malik-Shāh is also attested to in the events following the campaign against Qāwurt, the sultan's uncle. Faced with rebellion from the Saljūq soldiers, Malik-Shāḥ stated, "I refer to you all the affairs, big and small. You are [like] a father [to me]" (*qad radadtu al-umūr kullahā kabīrahā wa saghīrahā ilayka, fa'anta al-wālid*).[111]

Most sources agree that this was indeed the apogee of Saljūq power. Using a beautiful image, al-Kātib al-Iṣfahānī clearly states that "the days of the reign of Malik-Shāh were the best times of the Saljūqid dynasty, indeed like the middle pearl in a necklace."[112] The imagery of a strung necklace made from pierced pearls recalls my previous discussion of the significance of Niẓām al-Mulk as one who "strings along" Saljūq institutions. Other historians have offered similar praise of this period of Saljūq history and directly credit Niẓām al-Mulk with being the real ruler who was responsible for the prosperity and order of this period:

> It was he [Niẓām al-Mulk] who raised the banner of Islam. He was not only a vizier, but had a rank even higher than a Sultan. Malik-Shah's realm extended from Transoxiana and Hayāṭila and Bāb al-abwāb and Khurāsān and Iraq and Syria and Anatolia . . . from Kāshghar, being the farthest city of Turkestan to Bayt al-Muqaddas [i.e., Jerusalem], and from close to Constantinople to the Indian Ocean.
>
> Even so, with the *khwāja* [being there], he [Malik-Shāh] had nothing [to do with the actual task of ruling] except the name. He occupied himself with hunting and life and lust. It was only the *Khwāja* who was completely absorbed [in these tasks], and he was the absolute ruler. No task, great or small, was far from his sight.[113]

According to some sources, the young king was free in these early years to occupy himself with hunting.[114] Other sources also convey a similar critical opinion of Malik-Shāh's priorities during these years. Rāwandī, who does not seem to have had the highest opinion of Sultan Malik-Shāh, describes the sultan as a "tyrant" (*jabbār*)[115] and an "absolute monarch."[116] Furthermore, he also mentions that while his fathers had seized and conquered the world, Sultan Malik-Shāh merely ruled over it.[117] What is implicit in this criticism is that he was not a warrior in the fashion that his father, Alp Arslān, and Ṭughril Beg had been.

The Apogee of Niẓām al-Mulk's Reign

It was immediately during the period before the marriage of Malik-Shāh to Tarkān Khātūn that Niẓām al-Mulk reached the apogee of his power. Rashīd al-Dīn Faḍl Allāh states that the vizier had "possessed authority to a great extent, and become paramount to the utmost degree."[118] Other sources also confirm this impression. Al-Kātib al-Iṣfahānī, in his usual style full of word plays and exaggerated tropes, offers the following praise of Niẓām al-Mulk's thirty-year reign: "All these felicities were due to the exalted nature of the incomparable vizier, the Grand Khwājā Qiwām al-Dīn Niẓām al-Mulk, Abū ʿAlī Ḥasan ibn ʿAlī ibn Isḥāq, *raḍī amīr al-muʾminīn*. The shadow [of his realm] stretched over all, and his grace was ample. The vizierate of Niẓām al-Mulk was the adornment of the government (*kānat wizāratuhu liʾl-dawlat ḥilyatan*), and his resplendence was the ornamentation of the country. It was as if God Almighty had molded him to be a paragon of Glory and Rule (*kaʾannamā khalaqahu allāhu liʾl-mulk wa ʾl-jalāla muṣawwaran).*"[119]

There were two episodes during this period that demonstrated his worth to the Saljūq rulers. They became somewhat proverbial, quoted even in popular poetic anthologies as parables of political wisdom. The first one concerns a trip that Malik-Shāh and Niẓām al-Mulk had taken to Transoxiana. When a boatman aided the sultan and the vizier in crossing the Oxus, the *khwāja* wrote their payment in form of a monetary note made payable in Anṭākiya (in Anatolia). The boatmen cried out, "We are a poor people (*mā qawm-i darwīshānīm*), and our livelihood is from this river. If we leave here for Anṭākiya in our youth, we will not return even after having reached old age." The puzzled sultan consulted the aged and able vizier, asking, "O Father (*pidar*),[120] why did you show them such cold-heartedness? Did we not have the means in this region that we had to send them to Anṭākiya?" The *khwāja* answered that there was no need for the boatmen to travel anywhere. Indeed the note issued could be easily redeemed as cash, even as gold coins. He went on to state in characteristic wisdom, "I stated this to aggrandize the king, and exalt [your] imperial rule so that the people of the world would know how far the expanse of our realm is, and how thorough the command of the king."[121]

Naturally this episode was staged for the benefit of the sultan, to impress upon him the extent of the Saljūq realm—extending from Transoxiana to the very borders of Byzantium—and the efficiency of the financial system Niẓām al-Mulk had set up there. While Malik-Shāh is depicted as being as puzzled as a common boatman, it is Niẓām al-Mulk who understands how to demonstrate the political, economic, and administrative organization of the Saljūq realm to the elite and the masses alike.

The second demonstration of Niẓām al-Mulk's political wisdom was in orchestrating yet another strategic marriage between the Saljūq family and the ʿAbbāsids. According to Ibn al-Athīr, Niẓām al-Mulk was present during the marriage arrangement of Malik-Shāh's daughter to the ʿAbbāsid Caliph in 480/1087. Significantly, the sultan himself was on a hunting trip, so it was once again up to the capable vizier to arrange the details. Never one to miss an opportunity to make a public demonstration of Saljūq might, Niẓām al-Mulk arranged for the dowry of the sultan's daughter to be carried to the ʿAbbāsid abode in *Dār al-khilāfa*. Ibn al-Athīr records that 130 camels were required to carry this impressive dowry. The content of the dowry is described as being largely gold and silver. Leading the impressive caravan of jewel-carrying animals were thirty-three fine horses carrying the prominent figures of the Saljūq state.[122] Clearly the purpose of this public spectacle was to emphasize on one hand the wealth of the Saljūq family and on the other hand the grand union of the Saljūqs and the ʿAbbāsids, which was never far from Niẓām al-Mulk's heart.

Parting of Ways between Malik-Shāh and Niẓām al-Mulk

As the young sultan matured, his relationship with Niẓām al-Mulk also became transformed. Whereas the aged and able vizier had been able to control the young Saljūq king at the beginning of his reign, Malik-Shāh eventually came to assert himself more and more. He resented the autonomous modus operandi of the vizier who had been administering the state for over thirty years. There is even a report of a clown figure, Jaʿfarak [dim. for Jaʿfar], who would parody Niẓām al-Mulk to the great amusement of Malik-Shāh. This harmless satire led to a serious conflict when one of Niẓām al-Mulk's sons, Jamāl al-Mulk, became offended by Jaʿfarak's antics and ripped out the clown's tongue. Malik-Shāh, for his part, took revenge on Jamāl al-Mulk by having the commander of Khurāsān murder him in 475/1082.[123] This episode marked the beginning of the parting of ways between the aged vizier and the young sultan who was increasingly seeking to assert his authority and throw off Niẓām al-Mulk's yoke.

Niẓām al-Mulk's longevity in the Saljūq court did not go unchallenged. Malik-Shāh's attempts to exert his own autonomy were greatly aided by new generations of court administrators who aspired to the same high rank that Niẓām al-Mulk had held for so long. The extent of Niẓām al-Mulk's influence and the long duration of his reign are all the more remarkable when one recalls the vast number of personal vendettas that were waged against him by individuals who coveted his exalted position. Time and time again, Niẓām al-Mulk proved to be shrewder than his competitors in negotiating his way through the minefield of personal relationships in the Saljūq court.

After the murder of his son Jamāl al-Mulk, another serious challenge was posed to Niẓām al-Mulk by his own son-in-law, Sayyid al-Ruʾasāʾ Abū ʾl-Maḥāsin. Malik-Shāh had become increasingly fond of Abu ʾl-Maḥāsin, to the point of expressing longing if they went for a day without meeting. In 476/1083, Niẓām al-Mulk's spies in the court informed him that Abū ʾl-Maḥāsin had attempted to persuade the king that Niẓām al-Mulk had been hoarding the king's finances and dividing the realm between his own sons. Furthermore, Abū ʾl-Maḥāsin had promised the king that if Niẓām al-Mulk and his sons were handed over to him for execution, the king would receive a million gold coins from the confiscated belongings of Niẓām al-Mulk.

Niẓām al-Mulk, ever the master of public ceremonies, arranged for a regal feast in honor of the king. He had all of his personal army (known as the *Niẓāmī*s) present on this occasion. He kissed the ground before the king and acknowledged the rumors being circulated about him. However, he went on to dispute that he had held any of the money for himself and instead stated that it was all being spent on the welfare of the realm. In a strategic display of piety, Niẓām al-Mulk asked to be allowed to retire to a *zāwiya*, wearing nothing but a patched frock (*khirqa*). Malik-Shāh became distraught at the thought of losing the services of his most capable administrator (not to mention the prospect of having to cut back on the time he spent hunting). Seeking to placate Niẓām al-Mulk, he ordered Abū ʾl-Maḥāsin to be killed[124]—or blinded and imprisoned in a castle named Sāveh, according to other accounts.[125] The very fact that Niẓām al-Mulk could even threaten to retire from courtly life into that of a *khirqa*-donning Sufi in a *zāwiya* is another indication of his clever deployment of the discourse of the Sufis to legitimize his own position.

The threat to retire into a life of pious seclusion was a trump card that the shrewd vizier called upon from time to time to remind the arrogant Saljūq Sultan of the value of his service. On another occasion, Niẓām al-Mulk wrote a letter to Malik-Shāh in which he stated that he had faithfully served Saljūq Sultans for forty years. Now that he was approaching the age of seventy-five, he wanted to give up the pen and paper and instead head to the deserts of Arabia. Niẓām al-Mulk stated that he wished his dying days to be spent in sweeping the Bayt al-Ḥarām and the Kaʿba.[126] Malik-Shāh once again wrote an appeasing letter, stating that the service Niẓām al-Mulk would perform by heeding the cry of one lowly person would be equal to the blessing of multiple pilgrimages performed on foot.[127] The pretense to abandon courtly life from a vizier who had literally grown up in the court for all of his life was a masterful display of piety designed to remind the brash Saljūq Sultan of the long service rendered to the Saljūq regime by the aged vizier. Malik-Shāh was no doubt also confronted with the real challenge of running the day-to-day affairs of the realm without the services of the one individual who for more than forty years had come to personify the administration.

The Rise of Tarkān Khātūn and Tāj al-Mulk and the Demise of Niẓām al-Mulk

No man (or woman) would be able to elude the endless cycles of intrigue and accusations of heresy in the Saljūq regime forever, not even the masterful Niẓām al-Mulk. Even though Niẓām al-Mulk was the architect of the whole regime, in the end he would fall prey to a younger generation of ambitious politicians whose training had benefited from watching Niẓām al-Mulk maneuver his way around political troubles. The final and successful challenge to Niẓām al-Mulk's position came from a new direction, one that he had less experience dealing with. While the vizier was most capable in dealing with theologians, caliphs, and soldiers, he had not had to come to terms with a powerful female personality in the sultan's harem up to this point. This successful challenge to Niẓām al-Mulk's position of power came from Tarkān Khātūn, a powerful and intriguing political figure who is prominently featured in many of the historical chronicles dealing with the Saljūq period.

As was customary with Turkish warlords, Malik-Shāh was married to more than one wife. They tended to be the daughters (or other relatives) of allies and even potential foes. The historical sources mention three of his wives. The first wife was Tarkān Khātūn[128] (Lady Tarkān),[129] the daughter of Ṭamghāj Khān,[130] the ruler of Samarqand.[131] Ibn al-Athīr affirms Tarkān Khātūn's royalty, stating that she, the daughter of "Ṭafghāj Khān," was descended from the famed *Tūrānī* king Afrāsiyāb.[132] It is important to recall that identical claims of nobility were made for the Saljūqs as a whole in the *Tārīkh* of Abū ʾl-ʿAlāʾ (ibn) Ḥassūl (d. 450/1058), which claimed that the Saljūqs' ancestry was traceable (through thirty-four generations) to the same mythic Turkish king.[133] The second wife was Tāj al-Dīn Khātūn Safarīya, who was the mother of two of Malik-Shāh's sons, Muḥammad and Sanjar.[134] The third wife was Zabīda Khātūn, Bark-yarūq's mother.

Tarkān Khātūn was far from a demure figure who influenced the sultan from a secluded harem. She had her own *divān* (administrative court) and her own administrating vizier, Tāj al-Mulk Abū ʾl-Ghanāʾim Pārsī (Fārsī).[135] She and the vizier founded a new *madrasa* to compete with the famous *Niẓāmīya*, patronized by Niẓām al-Mulk. Furthermore, when her son was not chosen as the next sultan, she conducted a face-to-face negotiation with the ʿAbbāsid

Caliph. She also negotiated with some Turkish military leaders and arranged a (failed) rebellion against the new sultan.

Part of the contentiousness of the Saljūq ruling family came in the intrigues initiated by the mothers of the princes, each mother desiring to have her own son designated as the heir-apparent. Far from fitting the Orientalist fantasy of "harem women" operating behind the scenes, these were powerful and highly influential women who manipulated the various political factions with skillful ease. While there was some power and prestige in being one of the many wives of a present sultan, that did not compare with the immense power that could come their way as the mother of a future sultan. It was precisely this position that Tarkān Khātūn strove to obtain, and in doing so she became Niẓām al-Mulk's main antagonist. The chroniclers unanimously uphold her position not as a "significant female persona," but simply as one of the most powerful politicians of the Saljūq era.

The Saljūq historian Rāwandī was in awe of the rank Tarkān Khātūn held in Malik-Shāh's court and describes her as having had "complete power and authority" over the sultan (*bar sulṭān istīlāʾ dāsht*).[136] Al-Kātib al-Iṣfahānī states that, after Malik-Shāh's death, "the young child Maḥmūd was given the Sultanate because of his mother, Tarkān Khātūn, who was in charge during the time of Malik-Shāh. When he passed away, her rule (*ḥukmuhā*) [alone] remained. All the military commanders and the viziers were among her protégés."[137] Other historical sources also detail Tarkān Khātūn's position of power. According to Ẓahīr al-Dīn Nīshāpūrī's *Saljūq-nāma*, Tarkān Khātūn was "connected to the network of the Sultan's commands; and belonged to it." Nīshāpūrī further describes her as having possessed a "perfect grace and beauty, sweetness, a high lineage, a hereditary modesty, and complete power (*qudrat-i tamām*)."[138] His description is quoted almost verbatim by Rashīd al-Dīn Faḍl Allāh in his *Jāmiʿ al-tawārīkh*.[139]

The competition between Niẓām al-Mulk and Tarkān Khātūn arose as a result of a fierce rivalry over who would get to be designated as the heir-apparent (*walī-i ʿahd*) of Sultan Malik-Shāh.[140] Rāwandī in particular identifies this as the real "cause" of the enmity between the vizier and the powerful queen.[141] According to Ibn Athīr, an eleven-year-old son of Malik-Shāh named Aḥmad, who had been designated the heir-apparent, died in 481/1088 in Marv.[142] If Rashīd al-Dīn Faḍl Allāh is to be trusted, the deceased prince Aḥmad was also a child of Tarkān Khātūn.[143] Malik-Shāh was thus faced with the task of designating another heir-apparent, and the two likely choices seemed to be the seven-year-old Bark-yāruq and the one-year-old infant, Maḥmūd. Tarkān Khātūn beseeched Sultan Malik-Shāh to designate her son, Maḥmūd, whereas Niẓām al-Mulk favored Bark-yāruq, who was the older son.[144] Bark-yāruq was born of another wife, Zabīda Khātūn, the daughter of Amīr Yāqūtī, and her brother was another Saljūq notable, Amīr Ismāʿīl.[145] In fact, as part of his "mirrors for princes"-style advice for the king, Niẓām al-Mulk specifically pointed out to Malik-Shāh that a sign of the arrival of a "good age" is that "boys are not promoted [to high office], advice is sought from men of mature wisdom."[146] As Hubert Darke has also recognized, this was no doubt a thinly veiled polemic against Maḥmūd and his mother, Tarkān Khātūn.[147]

In her vendetta against Niẓām al-Mulk, Tarkān Khātūn was ably assisted by her capable vizier, Tāj al-Mulk. Rāwandī describes Tāj al-Mulk as having been a man possessed of a "[notable] countenance, information [of affairs of the realm], virtue and excellence, and aspiration" and as having served as the caretaker of the royal robes (*khadh-khudhā-yi jāma-khāna*).[148] According to both Rāwandī and Rashīd al-Dīn Faḍl Allāh, part of Tarkān Khātūn's plan was to get Malik-Shāh to remove Niẓām al-Mulk from power and appoint Tāj al-Mulk in his place. To do so, she would speak ill of Niẓām al-Mulk at every opportunity, in order to turn the sultan against him. She is reported to have diligently searched for any minor slip Niẓām al-Mulk committed.[149] Tāj al-Mulk was clearly her accomplice in this typical game of political backstabbing. Some of the sources, such as Ibn al-Athīr's *al-Kāmil*, which are somewhat more sympathetic to Niẓām al-Mulk, state that while Tāj al-Mulk clearly did have some worthy virtues, all of them were eclipsed by his role in the murder of Niẓām al-Mulk.[150]

Tāj al-Mulk must have risen through the ranks quickly, as Iṣfahānī states that the sultan bestowed upon him the vizierate of his own children, put the treasury at his disposal, entrusted the affairs of his harem to him, and gave him control of armies in some areas. Furthermore, he assigned him as the head of two posts, that of *ṭughrā* (royal seal) and *inshāʾ* (royal correspondence).[151] It is precisely this situation of Tāj al-Mulk being appointed to so many posts which leads Niẓām al-Mulk to lament in the *Siyāsat-nāma*, "Enlightened monarchs and clever ministers have never in any age given two appointments to one man or one appointment to two men, with the result that their affairs were always conducted with efficiency and lustre. When two appointments are given to one man, one of the tasks is always inefficiently and futiley performed, because if the man performs one task properly and diligently, the other one will be spoiled and neglected; and if he carries out the other task well and attentively, the first one will sure to suffer damage and failure . . ."[152] That this chapter is not just a timeless "manual of administration" but in fact a sustained and *timely* polemic against Tāj al-Mulk is made

2.1. The dome of Niẓām al-Mulk (the south dome). (Walter Denny, 1984, Courtesy of the Aga Khan Visual Archive, M.I.T.)

2.2. The dome of Tāj al-Mulk (the north dome). (May Farhat, 1992, Courtesy of the Aga Khan Visual Archive, M.I.T.)

all the more clear when later on in the same chapter Niẓām al-Mulk adds,[153] "Now in actual there is just such a one who is seeking to ruin this country by recommending economies."[154]

The "economies" suggested seem to have been aimed at cutting the number of soldiers in Malik-Shāh's army. Niẓām al-Mulk, who always favored keeping a large army employed so that they would remain under control, opposed this advice and, perhaps even more, its source: "When the Master of the World spoke in these same terms, I knew whose words they were—the words of one who wishes to ruin the country."[155]

The competition between Niẓām al-Mulk and Tāj al-Mulk can be documented through their patronage of additions to religious monuments. One of the best examples is to be found in the Friday Mosque in Isfahan. Niẓam al-Mulk had the south dome of the mosque built to house the miḥrāb of the mosque. The south dome was said to be among the largest domes at the time. The north dome, built through the patrongage of Tāj al-Mulk, is smaller than the south dome although its interior is far more refined.[156] The north dome, which is situated outside the proper boundaries of the mosque, is obviously set up as a competition to the south dome. These competitions, in other words, reshaped not only court politics but also the very physical appearance of Saljūq cities such as Isfahan.

Niẓām al-Mulk's Advice against the Political Involvement of Women

There is another important consequence of these powerful women and their actions for the medieval Islamic world: their impact on theological and political Muslim writings about the participation of women in society and politics. It was in response to this remarkable woman that Niẓām al-Mulk and the scholar who is forever linked with him, Abu Ḥāmid al-Ghazālī, speak so vehemently against the participation of women in politics. When Niẓām al-Mulk and al-Ghazālī warned the sultan of the evils of listening to women's advice and the deficiencies of women's intellects, it was less out of a universal distrust of all women and more in response to this one specific woman, Tarkān Khātūn, who threatened their own political standing. Given the prestige al-Ghāzālī and Niẓam al-Mulk have acquired in later Islamic thought and the tendency to view their statements as somehow normative, it is imperative to recall the context of these statements and the one woman who was the embodiment of the politically powerful Saljūq woman. To demonstrate this, we must analyze the sustained polemic ostensibly against all women, but in fact against Tarkān Khātūn, that Niẓām al-Mulk offers in his *Siyāsat-nāma*. The following material is from the chapter titled "On the Subject of Those Who Wear the Veil":

> The king's underlings must not be allowed to assume power, for this causes the utmost harm and destroys the king's splendour and majesty. This particularly applies to women, for they are wearers of the veil and have not complete intelligence. Their purpose is the continuation of the lineage of the race, so the more noble their blood the better, and the more chaste and abstemious their bearing the more admirable and acceptable they are. But when the king's wives begin to assume the part of rulers, they base their orders on what interested parties tell them, be-

> cause they are not able to see things with their own eyes in the way that men constantly look at the affairs of the outside world . . .
>
> Naturally their commands are mostly the opposite of what is right, and mischief ensues: the king's dignity suffers and the people are afflicted with trouble; disorder affects the state and religion; men's wealth is dissipated and the ruling class is put to vexation. In all ages nothing but disgrace, infamy, discord and corruption have resulted when kings have been dominated by their wives . . .
>
> The first man who suffered loss and underwent pain and trouble for obeying a woman was Adam (upon him be peace) who did the bidding of Eve and ate the wheat with the result that he was expelled from paradise, and wept for two hundred years until God had mercy on him and accepted his repentance.[157]

After offering the above bit of polemics couched in the language of political wisdom, Niẓām al-Mulk systematically moves through all the discourses which could possibly have been esteemed in the eyes of a Saljūqid ruler. He offers the examples of pre-Islamic Persian rulers, Alexander the Great, Sasanian viziers, Prophetic ḥadīths, and ʿAbbāsid paradigms. Clearly the purpose here is not to offer an "objective" lesson on the attitude of Islamicate rulers toward "women and politics," but rather to offer a seemingly exhaustive proof that *all* rulers (Muslim as well as pre-Islamic Iranian) have fallen into trouble by heeding the advice of women. The only conclusion that Niẓām al-Mulk is hoping Malik-Shāh will draw from all of this is that he must shun Tarkān Khātūn's political advice and instead follow the aged vizier's suggestion.

To begin with, Niẓām al-Mulk provides anecdotes of Sūdāba and Siyāvush and of the troubles which befell the king KayKāvūs because Sūdāba "had power over him."[158] The moral of the story, Niẓām al-Mulk asserts, is quite simple: "Kings and men of strong judgment have always ordered their lives in such a way, and followed such a path that they never let their wives or maid-servants know their feelings."[159] He then moves on to a story of Alexander, who after having conquering Darius, the king of Persia, is said to have avoided Darius's "moon-faced" daughter, stating "We vanquished their men; let us not be conquered by their women."[160]

The next "proof" in Niẓām al-Mulk's sustained polemical narrative is provided by the Sasanian vizier, Buzurgmihr, to whom Niẓām al-Mulk loved to compare himself. Buzurgmihr is said to have offered two reasons why the Sasanian empire fell to ruin: "firstly, the Sasanians entrusted weighty affairs to petty and ignorant officers, and secondly they hated learning and learned people. Men of stature and wisdom should be sought out and put into office; I had to deal with women and boys."[161] Fully concurring with Buzurgmihr, Niẓām al-Mulk offers this observation: "This is the very opposite of prudence and wisdom, for be assured that whenever a king leaves affairs to women and boys, the kingship will depart from his house."[162] It is impossible to miss the reference of "women" to Tarkān Khātūn and of "boys" to the infant Maḥmūd.

Having presented the ancient Persian precedent, Niẓām al-Mulk did not ignore the Islamic discourse: "There is a tradition that The Prophet (upon him be prayers and peace) says, 'Consult women, but whatever they say, do the opposite, and that will be right.' The words of the tradition are [in Arabic], 'Consult them but oppose them.' Had women possessed complete intelligence, The Prophet (upon him be peace) would not have commanded people to go against their opinions."[163] As Denise Spellberg and Rkia Cornell have amply demonstrated, the tradition of women "not possessing complete intelligence" tends to be invoked in Islamic polemics whenever a female authority challenges a traditional system, be it political or spiritual.[164] After having invoked Prophetic authority, Niẓām al-Mulk further solidifies this claim by appealing to the ʿAbbāsid paradigm, this time quoting the Caliph al-Maʾmūn: "The Caliph al-Maʾmūn one day spoke as follows: 'May there never be a king who allows the people of the veil to speak to him about the state, the army, the treasury and the government or to interfere in such matters, or to patronize particular persons.'"[165]

Niẓām al-Mulk's warning (put in the mouth of al-Maʾmūn) against "the people of the veil" patronizing "particular persons" has to be read as being directed against Tarkān Khātūn's patronage of Tāj al-Mulk. In the culmination to this sustained polemic, Niẓām al-Mulk returns to one of his favorite themes by recalling the typically Saljūq themes of the rise of heretics and evil men. He impresses upon the sultan that listening to women might lead to an uprising of heretics, as women are easily impressionable.

Another interesting point to note about the above polemic is where it is situated in the *Siyāsat-nāma*. It is placed immediately after the section titled, "On Not Giving Two Appointments to One Man,"[166] which, as we have seen, seems to have arisen out of his concern regarding Tāj al-Mulk being appointed to several different posts. The section is also placed before the chapter titled, "Exposing the Facts about Heretics Who Are Enemies of the State and of Islam."[167] After having composed one chapter against Tāj al-Mulk and one against Tarkān Khātūn, it is in this subsequent chapter that Niẓām al-Mulk sums up everything for Malik-Shāh: "There are certain persons who on this very day hold privileged positions in this empire."[168] After the obligatory accusation of labeling the "certain persons" (i.e., Tāj al-Mulk and Tarkān Khātūn) as secret Ismāʿīlīs, Niẓām al-Mulk correctly recognizes that "as a result of their representations The Master of the World has become weary of his humble servant, and is not prepared to take any action in the matter, because of the economies which these people recommend, thereby making the Master of the World greedy for money. They make out that I am interested in my private advantage and so my humble advice finds no acceptance."[169]

It is with sad—and almost prophetic—irony that Niẓām al-Mulk concludes this chapter, surely the most emotional in all of the *Siyāsat-nāma*, with the following words: "One day The Master will realize their iniquity and treachery and criminal deeds—when I have disappeared. Then will he know the measure of my devotion and loyalty to this victorious empire . . ."[170] The reference to "when I have disappeared" brings us to the event that marks the beginning of the demise of the Great Saljūqs: the assassination of Niẓām al-Mulk al-Ṭūsī.

Toward an Alternative Theory of Niẓām al-Mulk's Assassination

Niẓām al-Mulk's assassination is arguably the most famous such act of terror since the early Islamic period when ʿUmar, ʿUthmān, and ʿAlī were assassinated. Almost every survey of Islamic history includes an account of Niẓām al-Mulk's assassination, often using it to introduce the "assassins" of Alamūt, that is, the Ismāʿīlīs. A representative and respected secondary source is *The Cambridge History of Islam*.[171] This sweeping two-volume collection brought together many of the top experts of Islamic history. The article that deals most directly with ʿAbbāsid and Saljūqid history in this period is that written by the noted German historian, Berthold Spuler. In this article, Spuler deploys the old myth of the *fidāʾī* Ismāʿīlīs, whom he labels "self-sacrificers." In describing the activities of the "grand master of Alamūt," he states, "The community did not shrink from the murder of religious opponents. One of the first victims of their revenge was Niẓām al-Mulk."[172] These types of depictions have been repeated so often that they are accepted as a truism. Bernard Lewis characteristically follows suit, citing later Islamic sources that have Ḥasan-i Ṣabbāḥ asking his followers, "Who of you will rid this state of the evil of Nizam al-Mulk Tusi?"[173] The problem with the above convenient characterizations of attributing Niẓām al-Mulk's death to the Ismāʿīlī agents is that they are simply not recorded in this way in many of the earliest and most reliable sources dealing with this period.

Our task here is to reexamine the whole historical context that led to Niẓām al-Mulk's assassination. Even if later Ismāʿīlī sources claim credit for having assassinated Niẓām al-Mulk, the earlier sources suggest a different context, which has not been sufficiently explored. It is my thesis that Niẓām al-Mulk's murder is not simply an act of the Ismāʿīlīs but was engineered by Malik-Shāh over his desire to do away with the ʿAbbāsid Caliphate, a plan that was sternly opposed by Niẓām al-Mulk. The Saljūqid Sultan was assisted in this plot by Tarkān Khātūn and Tāj al-Mulk.

I have already examined the growing tensions between Malik-Shāh and Niẓām al-Mulk and the rise of Tarkān Khātūn and Tāj al-Mulk as forces competing against the aged vizier. As early as the time of ʿAmīd al-Mulk Kundurī, there were views that challenged Niẓām al-Mulk's approach to working with the caliphate. In particular, many of the Saljūq Sultans—especially Malik-Shāh—wished to challenge and perhaps do away with the caliphate as a whole. There had been allusions to this in the usage of certain titles, such as a divinely appointed *khalīfa*[174] and "the shadow of God" (*sulṭān sāya-yi khudā-st)*[175] in referring to themselves. What is detailed below, however, is a full-blown Saljūq plan to remove the ʿAbbāsid Caliphate from Baghdad.

The sources allude to an "estrangement" (*waḥsha*) between the powerful sultan and the caliph. Malik-Shāḥ "suggested" to al-Muqtadī that ʿAbbāsid Caliph move from Baghdad to any city he chose in "Damascus or Ḥijāz."[176] Baghdad and Samarra had served as the center of ʿAbbāsid Caliphate since the middle of the eighth century, and it was clearly identified with the *dār al-khilāfa*. While by this time Baghdad was clearly no longer the undisputed central city of Islamdom,[177] it was still the symbolic abode of the caliphate that provided unity (at least in a symbolic sense) to the expanding *dār al-islām*. The Saljūq Sultan's suggestion that the caliph move to Damascus or Arabia was intended to relegate the ʿAbbāsids to a more peripheral position of power. From a more strategic perspective, it was also meant to situate the ʿAbbāsids even further away from the Saljūq stronghold on the eastern lands of the Iranian plateau.

Ibn Kathīr provides more thorough information on this event: the sultan arrived in Baghdad in Ramaḍān of 485/(October) 1092 with an "unrighteous intention" (*bi nīya ghayr ṣāliha*). He sent a messenger to the caliph, informing him that it was imperative for the caliph to "resign for my sake from Baghdad" (*lābudda ʿan tanazzala lī ʿan Baghdād*) and remove himself to whichever land he so desired, so long as it was outside of Baghdad. The caliph wrote back, asking for a month's reprieve; the sultan refused him even "a single hour" (*wa lā sāʿatan wāḥidatan*).[178] The sources do not dwell on the cause of this *waḥsha*, yet it is hard to interpret it as anything other than the Saljūq Sultan wishing to assert a monopoly of authority over Baghdad without the presence of the caliph. It is intriguing to note that Ibn Kathīr lists this *waḥsha* immediately after the narrative dealing with Malik-Shāh's poisoning, as if to suggest the possible role of the ʿAbbāsid Caliph.

It is imperative to read this account in line with what Niẓām al-Mulk reveals about advice given to the sultan by certain viziers (probably Tāj al-Mulk) to remove the caliph altogether: "They try to persuade The Master of the World to overthrow the house of the ʿAbbasids, and if I were to lift the lid from the top of that pot—Oh! The disgraceful things that would be revealed."[179] The most direct pieces of evidence which connect Niẓām al-Mulk's murder to the above context are provided by the Shāfiʿī biographer al-Subkī[180] and the Saljūq historian al-Kātib al-Iṣfahānī.[181] Given that this theory of Niẓām al-Mulk's assassination has so far not received adequate scholarly attention, I will offer a systematic analysis of what the various sources state regarding this event. Our first evidence comes from al-Subkī, who specifically states that the Saljūq Sultan knew that Niẓām al-Mulk would oppose this move against the caliph and so prepared to have the aged vizier killed.[182] This is not the only explanation al-Subkī provides in his account of Niẓām al-Mulk's murder, even stating that the Ismāʿīlī theory is "closest to truth" in his own opinion. Yet he concludes his account with the Malik-Shāh conspiracy theory, and he dedicates by far the longest narrative in the whole section to this account. Al-Subkī's narrative is shockingly direct: "There was an estrangement (*waḥsha*) between Malik-Shāh and Niẓām al-Mulk. As we have stated, this was because Niẓām al-Mulk was in the habit of exalting the command of the Caliphate. Whenever the Sultan desired to remove the Caliph, Niẓām [al-Mulk] would prohibit him from doing so (*wa kullamā arāda ʾl-sulṭān nazʿa ʾl-khalīfa, manaʿaha al-niẓām*). He would secretly send a warning to the Caliph, asking him to strive to make the Sultan inclined towards him again."[183]

Al-Subkī goes on to offer a thesis that in the Ramaḍān of 485/1092, the sultan turned from Isfahan toward Baghdad. His intention is specifically stated as "changing of the Caliph": "He [Malik-Shāh] set out to change the Caliph (*ʿāziman ʿalā taghyīr al-khalīfa*). He knew that this would never come to pass so long as Niẓām al-Mulk was still living, so he had him killed, as we have explained, before reaching Baghdad (*wa ʿarafa anna dhālika lā yatimmu lahu wa niẓām al-mulk fī ʾl-ḥayāt, fa ʿamala ʿalā qatlihi qabl al-wuṣūl ila ʾl-baghdād, ḥasabamā sharaḥnāha*)."[184]

To those whose impression of the Great Saljūqs has been shaped by secondary sources, that is to say, those who have accepted the Great Saljūq Myth discussed in chapter 1 of the present study as historical reality, the above statement will no doubt seem shocking; the Saljūqs, allegedly the protectors of "orthodox" Islam, were embarking on removing the Sunni Caliphate. When prevented by Niẓām al-Mulk from doing so, the Saljūq Sultan planned to have him killed. This is yet another situation of the actual material in the historical chronicles departing from the carefully constructed image of the Great Saljūqs as upholders of peace, champions of "orthodox" Islam, and defenders of the Sunni Caliphate.

As shocking as al-Subkī's narrative might seem at first sight, it is corroborated by other sources which discuss the same event. Rāwandī and Nīshāpūrī state that it was at this point that Malik-Shāh abandoned Niẓām al-Mulk to Tāj al-Mulk, in effect leaving the aged vizier to be killed.[185] If we are to believe Rāwandī's account, Niẓām al-Mulk *was* murdered by the Ismāʿīlī "heretics,"[186] but all of this was on the instigation of Khwāja Tāj al-Mulk.[187] According to Nīshāpūrī, the act of the *fidāʾīs* was based on the "instigation and evil suggestion" (*ighrāʾ wa ighwāʾ*) of Tāj al-Mulk, as—Nīshāpūrī alleges—"he had a secret familiarity and connection with the heretics."[188] Rashīd al-Dīn Faḍl Allāh also confirms the connection between Tāj al-Mulk and the *malāḥida* (atheists, i.e., Ismāʿīlīs).[189] Also, Ibn Khallikān states that although the assassin was connected to the Ismāʿīlīs, he was "suborned against [Niẓām al-Mulk] by Malik-Shāh," and further acknowledges that Tāj al-Mulk was also suspected of a role in this murder.[190] Furthermore, Ibn Khallikān states that Malik-Shāh "was fatigued to see him [Niẓām al-Mulk] live so long, and coveted the numerous fiefs which he held in his possession."[191] Among these early sources, it is Qazwīnī alone who mentions Niẓām al-Mulk's assassination by the "heretical assassins" (*fidāʾī-yān-i mulḥid*) without mentioning the role of Tāj al-Mulk or Malik-Shāh.[192] It seems strange that so many of the secondary sources have followed the pattern of ascribing Niẓām al-Mulk's assassination entirely to the Ismāʿīlīs when there are so many relevant chronicles which present alternate theories, implicating Malik-Shāh himself.

The Last Exchange

At this point many of the sources offer the (in)famous last exchange between Niẓām al-Mulk and Malik-Shāh, which represents the culmination of decades of tension between the two. According to Rāwandī, Tarkān Khātūn at long last had succeeded in turning Malik-Shāh against the venerable vizier. With the sultan sufficiently suspicious of Niẓām al-Mulk's power and prestige, he sent a letter reproaching Niẓām al-Mulk: "You [operate as if you] share the kingdom with me! Without consulting with me, you make any changes that you desire, and you give much authority and land grants to your own children. You will see that I am going to order for the *dastār* to be removed from your head."[193]

Qazwīnī also records the above letter, except that he makes Malik-Shāh's threat even more explicit. He concludes the above quotation with the line, "That is, I will have you killed."[194] At this point, according to Rāwandī, a frustrated and agitated Niẓām al-Mulk replied in the following defiant note: "He who gave the crown (*tāj*) to you has placed this *dastār*[195] on my head. The two are wrapped up together, and linked to one another."[196] Another source, Nīshāpūrī's *Saljūq-nāma*, offers the complementary reading: "My ink-bottle and the crown are linked together."[197] Al-Subkī and other Arabic sources record a similar narrative in which the sultan became frustrated by Niẓām al-Mulk and all of his children virtually running the empire. Malik-Shāh is said to have stated, "It is as if you are my partner in the empire . . ." Al-Subkī records Niẓām al-Mulk as having replied, "If he has not known that I am his partner in the empire, let him know now."[198]

Whereas al-Subkī had been more cautious, presenting Malik-Shāh's jealousy as one out of a number of possible causes for Niẓām al-Mulk's murder, the astute al-Kātib al-Iṣfahānī is less equivocal. His account mirrors the narratives of Rāwandī, Nīshāpūrī, Qazwīnī, and al-Subkī. He states that the longevity of Niẓām al-Mulk's vizierate had been weighing on Malik-Shāh. The sultan sent a note to the vizier, stating, "You have had established yourself in a position of authority over my realm (*innaka istawlayta ʿala mulkī*), and you have divided up my areas among your children, your grooms, and your servants. It is as if you are my partner in rule (*faʾannaka lī fi ʾl-mulk sharīkun*)! Do you want me to order the ink-bottle of the vizierate (*dawāt al-wizāra*) to be removed from you, and to free people from your oppression?"[199]

According to al-Kātib al-Iṣfahānī, the Khwāja responded in a firm and bold tone: "[You act] as if you have just found out that I am a share-holder with you in rule, and your partner in the government. Indeed my ink-bottle is tied to your crown. He who removes the inkbottle, will [also] remove the crown [from your head]" (*kaʾannaka al-yawm ʿarifta annī fi ʾl-mulk musāhimaka, wa fi ʾl-dawlat muqāsimaka, wa inna dawātī muqtaranatun bi tājika. Fa man rafaʿatahā, rufiʿa*).[200]

A further verification of this narrative is provided by Ibn al-Athīr, who presents an almost identical account in the *al-Kāmil*.[201] This heated exchange provided Niẓām al-Mulk's enemies with ample opportunities to exaggerate it, and use it to raise the sultan's wrath.[202] In particular, Qazwīnī directly blames Tarkān Khātūn for having used this exchange to initiate the Niẓām's murder.[203] Al-Kātib al-Iṣfahānī reiterated that "the assassination that happened to Niẓām al-Mulk was covertly through the Sultan's permission" (*mā jarā ʿalā niẓām al-mulk min al-ightiyāl tajwīzan min al-sulṭān muḍmaran*).[204]

The cumulative evidence of all the above sources supports my thesis that, at least for the premodern chroniclers, the person most directly responsible for the assassination of Niẓām al-Mulk was Malik-Shāh. The main reasons for the assassination are held to be his jealousy of Niẓām al-Mulk's long reign and control over the country as well as his desire to challenge (and perhaps ultimately do away with) the ʿAbbāsid Caliphate.

After Niẓām al-Mulk

Malik-Shāh wasted no time after the assassination of Niẓām al-Mulk to follow through with his plans to challenge the ʿAbbāsid Caliphate. We have previously mentioned Malik-Shāh's desire to have the ʿAbbāsid Caliph exiled from Baghdad. Upon arriving in Baghdad, Malik-Shāh proceeded to the second phase of his plan. He asked the caliph to denounce his son Mustaẓhir as the heir-apparent and instead appoint another son, Jaʿfar, as the designated successor to the caliphate.[205] It is crucial to recall that this son, Jaʿfar, was a maternal grandson of the Saljūq Sultan: Jaʿfar's mother was Malik-Shāh's daughter.[206] The purpose of this request seems clear enough: the appointment of a child who would be both caliph and sultan, both Saljūq and ʿAbbāsid. Not being able to theoretically wrestle religious legitimacy from the ʿAbbāsids, Malik-Shāh seemed to be on the verge of genealogically steering the caliphate towards his own family.

At the same time, Malik-Shāh wasted no time in going through with a wholesale changing of the "ancient" members of the *dīvān* with new ones: Niẓām al-Mulk was replaced by Tāj al-Mulk, the *mustawfī* Sharaf al-Mulk Abū Saʿd was deposed in favor of Majd al-Mulk Abū ʾl-Faḍl al-Qummī, and lastly Kamāl al-Dīn Abū Riḍāʾ al-ʿĀriḍ's post was assumed by Sadīd al-Mulk Abū ʾl-Maʿālī.[207] A certain (A)bū ʾl-Maʿālī Naḥḥās wrote a poem on this occasion, addressed to Malik-Shāh: "Even if you were tired of Niẓām [al-Mulk], Kamāl [al-Dīn], and Sharaf [al-Mulk] look what has come your way from Tāj [al-Mulk], Majd [al-Mulk], and Sadīd [al-Mulk]!"[208] A more scolding critique of Malik-Shāh is offered by a later literary historian, the somewhat unreliable yet always amusing Dawlat-shāh: "The King, alas! Ignored that lucky fate which granted him a Minister so great; o'er his domains he set the cursed Tāj and jeopardised for him both Crown (*Tāj*) and State (*Mulk*)."[209] In a rather understated manner, Rāwandī and other historians state that this turnover would not prove "blessed" for the sultan.[210] Malik-Shāh died mysteriously after Niẓām al-Mulk's assassination; Rāwandī reports the time between the two deaths as having been less than a month,[211] al-Kātib al-Iṣfahānī as thirty-three days,[212] and Ibn Khallikān as thirty-five days.[213] Qazwīnī and Hindū-Shāh Nakhjavānī interpret this as the fulfillment of Niẓām al-Mulk's prediction that his own fate and that of Malik-Shāh would be linked together.[214] The sequence of passing away inspired Muʿizzī to compose the following poem: "The aged [Niẓām al-Mulk] departed to the Paradise of eternity. In another month, the youthful king followed. Divine Authority made the incapacity of the Sultan manifest. Look now at the Sultan's incapacity, now at Divine Authority."[215]

It cannot be entirely dismissed that Malik-Shāh's timely death—from the perspective of the ʿAbbāsids—might have been due to a more sinister plot, perhaps even a caliphal plot. Abu ʾl-Ḥasan Bayhaqī stated that Malik-Shāh was poisoned by a servant who fed him a fatal serving of cooked rabbit.[216] The author of *Majmal al-tawārīkh* also states, "It is said that Malik-Shāh was given a potion (*dārū*)."[217] The fortuitous passing of Malik-Shāh provided the ʿAbbāsids with a respite from Saljūq oppression. The uneasy cooperation between the Saljūqs and the ʿAbbāsids thus continued.

As for Tarkān Khātūn, her political activities only intensified after Malik-Shāh's death. The sources allude to her having hidden her husband's death and arranging military deals with certain Turkish *amīr*s.[218] Perhaps her most ambitious plan was to have the ʿAbbāsid Caliph recognize her son Maḥmūd as the sultan. The caliph refused to do this as he correctly recognized that a mere child would not be able to provide the caliphate with the needed military protection.[219] After a series of failed plots against Sultan Bark-yāruq, Tarkān Khātūn passed away in the Ramaḍān of 487/1094.[220]

As has already been mentioned, Hindū-Shāh Nakhjavānī states that after Niẓām al-Mulk's passing, the death of Malik-Shāh did not have a great impact on the populace.[221] If this account is to be believed, it is yet another indication that the people looked as much (and perhaps more) to Niẓām al-Mulk as the effective ruler of Islamdom than any Saljūq Sultan or ʿAbbāsid Caliph. Nor were the masses the only group to mourn the Niẓām's passing; even after his death, Niẓām al-Mulk was remembered fondly through panegyrics. E. G. Browne correctly recognizes that "a fallen Minister is seldom praised by Eastern poets," as most would be quick to offer their panegyrics to the next vizier. Niẓām al-Mulk proved to be an exception in this area, as in so many others. Shibl al-Dawla composed a lovely poem in his honor, which is featured prominently in Ibn al-Athīr's account: "The vizier Niẓām al-Mulk was a peerless pearl, (*kāna al-wazīr niẓām al-mulk lu'lu'atan*) which the All-merciful God esteemed as of great price, but, precious as it was, the age knew not its value, so in jealousy He placed it in its shell."[222]

Another indication of the degree of loyalty that Niẓām al-Mulk inspired in those around him was that, after his passing, his personal military servants (*niẓāmī*s) took revenge by attacking Tāj al-Mulk and killing him by cutting him to pieces.[223] Subsequently, the *khwāja*'s servants and family members removed his body to Isfahan, and buried him in the Karān neighborhood that came to be known as the *Turbat-i niẓām*.[224] Unlike most kings and sultans of premodern Perso-Islamic society, Niẓām al-Mulk's legacy came to be felt not through a regal mausoleum, but rather through the administrative and genealogical legacy he left behind. In chapter 3 of the present study, I will analyze the institutions that were "strung together" by Niẓām al-Mulk. However, it is also important to note that part of the Niẓām's legacy is genealogical. Many of his children, grandchildren, and great-grandchildren also ascended to prominent positions in the vizierate. (I have provided a list of Niẓām al-Mulk's descendants who attained to high administrative positions in the appendix.)

Having covered the rise and demise of Niẓām al-Mulk and his genealogical legacy, we are now positioned to examine his even more long-lasting legacy, that of the institutions he "strung" together to buttress Saljūq ideology: the land-grant system, the surveillance network, the khānaqāh, and most importantly for our purposes, the madrasa network which bore his name, the *Niẓāmīya*.

Chapter Three

Saljūq State Apparatuses

In the two preceding chapters, I identified the rise of the Great Saljūqs and the formulation of the Great Saljūq ideology, constructed mainly by the über-administrator Niẓām al-Mulk. In this chapter, I explore the most important institutions they used to establish and extend their authority. These institutions would prove to be of historic significance for the Iranian region. As Lambton has stated, "Many Saljūq institutions lasted in their outward forms (though the terminology was in some cases changed) until the twentieth century."[1] How these various institutions were connected to Saljūq ideology is the question that concerns us here.

What unifies multiple state apparatuses is their function to support the ruling ideology, which is none other than the ideology of the ruling class—that is, the Saljūqs. In looking at the connections between state institutions and ruling ideology, I am of course indebted to the work of Louis Althusser.[2] Althusser argued that ideology should not be collapsed to concern with material interests, even though material interests of a ruling-class ideology could be projected through a number of other institutions, with important consequences. In looking at state apparatuses broadly, one can come to see that some institutions operate through repression, whereas others operate through ideology. I am here mainly concerned with the latter examples, apparatuses that advance the ruling elite's ideology. These institutions consist of the land-grant system (*iqṭā*ʿ), surveillance, madrasa, and khānaqāh. I will therefore examine how each of these apparatuses works to support and legitimize Saljūq religious ideology. In the next two chapters, I will discuss various ways in which the patronized ʿulamāʾ (chapter 4) and Sufis (chapter 5) returned the favor by acknowledging Saljūq power. The conclusion of this chapter (as well as chapter 6) deals with the contesting of these same ideological state apparatuses.

Niẓām al-Mulk and Saljūq Apparatuses

One of the more intriguing accounts linking together a number of the ideological state apparatuses deployed by Niẓām al-Mulk comes up in ʿImād al-Dīn al-Kātib al-Iṣfahānī's *Nuṣrat al-fatra* (through Al-Bundārī, *Zubdat al-nuṣra*). The climax of this account is a pun on Niẓām al-Mulk's name, claiming that the realm (*mulk*) was returned to order (*niẓām*) and that the religion was returned to its proper condition of strength and correctness (*qawām*).[3] The linkage between social order and religious correctness is of course the hallmark of Saljūq state ideology, as we have previously seen. What is new here is that the historian ʿImād al-Dīn discusses a number of ways in which Niẓām al-Mulk worked to bring order to the realm, including his patronage of religious scholars and Sufis across the whole realm, his establishment of madrasas, and his reorganization of the land-grant system (*iqṭāʿ*).[4] If establishing social order and religious correctness are part of the discourse of Saljūq state ideology, the above institutions constitute the ideological state apparatuses of that same ruling class ideology. This chapter will deal with these ideological apparatuses and how they contributed to the larger process of legitimizing the Saljūqs.

Surveillance and Reconnaissance

Contemporary critical theorists such as Michel Foucault have persuasively argued that, since the eighteenth century, regimes of power and knowledge have been linked in European civilizations.[5] Furthermore, they have also pointed out the methods of control, surveillance, and regulation that are necessary for the enforcement of these systems. Foucault's own thesis grew out of research on various institutions of European society, such as clinics, prisons, and hospitals. He analyzed the ways in which a powerful minority can construct a definition of the normal and impose that definition upon the rest of society. Foucault was particularly fascinated by strategies of control and surveillance, epitomized in the Panopticon.[6] Given that his theories emerged from his research on European institutions in a modern era, one may legitimately question how successfully these theories can be applied to non-European and, perhaps more importantly, premodern civilizations. In other words, without assuming that they are necessarily a positive (!) or desired institution, one should seek to explore whether such systems of surveillance are uniquely a feature of modernity or possible only in a post-Enlightenment

European context. Our evidence suggests that already in fifth-/eleventh-century Islamdom, Niẓām al-Mulk had anticipated the importance of the systems of surveillance and reconnaissance for imposing the Saljūq view of normative Islam and normative social order on the whole society. While in practice these systems may not have become as fully materialized as Niẓām al-Mulk would have liked, his theoretical articulation of the need for them reveals a great deal about his model of a centralized state and the ideological apparatuses needed to support its religious ideology.

The aim of Niẓām al-Mulk's system of surveillance and reconnaissance was to keep a watchful eye on two groups: those who were likely to rebel against Saljūq authority and those within the Saljūq regime who were in positions of power/knowledge. Niẓām al-Mulk had provided a mechanism for this system of surveillance: a postal service (*barīd*) that doubled as a spy-highway network. This represented a new development in the well-established institution that went back to Umayyad times. He had also instructed the surveillance agents (*ṣāḥib khabar*) to go undercover as mendicants and Sufis, so as not to attract attention and to be able to wander freely.[7] Among the disguises listed, Niẓām al-Mulk specifically identifies *ṣūfīyān* (Sufis) and *darwīshān* (dervishes). The aim of these espionage agents (*jāsūsān*) was to "bring back news of whatever they [had] heard, so that nothing [remained] hidden" in any corner of the realm.[8] As Foucault might have argued, this was an exercise of Saljūq power as well as a means of registering knowledge and an attempt to extend the penetrating gaze of the central authority.

The reconnaissance system was, of course, not begun by Niẓām al-Mulk, nor was he the only one to make use of it. Ibn al-Athīr records an account in the year 465/1072–73 in which the enemies of the able vizier gathered some secret information about him and placed it under the prayer mat of Alp Arslān.[9] Even though this system had been used against him personally, Niẓām al-Mulk went on to state in his *Siyāsat-nāma*, "It is better to have surveillance agents (*ṣāḥib khabar*), since having postal agents (*ṣāḥib barīd*) is from the rules of statecraft."[10] As we will see with the iqṭāʿ and the madrasa system, what is new with Niẓām al-Mulk is not the *what* but the *how*. The novel aspect of Niẓām al-Mulk's system of surveillance and reconnaissance is in using it as an ideological apparatus toward supporting the dominant Saljūq ideology.

The Function of the Surveillance and Reconnaissance Mechanism

Given the prominence of the *Siyāsat-nāma*, it is surprising that other scholars have not focused on Niẓām al-Mulk's information-gathering machine.

This system of reconnaissance and surveillance—essentially a spy network—was to be spread throughout the whole Saljūq realm. Certain social groups are identified by Niẓām al-Mulk as specific targets of surveillance. In the fourth chapter of the *Siyāsat-nāma*, Niẓām al-Mulk states that one must always secretly (*dar sirr*) inquire about the tax collectors, the viziers, and the trusted ones. Deploying the distinctly Saljūq discourse of social corruption, Niẓām al-Mulk states, "This is because the well-being and *fasād* of the king and the realm are dependent on it."[11] In a later chapter, Niẓām al-Mulk states that the king must be aware of the condition of "his flock and army, both near and far. He has to know about everything that is going on, both grand and trivial."[12] Using the fiqh terminology that formed the basis of Niẓām al-Mulk's legal training, he identifies this duty as *wājib* ("obligatory") upon the king. He informs the king that should he not do so, the people would attribute the *fasād* in the land to him.

What the above narrative reveals is that Niẓām al-Mulk sought to expand the gaze of the Saljūq surveillance system beyond the royal court to encompass the army and the *raʿyat* ("flock"). No segment of society was to be left unwatched. The gaze of the Saljūqs would cover the entire realm, if Niẓām al-Mulk had his way. Of all the groups that were to be under surveillance and reconnaissance, Niẓām al-Mulk seems to have had a particular fascination with judges. He stated in the *Siyāsat-nāma* that kings must know about the affairs of each and every judge (*bāyad ki aḥwāl–i qāḍīyān-i mamlakat yagān-yagān bidānand*).[13] Niẓām al-Mulk went on to elaborate on the above, stating that the judges were in reality the deputies of the king (*nāʾib-i pādshāh*). Here the judges are represented as interpreters of legitimacy. It is crucial to recall here that one of the key functions of the judges in this period was to administer punishment. In Althusserian categories, their function also contains elements of both the repressive and coercive state apparatuses. Niẓām al-Mulk regarded watching the judges as particularly relevant "when the king is a Persian or a Turk, or one who does not know Arabic and has not studied the commandments of the sharīʿa. He is then in need of a deputy who can perform the function [of giving judgment] on his behalf."[14] The Saljūq Sultans were precisely such a group: Turks who were largely ignorant of the commandments of the sharīʿa. In directly identifying the judges as the king's deputies, Niẓām al-Mulk was bringing them—willingly or unwillingly—under the direct subjugation of the king. Judges were implicated in a political loop. Their role had a social and thus by definition political significance. In Niẓām al-Mulk's system, they had the overtly political role of representing the king.

I will return to the question of judges being under surveillance and reconnaissance in chapter 6 of the present study, regarding charges of heresy that were brought up against one specific judge and Sufi in the Saljūq era, ʿAyn al-Quḍāt Hamadānī, who challenged the dominant state ideology. Is it possible that he too was under surveillance? Could it be that surveillance agents had infiltrated his sermons and *samāʿ* sessions, dressed in the attire of Sufis, just as Niẓām al-Mulk had instructed them? In lieu of certain evidence, we can only raise the distinct possibility and look for potential clues.[15]

In an ironic though not unexpected twist, Niẓām al-Mulk stated that even the watchers were to be watched. Niẓām al-Mulk stated that in every city a watchful eye had to be kept out for those who were involved in religious matters and were seen as particularly pious. These individuals were to be given the task of gathering reconnaissance on "judges and tax-collectors, the police-chief and the flock, the old and the young." If these potential agents of surveillance and reconnaissance should refuse to do so, Niẓām al-Mulk specifically stated that they "must be forced to do so, even if they loathe to do it" (*īshān rā iltizām bāyad kard, wa bi ikrāh bibāyad farmūd*).[16] This, like so many other systems of surveillance, was a compulsory one, for both the watcher and the watched.

Charles Tilly has argued for the necessity of reading war making and state making as different aspects of the same process: organized crime. He locates "banditry, piracy, gangland rivalry, policing, and war making all . . . on the same continuum."[17] The Saljūqs would seem to confirm this, being essentially a Turkic tribe ("gang" in the above consideration) who moved from inter-tribal fighting to war making to state making. As Tilly correctly recognizes, part of the move toward state making is the production of "durable instruments of surveillance and reconnaissance within the territory."[18] Tilly's thesis would then urge us to look at the administrative efforts of Niẓām al-Mulk and the military conquests of the Saljūq warlords as being part of a broader spectrum.

How successful were the Saljūqs in establishing such a regime of surveillance as part of their state making? We cannot be entirely certain. Systems of surveillance and reconnaissance, by design, are to remain invisible. If they are visible to the point of being identified and recognized in contemporary premodern texts, they have by definition outlived their usefulness. The lack of explicit evidence of their presence should not be taken as a sign of their lack of existence, nor should it be read as their omnipresence. Commenting on the same point, Marshall Hodgson has stated that while it had been part of Niẓām al-Mulk's centralization agenda to institute the *barīd*, which he astutely recognizes as "the central information service," he questions its efficacy, stating instead that "a proper information service was not maintained. Instead, the Seljuḳ Sultans depended on their vast power and mobility to crush any rebellion after it had appeared."[19]

Indeed, the only evidence we possess which specifically talks about the effectiveness of such a system of surveillance and reconnaissance comes from the realm of one of their vassals in Kirmān. A local historian, Muḥammad b. Ibrāhīm, documents precisely such a system during the reign of Sultan Muḥammad b. Malik-Shāh (from 537/1143 to 551/1156). This system is said to have been very successful both within Kirmān and outside, even extending to regions such as Iṣfahān and Khurāsān.[20] If the Kirmān Saljūqs were able to establish such a system over a vast area with great success, could the Great Saljūqs have done the same? We can only hypothesize at this point until further evidence emerges.

Iqṭāʿ

Iqṭāʿ has probably been the single most misunderstood Saljūq institution. There are many reasons for the confusion, perhaps the most serious being the tendency to see the iqṭāʿ as a Nile-to-Oxus equivalent of a European fiefdom and to connect it to feudal systems there. Claude Cahen has offered the most thorough critique of this tendency.[21] Rather than comparing the iqṭāʿ with European feudalism, Cahen suggests that a more fruitful comparison might be made with the Byzantine *pronoia*.[22] In contrast to the European model, the iqṭāʿ system was generally not hereditary. Furthermore, Marshall Hodgson observed, "The iqṭâʿ system implied in none of its more usual forms a system of mutual obligations of lord and vassal, each of whom had its own indefeasible rights rooted as much in the lands as in military service, which is properly called 'feudalism'."[23] Hodgson suggests terms such as "revenue assignment" or "land grant" to translate iqṭāʿ.[24] He regards such translations as less misleading than "Islamic feudalism."

As is the case with the madrasa and the khānaqāh, there are vigorous debates about the origin of the iqṭāʿ system. The historian ʿImād al-Dīn al-Kātib al-Iṣfahānī (or, al-Bundārī) claimed that Niẓām al-Mulk initiated the practice of assigning land grants.[25] Again, similar to the madrasa (and its attribution also to Niẓām al-Mulk) and the khānaqāh controversy (and its attribution to Abū Saʿīd-i Abī ʾl-Khayr), this is a retrospective projection. We know for sure that the iqṭāʿ system existed under the Buyids, before the Saljūqs. Even Niẓām al-Mulk's *Siyāsat-nāma* refers to how "previous kings" utilized the iqṭāʿ.[26] What the debate seems to indicate is that Niẓām al-Mulk is seen as having initiated a great change in its protocol and administering it efficiently, to the point that later regimes came to associate the model of the iqṭāʿ with him. Niẓām al-Mulk's innovation seems to have consisted of merging together different types of iqṭāʿs that had existed before. The military type of iqṭāʿ and the administrative variety—which had been distinct before—were now merged into one.[27] As Ann K. S. Lambton has correctly recognized, the immediate consequence of this was the militarization of the state.[28] The result, as was the case with the *barīd* system, was the adaptation of an existing practice to meet new demands.

It is clear that Niẓām al-Mulk had envisioned the system of the iqṭāʿ as a form of payment for the Saljūq military. In discussing the payment due to the army, he states, "One has to make clear the payment of the army. As for those who are the people of iqṭāʿ, their payment is determined and appointed."[29] It seems that, in Niẓām al-Mulk's design, only the accomplished soldiers would be assigned land grants. He specifically states that the "servants" are not worthy of iqṭāʿ.[30]

Niẓām al-Mulk was not merely the redesigner of the iqṭāʿ system, he was also one of its greatest beneficiaries. Ibn Khallikān's biographical dictionary claims that Saljūq viziers received one-tenth of the produce of the whole realm in the form of iqṭāʿ.[31] Nor did this arrangement prevent the sultan from occasional displays of generosity by granting more iqṭāʿs to the vizier. A rare letter preserved from Sulṭān Alp Arslān to Niẓām al-Mulk documents the bestowal of an additional land grant worth fifty thousand gold coins to the vizier.[32]

The Function of Iqṭāʿ

What was Niẓām al-Mulk's aim for instituting such a system? Primarily, it was to bring land assignments under central bureaucratic control. As he had recommended doing with tax collectors, he suggested that the *muqṭiʿs* (land-grant assignees) be moved from site to site every few years so that they did not build up too much power in any one location. In addition, this system seems to have been designed to curb excessive abuses of the peasants by the assignees. The theoretical points identified by Niẓām al-Mulk in the *Siyāsat-nāma* provide us with important insights into existing social problems. For example, he reminds those who have been assigned iqṭāʿs that they have no rights over the peasants except collecting that which is their due. They are not, Niẓām al-Mulk emphatically repeats, to take the peasants' lives, possessions, wives, or children.[33] The fact that he has to remind them of this demonstrates precisely that some land-grant assignees did in fact take freely of the peasants' possessions and families. In order to threaten the assignees, Niẓām al-Mulk reminds them that the whole realm and the peasants belong to the sultan (*mulk wa raʿyat hama sulṭān rā-st*).[34] In deliberately ominous terms, the vizier reminds the assignees that by following his advice they can spare themselves the wrath of the pādshāh and the torment of the Hereafter. The historian ʿImād al-Dīn al-Kātib al-Iṣfahānī also points out that Niẓām al-Mulk intended to curb the assignees' abuse of peasants. This is noted as a common practice of the Saljūq family members, who would take advantage of their association with the rulers to justify their pillage.[35]

In addition to the above, the iqṭāʿ system was an important fiscal policy for the Saljūqs. The Saljūq regime, like most other premodern Muslim states, experienced a shortage of cash funds from time to time. The iqṭāʿ system enabled Niẓām al-Mulk to pay the army and scholars without needing to have cash on hand. The iqṭāʿ was part and parcel of Saljūq patrimonialism. The importance of this fiscal policy to the overall operation of the Saljūq regime cannot be overstated.

Another desired aim of the iqṭāʿ system was to settle the wandering Turkic nomads. Niẓām al-Mulk was keenly aware of the problem of disgruntled nomadic *Türkmen*. At best, they could roam freely and bring disorder to the realm. At worst, they could align themselves with challengers to the Saljūq regime. By assigning them a land grant, Niẓām al-Mulk was in a way assigning them to a land as well. This seems to have been part of Niẓām al-Mulk's plan to settle, or at least denomadize, the Türkmen.[36] He states, "Then they will settle down with other people and with growing devotion serve as pages, and cease to feel that aversion [to settled life] with which they are naturally imbued."[37] Although the land-grant recipients did not often live on the very land they had been assigned, this was a move toward identifying them with a particular, identifiable land to which they were connected, indeed tied. It would be reasonable to expect that they would visit their land grant at least for the purpose of collecting revenues. By settling them, they could be brought under a central surveillance and made accountable to the Saljūq regime. It is consistent with his policy of recognizing the debt the Saljūq regime owed to the *Türkmen* who had helped bring the Saljūqs to power. In theory, the iqṭāʿ would help guarantee the political fidelity of the fickle tribesmen.

A passage in the *Siyāsat-nāma* connects together the iqṭāʿ and the previously mentioned ideological state apparatus, the system of surveillance and reconnaissance. The thirty-seventh chapter of this work deals with the none-too-hypothetical situation of when an assignee of a land grant is taxing his peasants too heavily, to the point that they are impoverished. To keep tabs on such abuses, Niẓām al-Mulk recommends that a secret agent should be sent covertly to the area to ascertain the truth of the matter and bring back reports.[38] As can be seen, in this case the two state apparatuses were linked together toward achieving the larger goal of a stable realm.

As Marshall Hodgson has pointed out, the iqṭāʿ went hand in hand with the other institution of assigning land revenues, the endowment (*waqf*). The *awqāf* were most frequently associated with establishing new madrasas, and historical sources have emphasized Niẓām al-Mulk's eagerness in establishing awqāf for great scholars near and far.[39] Hodgson goes on to state, "As the ʿulamāʾ scholars became increasingly dependent on the waqf endowments, they found themselves in a position largely independent of but complementary to the amîrs, as the chief alternative beneficiaries of the land revenues, and to that degree they were prepared to sanction the system as a whole."[40]

One result of the increasingly sanctioning role of the ʿulamāʾ was the inevitable diluting of the "oppositional role of the ʿulamāʾ in political life."[41] The sanctioning and legitimizing role of the ʿulamāʾ is an aspect to which I will return to the next chapter, by focusing on the foremost madrasa scholar, Abū Ḥāmid al-Ghazālī. However, I will first discuss the rise of the madrasa and the khānaqāh as institutions of religious knowledge patronized by the Saljūqs.

Madrasa, Saljūq Patronage, and Empowering Knowledge

In dealing with a later Ayyubid period, a historian of premodern Islam has stated, "In short, regimes without legitimacy could assure acceptance by and the cooperation of their subjects only by supporting Muslim religious life."[42] Without ignoring the power of the discourses of kingship and royalty, the above statement could just as easily have been made about the Saljūqs. Virtually every major chronicle of Saljūq history includes examples of institutions of Muslim religious life that the Saljūqs founded and patronized. We have previously encountered Rāwandī's parable, comparing the Saljūqs to a tree whose fruit was the establishment of madrasas and khānaqāhs, among other social institutions.[43] This patronage is to be seen as a state apparatus to legitimize the Saljūqs' religious ideology.

The account provided by the fifteenth-century historian Ḥāfiẓ Abrū (d. 833/1430) is a perfect example of the way the Saljūqs came to be represented as patrons of Islamic learning in subsequent centuries. According to this narrative, when Alp Arslān was visiting Nīshāpūr, he came upon a group of jurists who were gathered in a mosque. The sultan asked Niẓām al-Mulk about them. The vizier replied that they were religious scholars who were "the best of humanity, as they have abandoned the pleasures of the ephemeral world" and had dedicated themselves to acquiring virtue and the perfection of themselves. The sultan was moved to provide for them and asked Niẓām al-Mulk to establish a place in "every city" for them so that they might gather and freely go about pursuing knowledge.

Being essentially a Saljūq hagiographic account—which must include an element of reciprocity[44]—the narrative ends with the sultan asking the jurists to offer their prayers on behalf of the "maintenance of the Sultan's realm." Ḥāfiẓ Abrū goes on to claim that, in that year alone, seventy madrasas were built through the Alp Arslān's generosity and that this sultan was the first one to have established such a beautiful example.[45] As with many other myths, the above narrative explains the origins of a practice in a way that is aimed to set a paradigm for the audience of the myth. Julie Meisami has astutely observed that in reality, the Saljūqs did not establish the many institutions of piety and learning that the chronicles ascribe to them or at least that evidence for these madrasas and mosques has not survived to today.[46] Again, what is important for our project is the ideological construction of such patronage that is depicted in the chronicles. While the above account occurs in a work of tārīkh, it is fair to call it a hagiography of patronage. In other words, it depicts the patronage of religious institutions as an ideological state apparatus used in legitimizing the Saljūqs. One of the key claims of my project is that historical narratives should be read not only (or perhaps even primarily) in a positivistic fashion but also as texts full of tropes and myth constructions. In short, the insights that scholars have developed about myths (not in the sense of something false but as scholars of religious studies use the term) should also be applied to these types of historical narratives as well.

Similar claims would be made on behalf of other Saljūq Sultans. A report by Nāṣir-i Khusraw indicated that already in 437/1046, Ṭughril had ordered the establishment of a madrasa in Nīshāpūr.[47] Ibn Kathīr reports that Malik-Shāh established a Ḥanafī madrasa.[48] However, the person most frequently associated with madrasa patronage under the Saljūqs is again, not surprisingly, Niẓām al-Mulk.

Niẓām al-Mulk and Patronage of Madrasas

Many later sources allude to the great vizier's fondness for scholars and saints. A typical narrative from a work dealing with the history of viziers recalls Niẓām al-Mulk as always keeping "the company of ascetics, scholars, and the great saints."[49] Even more instructive are the comments of ʿImād al-Dīn al-

Kātib al-Iṣfahānī. He states that Niẓām al-Mulk rewarded people according to their level of knowledge. Whenever he would find someone in a city from "the people of religion, learning, and virtue," he would patronize them. This form of patronage is specifically identified as a madrasa: he would establish a madrasa for the scholar, establish an endowment (waqf) for that madrasa, and provide for a library (*dār al-kutub*) there.[50]

The best-known madrasa established by Niẓām al-Mulk was the Baghdad Niẓāmīya.[51] According to Ibn al-Athīr, the construction of this madrasa began in 457/1065[52] and was finished in 459/1067.[53] Upon its completion, Niẓām al-Mulk is said to have visited it from time to time, narrating Prophetic traditions for the scholars there.[54] Niẓām al-Mulk obviously took a very personal interest in the madrasa that bore his name in the caliphal city. We are told that he went through the library (*dār al-kutub*) of the Niẓāmīya and examined all the volumes there. He even made suggestions for the improvement of the library.[55]

Given the prominence of the Baghdad Niẓāmīya, it is almost easy to forget that it was not the first madrasa founded, not even the first madrasa established by Niẓām al-Mulk. Already during the time Alp Arslān was a governor (450/1058 to 455/1063), Niẓām al-Mulk had founded the Niẓāmīya in Nīshāpūr. We are also told that when Imām al-Ḥaramayn Juwaynī died in 478/1085 he had been the director of the Nishāpūr Niẓāmīya for almost thirty years. Both of these would put the date of the founding of the Nīshāpūr Niẓāmīya a few years before the opening of the Baghdad Niẓāmīya (459/1067).[56]

Still, due to the prestige of the Baghdād Niẓāmīya, Niẓām al-Mulk and the patronage of madrasas became so synonymous that many later scholars would come to erroneously assume that he had invented the whole madrasa system.[57] Among the first to have noticed this error was the Shāfiʿī bibliographer, al-Subkī (d. 771/1369). He states that Niẓām al-Mulk had established madrasas in a number of different cities, including Balkh, Nīshāpūr, Herat, Baṣra, Marv, Āmūl, Mawṣil, and Ṭabaristan. Al-Subkī adds, "It is said that there is a madrasa patronized by him in every town in the regions of Iraq and Khurāsān." At this point the Shāfiʿī bibliographer notes the error of his own teacher, Dhahabī, who "believed that Niẓām al-Mulk was the first to patronize and establish madrasas. However, this is not the case."[58] In supporting his own position, al-Subkī gives a list of madrasas that had existed before Niẓām al-Mulk. These include the Bayhaqīya madrasa, which is stated to have been established even before the birth of Niẓām al-Mulk;[59] the Ṣāʿidī in Nīshāpūr, which was established by the Amīr Naṣr ibn Sabuk-tagīn in 390/1000;[60] and two more. Al-Subkī concludes, "When I [Subkī] reflected on this matter, this thought occurred to me that Niẓām al-Mulk was the first person to have devoted a predetermined and fixed stipend for the students, since I have no evidence that before Niẓām al-Mulk there was a fixed stipend for the students of [religious] knowledge. In all likelihood, there was no such arrangement until the time of Niẓām al-Mulk."[61]

If madrasas had existed before Niẓām al-Mulk, how did they later contribute to supporting the dominant state ideology? It is to this question that we now turn.

Madrasa Patronage in a Sectarian Milieu

In addition to Sunni-Ismāʿīlī conflicts, another dominant form of intellectual sectarianism in the Saljūq era arose within the various schools of Sunni thought. While the Saljūqs depicted themselves as the enemies of the Ismāʿīlīs, an overview of the historical chronicles dealing with this period demonstrates that most of the intellectual turmoil of this period was between Sunni madhhabs, particularly between the Shāfiʿīs and Ḥanafīs.

I propose to locate Niẓām al-Mulk's patronage of various Niẓāmīya madrasas in the sectarian context of Sunni squabbles in the fifth/eleventh century. The evidence is at times contradictory: some sources depict Niẓām al-Mulk as a fanatic patron of Shāfiʿī-Ashʿarīs. Others portray him as a sensible (though partial) patron seeking to restore harmony among the various madhhabs after the balance had been disturbed through the Saljūq ruling family's exclusive patronage of the Ḥanafīs. I believe that the cumulative weight of the evidence favors the second perspective. It is well-known that the Saljūq Turks themselves were staunch followers of the Ḥanafī legal madhhab. In doing so, they were continuing a long-standing tradition that linked the Turks with the Ḥanafī madhhab.[62] Prior to the Saljūqs, the Sāmānids had designated Ḥanafism as the official madhhab of the state and acted as patrons for Ḥanafī scholars in Samarqand, Bukhara, and other Transoxiana cities.[63] Wilferd Madelung has established that, prior to the rise of the Saljūqs, there had been a general balance of power between the Shāfiʿī and Ḥanafī madhhabs. The rise of the Saljūqs, accompanied by their exclusive patronage of Ḥanafīs, disturbed this balance. Madelung labels this the "overt partisanship of the Saljūq rulers and the crude Ḥanafite fanaticism and anti-Shāfiʿite bias of many of the Turks settling in the garrison towns of Iran."[64]

Niẓām al-Mulk sought to curb both the Saljūqs' exclusive patronage of the Ḥanafīs as well as the more extreme elements of polemical Shāfiʿī thought. Of the two, the first would prove to be his greater challenge. The policies of Ṭughril and his vizier al-Kundurī had led to a disproportionate rise in the prominence of the Ḥanafīs. I have already documented in the last chapter Kundurī's exile of Shāfiʿī-Ashʿarī scholars from Khurāsān. In Isfahan, a city that had traditionally been Shāfiʿī, Ṭughril had appointed a Ḥanafī judge (ʿAlī b. ʿUbayd Allāh al-Khaṭībī) as the chief qāḍī. In Rayy, the Saljūq warlord had established a second Ḥanafī mosque and brought with him Ḥanafī chief judges from the Ṣāʿidī family of Nīshāpūr.[65]

Such tendencies continued under the next Saljūq Sultan, Alp Arslān (d. 1075), who was so attached to the Ḥanafī madhhab that he carried his own personal Ḥanafī jurist (*faqīh*) with him during battles.[66] Furthermore, Alp Arslān had also established a madrasa for Ḥanafīs in 457/1067.[67] Niẓām al-Mulk's own accounts in the *Siyāsat-nāma* confirm that Alp Arslān used to bemoan the fact that his trusted vizier was not Ḥanafī and instead followed a Shāfiʿī madhhab: "Alas! Would that my vizier were not Shāfiʿī in his madhhab." In the very next sentence, Niẓām al-Mulk goes on to describe Alp Arslān as possessing great "power of discipline, and inspiring awe" and having disapproved of the Shāfiʿī madhhab. The vizier reveals that he was always "fearful" (*tarsān*) of the sultan on this account.[68] The linking of opposition to Shāfiʿī thought and the threat of discipline was no idle fear. The following sultan, Malik-Shāh (d. 1092), is also recorded as having founded a madrasa, a mosque, and a marketplace exclusively for the Ḥanafīs.[69]

To counter the above, Niẓām al-Mulk would emphasize that "in the whole world there are two good madhhabs: the Shāfiʿī and the Ḥanafī. Everything else was heretical innovation (*bidʿat*)."[70] The primary context of the above statement was a critique of the Ismāʿīlīs. However, it also reveals his attitude toward the tensions between the Shāfiʿī and Ḥanafī madhhabs. His exclusive patronage of Shāfiʿī scholars may be seen as an attempt to restore balance to the Saljūq Turks' exclusive patronage of Ḥanafī scholars. The primary way in which he accomplished this was by establishing the network of Niẓāmīya madrasas that were identified with the instruction of Shāfiʿī teachings. The first step in this process was the bringing back of the exiled Shāfiʿī-Ashʿarī scholars, including Imām al-Ḥaramayn Juwaynī and Qushayrī, and establishing honorable posts for them in his Niẓāmīyas.

If Niẓām al-Mulk had to counter the Ḥanafī fanaticism of his Saljūq patrons, he also had to deal with the extremism of some members of the Shāfiʿī madhhab who sought to engage in more vicious polemics against other schools of thought. We can document at least two situations that demonstrate Niẓām al-Mulk's commitment to curbing the fanaticism (*taʿaṣṣub*) of these Shāfiʿī partisans. The first recorded instance was in 456/1063. Some of the

Shāfiʿī detractors of Khwāja ʿAbd Allāh Anṣārī (d. 481/1089) brought charges against him to the vizier. Niẓām al-Mulk calmly dismissed the charges against him, thus disappointing many of his own Shāfiʿī-Ashʿarī clan.[71] Niẓām al-Mulk's support of the aged Anṣārī is all the more remarkable given the well-known polemics Anṣārī had waged against Ashʿarī theology (*kalām*), which was favored by Niẓām al-Mulk (and most Shāfiʿīs).[72] The second narrative comes from his interaction with Abū Isḥāq Shīrāzī, who in 470/1078 had requested permission to conduct polemics against the Ḥanbalīs. Niẓām al-Mulk refused, stating, "The administrative policy of the Sultan and the principle of justice do not justify us favoring towards one madhhab over another. I have established this madrasa only for the sake of supporting the people of knowledge and for the common good—not for creating difference and partitions."[73]

The above two narratives confirm Niẓām al-Mulk's own stated position in the *Siyāsat-nāma*, affirming and balancing the Shāfiʿī and Ḥanafī madhhabs. Niẓām al-Mulk was interested in using madrasas to balance the sectarian interests while providing a great place of prominence for scholars who followed Shāfiʿī Ashʿarism. The best assessment in this matter rests with Richard Bulliet: "All of Niẓām al-Mulk's madrasas were Shāfiʿī institutions, but none of them were allowed to become a bastion of militant Shāfiʿī politics. Niẓām al-Mulk was a patron of the Shāfiʿīs because they were the underdogs at the time of his accession to power, and bipartisan patronage would not have been acceptable in the overheated climate of patrician politics. He was not, however, a Shāfiʿī fanatic. . . . His object was to restore and maintain a balance between patrician factions of every stripe, but he was constrained to work through one faction only."[74]

Our evidence suggests that the tenuous balance of madhhabs achieved by Niẓām al-Mulk came to an abrupt end with his death in 495/1092. Soon after Niẓām al-Mulk's murder, Sultan Muḥammad ibn Malik-Shāh had many of the Shāfiʿīs killed. He sent an army to the Jāmiʿ mosque of Isfahan, which Niẓām al-Mulk had made into a center of Shāfiʿī activities. The sultan ordered the Ḥanafīs to lead the prayer there and suppress the Shāfiʿīs. The sultan also repeated the same pattern of actions in Hamadān.[75] As I have previously documented, contestation characterizes Saljūq culture, and not even the great vizier was exempted from it. Yet the establishment of the Niẓāmīya madrasas would ensure the Shāfiʿīs a stronghold in the turbulent and sectarian world of Saljūq politics and intellectual inquiry. The restoring of balance and the curbing of intellectual (and social) *fitna* all contributed to the larger Saljūq aim of maintaining social order.

The Function of the Madrasa

There has been a long-standing debate dealing with the precise function of the madrasa system under the Saljūqs. Some have stated that the main purpose of the madrasa was countering the propaganda of the Ismāʿīlīs, who had established their own institution of learning (the *dār al-ḥikma*) in Cairo in 395/1005.[76] Other scholars have preferred to see madrasas as institutions for the manufacturing and dissemination of an allegedly normative Islam, which would consist of a synthesis of Ashʿarī *kalām* and Shāfiʿī *fiqh*.[77] The endowment charter of the Niẓāmīya madrasa makes no mention of instruction in Ashʿarī thought, only providing for the teaching of Shāfiʿī *fiqh* and *ʿuṣūl al-fiqh*.[78] In short, there is no evidence that the Niẓāmīya was designed to offer instructions in Ashʿarī kalām. As George Makdisi has stated, the "Niẓāmīya had no 'public chairs' of theology."[79] The theory that Niẓām al-Mulk had envisioned the Niẓāmīya as a place for fostering Ashʿarī thought can be refuted by recalling that the first invited lecturer of the madrasa, Abū Isḥāq Shīrāzī, was known for having been *anti*-Ashʿarī in his methodology.[80] The "orthodoxy" propagated in the Niẓāmīya madrasa, then, was not centered around questions of kalām but was rather designed to support an *uṣūl*-ized (systematic, based on identifying the principles [*uṣūl*] of each discipline) approach to Shāfiʿī legal thought.[81]

Others have preferred to look at madrasas as primarily training facilities for a new administrative class, labeled by H. A. R. Gibb "the orthodox bureaucracy," which is stated to have replaced the earlier ʿAbbāsid secretarial class.[82] This last view, in more or less modified interpretations, has been accepted by many scholars of Saljūq history, including Ann K. S. Lambton.[83] Marshall Hodgson has advanced the argument by stating that, while the madrasas may not have provided good Sunni clerks for a centralized bureaucracy, they did aid in preserving a sense of "Muslim unity" throughout the lands of Islamdom.[84] The madrasa institution did succeed in bringing together the class of the ʿulamāʾ and the court administrators, who in earlier times had operated separately. It also worked to lend yet another aura of legitimacy to the recently converted Saljūqs by portraying them as generous patrons of Islamic learning. This, it will be recalled, was one of the main ideological claims of the Saljūqs.

We still know little about the nature of the madrasa as a social institution. We are just beginning to have a clearer understanding of the curriculum and how the institution was patronized and administered. However, for the time being, we can state with certainty that the madrasas patronized by Niẓām al-Mulk succeeded in the following:

1. temporarily restoring the balance between the various schools, thus
2. restoring social order, that most indispensable of Saljūq motifs;
3. training some faithful administrators for the Saljūq regime,[85] and
4. contributing to the reestablishment of Muslim social unity.

All of the above contributed to the larger goals of preserving social cohesion and unity, which went hand in hand with the Saljūqs' state ideology. I will now move on to the other institution of Muslim religious life with which Niẓām al-Mulk was greatly concerned, the khānaqāh.

The Khānaqāh

The madrasa was not the only institution of higher learning in the fifth/eleventh century. As Roy Mottahedeh has recognized, an examination of bibliographical dictionaries dealing with Saljūq figures reveals that many of the ʿulamāʾ did not receive madrasa educations.[86] George Makdisi has gone to great lengths in emphasizing the role of other institutions, such as the *jāmiʿ*, the *masjid*, and the *mashhad*.[87] Somewhat surprisingly, he does not consider the contribution of the khānaqāh in this context. Along with the madrasa, the khānaqāh proved to be a crucial institution for the Saljūq state in patronizing certain Sufis—those who were open to legitimizing the Saljūqs in return. The boundary between the khānaqāh and the madrasa was very fluid in this age. Many of the highest-ranking scholars were deeply immersed in Sufism, while many of the most notable Sufis were acknowledged religious scholars. Given the importance of the khānaqāh patronage and its understudied nature, I will devote a portion of chapter 5 to it. However, in the subsequent section I will make some preliminary remarks about the rise of the khānaqāh, and the fluid boundary between the madrasa and the khānaqāh in this time period.

Rise of Khurāsānī Sufis as a Distinct Social Group

In his groundbreaking social history of the ʿulamāʾ in Nīshāpūr, Richard Bulliet has documented how Sufism gradually emerged as a dominant label for those inclined toward the spiritual life in Khurāsān. In the beginning of the third/ninth century, the sources refer only to *zuhd* (asceticism). Gradually, alternate designations such as *ʿibāda* (pietistic worship) and *taṣawwuf* (Sufism) are introduced. By the fifth/eleventh century, Sufi becomes the clear designation for those inclined to the spiritual life.[88]

Just as there were various terms that designated individuals who gravitated toward a life of piety, there were also multiple designations for spaces where such individuals could gather. There is a great deal of flexibility in the usage of the terms *ribāṭ, zāwiya*, and khānaqāh in referring to the Sufis of Khurāsān in the fourth/tenth and fifth/eleventh centuries.[89] In addition to those well-known terms, the Sufis of Khurāsān also utilized another type of a structure known as a *duwayra* (little house), which was a smaller space attached to a larger khānaqāh. A *duwayra* was usually set aside for itinerant dervishes. We have reports of Abū ʿAbd al-Raḥmān al-Sulamī, Abū Saʿīd-i Abī ʾl-Khayr, and Abū ʾl-Qāsim Qushayrī all using *duwayra*s.[90] However, as had been previously the case with the term Sufi, the term khānaqāh became more prominent in Persian sources of the fifth/eleventh century and beyond, particularly when issues of patronage were concerned.

Later sources came to credit Abū Saʿīd-i Abī ʾl-Khayr with having founded the first khānaqāh in a similar fashion to how Niẓām al-Mulk would be (erroneously) acknowledged as the founder of the first madrasa. These are both indications not of historical fact but of the way in which institutions associated with the two Saljūq figures came to be seen as paradigmatic by later authors. Zakariyā Qazwīnī's *Āthār al-bilād*, composed in 661/1263, is typical of this tendency: "Abū Saʿīd-i Abī ʾl-Khayr was the first to establish a khānaqāh. Every day he would set up two spreads [*sufra*, for feeding the poor and the itinerant]. All the manners of the Sufis are based on him, as is abandoning the world. He laid down the foundations of the spiritual path (*ṭarīqa*) and the manners of Sufism. All the great Sufi saints are his students."[91]

In spite of the above assertions, it is clear that there were many khānaqāhs before the time of Abū Saʿīd. *Asrār al-tawḥīd*, the very hagiography written for Abū Saʿīd, points to Abū ʿAbd al-Raḥmān al-Sulamī (d. 412/1021), Imām Qushayrī (d. 465/1072), and ʿAbd Allāh Bākū (d. 420/1029 to 442/1050) as individuals who visited khānaqāhs.[92] Other contemporaries of Abū Saʿīd are also reported to have received him in their own khānaqāhs, thus dismissing the notion that Abū Saʿīd established the first such institution.[93]

Fluidity of the Boundary between Khānaqāh and Madrasa

An important aspect of the intellectual milieu of fifth-/eleventh-century Khurāsān was the fluidity of the boundary between ʿulamāʾ and Sufis, the madrasa and the khanāqāh. Recent studies of the Saljūq era that continue to rely on outdated models of "metaphysical bipolarity" between the two groups are surely misleading in this regard.[94] The fluidity and movement between the two groups was well in place before the rise of al-Ghazālī and Niẓām al-Mulk. Some individuals who are identified as both Shāfiʿī and Sufi, such as Abū Saʿd al-Astarābādī (d. 440/1048–49), established madrasas.[95] Another patron, Abū Saʿd al-Kharkūshī (d. 404/1013 or 407/1016) established both a madrasa and a khānaqāh.[96] The relationship between Sufis and ʿulamāʾ is one of overlapping spheres of identity, and not a mutually exclusive one.

There is ample anecdotal evidence to suggest the fluidity of the movement of scholars between the khānaqāh and the madrasa. Abū ʿAlī Daqqāq (d. 1015) is said to have established a khānaqāh in the city of Nasā.[97] His son-in-law and disciple, the famed Abū ʾl-Qāsim Qushayrī, is depicted as having received people in his *ribāṭ* and as having retreated to his own *zāwiya* for more personal matters.[98] Both Daqqāq and Qushayrī also operated through a madrasa that later came to be known as the Qushayrī madrasa, established in 391/1001.[99] The son of Qushayrī, Imām Abū Naṣr, is stated to have spoken both in the Niẓāmīya madrasa and in the ribāṭ of the Sufis.[100] The famous al-Ghazālī (d. 505/1111), who is in many ways the archetypal madrasa intellectual of premodern Islam, is depicted in later sources as having spent his last days in "a khānaqāh for the sake of Sufis, and a madrasa for sake of those who seek knowledge."[101] Later sources such as Ibn Kathīr remember him in the following way: "Every day, many people would gather in the ribāṭ to listen to him."[102] The marker between khānaqāhs and madrasas is depicted not as a wall but as a porous membrane that would allow for an infusion of ideas from and across both sides.

There are even anecdotes that seek to capture the very moments of movement for particular scholars from one institution to the other. One such account is told by Khwāja Abū ʿAlī Fārmadī (d. 1082), who records that in his youth he had gone to Nīshāpūr to study in the Sarājān madrasa. He states that he fell in love with Shaykh Abū Saʿīd-i Abī ʾl-Khayr upon meeting him and that the love for the Sufi folk was greatly increased in his heart. He eventually took his books and possessions "from the madrasa to the khānaqāh."[103] This physical *hijra* symbolizes the opportunity for some scholars to pursue knowledge both in the madrasa and in the khānaqāh, now tending to one, now to the other. In the case of Fārmadī, the khānaqāh education is seen as completing his earlier madrasa training. Abū ʿAlī Fārmadī was the teacher of both Abū Ḥāmid Ghazālī and Aḥmad Ghazālī, two other scholars who would also navigate between the madrasa and the khānaqāh.[104] The hagiography of Abū Saʿīd-i Abī ʾl-Khayr also features narratives from other figures who were moving back and forth between the madrasa and khānaqāh.[105]

Important Saljūq madrasa intellectuals, most notably Abū Ḥāmid al-Ghazālī, also concerned themselves at this period with the proper behavior of those in a khānaqāh. Al-Ghazālī issued two fatwās, one in Persian and one in Arabic, in which he dealt with questions, such as whether it was proper for those who resided in a khānaqāh to be fed through the endowments set up for these establishments, and sins, such as being alone with women, wearing silk, or wearing gold rings. He also included associating with unbearded youths in these offenses. Significantly for our purposes, al-Ghazālī also points out that a Sufi who seeks the financial resources of a sultan who has attained to riches in a forbidden manner (*ḥarām*) is no longer to be considered one of the Sufis, and the endowment of the Sufis are then forbidden for him.[106] As we will see in the case of Shīrāzī's objection to working in the Niẓāmīya madrasa, these are not mere theoretical points.

To conclude, both the madrasa and the khānaqāh were important centers of Muslim religious life in fifth-/eleventh- and sixth-/twelfth-century Islamic Iran, and the Saljūqs neglected neither. Saljūqs' patronage of Muslim religious life in all sites was a key component of Saljūq ideology.

Contesting Saljūq Apparatuses

All of the above apparatuses—the iqṭāʿ, the madrasa, the khānaqāh, and the system of surveillance and reconnaissance—were vital state apparatuses under the Great Saljūqs. Given the contested nature of Saljūq culture as a whole, it should not come as a surprise that every one of these apparatuses was challenged.

While Niẓām al-Mulk repeatedly argued for the importance of the postal-spy (*barīd*) system and the role of the spy (*ṣāḥib khabar*), it seems that the Saljūq Sultans did not share his vision. There was no perfectly uniform or uncontested model of Saljūq state or Saljūq rule. All these were contested from within and without. One may legitimately say that Niẓām al-Mulk's plan for orchestrating state apparatuses was impeded by the very Saljūq Sultans he served. It is with palatable frustration that Niẓām al-Mulk notes that the Ghaznavids had posted espionage and surveillance agents everywhere, as had been the habit of the kings since ancient times. However, he goes on to state that the house of the Saljūqs had not been enamoured of this practice.[107] This information can also be verified through ʿImād al-Dīn al-Kātib al-Iṣfahānī, who records that Alp Arslān had not been in favor of having undercover surveillance agents, nor of the network of postal agents (*ṣāhib barīd*) who would work for this goal.[108] In this case the challenge to Niẓām al-Mulk's vision came from within the Saljūq state, from the Saljūq Sultans themselves. Also, if we recall that Niẓām al-Mulk had provided for the possibility of forcing potential surveillance agents to undertake such a role, one might legitimately consider some of the would-be agents among those who contested and resisted this particular ideological state apparatus.

The next state apparatus to be contested was the iqṭāʿ. Under the Saljūqs, the iqṭāʿ became a crucial institution, in the opinion of one scholar "the dominant institution of the Great Saljūq Empire."[109] However, this did not mean that it went unchallenged. As we will see in chapter 6, one of the main Sufi intellectuals and judges of this time period, ʿAyn al-Quḍāt Hamadānī (d. 525/1131), challenged the legitimacy of the whole iqṭāʿ system, equating it with outright plunder. He wrote to his disciple ʿAzīz al-Dīn Mustawfī, who was the main treasurer of the Saljūqs, and reminded him that the lands either belonged to the dervishes (meaning here both the Sufis and the poor people) or to their specific owner. In the latter case, ʿAyn al-Quḍāt warned, the iqṭāʿ was a form of usurpation (*ghaṣb*).[110] The historical sources dealing with this time period reveal that ʿAyn al-Quḍāt's objection was not a hypothetical one, as there were many administrators who illegally confiscated the personal property of landowners, claiming it as their private iqṭāʿ.[111] ʿAyn al-Quḍāt's critique undermined the primary way the Saljūqs could pay their military and thus challenged the main fiscal policy of the Saljūqs.

The accusation of usurpation (*ghaṣb*) was also one repeated against the madrasa system. One of the more telling challenges to the madrasa system came from the first would-be appointee to the Baghdad Niẓāmīya, Abū Isḥāq Shīrāzī. When Niẓām al-Mulk had first contacted Abū Isḥāq to assume the post of leadership of the Baghdad Niẓāmīya, the learned scholar refused to accept the offer. It seems certain that Abū Isḥāq had serious reservations about the legitimacy of the ways that the land and material for the Niẓāmīya had been obtained. Ibn Khallikān states, "At the hour of prayer, Abû Ishak used to quit the college [i.e., Nizāmīya madrasa] and perform his devotions in a mosque; 'because,' he said, 'I have been informed that the greater part of the materials employed in the construction of the college have been procured illegally.'"[112]

Ibn Khallikān's account of Abū Isḥāq's hesitation to offer his prayer on grounds that might have been obtained through illegitimate means can also be verified through Sibṭ ibn al-Jawzī's *Mirʾāt al-zamān*.[113] George Makdisi astutely observes that Abū Isḥāq's own juridical text, the *al-Tanbīh fī ʾl-fiqh ʿala madhhab al-Imām al-Shāfiʿī* includes an injunction against praying on usurped grounds.[114] Ibn al-Athīr offers a complementary narrative. He records that, when the construction of the Niẓāmīya was concluded in 459/1067, the teaching post was offered to (and expected of) Abū Isḥāq Shīrāzī. He, however, was nowhere to be found. The reason for his delay was that, when he was headed to the school, he ran into a youth who posed a challenge to the learned scholar: "How can you teach in a place which has been usurped?" (*kayfa tudarrisu fī makānin maghṣūbin?*) Shīrāzī changed his mind and did not attend the ceremonies.

While the above narratives do document a challenge to the legitimacy of the Saljūq patronage of the madrasa system, their resolution also reveals a great deal about Niẓām al-Mulk's forceful powers of persuasion. When Shīrāzī did not show up for his appointed chair, the teaching post was offered to Shaykh Abū Manṣūr ibn Yūsuf ibn Ṣabbāgh, the author of the *al-Shāmil.* He only taught at the madrasa for twenty days, when Abū Isḥāq Shīrāzī took over the teaching responsibilities there.[115] He had been persuaded to accept the appointment. Once again Niẓām al-Mulk had gotten his way, defusing a challenge to one of his state apparatuses.

Reading Contests to Legitimacy as Piety

A sign of the complete success of the ideological operations of Niẓām al-Mulk is the way in which even challenges to his state apparatuses—and ultimately his own authority—were interpreted as virtues by later historians. As we have seen, Abū Isḥāq Shīrāzī had reservations about working at the Niẓāmīya. Hindū Shāh Nakhjavānī's *Tajārib al-salaf*, which was composed in 724/1323, records an episode from the end of Niẓām al-Mulk's life. A few lines of this document, which is replete with Saljūq ideological claims of correct belief, will be quoted here:

> It is said that the Master [Niẓām al-Mulk] was pure of belief (*pāk-iʿtiqād*) and had a Muslim heart (*musalmān-dil*). He was more concerned and suffered more for the Hereafter than for This world. At one point, it occurred to him to write down how he had dealt with all of God Almighty's servants, and asked all the religious scholars and the great ones of the faith to sign it as witnesses. He would then have that document buried with him.
>
> Even though such documents are unprecedented, and are not mentioned in the purified Sacred Law (*sharīʿa*), they wrote it down on the

> account of the Master's orthodoxy (*nīkū iʿtiqādī*). Every one of the great ones of the faith recorded his testimony on this document. As for Imām Abū Isḥāq . . . even though he was the lecturer at the Niẓāmīya and had received the generosity and blessing of the Master . . . when his turn came up, he wrote on it: "Ḥasan is the best of the tyrants." (*ḥasan khayr al-ẓalama*)
>
> When they brought this document before the Master, and he saw Abū Isḥāq's hand-writing, he cried and said: "None of these great ones have said the truth the way that he has." After the Master's passing away, someone had a dream of him in which he said: "God Almighty has forgiven me, and shown me mercy—all on the count of the true words of the master Abū Isḥāq."[116]

In the above account, what had been undoubtedly a critique of usurpation is recast. The whole episode is retold from the perspective of Niẓām al-Mulk's *nīkū iʿtiqādī*—the quality of "correct-belief," that is, orthodoxy. Abū Isḥāq addresses Niẓām al-Mulk not by his honorific or as *khwāja* (the title the rest of the narrative uses in referring to him) but simply as what he was when he came into this world and when he would leave it: Ḥasan. Ḥasan (Niẓām al-Mulk) might be the best of the tyrants, but he was still a tyrant. In a typical hagiographic move, this critique is said to have earned Niẓām al-Mulk's salvation. What is not dealt with, of course, is Abū Isḥāq Shīrāzī's historical challenging of the legitimacy of the Niẓāmīya madrasa. In this case, Abū Isḥāq's challenge is probably part of a much wider objection to all madrasas, all government-sponsored institutions that may have been illegitimately set up through usurpation of funds. It was part of the premodern piety of many scholars to refuse to work or to live in places acquired through usurped funds.

All of the above might be seen as individual challenges to the state apparatuses set up by Niẓām al-Mulk. As I will document in chapter 6, there would be one figure, ʿAyn al-Quḍāt Hamadānī, who challenged at a more basic level not merely the individual state apparatuses but the whole foundation of Saljūq religious ideology. He critiqued the iqṭāʿ and the madrasa, the association of the ʿulamāʾ with the state as well as the injustice of the Saljūq Turks. However, before we get to that material, we have to document the reciprocity of state apparatuses under the Saljūqs. Many of the above apparatuses, such as the establishment of the madrasa and patronage of scholars, may be seen as the Saljūqs' attempt to empower knowledge. There would be a corresponding move on the behalf of the religious scholars to acknowledge Saljūq power.

These two components, empowering knowledge and acknowledging power, are linked, being mutually dependent on one another. The acknowledging of Saljūq power grew out of and in response to Saljūq attempts to empower knowledge. I will now turn to the attempts of the arch-madrasa scholar, Abū Ḥāmid al-Ghazālī, to offer successive legitimization theories of the Saljūqs.

Chapter Four

The Shifting Politics of al-Ghazālī

In the last chapter I presented many of the apparatuses used by Niẓām al-Mulk and his descendants in the ideological legitimization of the Saljūqs. The madrasa and the khānaqāh constitute the two main religious institutions patronized by the Saljūqs. Chapters 5 and 6 will discuss the relations between Sufis and the Saljūqs, both in terms of legitimizing the state and contesting it. In this chapter, however, I will focus on the most well-known representative of the madrasa system, Abū Ḥāmid al-Ghazālī, and his attempts at legitimizing the Saljūq state and its dominant religious ideology.

The life of Abū Ḥāmid al-Ghazālī is well documented in biographical dictionaries and has received a lot of attention from contemporary scholars.[1] As such, only the broad outlines of his life will be provided here, emphasizing the details relevant to our concern with documenting his political treatises used in legitimizing the Saljūqs.

Al-Ghazālī was born at Ṭūs in the year 450/1058. He received much of his training through Imām al-Ḥaramayn al-Juwaynī until the latter passed away in 478/1085.[2] His first interaction with the Saljūqs came when he went to the military encampment (*ʿaskar*) of Niẓām al-Mulk, where he was received with honor. Starting with this formative event, there is a close association between political power and religious inquiry in the life of al-Ghazālī. Even at this early stage, al-Ghazālī acted as a *rasūl* (mediating messenger) between Sultan Malik-Shāh and the Caliph al-Muqtadī.[3] This mediating presence between the caliphate and the sultanate would only become more significant with the passing of time.

Al-Ghazālī and Niẓām al-Mulk were entrusted with the dubious yet essential task of negotiating between the contending political factions: the Saljūq Sultans and the ʿAbbāsid Caliphs. In chapter 2, I documented Niẓām al-Mulk's advice that the two should work in tandem. While Niẓām al-Mulk's advice with respect to the relationship between the sultanate and the caliphate remained more or less constant, I will demonstrate that al-Ghazālī's political thought with respect to this issue underwent a gradual transformation. Furthermore, Niẓām al-Mulk and al-Ghazālī were both entrusted with the task of dealing with contending intellectual claimants to religious knowledge: Sufis, jurists, dialectical theologians, philosophers, and Ismāʿīlīs. Given the role of Niẓām al-Mulk as al-Ghazālī's main patron up until the vizier's death in 485/1092, it should not come as a surprise that the patrons of Niẓām al-Mulk were also the patrons of al-Ghazālī and were legitimized by him. Likewise, the enemies of the great vizier were likely to receive the skillful critique of Ghazālī, the most prominent scholar of this age.

As had been the case with Niẓām al-Mulk, al-Ghazālī also carried on vigorous polemics against the Ismāʿīlīs. While the Saljūqs fought the Ismāʿīlīs on a military front, al-Ghazālī carried on the intellectual component of this same assault. Among his most well-known critique of Ismāʿīlī teachings is the *Faḍāʾiḥ al-bāṭinīya wa faḍāʾil al-mustaẓhirīya*.[4] This text has received a great deal of attention from western scholars, perhaps even before Goldziher's edition of this text appeared as *Streitschrift des Gazāli gegen die Bāṭinijja-Sekte* in 1916. A lesser-known, though no less important, treatise he wrote against the Ismāʿīlīs was the *Ḥimāqa ahl al-ibāḥa*, which was edited by Otto Pretzl as *Die Streitschrift des Gazālī gegen die Ibāḥīja*.[5] In this text, al-Ghazālī accuses the Ismāʿīlīs of many conventional polemical tropes, such as drunken behavior, fornication, and mass orgies. In general, the Ismāʿīlīs are depicted as breaking all the commandments of the Sharīʿa.[6]

In addition, al-Ghazālī repeatedly wrote against the philosophers. Of these writings, the most well-known is the *Tahāfut al-falāsifa*.[7] In this treatise, he specifically refuted a number of points held by the philosophers, including the claims that the world is preeternal,[8] that God does not have knowledge of particulars,[9] and that the body is not resurrected in the Hereafter.[10] While he raises a number of other objections against the philosophers, it is these three criteria that he returns to in the conclusion of the book. Furthermore, according to al-Ghazālī, it is based on these three criteria that the philosophers must be declared infidels (*takfīruhum lābud*).[11] He returns to the same conclusion in his *al-Munqidh min al-ḍalāl*[12] and reiterates his position that Muslim *faylasūfs* such as Ibn Sīnā and al-Fārābī must be reckoned as infidels.[13] Elsewhere, al-Ghazālī had critiqued much of kalām, stating that it was useful only as a defense of the faith in polemics and for a person whose weak faith could use such rational disputations. Beyond this limited utility, however, he recognized little of value in kalām.[14]

Al-Ghazālī's ranking of the various intellectual disciplines has already received a great deal of attention, perhaps most insightfully through the work of Marshall Hodgson, who concludes, "Ghazālī assured kalām a necessary but not very honourable niche in Islam."[15] Hodgson is certainly correct in reminding us that the *al-Munqidh* should not be read as a "straight forward autobiography."[16] Anticipating a point that I will return to in chapter 6, Hodgson correctly points out that "the doubts [al-Ghazālī] was repeatedly tormented with, all seem to have been directed not only toward achieving a personal religious certainty but also toward giving him a sound basis for religious leadership."[17]

Al-Ghazālī's quest for religious leadership brings us inevitably to the institution he was situated in, where his post was established for him by Niẓām al-Mulk to serve as the pulpit for the propagation of the Saljūq-sponsored interpretation of Islam. This institution, the Niẓāmīya madrasa, would be both al-Ghazālī's greatest podium and his prison.

Escape from Madrasa

In the year 484/1091, al-Ghazālī was appointed as the *mudarris* of the Baghdad Niẓāmīya. This appointment is noted in historical chronicles with great pomp and circumstance. In the typically hyperbolic prose of *Zubdat al-nuṣra*, ʿImād al-Dīn states, "In the year 484 [i.e., 1091 C.E.] al-Ghazālī came to Baghdad to teach in the Niẓāmīya madrasa. In terms of knowledge, he was an overflowing ocean (*baḥran ẕākhiran*), and a luminous full moon (*badran ẓāhiran*). The wonders of his knowledge have radiated to the East and the West."[18] Clearly, this was a moment of great prestige for al-Ghazālī as well as the Saljūqs. At this stage, the Niẓāmīya madrasa was arguably the most prestigious institution of higher learning in Islamdom, and al-Ghazālī its brightest star.

Soon after this appointment, the stability of the Saljūq regime was severely undermined by the assassination of Niẓām al-Mulk in 485/1092 and the passing away of Malik-Shāh about a month after that. To make matters worse, the Caliph al-Muqtadī also passed away in 487/1094. With the head of the Saljūqs and the ʿAbbāsids gone, and his own patron assassinated, al-Ghazālī did the unthinkable by giving up his post as the *mudarris* at the Niẓāmīya in 488/1095.

Al-Ghazālī's own account of this event comes up in his *Munqidh min al-ḍalāl* and needs to be read with great skepticism. W. M. Watt and others have recognized that al-Ghazālī's schemas and record of the unfolding of developments are hard to justify with respect to chronological data from other sources.[19] In the *Munqidh*, al-Ghazālī talks about his decision to leave the Baghdad Niẓāmīya in the section dealing with the path of the Sufis. He states that it was after having studied the works of the theologians, philosophers, and Ismāʿīlīs and having despaired of the possibility of attaining to certainty (*yaqīn*) that he became aware of his own attraction to worldly desires, in distinction to the longing to follow on the spiritual path. He goes on to state that he eventually grew unable to speak at his lectures and could "hardly swallow or digest a single mouthful of food."[20] Furthermore, he discusses that in order for him to be able to leave Baghdad, he had to come up with a ruse, pretending to be traveling to Mecca while in reality making plans to go to Damascus. He states, "I took this precaution in case the Caliph and all my friends should oppose my resolve to make my residence in Syria."[21]

Many of the later sources have also reported this narrative and interpreted it as al-Ghazālī's setting out on the spiritual path. An example is the historian Ibn Kathīr, who states, "In the Dhu ʾl-qaʿda of 488 [i.e., 1095], Ghazālī left Baghdad for Jerusalem. He left his teaching post at the Niẓāmīya, and became an ascetic in the world. He would only wear rough garments."[22] The reference to rough garments is evocative of the Sufis' penchant for donning wool (*ṣūf*). Ibn Kathīr's account also depicts him as having spent every day with many people in a Sufi hospice (*ribāṭ*).

Some contemporary scholars have been more skeptical, leading to a divergence of opinions offered as to the cause of al-Ghazālī's abandoning of his post at the Niẓāmīya. Many have argued for the necessity of reading this event in light of political events in Baghdad at that time. Duncan Black MacDonald argued that al-Ghazālī's departure might have something to do with tensions between him and the Saljūq Sultan Bark-Yāruq.[23] Alternatively, F. Jabre has suggested that this departure was due to al-Ghazālī's fear of being assassinated at the hands of Ismāʿīlīs.[24] Others scholars have offered more spiritual explanations for this event, more or less taking al-Ghazālī at his word. R. J. McCarthy interprets al-Ghazālī's sudden departure as having been due to "a true *conversion* [emphasis his], a real *tawba* [turning to God], a genuine *metanoia* [change of mind and heart]."[25] In attempting to strike for a middle ground, W. M. Watt argues that the fear of Ismāʿīlīs could be seen as one factor among many.[26]

I would like to add another perspective on this issue: why would it have been so important for al-Ghazālī to mislead people about his plans to leave Baghdad? While I have a great deal of skepticism about reading the *Munqidh* as a straightforward work of autobiography, I do take al-Ghazālī quite seriously about the one point that most scholars have not noted so far: the real possibility that the "Iraq regime" (which he identifies with the caliph) might prevent him from leaving. In looking back on our discussion of the state apparatuses introduced by Niẓām al-Mulk in support of the dominant Saljūq state ideology, I discussed Niẓām al-Mulk's plans for a system of surveillance and reconnaissance. Here is one situation where the madrasa can obviously be much more than simply a place for learning and teaching. Following Foucault's lead, I suggest that the madrasa is also a watchtower. It is a place for those scholars notable enough to deserve their own appointment to watch and intellectually discipline younger scholars—and be watched. So long as al-Ghazālī was the *mudarris* of the illustrious Niẓāmīya madrasa, his words, actions, and whereabouts would be easily known to the administration of the Saljūqs and ʿAbbāsids. Al-Ghazālī's escape is not simply that of one yearning for a spiritual life, it is also the desire to escape the gaze he was under at the madrasa. A recent Iranian scholar, ʿAbdul Ḥusayn Zarrīnkūb has written a thought-provoking work on the life of al-Ghazālī called *Farār az madrasa* (*Escape from Madrasa*). While it might be an exaggeration to equate the madrasa with a prison outright, Zarrīnkūb's work does allow us to contemplate the pressures that Ghazālī felt under the gaze of the Saljūq system.

Al-Ghazālī's desire to distance himself from the watchful eye of both the political and intellectual aspects of Saljūq administration is evident through a vow he made at the shrine of Abraham in Hebron/Khalīl in the year 489/1096. He states that he promised to follow through with three promises: 1) not to accept contributions from "any Sultan"; 2) to never go to greet "any Sultan"; and 3) not to engage in any dialectical disputation (*munāẓara*).[27] There are two telling points about the vow. One is the linkage again between patronage of the sultans and engagement in intellectual disputations. Al-Ghazālī's vow is to avoid both, as they are so clearly entangled. The second point is a bit subtler and more indicative of al-Ghazālī's inability—whether through his own volition or the overpowering will of others—to stay aloof of politics and political institutions completely. We know about the above vow through al-Ghazālī's collection of private letters. This collection, titled the *Faḍāʾil al-anām* consists mainly of letters al-Ghazālī wrote to various Saljūq notables toward the end of his life. The irony is inescapable: in a letter written to Saljūq administrators, al-Ghazālī is reminding them of his earlier vow never to have anything to do with the head of the Saljūq state! We might surmise that either al-Ghazālī was unable to keep the vow he had made or that at best the distinction between avoiding sultans while engaging Saljūq administrators is a bit too facile. Ghazālī was, and remained forever, a political creature.

The scenario al-Ghazālī himself presents is that he had to be coerced back to a more public role in the Saljūq regime after twelve years. The mediating party is held to be Fakhr al-Mulk, Niẓām al-Mulk's son, who pleads with al-Ghazālī to return to the Niẓāmīya. Al-Ghazālī repeatedly refuses to return to the Baghdad Niẓāmīya. As reasons for this refusal, he states that his homeland (*waṭan*) is Khurāsān, that by that stage of his life he was married with children (thus making it harder for him to travel to ʿIrāq), and that there were 150 students under his care there.[28] Perhaps more interestingly, he states that he would not be able to honor his vows in Baghdad, since "in Baghdad one has to engage in disputations, and one cannot refuse going to the Caliphal Abode to offer greetings." Could it be the case that Baghdad had an even more active surveillance scene? It is obvious that it was far more contentious and polemical. For whatever reason, al-Ghazālī's actions indicate that he felt freer in Khurāsān than in Baghdad.[29] He does, nonetheless, agree to teach at the Nīshāpur Niẓāmīya in 499/1106. Towards the end of his life, al-Ghazālī felt more comfortable being away from Baghdad (the center of the ʿAbbāsids) and closer to Khurāsān (the center of the Saljūqs). As I will demonstrate, this geographical preference away from the ʿAbbāsids and toward the Saljūqs was mirrored in his political theories as well.

It is against the above turbulent background that we need to contextualize al-Ghazālī's important political treatises. These were not simply abstract texts written about timeless principles of government but rather quite timely—and as I will argue, shifting—responses to the political scene. It is to these writings that we now move, as they mirror the above tendency of al-Ghazālī to distance himself from the ʿAbbāsids and move closer (both rhetorically and geographically) toward the Saljūqs.

Al-Ghazālī's Political Writings

Given the great scholarly attention previously devoted to madrasa intellectuals such as al-Juwaynī and al-Ghazālī, it is not my aim to offer a comprehensive overview of their thought. Rather, my concern is with their role in justifying Saljūq state ideology through writing political treatises detailing the necessity for the sultanate.

Given Al-Ghazālī's prominence in Islamic studies, his political thought has already received a great deal of attention from a number of scholars as varied as Henri Laoust,[30] Leonard Binder,[31] Ann Lambton,[32] and Caroline Hillenbrand.[33] While my analysis of Ghazālī's political theory—or rather, theor*ies*—is indebted to all of the above, it also seeks to advance my argument. Many of the previous approaches to al-Ghazālī's political theory suffer from the problematic of focusing on one of his political treatises and developing a political philosophy out of that one text. While that approach is valuable in its own right, it only takes a snap shot of a thinker who was perpetually shifting and adjusting his articulation based on the world around him. For example, Lambton's work deals primarily with the *Naṣīḥat al-mulūk*. Likewise, Binder's work focuses mainly on the *Iqtiṣād fi 'l-iʿtiqād*. My own approach most closely approximates that of Hillenbrand, who correctly recognizes the necessity of following the chronology of al-Ghazālī's political writings. However, I do take issue with her conclusion that "there is a considerable degree of consistency in al-Ghazāli's view on government."[34] I am as interested in the consistency and unity in al-Ghazālī's political thought as I am in the shifts and the disjunctions.

There is still the need to document the fundamental change that al-Ghazālī's political theory undergoes in his successive writings. He gradually shifts from talking about the caliphate to a cooperation of the caliphate and the sultanate and ends with a frank justification of Saljūq Turks as being the people to whom God has given "raw power" (*shawka*). It is well-known that in more philosophical and theological matters, Ibn Rushd criticized al-Ghazālī for having been "all things to all men."[35] That criticism could just as easily have been made about his political theories. I will document his successive political writings, going through the *Faḍā'iḥ al-bāṭinīya, al-Iqtiṣād fi 'l-iʿtiqād, Iḥyā' ʿulūm al-dīn*, and *Naṣīḥat al-mulūk*, before concluding with the *Tuḥfat al-mulūk* and *Pand-nāma*.

Faḍā'iḥ al-bāṭinīya wa faḍā'il al-mustaẓhirīya

This text has long been recognized as one of al-Ghazālī's authentic texts and was discussed by Goldziher as far back as 1916. The *Faḍā'iḥ* is a great indication of the *timely* and ideological nature of al-Ghazālī's political writings. The treatise was composed at the request of the ʿAbbāsid Caliph al-Mustaẓhir (d. 512/1118). Al-Mustaẓhir ascended to the caliphate upon his father's death in Muḥarram 487/February 1094. Al-Ghazālī composed this text prior to his leaving Baghdad in Dhū 'l-Qaʿda 488/November 1095. Therefore, we can pinpoint the composition of this *Faḍā'iḥ* to sometime around 488/1095.

When both Niẓām al-Mulk and Malik-Shāh passed away in 485/1092, Saljūq administration was at a transition point and somewhat more vulnerable. As a result, there is hardly any mention in this text of the Saljūq Sultanate apart from a discussion of the "Turks" possessing power. The very title of the work is rather revealing, linking together his sustained polemic against the Bāṭinīya (Ismāʿīlīs) to his praise for the Caliph al-Mustaẓhir. The work proceeds through ten chapters, the first eight of which are concerned with establishing al-Ghazālī's refutation of the Ismāʿīlīs. This refutation is not carried out in abstract: it leads directly to the last two chapters of the work in which al-Ghazālī claims that the Imām who "stands on Truth" and is to be obeyed in that age is none other than Imam al-Mustaẓhir.[36]

This text also discusses the "Turks," but not in a way that the Saljūqs would have found appealing. They are outsiders to the conversation between al-Ghazālī and the caliph. They are treated not as the holders of the sultanate—an institution that does not figure into this treatise—but simply as holders of power. Al-Ghazālī's presentation of the Turks is frank and not very flattering.

He begins with a discussion of qualities that the caliph must possess inherently (*khuluqī*), before moving on to those that he can acquire (*iktisābī*). The first "acquirable" quality presented by al-Ghazālī is what he terms *najda*, "efficacy."[37] It is under the rubric of the caliph's *najda* that al-Ghazālī brings up the Saljūqs, simply called "the Turks" here.[38] He states, "What is intended by *najda* in the case of the Imāms [i.e., caliphs] is the manifestation (*ẓuhūr*) of force (*shawka*)."[39] There is obviously a pun here between *ẓuhūr* and the name of the caliph, al-Mustaẓhir. However, key to al-Ghazālī's argument is the concept of raw force, *shawka*. He honestly admits, "In our age, *shawka* is one of the inherent traits of the Turks" (*fa ʾl-shawka fī ʿaṣrinā hādha min aṣnāf al-khalāʾiq li ʾl-turk*).[40] This association of brute, raw force with the Saljūq Turks is greatly reminiscent of Alp Arslān's declaration in the *Siyāsat-nāma* that "we have conquered this country only through the sword, and by force."[41]

In the subsequent passages, al-Ghazālī argues that God has so inclined the Turks to love the caliph and serve him by suppressing the enemies of his *dawla*. He goes on to state that should there be any insurrection against the ʿAbbāsids, the Turks would wage jihād against the rebels, even if it meant their own deaths. Al-Ghazālī rhetorically ends by asking, "What *shawka* in the world can match this?" (*wa ayya shawka fi ʾl-dunyā taqābalu hādha ʾl-shawka*"?)[42]

While the above does recognize the usefulness of the Saljūqs, it is far from incorporating them into the same discourse of legitimacy that is afforded the caliph. That development would gradually come in al-Ghazālī's subsequent political writings.

Al-iqtiṣād fi ʾl-iʿtiqād

This treatise covers a range of topics from the necessity of theological discourse to a discussion of God's being, essence, attributes, and actions.[43] Al-Ghazālī composed this text sometime around 488/1095, although it came after the *al-Mustaẓhirī*.[44] Unlike that text, *al-Iqtiṣād* was not dedicated to a caliph or a sultan. Hillenbrand postulates that the absence of a patron might have freed al-Ghazālī to discuss political matters with greater freedom in this text.[45]

The most relevant part of this text for our purposes is the last segment, which is composed of four chapters dealing with prophethood, the imamate (i.e., caliphate), resurrection, and charging with unbelief. The chapter on the imamate starts out by mentioning that questions about the imamate are not a matter of intellectual disputation (*maʿqūlāt*) or transmitted disciplines (*manqūlāt*) but rather belong to the domain of jurisprudence (*fiqhīyāt*).[46] A key phrase in the whole chapter is the term *sulṭān muṭāʿ* (a "sultan who is obeyed"), which impregnates the whole discussion. It might be argued that al-Ghazālī is using the term *sulṭān* to refer to an abstract notion of authority. While that is a possibility, it is hard to believe that a figure as politically shrewd as al-Ghazālī would have ignored the ramifications of such a phrase in an era when Saljūq Sultans had been present for over 40 years. As Hillenbrand has astutely noted, the chapter starts out with the phrase *imām* and moves on to a section where the "obeyed imām" and "obeyed sultan" are used interchangeably. The next phrase refers to them in conjunction: "death of sultans and imams." At the end of the discussion, al-Ghazālī reverts to the term imām yet again.[47]

There is no clear theoretical model here for the joint cooperation between the sultanate and the caliphate. However, it is a thought-provoking and perhaps playful indication of the direction al-Ghazālī's political thought had moved in a short year since the composition of the *al-Mustaẓhirī*. The next text, al-Ghazālī's magnum opus, would extend this discussion even further.

Iḥyāʾ ʿulūm al-dīn

This massive collection is universally held to be al-Ghazālī's masterpiece, and was most likely composed between 489/1096 and 495/1102. The *Iḥyāʾ (Revivification of the Religious Sciences)* is rightly held up as a highly influential compendium of ethical teachings. Given its prominence, it is thus surprising that more scholars have not analyzed its political discourse. The relevant political sections of the *Iḥyāʾ* come up in the chapter dealing with licit and illicit matters (*ḥalāl wa ḥarām*). This chapter is composed of seven segments, the fifth of which deals with sultans. Much of the discussion revolves around whether or not it is licit to accept money from sultans, given that most of the possessions of sultans have been obtained through usurpation.[48]

The discussion moves to what must surely have been a resonant reality in premodern Islam: that of an ignorant and tyrannical sultan (*al-sulṭān al-ẓālim al-jāhil*).[49] Al-Ghazālī considers the case of such a sultan who is in possession of brute force (*shawka*) and where attempts to remove him would inevitably lead to social strife (*fitna*). It is al-Ghazālī's view that public good demands that obedience be accorded to him. One has to obey him (*wa wajibat al-ṭāʿa lahu*) as one has obeyed military commanders.[50] In short, it is better to obey an unjust ruler than to undergo the social strife that would result in the process of trying to remove him. Even if one objects that the Saljūq Sultans are unjust, the interest of the public good deems it better to put up with them than to revolt against them. In other words, the argument has shifted subtly from the argument of justice/injustice to merely one of the broader social consequences of standing up to the admittedly unjust sultan.

Al-Ghazālī then moves on to a discussion of the relationship between the caliphate and the sultanate, here spelled out more clearly than in his previous works. He states that the caliphate belongs to the ʿAbbāsids, as he has previously stated in the *al-Mustaẓhirī*. Furthermore, the caliph is the person acknowledged by the possessors of force (*ṣāḥib al-shawka*). Likewise, the sultan is one who possesses command (*ḥukm*) and judgment (*al-qaḍāʾ*). He has to seize the *shawka* and be obedient to the caliph. He will be recognized through the *khuṭba* and the issuing of coins in his name.[51] The remarkable aspect of the above work is the way in which the caliphate and the sultanate are portrayed in a symbiotic relationship. Once again, there is a realistic acknowledgment that in his own age real power rested with the Saljūqs. However, this *shawka* is made—in theory—to serve the ʿAbbāsid Caliphate and protect it. Likewise, the caliphate is depicted as bestowing honorific titles and legitimization upon the brute force of the sultans. Ideally, the two would support and legitimize each other. In practice, however, the passage certainly leaves the possibility open for the Saljūqs to appoint anyone they wished from the ʿAbbāsids to the caliphate, so long as they professed loyalty to that figure. As al-Ghazālī himself states in an understated fashion: *wilāya* [authority of the Caliph] in this age follows from *shawka* (force): *al-wilāya al'ān lā tatabbaʿu illa ʾl-shawka* (*wilāya* [authority of the caliph] in this age follows from *shawka* [force]).[52]

The brute force of the Saljūqs, which in its most destructive manifestation had led to the devastation of so many Iranian cities in Khurāsān, is now interpreted as something slightly more than a necessary evil and slightly less than a virtue. Al-Ghazālī in fact deems its existence necessary for the caliphate to exist. The most powerful intellectual of the day thus acknowledges the power of the Saljūqs. Raw force, which by itself would only be a partial legitimizing source, is thus brought under the sacrosanct aura of religious legitimacy.

This theoretical model of cooperation between the Saljūqs and the ʿAbbāsids would be tilted even more in the favor of the Saljūq sultans in al-Ghazālī's next treatise, his *Naṣīḥat al-mulūk*.

Naṣīḥat al-mulūk

This is al-Ghazālī's best-known and most frequently cited political treatise. While the Persian original was rarely seen after its composition, the Arabic translation of the text, titled *al-Tibr al-masbūk fī naṣīḥat al-mulūk*, was frequently circulated in Mamlūk and Ottoman times.[53] (For a particularly fine example of this Arabic translation, see illustration 4.1.) One of al-Ghazālī's personal letters states that he composed the *Naṣīḥat al-mulūk* in the year 503/1109–10, which would make it one of his last works. There has been a vigorous debate regarding the patron to whom the treatise was dedicated. Some have seen the text as having been written for the Saljūq Sultan Sanjar immediately prior to his rise to power while others have preferred to see it as being addressed to Sultan Muḥammad b. Malik-Shāh.[54] The Arabic translation, *Al-Tibr al-Masbūk*, opens with a dedication to Sultan Muḥammad b. Malik-Shāh, leading to a likely date of after 499/1105 for its composition. However, the Persian original only addresses the patron as *malik-i mashriq*, "ruler of the East," which leaves open the possibility of it having been composed for Sanjar prior to his assumption of the title of sulṭān.[55] If the later date for its composition, mentioned in the aforementioned letter, is to be trusted, that would also favor a dedication to Sultan Sanjar.

Aside from the question of attribution, there is also a vigorous debate about the authenticity of *Naṣīḥat al-mulūk*. The present Persian text of the *Naṣīḥat al-mulūk* exists in two parts. All scholars agree that the first part of the *Naṣīḥat al-mulūk* is authentic. The debate is about the second part of the text. The editor of the text, Humā'ī, wrestled with the question of its authenticity for over thirty years. In the beginning, he stated that both parts were authentic. While thirty years later he came to have some reservation about the second part, he still felt that on the whole the evidence favored the authenticity of this part as well. Furthermore, given that the Arabic translation, *al-Tibr al-Masbūk*, almost always features both parts, Humā'ī concluded, "Until there is sure, beyond-doubt proof that the second part is from other than Imām Ghazzālī, we too will consider it from his writings—until the opposite of such can be determined."[56]

After Humā'ī, scholars have debated the authenticity of the second part. Recent scholars of Iranian Sufism, such as ʿAbd al-Ḥusayn Zarrīnkūb[57] and Nasrollah Pourjavady, have also argued against the authenticity of *Naṣīḥat al-*

4.1. Al-Ghazālī's *Naṣīḥat al-Mulūk* (*Counsel for Kings*), a fifteenth-century Mamluk manuscript. (Courtesy of American University of Beirut/Library Archives)

mulūk.[58] Pourjavady in particular presents a convincing case that the second part of the *Naṣīḥat al-mulūk* cannot be authentic. Yet the most detailed argument against its authenticity was from Patricia Crone.[59] Crone bases her argument on a number of points: first, that al-Ghazālī omits a discussion of the caliphate/imamate.[60] Second, that the second part of *Naṣīḥat al-mulūk* is heavily critical of women.[61] And lastly, that the preoccupations of this text are "as thoroughly Iranian as those of al-Ghazālī are Islamic."[62] While Crone does raise some valid points, each of her objections can be answered persuasively. Al-Ghazālī's omission of the imamate would be consistent with a gradual move away from the imamate towards the sultanate, something we have already seen in the *Iqtiṣād* and the *Iḥyā'*. A negative view of women would be consisted with similar statements made by al-Ghazālī's patron, Niẓām al-Mulk, after the ordeal with Tarkān Khātūn. Lastly, the argument that the treatise reflects an "Iranian" rather than an "Islamic" norm already presupposes a reified notion of these two discourses. As we have seen, one of the tropes of historical and political writings of this time period is the extent to which various Persian and Central Asian motifs were integrated into existing Islamic discourses of authority. Niẓām al-Mulk's *Siyāsat-nāma* is a very good example of this newly emerged hybrid writing. Indeed, it is easy to show many direct borrowings from Niẓām al-Mulk's *Siyāsat-nāma* into the *Naṣīḥat al-mulūk*.[63] The argument against the authenticity of the *Naṣīḥat al-mulūk* and other writings that use Persian tropes of political authority is somewhat circular, and goes like this: Al-Ghazālī used only Islamic tropes, so *Naṣīḥat al-mulūk* cannot be deemed authentic. Since the *Naṣīḥat al-mulūk* is not authentic, al-Ghazālī only used Islamic tropes of authority. I am more open to the possibility of flux, change, and indeed hybridity in al-Ghazālī's thought.

In contrast to Patricia Crone, a number of other scholars who specialize in the Saljūq period have accepted the authenticity of both parts of the *Naṣīḥat al-mulūk*. These include Henri Laoust,[64] Ann Lambton,[65] F. R. C. Bagley (the translator of the *Naṣīḥat al-mulūk*),[66] Maurice Bouyges,[67] 'Abd al-Raḥmān Badawī,[68] and Jawād Ṭabāṭabā'ī.[69] Given the lack of consensus, and the objections to Crone's thesis, I propose that there is a good possibility that the second part of the *Naṣīḥat al-mulūk* might be authentic; there is still need for further research into the matter.

In terms of content, the *Naṣīḥat al-mulūk* marks a significant departure from al-Ghazālī's earlier political treatises such as *al-Mustaẓhirī* and *al-Iqtiṣād*. Ann Lambton attributes this to al-Ghazālī's concern with "practical duties of the ruler rather than the underlying theory."[70] I am not entirely convinced of this facile dichotomy. Attempts like Lambton's underestimate the extent to which al-Ghazālī's "underlying theory" itself might have undergone transformations and shifts in the turbulent decade since the composition of the *al-Mustaẓhirī*. Such tendencies attempt to impose an artificial continuity when the sources do not warrant it.

As documented above, there has been a great deal of scholarly debate over the authenticity of the second part of the *Naṣīḥat al-mulūk*. In the interest of clarity, I will treat the two parts separately. Lost in the controversy about the authenticity of the second part is that the first part—which is unanimously seen to be authentic by all scholars—already contains material in favor of the Saljūqs, justifying and legitimizing them so long as they maintain justice. In other words, justice by itself is seen as sufficient in legitimizing the Saljūqs, not service to the imamate. Furthermore, as we shall see, the Saljūqs' rule is seen as being determined by God.

In the undoubtedly authentic first part of the *Naṣīḥat al-mulūk*, al-Ghazālī starts out with a number of ḥadīths attributed to Prophet Muḥammad (Ṣ) focusing on the virtues of a just sultan. Among these is the statement that the closest and most beloved person to God is a just sultan (*sulṭān-i ʿādil*), whereas the lowliest and most inimical one to God is a tyrannical sultan (*sulṭān-i ẓālim*).[71] Al-Ghazālī records another tradition stating that in the Day of Resurrection God will not cast any glances in the direction of a tyrannical sultan.[72] Another attributed ḥadīth which links together political righteousness and religious orthodoxy—the hallmark of Saljūq religious ideology—states that two groups will be bereft of the Prophet's intercession in the Hereafter: tyrannical sultans and innovators (*mubtadiʿ*) in the affairs of religion.[73] Likewise, the most difficult of torments in the Hereafter is reserved for a tyrannical sultan.[74] Significantly, al-Ghazālī states, it is God Almighty who grants the rank of authority and sultanate (*daraja-yi wilāyat wa sulṭānī*) to someone, and in this rank an hour of their life has the same worth as the totality of the life of others.[75] Explicit in these discussions, which are again accepted as authentic by all al-Ghazālī scholars, is already the notion that it is God who has raised the Saljūq sultans to the rank of sultanate. It is not raw power that is responsible for the Saljūqs' rule but God's own selection of the sultans.

One of the last significant points in the first, undoubtedly authentic, part of the *Naṣīḥat al-mulūk* recalls one of the main points of Saljūq ideology: that of the sultans' patronage of religious scholars. Here al-Ghazālī states that while rule and authority carry many spiritual dangers for the sultans, they can find well-being by keeping close to "those religious scholars who keep the faith" (*ʿulamāʾ-yi dīn-dār*) so that the sultans can learn justice from these scholars. Furthermore, the sultan is to "thirst after" visiting religious scholars and yearn for advice from them. In addressing what must surely have been a common problem, al-Ghazālī also warns the king to stay away from the "religious scholars who anxiously yearn after the material world" (*ʿulamāʾyi harīṣ bar dunyā*), those who praise the king and lust after him only so that they can gain some of the "corpse" (i.e., worldly possessions) that the sultan holds.[76]

Even if one were to agree with Crone and Pourjavady (among others) that the second part of the *Naṣīḥat al-mulūk* is indeed spurious, there is already ample material in the above section to document a further shift if not outright rupture in al-Ghazālī's political thought. As we will see shortly, one of the later disputed texts, the *Tuḥfat al-mulūk*, draws heavily on this undisputed first part of the *Naṣīḥat al-mulūk*, thus increasing the possibility that it too is authentic.

If, on the other hand, we are to agree with Humā'ī and others that the second part of the *Naṣīḥat al-mulūk* is also to be seen as authentic, it further amplifies the point above about the rupture in al-Ghazālī's political thought. The discussion in part two of the *Naṣīḥat al-mulūk* recalls the importance of *dīn-i durust* (right religion) for an emperor. Al-Ghazālī states that the best quality an emperor can possess is right religion. He goes on to state that *dīn* and *pādshāhī* (emperor-ness) are twin brothers, having emerged out of the same mother's womb. The classical formulations of this well-known statement link *dīn* and *dawla*. Al-Ghazālī has clearly come to qualify *dawla* as *pādshāhī*: the model of state rule is simply collapsed into that of an emperor without considering alternate models. There is no mention of a caliph or caliphate as having a part in the *dawla* here. The state begins, emanates from, and is quintessentially represented in the person of the sultan/emperor.

Furthermore, al-Ghazālī stated that it would be imperative for a sultan to look throughout his realm for one who is *bad-dīn* (bad-religion). The sultan would have to intimidate such a person until he repented or, alternatively, exile him from the realm. In doing so, the realm would be cleansed (*pākīza*) from the folk of heretical innovation.[77] In such a series of linkages, religion and the realm are linked, and they are both capable of being good or bad, pure or impure. Like any other discussion of a system of purity, this will inevitably lead to a differentiation between the pure and the impure, and how they must be kept separate.[78] The realms of religious thought and the Saljūq realm both need to be purified through the linked association of religion and state. The discourse of *bad-dīn* (bad religion) versus *dīn-i durust* (right religion), along with the linkage of the *dīn* and *pādshāhī*, clearly mark the writing of these political treatises as an ideological state apparatus legitimizing Saljūq religious ideology.[79]

Al-Ghazālī's political theory in the *Naṣīḥat al-mulūk* differs from his own earlier theories as well as those of earlier figures such as al-Bāqillānī (d. 403/1013) and al-Baghdādī (d. 429/1037).[80] This can be documented through al-Ghazālī's attribution of titles that were traditionally reserved for the 'Abbāsid Caliphate to the Saljūq Sultans. At one point, al-Ghazālī states that the sultan is God's caliph (*khalīfa-yi khudā*).[81] In another passage, he records a prophetic tradition (*akhbār*) stating that the sultan is the shadow of God on Earth (*al-sulṭānu ẓillu 'l-lāhi fi 'l-arḍ*).[82] We know from Saljūq court documents, most importantly the *ʿAtabat al-kataba*, composed during Sultan Sanjar's reign, that the Saljūqs referred to themselves in precisely such a fashion. The *ʿAtabat al-kataba* records a diploma (*taqlīd*) issued to appoint a certain ʿImād al-Dīn Muḥammad ibn Aḥmad ibn Ṣāʿid to the post of *qāḍī* in Nīshāpūr. In this document, Sanjar is referred to as the "Shadow of God on Earth."[83] What is significant here is that al-Ghazālī would describe the sultans in the same way. The attribution of such conventionally caliphal titles to Saljūq Sultans must be seen as an undermining of ʿAbbāsid authority in this new political model. A further indication of al-Ghazālī's departure from his older model of political theory is his invocation of pre-Islamic Iranian models of kingship, such as the *farr* (Divine light seen as surrounding the ancient Iranian kings).[84] Al-Ghazālī holds, "It is incumbent on people to love one whom God has bestowed *pādshāhī* and Divine *farr*. One must obey the emperors."[85]

Having appropriated the legitimacy of the prophetic paradigm and that of pre-Islamic kings, al-Ghazālī does not ignore that of the ultimate trump card, the Qurʾan. In a remarkable display of an esoteric reading of the Qurʾan to suit his political interests, al-Ghazālī states that in the Qurʾanic verse, *Obey God, the Messenger, and those in charge*,[86] the phrase "those in charge" (*ūli ʾl-amr*) refers to the people's commanders. Therefore, al-Ghazālī concludes, "Whoever has been given religion through God Almighty must love his own emperor, and remain obedient to him."[87] The phrase *ūli ʾl-amr* has been subject to a great amount of legal, political, and mystical inspection and had previously been interpreted as referring to Shīʿa imams, Sufi teachers, etc. Here al-Ghazālī simply concludes that it refers to the holders of military power and command. As was the case with Niẓām al-Mulk's usage of the *barīd* and iqṭāʿ systems, al-Ghazālī was not the first scholar to offer these interpretations of the *ūli ʾl-amr* verse. Scholars as far back as Ṭabarī had already interpreted the *ūli ʾl-amr* to refer to the actual rulers. What is significant about al-Ghazālī's usage, rather, is the way in which his interpretation supports the Saljūq ideological project. The value of the legitimization brought by the most recognized intellectual of the age to Saljūq state ideology can hardly be overstated.

Up to this point in the discussion, al-Ghazālī has made two points. First, he has made a case for the preordained nature of Saljūq rule, since "God grants rule to whomever He wishes."[88] Secondly, he has argued for the necessity of a ruler to maintain justice, since "the realm can outlast infidelity but not injustice."[89] The only remaining step is for al-Ghazālī to directly legitimize the Saljūqs' possession of brute force. This he does with typical rigor and persuasiveness. He states that the well-being and cultivation of the world is intrinsically tied to the emperors and also that the moral rectitude of his own age was in ruin.[90] Furthermore, al-Ghazālī states, "The people of today are unlike the people of yesteryears. They have no shame, no good manners, and no compassion." Therefore, he concludes, it is imperative (*wājib*) for a sultan to demonstrate *siyāsat*, meaning both discipline and punishment in the context of political authority. A sultan must both possess *siyāsat* and execute it, since he is the "shadow of God on Earth." He must inspire such awe and fear in his flock (*raʿyat*) that when they see him from a distance they dare not rise. In a typically Saljūqid invocation of the concept of *fasād* (social strife, discord), al-Ghazālī states that once upon a time, the whip of ʿUmar ibn Khaṭṭāb would have been sufficient to keep the whole world safe. However, in his own age if the people lived in such a situation, then *fasād* would arise. So the sultan *must* possess the power of fear and *siyāsat*, so that the people will be safe from one another. Citing ʿAlī b. Abī Ṭālib (A), al-Ghazālī concludes by saying that the people will not achieve obedience and virtue until they are afraid of the power of the sultan to punish them.[91]

Shawka (raw power) and the power to punish, which the Saljūqs possessed in great abundance, could have been and were seen by some as a vice. Al-Ghazālī first makes of them a virtue, and then a necessity. That this legitimization comes from the foremost theologian and intellectual of the day only makes it more valuable to the Saljūqs. However, this would not be his last word on this subject. He repeated some of the same themes in his last political treatise, the *Tuḥfat al-mulūk*.

Tuḥfat al-mulūk

The inclusion of material from the undisputedly authentic first part of the *Naṣīḥat al-mulūk* in this text dates it after the composition of the former (499/1105), making it one of al-Ghazālī's last major compositions. The inclusion of the authentic material also increases the probability that it might be authentic, in my estimation. It is my contention that the scholars who have compiled lists of al-Ghazālī's *oeuvre* (such as M. Bouyges and ʿAbd al-Raḥmān Badawī) have not sufficiently recognized the importance of this work.[92] Some, such as Bouyges, have even mistaken it for the *Naṣīḥat al-mulūk*.[93] Iranian scholars such as Jalāl al-Dīn Humā'ī and Mujtabā Minūwī have mentioned this treatise, though they have not offered any analysis of it. The Iranian bibliophile Muḥammad Taqī Dānishpazhūh was the first to publish an edition of this text.[94] There is a more recent reedition of this text by the masterful Iranian scholar Nasrollah Pourjavady.[95] While the Dānishpazhūh edition was published in Iran thirty-five years ago, I am not aware of any work of Western scholarship that has analyzed it.

As is the case with some of the other writings of al-Ghazālī, there is a scholarly debate about the authenticity of this text. Its original editor, Dānishpazhūh, considered it an important text for situating al-Ghazālī, while its recent editor, Pourjavady, considers the *Tuḥfat al-mulūk* to be spurious.[96] Some scholars such as ʿAbd al-Ḥusayn Zarrīnkūb have doubted the authenticity of this work as well, while others such as Charles-Henri de Fouchécour, Mujtabā Mīnawī, Peter Avery, and Badīʿ al-Zamān Furūzānfar have accepted it as authentic.[97] Given the level of scholarly disagreement, I am inclined to treat it as authentic unless it can be determined that it is not from al-Ghazālī.

This treatise is composed of eleven chapters, dealing with various topics ranging from belief (*iʿtiqād*) to the difference of opinion among scholars to a discussion of purity and stories of the prophets. There are a number of intriguing points about this text that make it of interest to the historian of premodern Islam. From a literary perspective, it mentions the story of Shaykh-i Sanʿān that ʿAṭṭār would later articulate so beautifully in his *Conference of the Birds*.[98] From a historical perspective, the last chapter of this text deals with *jihād*. The context of the *jihād* here is clearly the Crusades, as it reports the *kāfirān* ("infidels") having taken over the lands of Muslims, removing pulpits, and allegedly having turned the shrine of Abraham into a pig sty. In deliberately evocative language, al-Ghazālī states, "The prayer-niche of Zakariyā and the birthplace of Jesus, peace be upon him, have been turned into the wine-house of the infidels. Today, it is as incumbent on the Sultan of Islam to rise up against them as it is for him to perform his prayers."[99]

If we are to accept this text as authentic, it would be a valuable source of information about the final direction of al-Ghazālī's political philosophy. There is no mention here of a caliphate, or of the ʿAbbāsids. The only positions of authority mentioned are the *sulṭān-i ʿādil* (just sultan) and the *pāk-dīn pādshāh* (the emperor whose religion is pure). In fact, the text starts outs by thanking God for His mercy in having sent such a figure to humanity. His description of the Saljūqs as being *pāk-dīn* (pure in religion) is part and parcel of the same discourse of legitimization that describes them as *nīkū iʿtiqād* (correct belief). Toward the end of his life, al-Ghazālī is perfectly situated to offer this consummate legitimizing of the Saljūq Sultans.

Nor is the above passage an isolated one. The third chapter, focusing on the theme of justice, gives al-Ghazālī another opportunity. There is praise of the just sultan, attributed to no less an authority than Prophet Muḥammad

(Ṣ) himself. Al-Ghazālī lists four statements, each attributed to the Prophet: first, that the justice of a just sultan is more virtuous than sixty years of worship. Second, that on the Day of Resurrection, seven people will stand in the shadow of God's throne. The first of these is said to be the just sultan. Third, that the most beloved and closest to God Almighty is a just sultan. The most inimical and farthest from God is the tyrannical sultan.[100] This element repeats almost verbatim the account from the *Naṣīḥat al-mulūk*, above. Fourth, the acts of worship of a just sultan equal the worship of all of his flock. Indeed, each of the just sultan's prayers are said to count as seventy thousand prayers of others. Given all these factors, al-Ghazālī concludes, it would be a shame for the sultan to gravitate to tyranny and pursue anything but the path of justice.[101] The discourse here is one of overlapping authorities. The authority of the Saljūq regime is reinforced by linking it to the authority of the Messenger of God.

Al-Ghazālī continues the chapter by stating that the parable of the pādshāh is like that of the lord of the house, with the world being the house.[102] According to al-Ghazālī, it is vital for the ruler to have compassion and mercy, to the point that "not even the Jew would be oppressed." He concludes this section by reminding the rulers that on the Day of Resurrection heretical innovators and tyrannical sultans will be deprived of the Prophet's intercession. Here again we have a Saljūq motif, linking together religious heresy with tyranny and, conversely, orthodoxy with justice.[103] The motif of justice here is of course reminiscent of Niẓām al-Mulk's directive in the *Siyāsat-nāma*.

Pand-nāma

The most recent political treatise attributed to al-Ghazālī to receive scholarly attention is the *Pand-nāma*, which has been reedited and published by Nasrollah Pourjavady.[104] Pourjavady mentions that the authenticity of this treatise is up for debate, though the title page of the *Pand-nāma* does claim that it was written by al-Ghazālī for a Saljūq sultan. According to Pourjavady, the *Pand-nāma* draws heavily from other authentic writings such as the *Kīmīyā*ʾ*-yi saʿādat* and the previously mentioned *Naṣīḥat al-mulūk*.[105] The *Pand-nāma* starts with the common trope of a supplicant (in this case, the Saljūq sultan) writing al-Ghazālī, asking for some spiritual advice of the same variety that had been offered before in the *Kīmīyā*ʾ*-yi saʿādat* and the *Iḥyā*ʾ. Al-Ghazālī obliges and offers the *Pand-nāma* in response. This treatise doesn't add anything to the theoretical discussion of sultanate, except for the fact that the king is addressed as "the mighty one of the age, the chosen of God" (*ʿazīz-i rūzgār,* *guzīda-yi parwardagār*),[106] titles that again suggest God's selection of the Saljūqs for rule.

With this text, al-Ghazālī's political writings came to an end. As we have witnessed, over a period of about fifteen years, he gradually changed his position from one squarely focused on the caliphate, to a model that envisioned cooperation between the ʿAbbāsids and the Saljūqs, to eventually focusing on the Saljūqs as the sole possessors of power and authority. Al-Ghazālī marks the most successful example of acknowledging Saljūq power through the writing of political treatises. As I have previously argued, this was the reciprocal element to the Saljūqs' empowerment of institutions of knowledge, such as the madrasa.

One might wonder about the impact such political writings had on the society at large. The writing of political treatises is essentially an elite phenomenon, affecting the rulers, their administration, and a select group of religious scholars. That does not make it irrelevant, of course, as most of what we do know about premodern Islamdom is a product of this group and reflects back on them. However, the Saljūqs recognized full well the need to legitimize themselves in the eyes of other social groups. Thus they turned to the most widely influential piety movement in premodern Islam, Sufism. Our concern here will be not with the metaphysical sophistication of Sufi thought and practice but rather with the power of Sufis to legitimize or contest the Saljūqs' religious ideology. The next chapter will focus on examples of successful cooperation between the Sufis and the Saljūqs, while chapter 6 will focus on a lone Sufi dissident.

Chapter Five

Bargaining with *Baraka*

One of the main aims of this chapter is to contextualize Sufi communities of the Saljūq era in their proper sociohistorical context—a context that includes interconnected networks of power and patronage.[1] There is no shortage of scholarly works that deal with Sufis who flourished in the Saljūq age. All too often, however, the studies of these mystics follow the (in)famous tripartite "Life, Time, and Works" genre.[2] Of the three categories, the segment dealing with "Time" receives the most cursory treatment. Scant attention is given to the historical context in which these Sufis lived, and even less analysis of the way in which they are depicted as having interacted with various social institutions, religious intellectuals, and political figures.[3] To a certain extent this is due to the textual training of most scholars of Sufism. We are trained to read philosophical and mystical texts written in a host of Muslim languages (Arabic, Persian, Turkish, Urdu, etc.). The writing of "definitive" studies of Sufis typically involves reading through and analyzing their writings, and extracting stories and anecdotes about them from various historical sources and hagiographies. Most scholars of Sufism do not, however, read through the important historical chronicles apart from the relevant references to the Sufis that they study.[4] This has significantly hampered the ability of many scholars of Sufism to have a nuanced grasp of the societies in which the mystics were situated.[5] The problem is only exacerbated in the case of the Saljūqs since there are few adequate secondary studies on the Saljūqs. The scholars of Sufism's neglect of the wider historical context is often mirrored in historians' own neglect of Sufi texts. Most historians have neglected to fully integrate the role of Sufis into their construction of the social landscape of premodern Islamdom. Many historians have dismissed Sufi hagiographies in toto, seeing them as "unreliable" material for a historical investigation.[6]

The present chapter aims to depart from the above approaches and revisit familiar mystics of the Saljūq era in a new framework. My goal in this chapter is not to offer exhaustive surveys of any of the Sufis covered here. Nor do I do intend to offer thorough presentations of their teachings or analysis of their multifaceted compositions. My main interest is in analyzing their positions as social and political beings in a hotly contested world of relations between political and religious figures. My aim is not to diminish the metaphysical and spiritual accomplishments of these saintly souls. Rather, I am primarily concerned with the ways in which the authority and charisma of these "friends of God" is appropriated by the Saljūq legitimizing discourse. The hagiographers and disciples of these saints used the legacy of the Sufi teachers as spiritual capital to offer a retrospective blessing of the raw force (*shawka*) which had brought the Saljūqs to power. In exchange for this service, the Sufi communities often received Saljūq patronage through having khānaqāhs built for them or having their philanthropic endeavors financed. The saints themselves are often depicted in both historical sources and hagiographies as extending their baraka to the Saljūqs in exchange for a promise that the people who lived under the saints' authority (*wilāya*) would be treated justly. This bartering of charisma for patronage is one of the more ubiquitous features of Saljūq Islam. Sufism in this period was not a marginal discipline being pursued only by world-renouncing ascetics. The process of legitimizing the Saljūqs through the saintly *wilāya* was one that wove together different saints and their communities, hagiographers and historians, rulers and viziers.

The sheer fact that a large number of historical and hagiographic texts describe such relationships between many Sufis and Saljūq politicians alone should warrant it as a suitable subject for a historical investigation. However, in order to appreciate the social and political significance of saints in this time period, we will first have to problematize the all too convenient and reified categories of mysticism as "privatized experience" which continue to be deployed in studying Sufism.

Beyond "Privatized Mysticism": Sufis in the Midst of Society

A charming story is told about the famed Persian Sufi Abū Saʿīd-i Abī ʾl-Khayr in the hagiographic collection *Asrār al-tawḥīd*:[7]

> They told the Shaykh: "So-and-so can walk on water!"
>
> He said: "That is easy! The frog and the finch[8] can do the same . . ."
>
> They said: "So-and-so flies in the air!"
>
> He said: "A fly and a sparrow[9] can as well . . ."

They said: "So-and-so can go from one city to the next in a single moment."

He said: "Satan can go in a span of one breath from the East to the West. There is not much value to such things. A [real saintly] man is he who sits and rises in the midst of people, eats and sleeps, conducts trade with people in the bazaar, and mixes with people—and yet for one moment does not become neglectful of God in his heart."[10]

This amusing account would seem to offer yet another indication that, for the Sufis, the true test for the men and women of God is to remain mindful of God while conducting their day-to-day affairs in the midst of society. The model of social interaction constructed here is not one of withdrawal from society, but rather one of being active in the world while resisting worldliness.

In spite of such accounts, which emphasize the importance of the social role played by the Sufis, the study of Islamic mysticism continues to borrow theoretical frameworks which relegate mysticism to a privatized realm, focusing on "mystical experience."[11] Many such frameworks are the result of a post-Enlightenment, Protestant worldview in which the realms of "religion" and "mysticism" have been privatized, removed from the public sphere, and defined in opposition to "rational philosophy."[12] Premodern Persian Sufis would have faced a great challenge in recognizing themselves and their religiosity in such restricted definitions of "mysticism," perhaps in many of the same ways as their premodern Christian counterparts. Another major aim of this chapter is to problematize such theoretical models for the study of "mysticism" by focusing on a group of fourth-/tenth- and fifth-/eleventh-century Sufis in Islamic Iran, who were intimately connected to the political and social institutions of that time period. In their dealings with sultans and viziers, police forces and merchants, and their own Sufi communities, they provide us with an opportunity to see the shortcomings of the models of mysticism that would privilege the mystics' "quest for a personal experience of God" over their larger social, political, and institutional roles.

Sufis Who Seek to "Rearrange" the World

In her classic study of mysticism, Evelyn Underhill stated that the aim of the mystic "is in no way concerned with adding to, exploring, re-arranging, or improving anything in the visible universe."[13] Quite to the contrary, we are concerned here with Sufis who saw it as their task and duty to be involved in the rearranging and improving of the affairs of humanity in this visible universe. Since the fourth/tenth century, Persian Sufis like other Muslims found themselves in a crucial and highly unstable point in Islamic history: the ʿAbbāsid regime had been overtaken by the Buyids, the threat of Ismāʿīlīs (military, doctrinal, and psychological) was felt everywhere, and a recently converted group of Saljūq Turks was dominating much of the political scene. Not content to simply "brush aside the visible universe," as Underhill might expect a mystic to do, the Persian Sufis entered a varied and complex set of relationships with the Saljūq regime. Some, such as the Sufis who will be covered in this chapter (Bābā Ṭāhir, Abū Saʿīd-i Abī ʾl-Khayr, and Aḥmad-i Jām) entered—or were depicted as entering—into rather amicable relations with it. Their relationship consisted of a reciprocal process in which the saintly figures lent their sanctifying power (*baraka*) to the political figures in exchange for promises that their behavior toward the masses would be rooted in justice (*ʿadl*) and spiritual excellence (*iḥsān*). In return, the political figures expressed their gratitude in the form of devotion to the Sufi masters as well as patronage (*irādat*) of the Sufi complexes.

Other Sufis, such as ʿAyn al-Quḍāt Hamadānī, had much more contentious relations with the Saljūq regime and paid for their criticism with their lives.[14] In both cases, as well as the less drastic middle possibilities, all of these mystics were intimately involved in the task of using their sanctity to rearrange, improve, challenge, and remain responsible for the affairs of the visible universe. Their social interactions far from nullify their credentials as "mystics" but in fact reinforce their status as holders of both *wilāya* (power and authority) and *walāya* (intimacy with God). Sainthood in Islam is no less than a social phenomenon: it can only be recognized when it exists and is acknowledged socially.[15]

Between Hagiography and Social History

If it is granted that saints had a significant social role in their own societies, then it is imperative for us to incorporate material dealing with lives of the saints in imagining the social context of a premodern Muslim society. The study of hagiographic material for a reconstruction of a larger sociohistorical context is not a new one in academic studies of Sufism. I am here indebted to the work of scholars as varied as Richard Eaton,[16] Simon Digby,[17] Devin DeWeese,[18] Carl Ernst,[19] Jo-Ann Gross,[20] and Vincent Cornell.[21] While some of the hagiographic passages I will be analyzing here have been translated before,[22] I do not believe they have received the critical reading they so richly deserve.

Reading Sufi Hagiographies: Patterns of Interactions between Sufis and Politicians

While there are many different narratives of reciprocally beneficial interactions between Sufis and political figures depicted in the sources, three main patterns stand out in the hagiographic sources. The first pattern is that of the firāsat-designating narratives in which the saint uses his divinely bestowed insight and clairvoyance (*firāsat*) to forecast great success for figures well before they have achieved notoriety.[23] The second pattern, baraka-legitimizing accounts, portrays a saint receiving political figures who have already achieved worldly power and blessing their success through his baraka. The third pattern, which reciprocates the above two, is the political figures' devotion (*irādat*) toward and patronage of the saints, their descendants, and the shrine-khānaqāh complexes associated with them. Not infrequently these acts of patronage are depicted as having occurred precisely during times that the Sufi complexes—philanthropically providing for hundreds of indigents—were most in need of such acts of generosity. It is intriguing to note—as much as it may strike our modern sensibilities as "unspiritual"—that these acts of patronage often came about after what might be termed spiritual blackmail!

Unlike our own contemporary wishes for saints to be men and women of infinite compassion and wisdom somehow isolated from any worldly attachments, the premodern Muslim saints were, as much as anything, men and women of power. Their power derived from their sanctity, which in Sufi discourse is associated with both *wilāya* and *walāya*: the former being associated with authority, and the latter with proximity to the Divine. They are saints because they are close to God; in Qur'anic language, *awliyā' Allāh*, "Friends of God, Clients of God." In a sense, they are passive with respect to God, being under His protection. Yet to humanity, they embody the power and authority that comes from being close to God. Without denying their spiritual states and station, the saints face the public as men and women of both *walāya* (intimacy with Divine) and *wilāya* (resultant authority and power).[24]

The hagiographies of these saints are replete with accounts of them manifesting this power and authority, bringing untold blessings to their supporters and disciples, and also surprisingly—perhaps only to a modern notion of "saintly behavior"—causing their ill-wishers to go blind, or mute, or to drop dead. The hagiography of a saint from a later period in Saljūq history, Aḥmad-i Jām (d. 536/1141), is a good example: a man who speaks ill of the Shaykh is struck mute.[25] A woman who was sneaking a peek at the saint from behind a door is blinded.[26] A man who attempted to have the saint expelled from the town drops dead.[27] Nor are the saint's powers limited to punishing: the saint is frequently depicted as being aware of other people's secret thoughts.[28] He saves a village's crop from a swarm of locusts.[29] He cures a whole host of ailments ranging from blindness[30] and madness[31] to infertility.[32] In perhaps the ultimate everyday miracle narrative, he also aids in finding a lost donkey![33]

These accounts have been approached in two conflicting ways, which nonetheless share a basic assumption. The first approach is characteristic of those who have fallen under the undeniable charm of these hagiographic narratives: the stories of the saints' wondrous deeds (*karamāt*) are told over and over again, as if the disciples' embellished and, more importantly, tropeladen accounts of these miracles simply and naively reproduce the saints' lives. The second approach, a positivistic reaction against the above, rejects miracle narratives and looks upon them with disdain. It dismisses these accounts as superstitious rubbish feeding the imagination of illiterate (and presumably ignorant) masses.

As disparate as these two perspectives seem, they share one important presupposition: they both read hagiographic accounts as straightforward biographical history, either to be accepted faithfully or to be dismissed scornfully. Both perspectives ignore recent developments in hagiographic studies that attempt to ask different questions from myths and mythological narratives. Such recent works in fields of myth and hagiography are concerned less with whether or not a narrative is "true" or "real" in a positivistic sense and more with the consequences for a community who believes that the mythic events are real. In such readings, a myth is not a false story, but rather a "story that is sacred to and shared by a group of people who find their most important meanings in it; it is a story believed to have been composed in the past about an event in the past . . . an event that continues to have meaning in the present because it is remembered . . ."[34]

I am not concerned with establishing the hagiographic narratives of interactions between saints and political figures as "real" or "false" in a positivistic historical fashion. Rather, my premise is that these myths contain a special relevance for those who retell them, and it is with these meanings that I am concerned. Furthermore, these myths are designed to shape the contemporary response of the hagiographers' community.[35] To put it differently, the saints' hagiographies are not transparently a reflection of the individual saint's abilities. Rather, the hagiographies aim to connect the saint, his/her community, and the audience of the myth (in a textual or performative context).[36] The stories about Abū Saʿīd are not designed to provide the modern reader with a "biography" of Abū Saʿīd as much as they were written to pass on these traditions to Abū Saʿīd's community and shape its behavior. Therefore, in reading these narratives, we will be concerned with how they construct and govern ideal paradigms of behavior.

If a hagiography claims that Bābā Ṭāhir met with Ṭughril (or Abū Saʿīd with Niẓām al-Mulk, or Aḥmad-i Jām with Sultan Sanjar) and blessed him, I am mostly uninterested if this meeting actually took place. Rather, I am concerned with the meanings given to such a meeting by those who tell the narratives and the response it is meant to elicit in those who hear/read the narratives.[37] Our own skepticism towards the possibility of the supernatural realm intervening in daily life should not blind us to the project of reconstructing the sociohistorical milieu of the Earlier Middle Period (950–1250) in Islamic history, to recall Marshall Hodgson's chronological schematization. Regardless of our belief (or lack thereof), these Sufis were surrounded by disciples who had full faith in the saint's power and transmitted such stories endlessly. Even the Saljūq historians (such as Rāwandī, the author of *Rāḥat al-ṣudūr*) had faith in the power of the saint to legitimize the Saljūq rulers. In this case the power focused on was not the ability to perform miracles but the power to lend legitimizing credibility and prestige to a newly converted group, the Saljūqs, who were of a questionable Islamic pedigree.

While not all Sufis entered into such mutually beneficial relationships with the Saljūq rulers, many did. Among the various Sufis who are fully appropriated by the Saljūq legitimizing discourse are the mysterious and perhaps illiterate Bābā Ṭāhir ʿUryān, the exuberant Abū Saʿīd-i Abī ʾl-Khayr, and the repentant and austere Aḥmad-i Jām. I will now turn to a close reading of the hagiographic narratives associated with each and an examination of the patterns that emerge from such myths.

Bābā Ṭāhir ʿUryān, "the Naked"

We know virtually nothing about the life of this saintly composer of heartfelt Persian *du-baytī* quatrains.[38] The sources are even in disagreement as to which century he lived in;[39] Riḍā-Qulī Khān Hidāyat claimed in *Majmaʿ al-fuṣaḥāʾ* that Bābā Ṭāhir lived during the Daylami era and had died before Firdawsī and ʿUnṣurī, that is, before 410/1019–20.[40] Other sources suggest that he might have been a contemporary of ʿAyn al-Quḍāt Hamadānī (d. 526/1131) or Khwāja Naṣīr al-Dīn Ṭūsī (d. 672/1273–74). The discrepancy of over two hundred and fifty years is a testament to the elusive nature of this historical personality.[41] What is not debatable, however, is the profound impact that Bābā Ṭāhir's poems have had on many segments of Persian society. His poetry was composed not in the classical Persian but in a vernacular tongue. The contemporary sources referred to the language of the quatrains as *Fahlaviyāt*, which seems to suggest a close connection between it and the Middle Iranian dialect Pahlavi.[42]

Ṭāhir's quatrains, not unlike the *oeuvre* of ʿUmar Khayyām and Abū Saʿīd, have been transformed from an oral collection to something of a genre, always inviting the sincerest form of flattery: imitations. It is virtually impossible to definitely separate Ṭāhir's own poems from the hundreds of those which were composed to imitate him. Whereas E. Heron-Allen's collections of the *du-baytī*s contained only eighty or so quatrains,[43] the collection of *du-baytī*s edited by the late Waḥīd Dastgirdī contained some 296 quatrains.[44] Almost none of these poems reveal any biographical details about Ṭāhir's life.

To establish the historical outlines of Bābā Ṭāhir's life, one could look to other hagiographic accounts, as there is no work devoted solely to him. Bābā Ṭāhir's fellow Hamadānian, ʿAyn al-Quḍāt, is linked to Bābā Ṭāhir in a number of ways. To begin with, there is a commentary—attributed to ʿAyn al-Quḍāt—on the *Kalimāt-i qiṣār*, allegedly written by Bābā Ṭāhir. Scholars have questioned the authenticity of this commentary as well as the original Arabic aphorisms. Yet the sheer attribution of this text to ʿAyn al-Quḍāt suggests that Bābā Ṭāhir was viewed as having lived before the former Hamadānī mystic. In support of this perspective, it can be noted that ʿAyn al-Quḍāt makes mention of Shaykh Fatḥa (the teacher of ʿAyn al-Quḍāt's own master, Shaykh Baraka) recalling the example of a certain Sufi saint called "Ṭāhir," also from Hamadān: "Fatḥa, may God have mercy on him, says: 'It has been seventy years that I have tried to show the type of devotion to Ṭāhir that he deserves; this I have not been able to do.'"[45] ʿAyn al-Qūḍat was killed in 525/1131. If we accept the premise that this Ṭāhir from Hamadān is in fact our "burnt-heart" (vernacular: *Del sūteh*; Classical Persian: *Dil Sūkhtah*) poet-saint, these narratives would tend to suggest that Bābā Ṭāhir lived about three generations before ʿAyn al-Quḍāt, or toward the middle of the fifth/eleventh century.[46] Other narratives also place him in the middle of the eleventh century.[47]

The only narrative that comes from a *tārīkh*-based source mentioning Bābā Ṭāhir is Rāwandī's oft-quoted account of the meeting between a mature, saintly Bābā Ṭāhir and the Saljūq Sultan Ṭughril in 447/1055 when the Turkish warlord was on his way to Baghdad. According to Rāwandī:

> When Sultan Ṭughril Beg came to Hamadān, there were three saints there: Bābā Ṭāhir, Bābā Jaʿfar, and Shaykh Ḥamshā.[48] They were stand-

> ing on a small mountain called Khiḍr close to the gate of Hamadān. The Sultan saw them (*naẓar āmadh*). He stopped the army and went to see them on foot along with the vizier Abū Naṣr al-Kundurī. He kissed their hands. Bābā Ṭāhir, the enthralled soul, said to the Sultan: "O Turk! What will you do with God's people?" The Sultan replied: "Whatever you state." Bābā said: "[Rather,] do that which God orders: *'Verily God commands justice and spiritual excellence'*." [Qur'ān 16:90] The Sultan wept, and said: "I will do so".
>
> Bābā held his hand and said: "Do you accept this from me?" The Sultan said: "Yes!" Bābā had a broken ewer, which for years he had used for ablutions, and kept the tip of it [as a ring] on his finger. He took it out and put it in the finger of the Sultan and said: "Thus, I have handed to you dominion of the world. Stand firm on justice." The Sultan kept that ring among his charms (*taʿwīdh-hā*). Whenever he would go on battle, he would put on this ring.[49]

There are many intriguing points about this narrative. It is simply the most well-known, succinct, and perfectly orchestrated narrative of the exchange of baraka between a saint and political figures in all of Saljūqid literature. Virtually all Iranian and Western scholars dealing with this episode have accepted the historicity of this account.[50] The remarkable feature of such consensus is that the story is clearly a hagiographic narrative, of the sort that one comes across frequently in Persian hagiographic works. One wonders whether the fact that this narrative is quoted in a *tārīkh* (rather than a hagiographic *tadhkira* or *manāqib*) text had led scholars to accept its "authenticity." This raises a number of interesting points about our own presuppositions in privileging the alleged historicity and authenticity of *tārīkh* narratives over hagiographic ones. Clearly, both genres in this time period include mythic narratives that have to be examined more closely.

My aim here is not to cast aspersions on the historicity of this event. Rather, I intend to analyze this narrative as a perfect Saljūq myth, especially as regards the exchange between a saint and a political figure. Hamid Dabashi has interpreted this narrative as "the prototype model for subordinating the political to the mystical."[51] Rather than viewing this narrative as a model for subordination, I prefer to read it as a model of negotiation. Neither the mystical power (Bābā Ṭāhir) nor the political power (represented by Ṭughril and his vizier) are depicted as being completely subordinated by the other. Rather, there is a nuanced negotiation of power and authority between them. This narrative clearly falls into the genre of the baraka-legitimizing narratives: the baraka of the saint legitimizes the military conquest of the warlord in exchange for promises of justice for the people.

The timing of the narrative is important. Immediately before the Turkish warlord enters Baghdad, he participates in one last rite of receiving a blessing from a *walī*. This exchange not only sanctifies the person of Sultan Ṭughril but also legitimizes the military conquest of Baghdad and, in a greater sense, the whole establishment of the Saljūq dynasty. There is no introduction of any of the three saints named there, and in fact we have no collaborating information about the other two *awliyā*ʾ. Even Bābā Ṭāhir appears out of nowhere, blesses the sultan, and disappears again. He is a perfect mythic character, one whose being explains, organizes, and shapes behavior and who acts as a paradigmatic presence. The whole reason for his presence in this narrative is to sanctify the warlord and be a reminder of the Qurʾanic paradigm for justice and spiritual excellence.

The saints are standing on a mountaintop, an elevated physical status that corresponds to their sublime spiritual station (*maqām*). The name of the mountain itself, *khiḍr*, is a sign of the mysterious knowledge-blessing that comes from God (*ʿilm ladunnā*). The name is surely evocative of the Qurʾanic narrative (18:60–82) in which "one of our [God's] servants," named as Khiḍr in the tradition, accompanies and admonishes Moses on a mysterious journey. In a sense, the saint may be said to fulfill the khiḍrian task of initiating the Moses-like sultan. The fact that there is more than one saint present (although only Bābā Ṭāhir takes part in the rite) provides witnesses, collaboration, and further acknowledgement. It is intriguing to note that many of the narratives dealing with the investiture of baraka in political figures feature at least the minimum number of witnesses the sharīʿa requires for a valid business transaction.

When the sultan comes upon them, he does not simply "see them"; rather, his *naẓar* (glance) falls on them. Naẓar has long been a Sufi trope, a subtle and amorous glance exchanged between a Sufi master and a disciple, a lover and a beloved.[52] The sultan dismounts from his horse, physically and spiritually humbling himself before the saint. Perhaps a most important feature of the exchange is that the sultan approaches Bābā Ṭāhir not alone but with his vizier, Abū Naṣr al-Kundurī. We have already seen that viziers were the ultimate arbiters of the political-intellectual realm in the Saljūq era. The vizier need not speak a word in the narrative, but his presence mediates the exchange.

Bābā Ṭāhir is described as being *shifta-gūna*, something of a wild and enamoured man. E. G. Browne associates this with the "consideration and respect still shown by the highest and noblest in Muḥammadan countries to half-crazy (*majdhūb*) dervishes with a reputation for sanctity."[53] Rather than reading this narrative as the tolerated ranting of a half-mad man, I would suggest that this conversation is one that the legitimizers of the Saljūq regime desperately sought. Without the blessing from saintly figures and religious scholars, Ṭughril would be just another warlord marching from the plains into the cities. With the blessing, he can claim to be the champion of "orthodox" Islam, what the Saljūq sources refer to as *nīkū iʿtiqād*.

The saint's addressing of the warlord as "Turk" is a reminder of Ṭughril's status as an outsider in the Perso-Islamicate world. The tone of the episode recalls Alp Arslān's warning to the nobles in his court: "I have told you over and over again that you Turks are the army of Khurasan and Transoxiana and you are foreigners in this region . . ."[54] What had been a civilization of Arabs and Persians had now become a multiethnic one, and the Turks had to be accounted for, reckoned with, and legitimized. Future episodes of saints addressing rulers simply as "Turk!" would follow down the centuries.[55] The key narrative moment is when the saint reminds the sultan of his duty to treat people with "justice and spiritual excellence" (*ʿadl wa ʾl-iḥsān*), a Qurʾanic commandment. The choice of the Qurʾanic verse is of course deliberate. The rest of the well-known verse reads, "And God forbids all *faḥshāʾ* (shameful deeds), *munkar* (abomination, injustice), and *baghy* (wickedness, rebellion). He instructs you, that you may receive admonition."[56] The saint becomes the mouthpiece for the divine admonition, embodying all the Qurʾanic authority. Words such as *faḥshāʾ* and *munkar* were no hollow words in those troubled social times. The choice of the verse can be read as the saint chastising the sultan for the abominations committed by the Saljūqs during their march through the Iranian plateau, prohibiting further atrocities, and calling him instead to justice and spiritual excellence toward the populace. The saint functions as a reminder of the highest ethic of *iḥsān*, an Islamic model of virtuous existence devoted to the actualization of goodness and the realization of beauty. As the narrative of the famous *ḥadīth Jibrʾīl* (Ḥadīth of Gabriel) states, it is to live in a state as if one sees God, and if one does not see God, to recall the Divine sees us.[57] The sultan assumes the role of the willing pupil.

The transmission of baraka is never a unilateral bestowal. It is always a mutually reciprocal transaction, even a barter. The exchange of glances and the transmission of ethical teachings need to be substantiated by two subsequent acts: first, the saint—acting as a divine agent—bestows the rule of the whole world to Ṭughril. The sultan is not depicted as having conquered the world through raw military might; rather, he is given the world to rule through the sagacious baraka of a friend of God. The world will remain in his hands so long as he deals with his subjects in justice and recalls his connection with the saint. All these are important components of the Great Saljūq myth.

Second, the exchange between the ruler and the saint is also commemorated in a tangible way through the transmission of a ritualized object: a ring obtained from an *ibrīq*, a pew used for ablutions. The sultan used this ritual object as a talismanic charm (*taʿwīdh*), which was said to aid him in battles. The ring serves as a physical and tangible documentation of the exchange of baraka for justice. The choice of the ring is itself significant; it carries connotations of both regal and saintly rule. The origin of the ring, from a water pew used for ablutions, recalls the religious injunction of ablutions necessary for prayers. The exchange with the saint purifies and prepares the sultan for the upcoming conquest of Baghdad, just as the ablutions purify and prepare one for prayers. Its usage as a taʿwīdh is as a ritualized object, a relic, which reaffirms the connection between the Saljūq warlord and the saint who has sanctified him. The episode with the taʿwīdh provides us with another opportunity to see the shortcomings of some recent notions of "mysticism." There is hardly any room in the "mysticism" of William James, Margaret Smith, and Evelyn Underhill for the Sufis' usage of relics and ritualized objects. The Sufis of medieval Islam problematize the above depiction greatly, as they are often seen as giving charms to their followers, yearning for a patched frock (*khirqa*) of a deceased saint, and even blessing them by putting their own spit in their mouths. The ring from a wash pew given to Sultan Ṭughril falls into this category: it is a physical object which is meant to recall the saint's legitimization, not only during the event itself, but also during each of the subsequent military campaigns undertaken by the ruler. The baraka of the saint follows the sultan to each victory and sanctifies those endeavors as well.

The conclusion of this narrative is a powerful and vivid example of the connection between mystics and Saljūq orthodoxy. At the end of the narrative, the historian Rāwandī adds that such was the "pure belief" (*iʿtiqād-i pāk*) and the "purity of creed" (*ṣafā-yi ʿaqīdat*) of Ṭughril in the "Muḥammadan religion" (*dīn-i Muḥammadī*), no one possessed more religion than the sultan. In the obligatory hyperbolic poem, Rāwandī compares Ṭughril to no less than Prophet Muḥammad (Ṣ) himself: whereas the Prophet was the Seal of Prophethood, Ṭughril is said to have been the Seal of Kingship; whereas the Prophet freed "religion" (*dīn*) from tyranny, Ṭughril is said to have cultivated the world through justice. All the tropes in the above—exchanges between mystics and rulers, claims of orthodoxy, the discourse of justice and religion, etc.—mark this as the ultimate example of Saljūq myth.[58]

Abū Saʿīd-i Abī ʾl-Khayr

Of all the Sufis in the Saljūq era, the one whose legacy is the most intricately connected with the Saljūqs is Abū Saʿīd-i Abī ʾl-Khayr (d. 440/1049) of Mayhana. Many of the other saintly figures of this period are depicted as having interacted with only one significant political figure: Bābā Ṭāhir with Sultan Ṭughril, and Aḥmad-i Jām with Sultan Sanjar. Abū Saʿīd, on the other hand, stands out by having interacted with a host of Saljūq notables from the political, administrative, and intellectual ranks. The political notables mentioned in his hagiography include—but are not limited to—Niẓām al-Mulk, Sultan Ṭughril, and Chaghrī Beg.[59]

Unlike many of the other saints of this time period, Abū Saʿīd had not one but two separate hagiographies written for him by his descendants. The first hagiography was composed by one of his descendants, Muḥammad b. Abī Rawḥ Luṭf Allāh b. Abī Saʿīd b. Abī Ṭāhir b. Abī Saʿīd b. Abī ʾl-Khayr. As can be deduced from his name, the author was a great-great-grandson of the famed saint. The *Ḥālāt u sukhanān-i Abū Saʿīd-i Abū ʾl-Khayr* was first published by the Russian Orientalist V. Zhukowski in 1899 and has since been reprinted.[60] Muḥammad b. al-Munawwar, a cousin of the above author and another descendant of Abū Saʿīd, utilized the *Ḥālāt u sukhanān* in composing his own hagiography, the well-known and often cited *Asrār al-tawḥīd fī maqāmāt al-shaykh Abī Saʿīd*, written between 574–88/1179–92.[61] Even apart from its hagiographic value and its importance in establishing the ambience of Persian Sufism in the twelfth century, the work has been unanimously described as one of the masterpieces of Persian literature.[62]

The *Asrār al-tawḥīd* is full of accounts of exchanges between the saint and a number of nobles. These accounts cover the full spectrum of the patterns we have indicated earlier: firāsat-designation, baraka-legitimization, and devotion-patronage. The writing of this hagiography, a full 130 to 150 years after the death of the saint, no doubt had the benefit of retrospectively forecasting Saljūq successes and attributing them to the blessing of Abū Saʿīd. Yet many of the accounts in the hagiography seem to be oral narratives which had circulated in the Sufi community for generations before they were written down. In addition, this hagiography was written in the unsettling and disturbing period that marked the beginning of the demise of the Great Saljūqs.[63] Part of its aim, being written in such troubled times, was to reshape the behavior of both the saint's community and the political figures along the lines of the paradigmatic behavior of Abū Saʿīd and the first generation of the Great Saljūqs.

A number of passages connect Abū Saʿīd to members of the merchant class such as Abū Jaʿfar Bāzargān Nīshāpūrī[64] and Abū ʿUmarū Ḥaskū[65] (head of the merchants in Nīshāpūr). A still greater number of narratives document his relationship with political figures. The Saljūq figure whose name is brought up most frequently is Niẓām al-Mulk. Numerous narratives connecting the earthly success of the famed vizier and the wilāya of the great saint easily allow one to find examples of all three patterns of hagiographic narratives. I will offer examples from each pattern.

Firāsat-Designating Narratives

The first account features many members of the family of the hagiographer (the hagiographer's uncle, grandfather, and great-grandfather) visiting Niẓām al-Mulk. The great vizier recalls the following episode from his childhood:

> I was [still] a child when Shaykh Abū Saʿīd—May God sanctify his awesome soul—came to Ṭūs. One day I was standing with another group of children at the alley of the Christians. The Shaykh, being accompanied by many people, approached us. When he came near to us, he looked at the crowd following him and said: 'Whoever wishes to see the master of the whole world (*khwāja-yi jahān*), here he is, standing right there!' And he pointed to me. We [the children] all looked at each other in astonishment, not knowing whom he meant by this. Today forty years has passed, and it is now evident that he was referring to me.[66]

This passage is a perfect example of a firāsat-designating narrative: the great saint points out the young Ḥasan (surely not yet worthy of the title *Niẓām al-Mulk*) in a crowd of children and predicts that he will someday be the *khwāja-yi jahān*, "Master of the world." Both the child's young age and his locale in the vicinity of the Christian neighborhood are designed to mark the lowly beginnings of young Ḥasan. The young boy has not sought this blessing and is not even sure to whom the great saint is referring. It is only forty years later (note the trope of forty) that the great vizier recognizes this firāsat-designation.

Two other features of this narrative also stand out: first, the crowd accompanying the saint. As we have seen with other hagiographic narratives (such as that of Bābā Ṭāhir), the narratives are placed in a *public* sphere. In Saljūq Islam, as indeed elsewhere, sainthood is a public discourse. The activity of the saint almost by definition involves others and demands acknowledgement from others. As Vincent Cornell has remarked, "Sainthood is a matter of discourse. It can be nothing else. Whether the other who bestows legitimacy on the saint is divine or human, learned or unlearned, a process of negotiation is invariably involved."[67]

The second feature of the above narrative is the emphasis on bridging the gap between the present (age of the hagiographer) and the source of authority, Abū Saʿīd. The figures that are mentioned as having been present in the vizier's audience include the saint's son (Abū Ṭāhir), his grandson Khwājā Abū Saʿd, and the latter's son Kamāl al-Dīn Abū Saʿīd. The naming of these individuals forms something of a *silsila*, reconnecting the hagiographer and the Sufi community (the audience of the narrative) to the Shaykh, who is the source of saintly authority. The charisma of the saint is remembered, perpetuated, and transmitted through the very recollection of these narratives.

Baraka-Legitimizing Narratives

The second pattern of narratives is that epitomized in the exchange between Bābā Ṭāhir and Ṭughril in which the saint with his God-given baraka sanctifies and legitimizes political figures. Baraka is a sacred power, which is both blessed and blessing. This is a key to understanding the social role of baraka. It might be seen as divine in origin, but it would be a great oversimplification to view it as a simple "spiritual" blessing bereft of any earthly ramifications. Baraka is, as much as anything else, about power: the spiritual power of the saint, the power of the saints to interact with mighty rulers, and the power to lend them legitimacy.

The baraka narratives in the *Asrār al-tawḥīd* are not limited to Niẓām al-Mulk. The hagiography is full of individuals who similarly credit the saint.[68] The hagiography also depicts Abū Saʿīd as legitimizing two Saljūq rulers, Ṭughril and Chaghrī. The narrative is historically contextualized during the time when Sultan Masʿūd Ghaznavī had neglected his realm and preoccupied himself with moral depravity. The Saljūqs emerged from an area near Bukhārā and came to Khurāsān proper. The Ghaznavīd ruler threatened them, to which they responded that the whole affair was a divine affair, and it would turn out as He had willed.

As is the pattern with *Asrār al-tawḥīd*, the narrative starts out with a historical situation that is public knowledge and then introduces the central role of the Shaykh to explain how his spiritual force was in reality the animating force behind the event. The narrative states:

Our Shaykh, Abū Saʿīd, may God sanctify his mighty spirit, was aware of this circumstance through his clairvoyance (*firāsat*). Then the two brothers, Chaghrī and Ṭughril, came to visit (*ziyārat*) the Shaykh in Mayhana. The Shaykh was seated on a sepulchral shrine, with some of his followers. The two Saljūq brothers came close to the Shaykh's throne, and offered their greetings of *salām*. They kissed the Shaykh's hand, and stood in front of his throne.

The Shaykh, as was his custom, lowered his head in reflection for some time, and then raised it. He said to Chaghrī: "I have given you dominion (*mulk*) over Khurāsān." He told Ṭughril: "I have given dominion over Iraq[69] to you."

They paid their respect, and departed.[70]

This account is a perfect example of the baraka-legitimizing narrative. It clearly situates the Shaykh as the intermediary divine agent who bestows dominion to the rulers. It is through him that the kings are made and—implicitly—deposed. The terminology used in the account is remarkable; the two Saljūq Sultans treat the saint as one would treat a king: they proceed to his *takht* (throne), kiss his hand, and remain standing. After being told of what has been given to them, they pay their respects and leave. Furthermore, the whole episode is described as a *ziyārat*, a term that in Persian religiosity is used for minor pilgrimages, visiting people and places where the presence of the Sacred is palatable.

The narrative moves to an account of the battle waged by Sultan Masʿūd against Mayhana in which he broke his promise of peace and cut off the hands of forty-one archers from Abū Saʿīd's hometown. The saint weeps upon hearing this and states that the Ghaznavīd ruler has just "cut off the hand of his own dominion (*mulk*)."[71] Clearly, the saint's powers include not just the making of kings but also predicting and bringing about their downfall. The saint is clearly not one to be trifled with: he giveth *mulk* and he taketh it away.

The account concludes with the downfall of the Ghaznavīds at Dandānqān in 431/1040. The conclusion is both historical and hagiographic, confirming the validity of the saint's experience and his legitimization: "Dominion was transferred from the family of Masʿūd [the Ghaznavīd ruler] to the house of Saljūq. Chaghrī became the emperor of Khurāsān, and Ṭughril that of Iraq. It was just as our Shaykh had predicted."[72]

This conclusion confirms that the realm of the saint is not just the "spiritual" but very much also that of mulk, earthly dominion and governance. He predicts and brings about the rise and fall of dynasties. The spiritual and political power held by the saint necessitates that the proper response of political figures to the saints' wilāya should be that of the third type of narrative: acts of patronage and homage.

The Proper Response of Political Figures: Devotion and Patronage

To a certain extent, the relationship between saints and political figures is meant to recapitulate the relationship between the human being and the Divine. The Divine provides immense blessings and grace towards humanity. Humanity's response is to be ever mindful and to show gratitude (*shukr*) toward the Divine.[73] Being agents of divine dispensation, the saints are also owed a measure of devotional discipleship (*irādat*) and gratitude. In hagiographic accounts, political nobles display their gratitude in two distinct forms. First, the politician perpetually recalls his debt to the saint for all of his earthly success, thus demonstrating his irādat. Second, the political figure is willing to patronize the operations of the saint's shrine and associated complex.

From the patron's perspective, this exchange is not simply an act of charity but a transaction. The patronizing of the saint is deemed to carry with it meritorious rewards for both life in this realm and in the hereafter. When Ṭughril's vizier, Khwāja Abū Manṣūr Varqānī, was close to death, he summoned both Abū Saʿīd and Imām Qushayrī and reminded them, "I love you. *I have spent much money on you*. Now I need you. When I pass away, I want you both to come to my grave, and stay by my tomb until I have successfully passed the questioning (*su'āl*)[74] with your help."[75] (emphasis mine) Clearly, the vizier is counting on his generous acts of patronage to warrant the presence of two saints by his graveside. It is his belief—and indeed the belief of many if not most premodern Muslims—that the baraka of saints could prove to be of assistance not merely during this life but even after death. The saint-patron relationship might be said to outlast both of their earthly lives: a patron could count on a saintly figure to ease his passing to the next world, and the descendants of a Sufi master could count on the continuous patronage of a political figure long after the earthly demise of the saint.

There are a number of narratives in the *Asrār al-tawḥīd* that demonstrate such responses of irādat and patronage. Some figures are named in isolated passages as having patronized the saint's feasts. Abū ʿAmr Ḥaskū, the head of merchants in Nīshāpūr, is said to have financed some of the elegant and expensive feasts of Abū Saʿīd.[76] However, it is once again the figure of Niẓām al-Mulk who is most frequently associated with patronizing the saint and his complex. Many such narratives start with a typical baraka-legitimization narrative before moving on to the documentation of the irādat relationship. In one such account, Khwāja Imām Abū ʾl-Futūḥ ʿAbbās (accompanied by his father) recalls having visited the great vizier in Isfahan. Niẓām al-Mulk informed his visitors, "Whatever I have attained to has been through Shaykh Abū Saʿīd [ibn A]bī ʾl-Khayr." The vizier reminisced about an episode in his youth in Nīshāpūr in which he was riding an inferior horse when he was summoned to the *khānaqāh* of Abū Saʿīd. The saint grabbed his hand and said, "You will be a good man." The vizier paid his respect to Abū Saʿīd and returned. This portion of the account seems to be a typical firāsat-designation. In the beginning, Niẓām al-Mulk is riding an inferior (literally: good-for-nothing) horse (*asbī lakāta-ī bad*), as if to underscore his lowly status before receiving his blessing from the saint. Niẓām al-Mulk receives this designation before he had achieved any political notoriety, thus underscoring the saint's firāsat. Furthermore, the story is told to the saint's son and grandson, reinforcing the link between the past and the present.

In the same gathering with the hagiographer's family, Niẓām al-Mulk recalled another episode in which he attended the Shaykh's assembly but hid behind a column so that the Shaykh could not see him. Abū Saʿīd says, "Ḥasan owes a debt." The vizier donates his belt, which the Shaykh takes, and twirls on his finger. He then prophesies, "Before too long, you will have four thousand men buckling their belts in your service, and of those, four hundred will have belts of gold."[77] The vizier then informs his visitors (Khwāja Imam Abū ʾl-Futūḥ and his father) that on that very day of their visit he had counted the men in his army, and they had numbered exactly four thousand. Furthermore, he states that of that four thousand, exactly four hundred of them were wearing golden belts, "not one more, and not one less." The vizier thoughtfully concludes, "Whatever I have attained to, it is through him (Abū Saʿīd). It is for this reason that I am the servant (*ghulām*) of all the Sufis in the world."[78] This account is a perfect example of the vizier paying his homage to the saint, and attributing all of his earthly success to the latter. Here the narrative shifts from an account of the vizier having received his designation and legitimization through the saint in the past to his ongoing devotion-patronage toward all the Sufis in the world in the present. The appeal to an authority in the past to bring about a change in the behavior in the present is characteristic of many mythological accounts, including Sufi hagiographies.[79]

Even the demise of Niẓām al-Mulk is told in another story in which before his assassination, the aged vizier recalls a conversation with the saint in which Abū Saʿīd asks him to promise that he will cherish the Sufis (*ṭāʾifa*) and provide for them. Niẓām al-Mulk allegedly responds in a pact (*ʿahd*) that he would be the "dust under their feet" (*khāk-i qadam-i īshān bāsham*).[80] The usage of the term *ʿahd* is significant, recalling the notion of covenant, even that of the Primordial Covenant (*ʿahd-i alast*) between humanity and the Divine.[81] The bond between Niẓām al-Mulk and the saint is not simply a personal relationship that may be forgotten with no consequence. It is a covenant: fulfilling it brings blessings and ignoring it has dire consequences. Apart from devotion and discipleship, the saint specifically asks the vizier to cherish all of the Sufi *ṭāʾifa*[82] and, significantly, to provide for them. Devotion is necessary but not sufficient: it must be accompanied by patronage.

Another feature of these narratives is to provide a spiritual connection between the generation of the hagiographer and the saint. These accounts in a sense legitimize the hagiographer's generation of Sufis and make their demands for patronage more credible. A perfect example of such an account is the one that recounts Niẓām al-Mulk defending the descendants of the saint from accusations laid against them by an anti-Sufi Ḥanafī ʿAlawī. The latter had critiqued Abū Saʿīd's descendants and disciples for being ignorant of the basics of Islam, even the Qurʾan. Furthermore, he had questioned the appropriateness of Niẓām al-Mulk patronizing such an ignorant bunch. The vizier had asked the saint's grandson, Abū ʾl-Futūḥ, to be made present in order to quiz him on his memorization of the Qurʾan. The specific chapter was not revealed until the public had gathered to witness this questioning. Niẓām al-Mulk asked Abū ʾl-Futūḥ to recite the forty-eighth chapter of the Qurʾan, which he did successfully. The partisan crowd rejoiced, and the humiliated and defeated ʿAlawī departed. It was only then that the grandson of the saint confessed that in fact he was ignorant of the Qurʾan—except for one chapter. It had been at the insistence of his grandfather, the great Abū Saʿīd, that he had memorized the very surah that he had been asked to recite on this day.[83] The saint's firāsat sanctifies the community and protects its reputation, even after his earthly demise.

While at first this narrative seems like an ordinary firāsat miracle, it serves a deeper purpose as well. In the course of the narrative, Niẓām al-Mulk insists that Khwāja Abū ʾl-Futūḥ was "the best of the Sufis of the age" and even "the Pole" (*quṭb*). Here the tables are turned—the vizier, who had been designated through the firāsat and legitimized through the baraka of the saint, is now in a position to acknowledge and legitimize the descendants of the saint. Furthermore, his patronage is the tie that binds the descendants and the political figures together. It is remarked that Niẓām al-Mulk was the disciple "of the Shaykh *and the Shaykh's children*" and the disciples of all the Sufis because of the Shaykh.[84] In the course of the prolegomena to the same narrative, it is revealed that the descendents of the saint had turned to the vizier because they had once again run up debts that they could not afford to repay. Niẓām al-Mulk is described as being the lone person who could have paid off these debts, and he did not disappoint them: he is said to have rewarded them in a measure "beyond limits and descriptions."[85] The past and the present are reconnected; the relations of patronage reconnect the disciples and their patrons, and the narratives recall both the spiritual merit of the patrons and the efficacy of this patronage.

Bābā Ṭāhir is utilized to legitimize the founding members of the Saljūq dynasty, and Abū Saʿīd is connected to the institutionalizing organizer of the Saljūq realm, Niẓām al-Mulk. There is yet another saint appropriated by the Saljūq legitimizing discourse: Aḥmad-i Jām is connected with the last of the Great Saljūqs, Sanjar. No period of Saljūq rule, beginning, middle, or end, is left bereft of the legitimizing presence of a Sufi master. It is to Aḥmad-i Jām that we now turn.

Aḥmad-i Jām

Aḥmad "of Jām" was born in the year 440/1048 in a small village called Nāmaq, close to Tarshīz in Quhistān.[86] While he is occasionally referred to by the appellation *Nāmaqī*, he is more frequently known by the place that his family migrated to: Jām. His numerous honorific titles include *Shaykh al-Islām, Quṭb al-awtād* (Pole of the four saintly props), and curiously, *ẓhanda pīl* (the great elephant). If one is to believe the hagiographic accounts of his life, Aḥmad-i Jām spent his youth in a drunken stupor. The hagiographic trope of the repentant drunkard turned saint is of course well-known in Sufi literature.[87] These stages of his life are referred to in the hagiography as the age of moral depravity,[88] a resonant concept in all Saljūq texts. According to the same source, the turning point in his life came when he, riding on a donkey carrying wine, had an experience not unlike that of Paul on the road to Damascus. He heard a great voice and repented from his life style. He retreated into a life of solitude for twelve years and devoted himself to ascetic practices. This repentance (*tawba*) is depicted in typically emphatic—not to say exaggerated—fashion in later hagiographic sources. ʿAbd al-Raḥmān Jāmī (d. 1492) claims that Aḥmad-i Jām was unlettered (*ummī*) until the age of twenty-nine but subsequently composed over three hundred works on various religious sciences.[89] Upon his return, Aḥmad turned to summoning those around him to a strongly sharʿī-oriented interpretation of Sufism. Aḥmad-i Jām died in the year 536/1141 in his khānaqāh, located in Jām.

The hagiography of Aḥmad-i Jām attempts to establish a spiritual transmission between him and Abū Saʿīd-i Abi ʾl-Khayr.[90] According to this claim, a disciple of Abū Saʿīd named Abū Ṭāhir-i Kurd is reported to have passed on to Aḥmad-i Jām the khirqa of the famous saint from Mayhana. Fritz Meier rightly questions the historicity of such a transmission.[91] From our perspective, however, what is important about this claim is not its historical veracity. Rather, this narrative is an important documentation of the attempt of Aḥmad-i Jām's descendants to link themselves with Abū Saʿīd, the most successful spiritual and earthly saint of the generation prior to Aḥmad-i Jām. Jāmī's *Nafaḥāt al-uns*, one of the most important later Persian hagiographies, devotes a detailed section to the transmission of this mythical khirqa from Abū Saʿīd to Aḥmad-i Jām via Abū Ṭāhir.[92] Regardless of the "authenticity" of the reports of the spiritual transmission from Abū Saʿīd to Aḥmad-i Jām, the descendants of Aḥmad-i Jām succeeded in documenting this link in the eyes of premodern Sufis.

Aḥmad-i Jām's writings

In distinction to the other saints considered in this chapter, Aḥmad authored a number of texts, many of which are still extant: *Rawḍat al-mudhnibīn, Anīs al-tāʾibīn, Miftāḥ al-najāt*, and others such as *Sirāj al-sāʾirīn*, *Kunūz al-ḥikma*, and *Biḥār al-ḥaqīqa*. Significant for our purposes, another treatise, titled the *Risāla-yi Samarqandīya*, includes a correspondence between Aḥmad-i Jām and Sultan Sanjar. Sanjar's letter was an inquiry about the signs through which God's saints can be identified.

An intriguing case is that of the collection of poems (*dīvān*) attributed to Aḥmad-i Jām. The authenticity of the *Dīvān* has been severely questioned by many scholars, as this *Dīvān* contains many poems which at face value contain audacious claims. The *radīf*, "rhyming words," at the end of one particularly poem are *man mulḥid-i dīrīna-am*, "I am ancient heretic!" In it, the composer claims to have been the actual agent of the *Miʿrāj*, the real Joseph at the bottom of the pit, Jonah in the belly of the whale, etc. He claims to be the cure to every ailment and the guide of every seeker. Furthermore, he lashes out against "judges" (*qāḍī-yān*), "jurists" (*muftī-yān*), "Muslims" (*islāmī-yān*), "the pious" (*pārsā*), "ascetics" (*zuhhād*), and "righteous ones" (*ṣāliḥ-ān*). He calls himself the "pure Light of Aḥmad"[93] and equal to both Muṣṭafā (Prophet Muḥammad) and God![94] The ecstatic and outrageous claims of this poem are in no way reconcilable with the image of the sharʿī-oriented, austere preacher we get from Aḥmad-i Jām's own writings. The editor of the texts of Aḥmad-i Jām, ʿAlī Fāḍil, believes that the overwhelming majority of these poems are later fabrications ascribed to the famous saint.[95] This provides an intriguing example of how the "public image" of a saint might often be constructed based on texts which have little or no connection to the saint's own writings.[96] For our purposes here, what is more of interest is not the above controversial poetry but rather connections of Aḥmad-i Jām with the political figures of his time. He too was willingly appropriated by the Saljūq legitimizing discourse that was centered on claims of *nīkū iʿtiqād*, "orthodoxy." I will first examine Aḥmad's own account of this relationship and then analyze hagiographic accounts about him composed by his disciples and descendants.

There is already a direct textual link between Aḥmad-i Jām's own writings and one of the mightiest of the Saljūq rulers, Sultan Sanjar (477/1084 to 552/1157). Fritz Meier mentions but does not explore the ramifications of this relationship.[97] It is precisely this investigation that informs our inquiry here: the text of *Rawḍat al-mudhnibīn* is dedicated to Sultan Sanjar. The long soliloquy that opens the book is a masterpiece of Persian panegyrics and deserves a thorough analysis. The narrative starts out by establishing the credentials of Aḥmad-i Jām himself and his relationship with Sultan Sanjar: "The Khwāja, the ascetic Imām, Shaykh al-Islam, the exemplar of the forty substitute saints, he who summons people to Truth, he who is full of sympathetic compassion for people, the governor of justice on God's earth, Abū Naṣr Aḥmad ibn Abī ʾl-Ḥasan al-Nāmaqī al-Jāmī (may God sanctify his mighty spirit),[98] had wanted to say a prayer for the Sultan of the whole world, the most great Shāhanshāh, may God make his rule and realm eternal. He had desired to do this out of a spirit of friendship, support, and invocation of prayers."[99]

Whereas with Bābā Ṭāhir and Abū Saʿīd the relationships between saints and political figures are portrayed in hagiographic accounts, the case of Aḥmad-i Jām provides us with a different scenario: the first-person voice of the saint. Aḥmad-i Jām reaches out to the sultan in a spirit of friendship (*dūst-dārī*), support (*hawā-khwāhī*), and invocation of blessings (*duʿā-gūʾī*). The saint does not identify himself as a servant of the king, but a "friend" (*dūst*). He comes not to beg, but to lend support; he brings not a plea, but blessings. While the overall tone of the panegyric quickly moves on to the expected praise of the king in typically hyperbolic terms, it is this initial self-identification of the more or less equal relationship between the saint and the king that is of interest. It confirms our contention that the transaction of baraka between the saint and the political figure is not a one-way transmission but a reciprocal process of exchange.

Having identified his endeavor as that of a pious soul wishing to show his "friendship and support" toward Sultan Sanjar, Aḥmad-i Jām moves on to a double praise of Sanjar and his royal court. Sanjar is praised in typical Saljūq terms: "Master of the East and the West," "refuge of dervishes," and "protecting friend of Muslims." Significantly, the court is praised not in terms of its material riches but as containing a host of "Imāms, viziers, intellectuals, and servants."

> The more he [Aḥmad-i Jām] looked into the matter, the less he saw himself worthy of adding anything whatsoever to what was already with the king.
>
> The court of that king of the world, the shadow of his realm, the throne of the Sultan of the universe, the most great Shāhanshāh, the master of the East and the West, the Khusrau of Khurāsān, the champion of the world, the Sun of the Earth and the epoch . . . the enemy of the faith-less ones, the protecting friend of the Muslims, the refuge of the dervishes, the support and shelter of the weak ones, Sanjar ibn Malik-Shāh ibn Alb Arslān, (may God make his realm eternal) was already so full . . .[100]

This portion of the narrative starts out with a description of the sultan's honorific titles and responsibilities. He is to protect the Muslims, to combat the irreligious ones, to fight for Islam, and, significantly, to act as the refuge of the dervishes. The relationship is clearly a mutual and a reciprocal one: so long as the king fulfills his task of protecting the Muslims, the weak ones, and specifically the ʿulamāʾ and Sufi dervishes, the saints will lend their friendship, support, and blessings to the sultan.

Despairing of having nothing new to bring to Sultan Sanjar's magnificent court, Aḥmad moves on to the pious trope of having to apologize for writing his work. This is a common trope in Persian mystical writings in which the author claims to be goaded into writing the work either at the earnest bequest of a friend or disciple or after having been inspired directly by a divine agency. In this particular case, Aḥmad claims then to be inspired through three sources: the king's divinely bestowed splendor (*farr*),[101] Providence, and the "realm and felicity of the Sultan of the world," that is, Sanjar. The specific agent of inspiration is stated to be the angel of Divine Inspiration (*ilhām-i rabbānī*), which told him, "If you wish to show your own characteristic at the gate of the Sultan of the world—may God make his realm eternal—so that from now until the Day of resurrection you and him will be thought of well, write a book in his name. That way, when the prayerful ones look at the book, they may make remembrance of you and him. The elite and the masses, the noble and the base, everyone will benefit from it."[102] Having been thus anointed by the divine agency of inspiration, Aḥmad proceeds to explicitly dedicate the book to Sultan Sanjar, who yet again is praised:

> The Sultan who keeps and adorns the world is the blessed king. Through his existence, the weak ones find solace. In his throne, in his fortune, and in his court Muslims find ease . . . To the believers and the dervishes, he is a luminous sun, a bright moon, a brilliant star, a beaming sun. Through him, every body is pure, and every person is fragrant . . .
>
> Aḥmad ibn Abī ʾl-Ḥasan al-Nāmaqī al-Jāmī will immediately start to write this book through the inspiration of God Almighty, in the name of the Sultan of the World [Sanjar], may God make his realm eternal, in the month of Muḥarram in the year 520 [i.e., 1126 C.E.].[103]

Having thus praised the ruler, asserted his own relationship to the sultan, and provided a pious apology for the writing of the text, Aḥmad-i Jām moves on to clarify the conditions incumbent on the reader. The key phrase used here, *iʿtiqād-i durust* (right doctrine) belongs to the same discourse of orthodoxy we have previously encountered in legitimizing the Saljūq Sultans: "It is imperative on whoever reads this book to do so using a right-doctrine (*iʿtiqād-i durust*)."[104] The Saljūqs were legitimized on the basis of having possessed "good and pure doctrine" (*nīkū iʿtiqād*), quite literally orthodoxy. Here the saint uses an almost identical language, that of "right doctrine" (*iʿtiqād-i durust*), in defining how his text is to be read. Nor is this an isolated reference; the totality of the above panegyric is filled with contrasting those who have "no-religion" (*bī-dīnān*) and those who have religion (*dīn-dārān*). One can see in such language the emergence of a concept of "belief" which one either possesses or not. Furthermore, this belief is one that has to be defined as "good" or "pure" as opposed to "bad" or "incorrect."[105] Yet again we are faced with the overlap of intellectual and political discourses in Saljūq Islam: the same rhetoric of orthodoxy which is found in historical and political texts is seen in mystical texts. The emphasis on "right," "pure" and "good" doctrine is a ubiquitous feature of Saljūq society at all levels: political, spiritual, and intellectual. Not only are the mystics and political figures of this time period directly engaged with one another, they both utilize the same discourse of legitimacy, "orthodoxy," and authenticity. In a sense, it is not so much that mystics are yielding to politicians, or that politicians have surrendered to saintly beings, but that both groups participate in a discourse of orthodoxy.

Aḥmad-i Jām and Hagiographic Material

The relationship between Aḥmad-i Jām and the Saljūq Sultan Sanjar did not have to be fabricated in the hagiographic narratives: Aḥmad-i Jām himself had dedicated one of his texts, the *Rawḍat al-mudhnibīn*, to Sultan Sanjar and carried on a correspondence with him in another (*Risāla-yi samarqandīya*). Aḥmad's descendants and hagiographers eagerly expanded and embellished this relationship. The main person responsible for this was his main hagiographer, Sadīd al-Dīn Ghaznavī, who composed the extant source *Maqāmāt-i zhanda pīl*.[106] This hagiography drew on an earlier (no longer extant) source written by Raḍī al-Dīn ʿAlī b. Ibrāhīm-i Tāʾabādī.[107]

The *Maqāmāt-i zhanda pīl* contains a host of wondrous deeds (*karamāt*) attributed to Aḥmad-i Jām, including healing, feeding, and punishing narratives. In addition, a significant part of this hagiography deals with establishing relations of power, protection, and patronage between the saint and political figures, in particular the powerful Saljūq Sultan, Sanjar. As mentioned above, there is no reason to doubt the historicity of a connection between Aḥmad-i Jām and Sultan Sanjar.[108] However, in the *Maqāmāt-i zhanda pīl* this connection is articulated in a series of narratives in which the saint saves the sultan's life from Ismāʿīlī threats and assassination attempts. What follows is an analysis of some of these narratives.

When History and Hagiography Converge—and Diverge

The most detailed narrative that documents the relationship between Aḥmad-i Jām and political figures is one that provides us with a perfect opportunity to examine how hagiographic narratives overlap with and yet remain distinct from historical ones. This narrative from the *Maqāmāt-i zhanda pīl* discusses an ominous situation, that of an Ismaʿīlī assassination attempt on the life of Sultan Sanjar.[109] According to this narrative, an Ismāʿīlī *dāʿī* (missionary) named Shaykh Asʿad ʿIrāqī, from Quhistān, came to Sultan Sanjar's capital, Marv. Shaykh Asʿad concealed his true identity and managed to befriend the sultan's personal wardrobe coordinator, Abū ʾl-Futūḥ. Having gained his trust, the Ismāʿīlī missionary asked Abū ʾl-Futūḥ to place a dagger underneath the sultan's pillow. To ensure the cooperation of his accomplice, he bribed Abū ʾl-Futūḥ with a thousand gold coins. When Sanjar saw the dagger, in his private chamber nonetheless, he was filled with real fear. He clearly recognized it as a tangible and ominous symbol of the ease of access his ill-wishers had to his most private chambers. Abū ʾl-Futūḥ naturally feigned ignorance of how the dagger had gotten there. The Sultan asked his wardrobe coordinator to keep the whole matter a secret.

Soon after, an Ismāʿīlī messenger from Quhistān arrived and brought many gifts for the sultan. Furthermore, he also asked the sultan for peace between the Saljūqs and the Ismāʿīlīs, in particular through a guarantee of safe passage for all the Ismāʿīlīs to Khurāsān. The messenger's request was accompanied by a threat, should the wishes not be granted. The sultan responded by stating that he had no reason to seek peace with "the heretics." The messenger of the Ismāʿīlīs (whom the narratives call "the infidels") reminded the sultan of the hitherto secret dagger, further stating that it would be no great matter to have him killed. The understandably fearful sultan made a pact with the Ismāʿīlīs and allowed them entry into the cities of Khurāsān. Soon the number of the Ismāʿīlīs greatly increased in Khurāsān, which is said to have caused great concern for many of the Saljūq religious leaders and military commanders. Yet the fear of assassination kept the once powerful sultan from acting against the Ismāʿīlīs. As a final insult, the Ismāʿīlīs even established a propaganda center (*daʿwat-khāna*) in the sultan's own capital, Marv.

What is remarkable about the above narrative is that up to this point it is in complete agreement with the most reliable historical sources of the period—a virtually identical account exists in *Jahān-gushā-yi Juwaynī [Juvaini]*. In this source, the noted historian ʿAlā al-Dīn ʿAṭa Mulk Juvaini reports that he had personally viewed Sanjar's regal decrees (*farmān*s) in which he had "conciliated and flattered" the Ismāʿīlīs.[110] However, whereas Juvaini insists that this peace lasted throughout Sanjar's reign in which "the Ismāʿīlīs enjoyed ease and tranquility,"[111] the hagiography insists on a different end to the narrative: the saintly—and political—intervention of Aḥmad-i Jām.

The rest of the narrative in the *Maqāmāt* diverges from the conventional historical narrative of this episode. Aḥmad-i Jām miraculously intervenes to save the king's life, the Saljūq kingdom, and indeed the well-being of Islamdom from the imminent Ismāʿīlī threat. The hagiographic narrative continues in the following fashion: one day, when Aḥmad-i Jām was discussing the issue of the infidels (Ismāʿīlīs) with his disciples in Nīshāpūr, he had an "unveiling" (*kashf*). The saint was told to go to Marv and inform the king of the evil of being so lax with "the infidels." Aḥmad-i Jām sensed that there was a great *fitna* in both "the religion and the world." The sultan welcomed him to Marv and received the saint warmly. Aḥmad severely criticized Sanjar for his lax dealing with the Ismāʿīlīs. The sultan responded that everything that he had done up to that point had been through consultation with the religious scholars but that from that point on, he would proceed only as the saint commanded. The saint, still not satisfied, protested, "Have you no fear of God Almighty? Have you no shame?" He further demanded that all the religious scholars (including the Ismāʿīlīs) be gathered in the court on the following day.

Upon convening the gathering Aḥmad had requested, the *dāʿī* of the Ismāʿīlīs posed a theological question. None of the Sunni religious scholars dared answer this challenge. It seemed that they wished for Aḥmad to take on the *dāʿī*, since the saint himself had insisted on that gathering. No doubt, they also wished for Aḥmad to shoulder any risks of publicly confronting the *dāʿī*. The Sufi saint stated that he, being a religious leader, loathed to speak to this "infidel dog" (*sag-i mulḥid*) and instead called on his own servant who had carried his shoes[112] to come and sit knee-to-knee in front of the Ismāʿīlī scholar. The unlearned servant answered the *dāʿī*'s question correctly. The court erupted into a joyous celebration. The *dāʿī* hung his head in embarrassment at having been defeated by a servant. The sultan asked the saint as to what should be done with the Ismāʿīlī leader. The Shaykh responded, "He has bad-religion (*bad-dīn*), he should be killed quickly so that we can move on to the other matters that need tending to." The king still hesitated to kill him, fearing the "infidels." An hour passed, and the sultan had still not ordered the *dāʿī* to be killed. The narrative states that this was due to the sultan's fear of the Ismāʿīlīs. Aḥmad-i Jām, at this point quite angry, erupted:

> What is this? Do you not see that you have clearly been trusted (*sipurda*) to me? It is through God Almighty's grace and permission that I have been and continue to protect (*muḥāfaẓat*) you . . . What has happened to make you so weak in your belief (*sust-ʿaqīda*)?
>
> If an ignorant one became deluded away from the right path by the promise of gold (coins), and followed an infidel's cunning to place a dagger under your pillow, why are you so afraid? Have you no shame? *So long as I am alive, you have no one to fear*. Tell them to kill this infidel so that you can see what moral corruption and strife has been established in Marv and other locations.[113]

The sultan responded that he knew nothing of the corruption and strife to which Aḥmad was alluding. The saint asked for a military commander named Muḥammad Marvazī to be made present. The saint ordered the commander to take ten of his trusted men and proceed to follow his very detailed instructions: they were to go to a certain neighborhood, such-and-such a street, and find a certain house. Once inside, they were to go to a dais on the south side and look for a curtain that was hiding a secret domed chamber. The *qibla* of this domed chamber contained another curtain, hiding another room. This room contained a niche, which contained a locked box. The commander was to break the lock and obtain the writings that were hidden inside.

Meanwhile Aḥmad-i Jām ordered a few of the famous people in Marv to be made present, claiming that they were some of the people whose names were included on the list to be discovered by the military commander. Many of the religious leaders expressed astonishment at this, as the names that Shaykh al-Islām was reading off included many of the most well-known and respected citizens of Marv. Eventually the sultan and the religious leaders apologized to the saint for having doubted him and confessed that they had been ignorant of the strife and moral corruption. Shaykh al-Islām commanded that all of the people on the list be made present and stated that any Ismāʿīlīs who would repent and return from that madhhab and belief (*iʿtiqād*) would be let go, whereas anyone who refused would be immediately killed. Most of the Ismāʿīlīs repented, except for eighteen of them who were killed.[114]

Thus ends one of the most remarkable and successful Saljūqid hagiographic myths. The myth is successful, not only because it was quoted subsequently by a number of historians, and certainly not because it survives a modern, positivistic scrutiny. In fact, many of the details in the latter half of the narrative are likely to be dismissed by many historians as the product of the fanciful imagination of a pious follower of the great saint who is seeking to exalt his ancestor. Yet from our perspective, the myth is successful because it weaves together so perfectly and harmoniously many distinct elements of the Saljūq mythology. The scene prior to the arrival of the great saint is one full of sociodoctrinal upheaval. The pernicious Ismāʿīlī threat is encroaching on the heartland of Saljūq power, Khurāsān. The heretical doctrine of the Ismāʿīlīs is combined with that other great fear of Saljūq administrators: the infiltration of Ismāʿīlī propagandists in the very court of the Saljūq rulers, leading to threats of assassination. This hagiographic narrative succeeds in linking together the well-being of Islamdom, that of the Saljūq kingdom, the king's rule, the intervention of the "orthodox saint," and the suppression of the socioreligious threat of heresy. It is the overlapping of all these factors that makes this narrative another perfect Saljūq hagiographic myth. Written by a follower of Aḥmad-i Jām long after the demise of the Saljūqs, it recapitulates and perpetuates the myth of the Great Saljūqs. The heresy of the Ismāʿīlīs is portrayed as being combined with psychological manipulation into allowing them to manhandle even the Saljūq Sultan. The background of this story fully recapitulates the historical background necessary for the Great Saljūq Myth. The recurring terms in this narrative, which fully recall that of the Great Saljūq Myth, are *fitna* and *iʿtiqād*.

Enter the saint. Unlike many of the king's servants and the Ismāʿīlīs who are "bad-religion" (*bad-dīn*), Shaykh al-Islām is described as possessing an insight (*firāsat*) that even the king's religious advisers did not. Even the king is criticized for having been weak in his *iʿtiqād*, a malaise that only the saint can remedy. He can expose the heretics and pushes for their punishment. He alone can vouchsafe the king's safety and Islam's "orthodoxy": "So long as I am alive, you have no one to fear." There is also a not so subtle implication that the sultan should fear the saint. The saint further claims that he alone is responsible for the protection of the sultan, a task that has been divinely bestowed upon him. The narrative ends, as expected, with the king rescued from danger, the Ismāʿīlīs subjugated, and everyone renewing their pact with the great saint.

Hagiography as Narrative That Shapes Behavior

In arguing for the reading of hagiographic narratives as mythic—as defined by Doniger, Heffernan, and others—I have stressed the importance of these narratives in shaping behavior and eliciting responses. The hagiographic narratives of Aḥmad-i Jām are no exception. Whereas the saint may be viewed as having lent his legitimizing baraka and life-saving insight (*firāsat*) to the Saljūqs, the Saljūq Sultan clearly reciprocated this favor through his patronage of the shrine complex. We are told that Sanjar visited Aḥmad-i Jām both before and after the latter's death. Sanjar is said to have visited the great saint after the saint retired from the city of Sarakhs to the village of Maʿd-Ābād,[115] and visited his shrine after the saint's passing. Furthermore, Sanjar also contributed to the upkeep of the shrine and its expansion and patronized learning circles around the *turbat*. He also supported the many charities associated with the shrine complex.[116]

What might be termed the career of a saint seems to continue even after his death—a skeptic might even say it only starts after his death. The example of authority and spiritual power (*baraka*) possessed by the saints allowed their descendants and disciples throughout the centuries to appeal to their example. This was indeed the case for the followers of Aḥmad-i Jām. Even after the generation of the hagiographer Ghaznavī, the descendants of the Shaykh explicitly invited the political figures of their own time periods to

5.1. The shrine of Aḥmad-i Jām. (Lisa Golombek and Donald Wilber, *The Timurid Architecture of Iran and Turan*, vol. 2. © 1988 Princeton University Press. Reprinted by permission of Princeton University Press)

emulate Sanjar by continuing to support and patronize the shrine complex of Aḥmad-i Jām. This would lead to them earning the continued baraka, support, and blessings of the long-deceased, but certainly not forgotten, Shaykh. The descendants of Aḥmad-i Jām seem to have been successful at achieving this goal, as we are told that the great warlord Timurlane visited the shrine.[117] The link between the great saint and his descendants is further accentuated by the numerous children and descendants of Aḥmad-i Jām who are buried in this ever-expanding complex.[118] In the subsequent years, divergent rulers ranging from Shāh ʿAbbās Ṣafavī[119] to the Moghul emperor Humāyūn have contributed to the upkeep of this shrine.[120] Furthermore, many of the descendants of the Aḥmad-i Jām also assumed the authority to address political figures in the same fashion as their pious ancestor had once addressed Sanjar. Here the charisma and baraka of a saint is not simply transmitted but also renewed. One of the distinguished followers of Aḥmad-i Jām, Muʿīn al-Dīn Jāmī,[121] addressed Timur (Amīr Taymūr Gūrgān) in the following fashion:

> When I put pen to paper, a joyous tiding came to me, saying: "Address him as 'child'! Your ancestors, may God's mercy and supreme pleasure be upon them, used to address emperors as 'child.' You too should address them in this fashion so that you may find felicity and prosperity. How grateful will that realm be in the tomorrow's Hereafter, when he will be gathered under the Banner of Aḥmad[122] and reckoned as one of his [i.e., Aḥmad-i Jām's] 'children.' They will strive to pursue justice, seek redress, and mind the flock, the worshippers, the great saints, scholars, and ascetics."[123]

In tracing his own practice of addressing a king as "child," Muʿīn al-Dīn Jāmī appeals to the example of Aḥmad-i Jām. In doing so, he reminds Timur of the spiritual relationship between Aḥmad-i Jām and Sultan Sanjar. No doubt the suggestion is that, just as the great Sultan Sanjar was devoted to Aḥmad-i Jām, so should the great Timur submit to a similar relationship with Muʿīn al-Dīn. He addresses Timur as *farzand* (child) just as Aḥmad-i Jām once addressed Sanjar, a connection he explicitly raises in the following: "The Great Sultan of Islam, the king who guards the kings of the world, the shadow of God, Abū ʾl-Ḥārith Sanjar ibn Malik-Shāh . . . who was the emperor of the whole world, and the Khusrau of the universe, was the child and disciple (*farzand va murīd*) of His Holiness, Shaykh Aḥmad (-i Jām), may God sanctify his innermost heart."[124]

Muʿīn al-Dīn further recalls a number of hagiographic accounts, which also document Sanjar's devotion to Aḥmad-i Jām. In one narrative, we are told that the sultan came to the *Khānaqāh* of the saint when the dervishes were carrying mud (mixed with straw, to make walls). The "Sultan with the beautiful name, him of the good-doctrine (*nīkū iʿtiqād*)" got up and helped them carry some mud. When the Shaykh asked the king why he was tending to such tedious tasks, the king answers:

> So that if tomorrow (i.e., on Judgement Day) God Almighty asks of me: "O you who was given the whole world, what did you do for Our sake?," I can say: "I too carried a bin of mud in the worship place of a saint from your saints."
>
> Sanjar was but a servant (*ghulām*) carrying a bin
> when he was with Zhanda Pīl, the holy one of God.[125]

A remarkable feature of this narrative is that once again the motif of the "good and pure doctrine" (*nīkū iʿtiqād*) sultan is brought up by the hagiographer, and we are told that it was due to this *iʿtiqād* that God rewarded him. Not only do the Saljūqs possess and propagate orthodoxy, God even rewards them directly for their orthodoxy. In this mutual relationship, "good doctrine" goes far beyond a simple list of theological creeds and includes devotion to Sufi masters. Orthodoxy and devotion-patronage are forever linked in Saljūq ideology.

Muʿīn al-Dīn concludes this remark by the following emphatic conclusion: "For this belief (*iʿtiqād*), God Almighty gave to Sanjar religion, the world, and a long life. For sixty plus years he freely ruled the age and the Earth, and none harmed him."[126] The message to Timur is clear: Timur can have the same long life, political might and religious peace that Sanjar enjoyed if he earns/receives the spiritual blessing of the saints, conveniently being offered by the descendants of Aḥmad-i Jām. The way to receive the baraka, naturally, is through devotion and patronage.

Thus unfolds the successful symbiotic existence of saints and Saljūqs in medieval Iran. Two elite communities, one rooted in raw political and military power (*shawka*), the other in spiritual power (*baraka*), largely came to coexist and support one another. It may be safely said that the Saljūq interest in the Sufis was not so much because of their mystical insight, poetic utterances, or teachings of love and divine knowledge. The Saljūqs sought out legitimization at the hands of Sufis (and their communities) because the awliyāʾ were seen as possessing baraka and wilāya—which means that they possessed power. Power, whether earthly or heavenly, was something with which the Saljūqs were familiar, and in which they were intimately interested.

Conclusion

The aims of this chapter have been threefold: first, to study three of the more important mystics of this time period, Bābā Ṭāhir, Abū Saʿīd-i Abī ʾl-Khayr, and Aḥmad-i Jām, in the sociohistorical context of their time period. Second, to offer close readings of hagiographic passages which have tended to be all too quickly dismissed by many historians and scholars of Sufism. I have argued for the importance of hagiographic works in reconstructing the sociohistorical world of premodern Islam. Third, I have sought to problematize the identification of post-Enlightenment categories of "privatized experience" as the essence of mysticism in the case of Sufism.

In this chapter we have documented some of the social roles of the Sufis in legitimizing Saljūq institutions. Yet not all the mystics of this period were so eager to lend their support to the Saljūq regime. Some, such as Khwāja ʿAbd Allāh Anṣārī, suffered untold harassment at the hands of the Saljūqs, and others, such as ʿAyn al-Quḍāt Hamadānī, deliberately took upon themselves the task of opposing Saljūqid rule, which they viewed as unjust, illegitimate, and oppressive. It is to these oppositional figures that we now turn.

Chapter Six

An Oppositional Sufi: ʿAyn al-Quḍāt Hamadānī

And then there were the oppositional figures. Edward Said has previously stated that the one adjective he would use not to modify but to emphasize the task of being a social critic would be "oppositional,"[1] and there were a few Saljūq notables who fully qualified as oppositional social critics. These were not a homogenous group but rather consisted of many figures operating outside the major religio-political alliances of this time period. While some Sufis (and more importantly, their descendants) such as Abū Saʿīd-i Abī ʾl-Khayr and Aḥmad-i Jām aligned themselves with the Saljūqs, others resisted lending their baraka to legitimizing the Saljūqs. Some of the "outsiders" were neither Shāfiʿī nor Ḥanafī but Ḥanbalīs, like Khwāja ʿAbd Allāh Anṣārī.[2] He was a pious soul who remained a perpetual outsider to the Saljūq regime and was regularly harassed. We are told that due to his critique of the Ashʿarī theologians, Anṣārī was threatened with death on five separate occasions and was exiled three times.[3]

This time period also witnessed the defiant figure of ʿAyn al-Quḍāt Hamadānī. He certainly had all the qualifications to be a powerful insider and an active participant in legitimizing the Saljūqs: he was Shāfiʿī-Ashʿarī, a judge, a Sufi, a popular preacher, etc. However, this was one dissident who used his baraka not to bargain with the Saljūqs but to rise against them, defiantly contesting their legitimacy. He called into question the association of religious scholars with them, the economic underpinnings of their system, and the very legitimacy of their rule. In doing so, he presented the most thorough contestation of Saljūq authority in this period. He was the embodiment of an oppositional social critic in the Saljūq era.

ʿAyn al-Quḍāt Hamadānī (492/1098–525/1131)

The life of ʿAyn al-Quḍāt is wrapped up in many myths and legends. The hagiographic accounts about his life and, more importantly, his death are so fantastic as to have almost eclipsed his real accomplishments: his teachings and writings. The legendary accounts of his martyrdom are well-known and will only be alluded to here. Many of the hagiographies and scholars who have analyzed the life and death of ʿAyn al-Quḍāt have imposed a Ḥallājian persona on ʿAyn al-Quḍāt, thus collapsing each man's distinctiveness as well as the circumstances that led to their death. Rahim Farmanish, the first twentieth-century scholar to have gathered together material on the life and writings of ʿAyn al-Quḍāt, was among the first to have noted the "similarity" between the two: "There is a complete similarity between the lives of these two ecstatic Sufis (Ḥallāj and ʿAyn al-Quḍāt), in terms of their endurance of torture and pain, accusations, conviction, and the quality of their martyrdom. This is why some have called him Manṣūrī [Ḥallājian] in terms of his path."[4] Another noted scholar who focused on the similarity between ʿAyn al-Quḍāt and Ḥallāj was the noted Russian orientalist, Y. Bertels, who stated, "It is possible to see the echoes of Ḥallāj's cry of *Anā ʾl-Ḥaqq* in many Iranian Sufis. However, in most cases this cry is turned to a meaningless formula, and loses its original depth and rapturous pride. Using all of his force, ʿAyn al-Quḍāt brought back to life this cry. Two hundred years after Ḥallāj's death, he repeated the latter's tragedy in all of its detail."[5]

The main problem of reading ʿAyn al-Quḍāt as an ethereal, timeless Ḥallājian martyr is that it rips him out of his own time period, the circumstances against which his discourse is situated, and the political intrigue which led to his death. Even the noted A. J. Arberry falls prey to this tendency, introducing ʿAyn al-Quḍāt as a middle member of a trinity of martyrs consisting of Ḥallāj, ʿAyn al-Quḍāt, and Shaykh al-Ishrāq Suhrawardī without analyzing the historical and/or political context of Saljūq Iran.[6] It is my aim in this chapter to provide a historical context for the challenge that ʿAyn al-Quḍāt represented to the Saljūq regime. Rather than reading his life as a mystical "quest for annihilation,"[7] I propose to contextualize him in his own time and place.

As we can best determine, ʿAyn al-Quḍāt was born in the western Iranian city of Hamadān, in 492/1098. His family was originally from the city of Miyāna[8] in Adharbāījān, which earned him the name by which he is often referred to in biographical dictionaries: al-Miyānajī. His grandfather, who became the Qāḍī of Hamadān, was educated in Baghdad. There are reports

6.1. A page from *Majālis al-ʿushshāq* (*The Gatherings of Lovers*), possibly depicting Ahmad Ghazālī and ʿAyn al-Quḍāt. Courtesy of the Bodleian Library.

that he too was a martyr: Ibn Samʿānī reports that in the year 471/1078, this grandfather figure was killed in the mosque he used to offer his juridical verdicts.[9] ʿAyn al-Quḍāt's father was also a Sufi, and there is evidence that he attended the samāʿ sessions of Aḥmad Ghazālī.[10] The Shāfiʿī historian al-Subkī reports that this father was a "*fāḍil* (virtuous man), son of a *fāḍil*, father of a *fāḍil*." He also mentions that the elder Hamadānī was a companion of the famed Abū Isḥāq Shīrāzī, whom we have already encountered in the opening of Niẓāmīya madrasa.[11] Given Abū Isḥāq's critique of the Saljūqs' usurpation of land, one is tempted here to notice a legacy of qāḍī-ʿulamā's, who critiqued and challenged the legitimacy of the Saljūqs. This group would consist of Abū Isḥāq Shīrāzī, the elder Hamadānī judge who was Shīrāzī's companion, and ʿAyn al-Quḍāt. Other sources also depict ʿAyn al-Quḍāt's father as an intelligent and pious man (*fāḍilan dhakīyan*) who was also a judge.[12] If all of the above accounts dealing with ʿAyn al-Quḍāt's father and grandfather are to be accepted, it seems safe to assume that ʿAyn al-Quḍāt came from a distinguished and scholarly family. We have precious little information about ʿAyn al-Quḍāt's childhood and early education, although his training reveals that he had complete mastery of Arabic and Persian, Qur'an and ḥadīth, poetry and kalām (dialectical theology) by an early age. He himself boasts that by the relatively young age of twenty he had already composed many works that baffled much more established scholars.[13]

Our best source in reconstructing ʿAyn al-Quḍāt's intellectual and spiritual journey is the set of narratives he provides in his own writings, namely the *Zubdat al-ḥaqā'iq, Shakwa 'l-gharīb*, and *Tamhīdāt*. However, in relying upon such seemingly straightforward "autobiographical" narratives, one is reminded of similar works by Ibn Sīnā and Abū Ḥāmid al-Ghazālī. There is little doubt that ʿAyn al-Quḍāt was familiar with those works. It is awfully tempting to read these works as the closest premodern Muslim analogue to a contemporary "spiritual autobiography," especially as all of them use the common tropes of an early genius and the inevitable middle crisis before moving on to the climactic solution. It might be tempting to do so, but I believe that this would be a fundamental misreading of them. These texts were not written to convey the "life and times" of the various intellectuals but rather to act as a sophisticated polemic against certain intellectual discourses. At the very least, they offer the author's "ranking" of the various disciplines. The "stages" each author claims to have moved through correspond to the rank the disciplines hold in the author's perspective. It is no surprise that in the *Sīra shaykh al-ra'īs*, Ibn Sīnā's difficulties were solved only after reading Fārābī's treatise on the objects of the *Metaphysics*.[14] In Ghazālī's *al-Munqidh*, he dismisses the works of Ismāʿīlīs and philosophers and relegates kalām to a clearly subservient position before settling on a Sharʿī view of Sufism. Similarly, ʿAyn al-Quḍāt struggles with kalām, reads Abū Ḥāmid Ghazālī's works, and finally attains to certainty upon meeting Aḥmad Ghazālī. These texts are not the self-evident confessions that the contemporary scholar would so dearly love to possess, although they are the closest we are likely to get to a "personalized" and personified polemic.

ʿAyn al-Quḍāt's personal narrative in the *Zubdat al-ḥaqāʾiq* is a similarly personalized ranking of the usefulness of the various intellectual disciplines. According to this text, in his early twenties he turned to the discipline of kalām. He states that he clung to kalām like one who is drowning and will attempt to hold on to anything to save himself. His intention, we are told, was to turn from "the lowliness of imitationism (*taqlīd*) to the exalted-ness of inner insight (*baṣīra*)." However, he confesses that he "did not attain to what [he] was seeking" in kalām. This plunged him into a serious crisis of intellectual and spiritual faith, which he describes as a frightening abyss as well as one "having mixed up the principles of different schools of thought."[15] He refuses to go into further detail, stating that the majority of people would not benefit from hearing his trials and tribulations and that it might even harm those who have "weak hearts and feeble intellects (*ḍararan ʿaẓīman li ʾl-afhām al-qāṣira wa ʾl-qulūb al-ḍaʿīfa*)."[16] It is at this point that he credits God, the "Guide of the bewildered ones" (*dalīl al-mutaḥayyirīn*), with having guided him to the right path. Part of his cure, he states, was having studied the works of Abū Ḥāmid Ghazālī: "What saved me from falling, apart from God Almighty's grace, was the study of the works of Shaykh Imām, the Proof of Islam, Abū Ḥāmid Muḥammad ibn Muḥammad ibn Muḥammad Ghazālī, may God be pleased with him. I studied his works for almost four years. In this time, the intensity of my [immersion in seeking] the religious sciences led me to see many wonders, which saved me from infidelity, going astray, bewilderment, and blindness."[17]

ʿAyn al-Quḍāt does not end his own spiritual odyssey with his reading of Abū Ḥāmid Ghazālī's texts. After four years of closely reading Abū Ḥāmid's writings, he met the latter's younger brother, Aḥmad Ghazālī. It is Aḥmad whom he calls "my master and lord, the Shaykh, the most sublime imām, the Sultan of the spiritual path (*sulṭān al-ṭarīqa*), the interpreter of spiritual reality."[18]

ʿAyn al-Quḍāt had a remarkable engagement with both of the Al-Ghazālī brothers, Abū Ḥāmid and Aḥmad. I will discuss his relationship with Abū

Ḥāmid at a later point. That relationship was mainly a textual and intellectual one. His relationship with Aḥmad was of a more personal and spiritual nature. Here the conventional hierarchy of a master-disciple relationship disappeared, and each soul became a polished mirror the other used to contemplate spiritual realities. In the correspondences exchanged between the two, ʿAyn al-Quḍāt asks Aḥmad in a straightforward manner what he should do if he ever sees hypocrisy in the latter. This type of rare candor is exceedingly rare in Sufi master-disciple relationship and was one that ʿAyn al-Quḍāt fostered in his own disciples as well.

Farmanish held that the initial meeting between ʿAyn al-Quḍāt and Aḥmad Ghazālī probably occurred in the year 515/1121.[19] ʿAyn al-Quḍāt's own account of meeting Aḥmad Ghazālī is worth citing:

> I remained in that station for one year, until my lord and master, the Shaykh, the Imām, the Sultan of the spiritual path, Aḥmad ibn Muḥammad ibn Muḥammad ibn Ghazālī, may God have mercy on him, came to my hometown, Hamadān. In twenty days of companionship with him such things became manifest to me that nothing remained of "me," and "my desires," except that which God has willed. Nothing occupies me now except a quest of annihilation in *that.* Even if I attain to Noah's [longevity] in life, and annihilate myself in this quest, it is as if I have done nothing—and that *thing* has taken hold of the whole world. My glance has not fallen upon any thing, without seeing *his face* in it. If any breath does not increase my "drowning" in it/him, may it not be blessed for me![20]

The meeting was so significant for later hagiographers that Jāmī included a Persian paraphrase of the above in his *Nafaḥāt al-uns*.[21] Other sources such as Hidāyat's *Majmaʿ al-fuṣaḥā'* also confirm the very close relationship between the two saintly figures, stating that "Aḥmad Ghazālī united in himself external and internal sciences, and ʿAyn al-Quḍāt, with all of his excellent qualities, was devoted to him."[22] It is not only the Sufi tadhkiras that focus on this event and the relationship it fostered. Even historical sources such as ʿImād al-Dīn al-Kātib al-Iṣfahānī's *Kharīdat al-qaṣr* connect the spiritual legacy of Aḥmad Ghazālī to ʿAyn al-Quḍāt. ʿImād al-Dīn states, "After [Aḥmad] Ghazālī, the sun of excellence never shone no bright as it did in the Qāḍī [ʿAyn al-Quḍāt]."[23] Given the vast internal and external evidence connecting the two, a recent scholarly study on ʿAyn al-Quḍāt that attempts to downplay this relationship appears oddly out of touch with the sources.[24]

Extant Writings of ʿAyn al-Quḍāt

ʿAyn al-Quḍāt's period of intellectual maturity lasted no more than about ten years, but even in this relatively short time he left behind many important works:

Tamhīdāt—ʿAyn al-Quḍāt's masterpiece. In terms of its own merits, the *Tamhīdāt* is one of the most important premodern Sufi texts, and it provides us with a great deal of information about many Sufis whose names and statements would not be known to us otherwise. This work has previously been described as "among the most important texts of Ṣūfī doctrine before Ibn ʿArabī."[25] (The present author is preparing a complete translation of this text for the Classics of Western Spirituality series of Paulist Press.)

Zubdat al-ḥaqāʾiq—"The Choicest of Spiritual Realities," an earlier kalām work of his. ʿAfīf ʿUsayrān, the editor of the *Tamhīdāt*, also edited this book.[26] This work has been frequently confused with the above, even though their content (and language) is vastly different.[27] The confusion is in all likelihood due to a line in the opening paragraph of the *Tamhīdāt* where ʿAyn al-Quḍāt states, "This book, the choicest of realities in unveiling of subtleties (*zubdat al-ḥaqāʾiq fī kashf al-daqāʾiq*) will be completed in ten chapters, so that its readers might benefit from it."[28]

Nāma-hā—Another important source of information about ʿAyn al-Quḍāt, a three-volume collection of over a hundred letters written from ʿAyn al-Quḍāt to various disciples.[29] This marks one of the most impressive extant collections of letters from a Sufi master from the premodern period, consisting of over a thousand pages in its current print version. We will pay particularly close attention to this source as it is our best source for documenting ʿAyn al-Quḍāt's critique of the Saljūq regime.

Shakwa ʾl-gharīb—The last work of ʿAyn al-Quḍāt, his prison memoir, translated by A. J. Arberry as *A Sufi Martyr*.[30] This apologetic text, written by ʿAyn al-Quḍāt in a futile attempt to exonerate himself from the charges of heresy cast against him, distances itself from the more audacious claims made in the *Tamhīdāt* and the *Nāma-hā*.

Lawāʾiḥ—Another text attributed to him, which was published by Raḥīm Farmanish.[31] The dubious *Majālis al-ʿushshāq* attributed it to Hamadānī, while H. Ritter questioned its authenticity. ʿAfīf ʿUsayrān rejects this attribution on stylistic grounds, while Farmanish supported it.[32] However, there are also internal evidences that the text cannot date from earlier than the thirteenth century: the text cites Shaykh Awḥad al-Dīn Kirmānī (d. 635/1238) by name.[33] C. A. Storey attributes the text instead to Qāḍī Ḥamīd al-Dīn Nāgawrī.[34]

Risāla-yi yazdān-shinākht—Another text attributed to ʿAyn al-Quḍāt, which has since been connected with Shaykh al-Ishrāq Suhrawardī.[35]

The above list details only the extant works of ʿAyn al-Quḍāt. Many other works including his extensive Qurʾanic commentary appear to be lost.[36]

ʿAyn al-Quḍāt's Death

In spite of the brilliance that ʿAyn al-Quḍāt demonstrated in the above treatises, most hagiographers—and to a large extent many contemporary scholars—have been more dazzled by the fantastic narratives that have been developed over the centuries to describe his passion. One cannot dismiss the impact of the *Shakwa ʾl-gharīb* here in setting the "mood" which was simply elaborated upon by later hagiographers. The *Shakwa*, an eloquent premodern Muslim prison memoir, may legitimately be considered an "autohagiography." The normally sober Shāfiʿī historian al-Subkī records Ibn al-Samʿānī as having seen a treatise from ʿAyn al-Quḍāt to his "companions and brethren" in Hamadān which, "if it were to be recited over rocks, you would see them become shattered—due to its tenderness and eloquence."[37]

Hagiographic narratives would soon follow, one of the more embellished of which records him as having entrusted the following poem to a disciple a week before his execution:

We have prayed for death, through martyrdom.
If the Friend[38] *would grant what we seek . . .*
Three worthless items:
Fire, oil, and kindling.[39]

More recent hagiographic sources develop the above poem into a full blown passion narrative in which ʿAyn al-Quḍāt is skinned alive, hung in front of the madrasa he used to teach in, then brought down, wrapped in a cloth doused with gasoline, and burned.[40] While one is hard pressed to accept these accounts from a factual level, they do offer an important testimony to the constructed persona of ʿAyn al-Quḍāt in later hagiographies.

The hagiographers resorted to many amusing myths to present ʿAyn al-Quḍāt's persona as a brash, brilliant, confident, and ecstatic soul. One particularly memorable exchange is cited in the *Tadhkirat al-ʿurafāt*. A certain Badīʿ "the theologian"[41] had an enmity with ʿAyn al-Quḍāt. When he heard that

ʿAyn al-Quḍāt had referred to God as "the Necessary Being" (*wājib al-wujūd*), Badīʿ claimed that the divine names should be limited [to those in the Qurʾan and the *ḥadīth*], and that the aforementioned term was one of the technical terms used by philosophers.[42] ʿAyn al-Quḍāt, undeterred, is said to have responded, "He is my beloved, and I will call him by whatever name I please!" (*maḥbūb-i man-ast, bi-har nām kih khwāham khwānamash!*).[43] While the historicity of the above account might well be doubted, it successfully conveys something of the defiance, even brashness, of the young, fiery, love-possessed mystic who was called by later Sufis the "Sultan of lovers" (*Sulṭān al-ʿushshāq*).[44] It is this style, above all else, that characterizes his writings, particularly the *Tamhīdāt*. To that extent it might be said that these hagiographic narratives, which one can dismiss from a postivistic historicist perspective, do faithfully represent the same spirit that animates ʿAyn al-Quḍāt's own bold writings.

One might imagine that the secondary studies on ʿAyn al-Quḍāt would have distanced themselves from such hagiographic approaches. While the scholarly sources on ʿAyn al-Quḍat come from a whole host of perspectives, many of them in fact can be considered neohagiographies perpetuating the same frameworks deployed by the above hagiographers. Others are also impoverished by theoretical problems. Both kinds of secondary sources on ʿAyn al-Quḍāt will be discussed.

The Treatment of ʿAyn al-Quḍāt in Secondary Sources

The classical study which reintroduced ʿAyn al-Quḍāt to the academic world was Raḥīm Farmanish's *Aḥwāl wa āthār-i ʿAyn al-Quḍāt*.[45] This source brought together all the hagiographic data available on ʿAyn al-Quḍāt in a catalogue fashion. However, Farmanish has at times been criticized for not analyzing these hagiographic accounts critically as well as for accepting certain attributed texts such as the *Lawāʾiḥ* as authentic.

Another source that gathered data on ʿAyn al-Quḍāt is Ghulām-Riḍā Afrāsīyābī's *Sulṭān al-ʿushshāq*. This work, more thorough than Farmanish's classic monograph, nonetheless suffers from some of the same weaknesses. As is the case with many Iranian works on Sufism, it is distorted by unwarranted tendencies to introduce Shīʿī and nationalistic elements into its analysis of Sufism.[46] A number of other works deserve to be mentioned as well: Nasrollah Pourjavady, in his usual meticulous scholarship, has authored the careful study, *ʿAyn al-quḍāt wa ustādān-i ū* (*ʿAyn al-Quḍāt and His [Spiritual] Teachers*).[47] Carl Ernst's *Words of Ecstasy in Sufism* contains an insightful chapter on ʿAyn al-Quḍāt's *shaṭḥīyāt*, which presents a thorough analysis of his paradoxical doctrine of "mystical infidelity,"[48] and Leonard Lewisohn has published a useful article titled "In Quest of Annihilation."[49]

The most recent scholar to have written extensively in English on ʿAyn al-Quḍāt is Hamid Dabashi. As far back as 1993, Dabashi had offered a tantalizing essay on ʿAyn al-Quḍāt and indeed the whole intellectual milieu under the Saljūqs in his "Historical Conditions of Persian Sufism during the Seljuk Period." However, he moved to a much more extensive discussion of ʿAyn al-Quḍāt and questions of authority and narrative in his massive *Truth and Narrative: The Untimely Thoughts of ʿAyn al-Qudat al-Hamadhani*. Dabashi's text defies convenient categorization. It is clear that Dabashi has set out not to write a conventional monograph on ʿAyn al-Quḍāt but rather to use the Hamadāni intellectual as a point of departure for presenting what he believes should be a new paradigm of intellectual studies. Dabashi is clearly a gifted and passionate intellectual in his own right, engaging postmodern theories, classical Sufi texts, historical chronicles, and contemporary philosophy with equal grace and ease. There are, however, a whole host of problems in this volume. One of the most serious is in the question of the relationship between ʿAyn al-Quḍāt and the larger Sufi tradition. Dabashi seeks to disconnect ʿAyn al-Quḍāt from the Sufi discourse in which the latter was situated. This much even Dabashi himself had admitted in his 1993 article on "Historical Connections," even speaking of ʿAyn al-Quḍāt's "Sufi voice." However, in *Truth and Narrative*, Dabashi no longer sees Sufism as a proper angle—or even as one angle—for studying the life of ʿAyn al-Quḍāt. Dabashi clearly admits, "The way I shall look at him with my own particular urges and fallibilities, will very much be a reflection of my own conditions and reasons for remembering him."[50] One cannot help but recall ʿAyn al-Quḍāt's own words here, that his discourse has a "mirror-like" quality: whoever looks at them, sees their own face being reflected.[51] In reading and writing about ʿAyn al-Quḍāt, Dabashi is working through some of his own angst as an expatriate, postcolonial Iranian intellectual.

Perhaps the foundational flaw of Dabashi's model is his tendency to construct an essential (and essentialized) dichotomy between jurists and Sufis. Dabashi mentions ʿulamāʾ-Sufi hostilities in his 1993 article, "Historical Conditions." He cites the hostility between the two groups as a

> reflection of two fundamentally opposed interpretations of the Koranic revelation and the Muḥammadan legacy. The positive nomocentricity of Islamic law found the language of Islamic mysticism as quintessentially flawed in nature and disposition. The feeling was mutual. The

> Sufis, too, rejected the rigid and perfunctory nomocentricity of the jurists as quintessentially misguided and a stultification of the Koranic message and the Prophetic traditions. The metaphysical bipolarity had, of course, an active political component with both the mystics and the jurists seeking to manipulate the powers-that-be in their respective interests and advantage.[52]

The "opposition" and "bipolarity" hinted at in "Historical Conditions" were developed in *Truth and Narrative* into an extensive discussion of the "rivalry" between the Sufis and the legal scholars, which depicts various Sufi masters as "subverting the nomocentricism of the clerical establishment."[53] The resulting image is none other than the trite characterization of an absolute dichotomy between Sufis and jurists. As far back as the mid-1960s, Hodgson had problematized with great sensitivity and nuance the very dichotomy deployed by Dabashi. In his chapter "Maturity and Dialogue among the Intellectual Traditions, c. 945–1111," Hodgson stated:

> In the High Caliphal Period Islamicate scholarship and science had flowed in a number of largely separate streams. The Sharʿī scholars, the Adīb, and the Faylasūf by no means lived in separate worlds; there were important intellectual contacts among them, increasingly as time went on. But the story of the intellectual development of each group can be told, in the main, separately from that of the other groups. This was much less true of the Middle Periods. In the tenth and eleventh centuries, all the different intellectual traditions were well matured . . . The Hellenists and the ʿulamāʾ fully confronted each other and the result was as stimulating in the intellectual field as the confrontation of the adībs with the Sharʿism of the ʿulamāʾ had been frustrating in the social fields . . .
>
> But the confrontation had borne fruit. And just as in the social and political life the various elements of urban society had worked out effective patterns consistent with the supremacy of the iqṭāʿ-amīrs, so in intellectual life by then, ways had been found to accommodate in practically all fields of thought a certain intellectual supremacy that had to be accorded the madrasah ʿulamāʾ. So was ushered in the intellectual life of the Middle Periods in which the intellectual traditions were *relatively interdependent*. The graduates of the madrasahs themselves eventually tended to blur the lines between the *kalām* of the ʿulamāʾ, the various sciences of the Faylasūfs, and even adab of the old courtiers. The Faylasūfs, in turn, adjusted their thinking, at least in secondary ways, to

the fact of Sharʿī supremacy. *And speculative Ṣūfism penetrated everywhere.*[54] [emphasis mine]

Dabashi's model of the "metaphysical bipolarity" between the jurists and the Sufis—along with his later full-blown dichotomy in *Truth and Narrative*—enjoys none of Hodgson's insight that the intellectual traditions of this time period were "mutually interdependent." Dabashi's reading of the Saljūq intellectual milieu would have benefited in this case from a closer reading and an engagement with—rather than a complete glossing over—of Hodgson's valuable insights.

Lastly, Dabashi categorically denies the connection later Muslim intellectuals had with ʿAyn al-Quḍāt. He states, "There is not the slightest indication that later philosophers and Sufis even read ʿAyn al-Quḍāt."[55] I have elsewhere offered extensive proof that Iranian, Indian, and Turkish Sufis, in particular the followers of the "Path of Love" (*madhhab-i ʿishq*), have read and engaged ʿAyn al-Quḍāt through the centuries.[56] Suffice it to say that Indian Sufis such as Hazrat Niẓām al-Dīn Awliyāʾ,[57] Naṣīr al-Dīn Chirāgh Dihlī,[58] Masʿūd Bakk,[59] Rukn al-Dīn Kāshānī,[60] and Gīsū Dirāz[61] engaged ʿAyn al-Quḍāt. An early fourteenth-century Indian historiographer named Baranī lists the books that were considered "fashionable" to purchase in Delhi at this time period. Among them were the letters of ʿAyn al-Quḍāt.[62] Apart from the Indo-Persian Sufi tradition of the Chishtīs documented above, various Persian Sufis and philosophers also engaged ʿAyn al-Quḍāt. Their list ranges from lesser-known figures such as Kamāl al-Dīn Khwārazmī[63] to the well-known Jāmī[64] and Mullā Ṣadrā.[65] There is also evidence that ʿAyn al-Quḍāt was known in Rumi's circle of followers in Konya.[66] In short, there is ample evidence that later mystical and philosophical traditions claimed ʿAyn al-Quḍāt as one of their own.

The Challenge of Situating ʿAyn al-Quḍāt Intellectually: The Real Maverick

ʿAyn al-Quḍāt challenges the convenient pigeonholes of "Sufi," "philosopher," "theologian," and "jurist" as no other figure in the Saljūq era. At times some scholars have wished to express the difficulty of classifying him by resorting to hyphenated and linked terms such as "mystic-martyr"[67] and "mystic philosopher."[68] The problem with such hyphenations, as indeed with most hyphenations, is that the hyphen becomes as much a barrier as bridge, keeping two essentialized qualities apart. A similar problem can be noticed in Henry Corbin's assessment of ʿAyn al-Quḍāt as "both jurist and mystic, philosopher and mathematician."[69] In such assessments, "jurist" and "mystic" become somewhat reified categories, which are quintessentially separate even though they are somehow brought together in the person of ʿAyn al-Quḍāt. Rather than using hyphenations and "both" statements, I suggest that we take up the challenge ʿAyn al-Quḍāt poses to our convenient categories by situating him against the dominant intellectual discourses of his time period. If he proves difficult to classify, it is our rigid categories that need refining.

Another dominant tendency in reading ʿAyn al-Quḍāt has been to view him as an "exception to patterns," a peerless voice who has no precedents and no followers.[70] I wish to add some nuance to both of the above tendencies. It is good to remember that ʿAyn al-Quḍāt does fit the pattern of what Marshall G. S. Hodgson had eloquently described as one of the identifying features of the "best thinkers" of this time period: "The best thinkers were not simply working out the consequences of the particular insights of their own immediate tradition, as often before, but now came frankly and honestly to grapple with the best insights that any accessible tradition could offer."[71] As we will see later on in this chapter, that is precisely the case with ʿAyn al-Quḍāt: while he was clearly rooted in Khurāsānī Sufism,[72] he was not reticent to side with Ibn Sīnā against the arch-Khurāsānī Sufi (Abū Saʿīd-i Abī ʾl-Khayr), or even with Ibn Sīnā against al-Ghazālī. He felt that he was more or less free to choose what Hodgson called the "best insights" offered by any of the dominant intellectual discourses of his time.

None of this is meant to explain away what makes ʿAyn al-Quḍāt so rare and so audacious. In previous chapters, I identified the tendency towards *uṣūl*-ization (systematization) of Islamic intellectual discourse starting in the tenth and eleventh centuries. As such, it had become a commonplace assertion for many members of the ʿulamāʾ and Sufis to state that their teachings and discourse were fully in accordance with the Sunna of the Prophet. When taken in this context, ʿAyn al-Quḍāt's rebellious statement below assumes an even greater significance:

> Everyone claims to be following the Sunna. But we are all far from the Sunna. I am not saying that *they* are far from it. I see many heretical innovations (*bidaʿ*) in my own self!
>
> O friend! Heretical innovations are in beliefs (*ʿaqāʾid*), attributes, and actions. Whoever believes something about God, the Messenger, the Grave, the Resurrection, and religious sciences that is not the same as what was held by the Messenger [of God], peace and blessings upon him, that person is committing a heretical innovation in beliefs. Until

one's knowledge is perfected in all the religious sciences, a man cannot be freed from this innovation. How is one to attain? I confess that I do not have it. I don't know about others.[73]

It is precisely this extraordinary intellectual capacity for self-criticism that was rare in Saljūq Islam. Far from claiming, as most if not all of his contemporaries did, that he too was a follower of the Sunna, ʿAyn al-Quḍāt was confessing something much more drastic and radical: the terminology, categories, and concerns of the various discourses of Islamic intellectual life represented an ongoing engagement with contemporary concerns that by definition would not have existed at the time of the Prophet. For ʿAyn al-Quḍāt, this is no reason to stop exploring these various disciplines. Rather, he had the intellectual honesty, and one might add courage, to confess the innovative nature of the discourse that he and his fellow ʿulamāʾ members were engaged in. One might suspect that there were others who felt the same, but we do not possess any extant sources to document this. ʿAyn al-Quḍāt was not so much an "exception to the pattern" as he was the most radical example of Hodgson's model of scholars who incorporated insights from various intellectual traditions.

In depicting this tendency to challenge the dominant discourses of his time, Dabashi deploys the term "maverick" in describing both ʿAyn al-Quḍāt and Abū Ḥāmid Ghazālī.[74] If by the term maverick one means a loner, a nonconformist, and one who stands apart from the mainstream powers that be, that would be an apropos label for ʿAyn al-Quḍāt. I am, of course, mindful that even such a designation is a relative one. One may legitimately ask how much of an "outsider" a figure like ʿAyn al-Quḍāt truly was: he was a Qāḍī, son of a Qāḍī, grandson of a Qāḍī. He had disciples in the Saljūq court (power) and was himself both recipient and transmitter of Sufi modes of authority (*baraka*). From those perspectives, one can say that he was not an outsider but a voice of dissent within the elite of power. He was a powerfully situated (and thus dangerous) dissenter who was not willing to lend his own legitimizing voice and baraka to the Saljūqs. In those regards, and in challenging the dominant intellectual discourses of his time period, he may legitimately be considered a maverick.

On the other hand, it is difficult, if not impossible, to justify applying the same label of "maverick" to Abū Ḥāmid Ghazālī. While it is true that he too was harassed, as Dabashi correctly recognizes, their life stories are completely different: Ghazālī was the main spokesperson for the Saljūq regime; ʿAyn al-Quḍāt was killed by the Saljūq regime. Ghazālī was situated at the top lectureship post in the most prestigious of all the Niẓāmīya madrasas; if we are to believe some of the hagiographic accounts, ʿAyn al-Quḍāt was killed in front of his madrasa. Ghazālī was patronized by the most powerful vizier of his day, Niẓām al-Mulk; ʿAyn al-Quḍāt was killed by the most powerful vizier of his day, Dargazīnī. Ghazālī's texts were read within ten years all over Islamdom, as far away as the Maghrib; ʿAyn al-Quḍāt's texts were destined for a more select audience. Ghazālī's synthesis became the point of departure for many future discussions of "orthodoxy," down to our own day; ʿAyn al-Quḍāt clearly excused himself from such a rhetoric and confessed that he saw many heresies in himself! Perhaps the clearest demarcation between the two is that ʿAyn al-Quḍāt had to defend himself against the charges of heresy which were laid out—not to mention accepted and applied within one generation—by Abū Ḥāmid Ghazālī. ʿAyn al-Quḍāt fits the label of maverick, and he would have perhaps worn that label like a badge of honor. As it has been presented in chapter 4 of the present study, al-Ghazālī represents a pinnacle of the *real-politik* ʿulamāʾ who worked with and for the Saljūq regime.

ʿAyn al-Quḍāt and the Two Ghazālī Brothers

The above gives us an opportunity to examine ʿAyn al-Quḍāt's complex relationship with the two Ghazālī brothers (Aḥmad and Abū Ḥāmid). ʿAyn al-Quḍāt's powerfully intimate relationship with Aḥmad has already been alluded to. ʿAyn al-Quḍāt had a more complex and uneasy relationship with Abū Ḥāmid Ghazālī. While I will be pointing out several charges that ʿAyn al-Quḍāt casts against Abū Ḥāmid, it is important to bear in mind that overall ʿAyn al-Quḍāt held *both* al-Ghazālī brothers in very high regard. Any such criticisms will have to be read against the background of that affinity. A statement in the *Tamhīdāt* offers us a powerful testimony to the above. ʿAyn al-Quḍāt identifies himself, Aḥmad, and Abū Hāmid Ghazālī as being among "the ten scholars firmly rooted in knowledge." He states, "O friend! For some time I have known about nine of the scholars who are firmly rooted in knowledge. Tonight, which is Friday night, the day for writing [letters], the tenth one was also made known to me: Khwāja Imām Muḥammad Ghazālī, May God have mercy on him. I knew about Aḥmad [Ghazālī], but I had not known about Muḥammad [Ghazālī]: Muḥammad is also one of us . . ."[75]

ʿAyn al-Quḍāt credited reading Ghazālī's *oeuvre* with rescuing him from his intellectual crisis brought about by reading too much *kalām*. ʿAyn al-Quḍāt continues to rely on Abū Ḥāmid Ghazālī, particularly in answering the challenges of the *mutakallimūn* (theologians). A clear example of this reliance on

Ghazālī occurs in the beginning of the tenth chapter of the *Tamhīdāt*, which is titled "The Principle and Reality of Heaven and Earth, Being the Light of Muḥammad [Ṣ] and [the Light of] Iblīs." Here ʿAyn al-Quḍāt attempts to answer theological objections to using the term *nūr* (light) in referring to the Divine. After explaining that by light he means something other than physical light, he states, "Alas! How well does the Proof of Islam, Abū Ḥāmid al-Ghazālī, may God be pleased with him, explain this! He has explained something of this light by stating, 'Light is that through which objects are seen.'"[76]

In a number of passages, ʿAyn al-Quḍāt identifies Abū Ḥāmid Ghazālī as one who has achieved the highest rank of acquired knowledge: "If someone wishes to acquire knowledge, so that he attains the ranks of Ghazālī . . ."[77] However, one cannot help but wonder whether in the above compliment there is not a subtle hint of the limitation of the knowledge reached by Abū Ḥāmid. Did ʿAyn al-Quḍāt not begin his *Tamhīdāt* by differentiating between the two types of knowledge, that which is acquired and that which is from God? Could it be that while he holds Abū Ḥāmid Ghazālī to represent the pinnacle of acquired knowledge, he relegates the famed Ghazālī to a rank below those who are freely given knowledge from God (*ʿilm ladunnī*)? In ʿAyn al-Quḍāt's view, it is precisely this type of knowledge that his own illiterate teachers, Shaykh Fatḥa and Shaykh Baraka, possessed.[78] Again, in this case, ʿAyn al-Quḍāt's assessment of Abū Ḥāmid Ghazālī would represent not a dismissal but rather a belief that while Ghazālī had no doubt reached the upper echelon of knowledge, he still assumed a subservient rank to those "who are given knowledge by God."

ʿAyn al-Quḍāt also offers more direct criticisms of Abū Ḥāmid Ghazālī. In some passages, he clearly demarcates his own theory of the Qurʾan from that offered by Abū Hāmid Ghazālī. According to ʿAyn al-Quḍāt, Ghazālī's theory is the familiar two-tiered theory of the levels of meanings of the Qurʾan. The first type is "closer to the understanding of the masses," whereas the second type is intended for the "elites." Fearing strife (*fitna*), ʿAyn al-Quḍāt alleges, Ghazālī did not discuss the level of meaning intended for the elites. ʿAyn al-Quḍāt concludes, "There is a great difference between what I am saying here, and that which he has said there—these two claims are opposite!"[79]

Perhaps the most intriguing critique of Abū Ḥāmid Ghazālī offered by ʿAyn al-Quḍāt was that the famed theologian showed neither fairness (*inṣāf*) nor manliness (*mardī*) in his polemics against other schools of thought. In a long and complex letter written to ʿAzīz al-Dīn Mustawfī, ʿAyn al-Quḍāt states one of his fundamental tenets, that the principle or root of all schools of thought and religions must be correct. Furthermore, ʿAyn al-Quḍāt holds that it is only the corruption of "bad transmitters" (*taḥrīf-i nāqilān-i bad*) that has led to the emergence of falsehood in these various *madhāhib*. In typically ʿAyn al-Quḍātian fashion of situating his own discourse, he states that to consider the very origin of different *madhāhib* false is "impossible from where I am."[80] ʿAyn al-Quḍāt then raises Abū Ḥāmid Ghazālī's discussion in *Maqṣad aqṣā*[81] regarding the debates over the relationship between the "Name" and the "Named" (*ism wa musammāʾ*). He states that Ghazālī had favored the perspective that the Name is not the same as that which is Named and had refuted the other two schools of thought.

What is significant for our purposes is not ʿAyn al-Quḍāt's position per se but his justification. He states that, from "where I am [situated]," all the various perspectives on the matter are true and that which the "Khwāja Imām" [i.e., Abū Ḥāmid Ghazālī] had expressed would be evident to even the common scholars, much less the elite among them.[82] It is at this point that ʿAyn al-Quḍāt accuses Abū Ḥāmid Ghazālī of the most serious intellectual charge. Hamadānī states that what Ghazālī had refuted was in fact *not* the perspective of that madhhab but something else that the founder of that school of thought himself would have refuted.[83] In other words, Ghazālī had trumped up a polemical straw man, only to refute it.

ʿAyn al-Quḍat then moves on to Ghazālī's assessment that ethics (*akhlāq*) are open to change. In doing so, ʿAyn al-Quḍāt reveals his detailed knowledge of Ghazālī's *Iḥyāʾ ʿulūm al-dīn*. However, here again he disagrees with Ghazālī: ʿAyn al-Quḍāt states that before refuting the perspective of a school of thought, one has to understand what its founders have been trying to express. Otherwise, ʿAyn al-Quḍāt charges, "speaking in affirming or refuting that madhhab has no fairness (*inṣāf*)."[84] This is clearly a serious charge, one that he returns to in the conclusion of this long letter. In the end, he records an Arabic line of poetry that to him suits Ghazālī's behavior: "You were incapable of hunting the wild donkey, and thus pointed your lance at the domesticated ass." The above lines might be taken to contain a sarcastic sexual undertone. In the subsequent paragraph, ʿAyn al-Quḍāt makes this theme even more apparent: "It is not manliness (*mardī na ān-ast . . .*) to engage the true discourse of those on the path in a hideous manner, so that one can then plunge into negating it. Manliness is that one represents all the schools of thoughts (*madhāhib*) in a true and correct fashion . . ."[85] ʿAyn al-Quḍāt charges Ghazālī with both unfairness and a lack of intellectual machismo. Given these critiques, one may legitimately consider ʿAyn al-Quḍāt the first real critic of the famed and accomplished Abū Ḥāmid Ghazālī. ʿAyn al-Quḍāt, who identifies himself as a "student of Ghazālī's books"[86] but never met him in person,[87] offers substantial critiques of Ghazālī less than twenty years after the famed theologian's passing.

Hamadānī's critique of Ghazālī brings us to the next group of Muslim intellectuals with whom he was engaged: the theologians. His critique of the theologians owed a great deal to the same Abū Ḥāmid Ghazālī.

ʿAyn al-Quḍāt and Theologians

We have already encountered ʿAyn al-Quḍāt's own narrative in which he recalls having been plunged into an intellectual and spiritual crisis when the works of kalām were insufficient in meeting and answering his inquiry. While he continues to use many of the terms appropriated by the theologians, on the whole he has a low opinion of kalām's potential to bring enlightenment to humanity. At one point he goes so far as to call kalām a "heretical innovation (*bidʿat*) and going astray (*ḍalālat*)."[88] In the context of a letter, he offers the following opinion of kalām:

> The example of those who have plunged themselves into kalām is like those whose ailment was not getting better through permissible medicines. Given the exigent circumstances, it is therefore permissible to cure them with forbidden medicines. In Islamic Law, drinking wine is forbidden. However, if there is a patient regarding whom physicians say that he can only be cured through drinking wine—and that if he does not drink it he will die—certainly the consensus of all religious scholars would be that wine is permissible for him. In fact, if he does not drink it, he is being disobedient . . . Likewise, it is not permissible for anyone to study kalām, except through necessity.
>
> In the age of the Prophet, Peace and blessings upon him, no one occupied themselves with kalām. Neither did anyone do so in the age of the companions, may God be pleased with them. It was after them that the heretically innovative sects came into being. The Prophet, peace and blessings upon him, said: "Whatever comes after me that is not traced to me is heretical innovation, and going stray. Avoid it."
>
> Therefore, plunging into kalām is only permissible for two groups, and forbidden to all else. One is a firmly rooted scholar,[89] who is walking on a firm ground in terms of religion. When he sees that innovators are in positions of authority, and that one cannot refute their discourse except through kalām, then it is permissible for him to learn enough kalām to offer a response to these enemies.

> The other person [who should be permitted to study kalām] is one whose belief in God and the Messenger is weakened due to the heretical teachings he has heard, which have influenced his heart. If the discourse of the preachers does not cure him, and the religious scholars say that he can study enough kalām to know that the innovator's discourse is all false, then it is permissible for him to do so.
>
> Apart from these two, if someone studies kalām and seeks to offer his own esoteric and allegorical interpretation, this person is a heretical innovator, and one who seeks to cause strife.[90]

It will be recalled here that this critique is almost identical to Ghazālī's own position on kalām. Ghazālī had identified the purpose of kalām as having been designed to "safeguard the articles of faith." He recognized that it was "indispensable in debating innovators and answers their heresies with what will remove and destroy their influence over the heart of the common man."[91] Once again, in confronting the *mutakallimūn*, ʿAyn al-Quḍāt betrays his continuous reliance on Abū Ḥāmid Ghazālī.

On a number of other occasions, ʿAyn al-Quḍāt critiques positions held by theologians. At one point he groups the *mutakallimūn* together with "ignorant scholars" as people who state that it is not appropriate to use the term *nūr* (light) to refer to God.[92] Not surprisingly, he contrasts here the ignorance of the theologians with the insight provided by Abū Ḥāmid al-Ghazālī. ʿAyn al-Quḍāt goes on to state that by the light of God he means something other than the light that one sees around us, and offers this as the true interpretation of the Qur'anic phrase "God is the light of the heavens and the Earth."[93]

As had been the case with Abū Ḥāmid Ghazālī before him, ʿAyn al-Quḍāt relegated kalām to a subservient position but saved a more extensive critique for the Ismāʿīlīs. It is to this group that we now turn.

ʿAyn al-Quḍāt and Ismāʿīlīs

It is understandable that ʿAyn al-Quḍāt would attempt to distance himself from the Ismāʿīlīs in the *Shakwa ʾl-gharīb,* which was composed when ʿAyn al-Quḍāt was already incarcerated. Previously, he had also attempted to demarcate his own thinking from that of the Ismāʿīlīs. One of the more sustained discourses against the Ismāʿīlīs, whom he calls the *taʿlīmīyān* (people of esoteric teaching), is undertaken in a long letter written to his disciple, ʿAzīz al-Dīn al-Mustawfī. ʿAyn al-Quḍāt begins this letter by noting that it is the custom of the *taʿlīmīyān* to begin their missionary activity by asking how one can attain to intimate knowledge of God (*maʿrifat*). The two options, according to the Ismāʿīlīs, are through the intellect and an *imām-i maʿṣūm* (immaculate Imam).[94] The Ismāʿīlīs would proceed to state that the intellect was not a reliable faculty in attaining to certainty and knowledge, and therefore one had to rely on the living, immaculate Imam. ʿAyn al-Quḍāt acknowledges that Abū Ḥāmid Ghazālī has dealt with this matter in some of his books. However, he states that Ghazālī's answer is still insufficient, failing to meet the Ismāʿīlī challenge. In a typically ʿAyn al-Quḍātian fashion, he adds, "Now, oh precious one [ʿAzīz], be all ears so that I can elucidate this matter for you."[95]

He proceeds to offer an extensive rebuttal of the framework of the Ismāʿīlī challenge, which includes problematizing the whole framework of an immaculate Imām since as ʿAyn al-Quḍāt states:

> It is not a condition incumbent upon the spiritual teacher that he be immaculately sinless, since even Muṣṭafā [Prophet Muḥammad], peace and blessings of God be upon him, who is the master of all the spiritual teachers and the head of all messengers, is not immaculately sinless![96] Hear it from the Qur'an: *[so that God might forgive you] your past sins, and those to follow.*[97] [Or, in another verse:] *And we removed from you your burden, the one that weighed heavily on your back.*[98] And [A]bū Bakr and ʿUmar also sin. And Junayd, Shiblī, and Uways Qaranī sin as well.
>
> Yes . . . The only condition incumbent on the spiritual teacher is that he has progressed on God's path, and has a type of compassion that leads him to guide the disciple to perfection.[99]

By stating that the Prophet was not *maʿṣūm*, ʿAyn al-Quḍāt is pulling the rug from under the Ismāʿīlīs and their claim for a sinless, immaculate Imām. He had argued earlier in the *Tamhīdāt* that a disciple should not seek sinlessness (*maʿṣūmī*) from a spiritual teacher, but here the argument is developed in full. Further debunking the whole framework of the Ismāʿīlī claim to religious leadership, ʿAyn al-Quḍāt states that there is no reason for there to be only one figurehead of religious authority. It is possible that there might be a thousand spiritual teachers who have attained to the rank of being a *pīr*, "spiritual teacher." He states, "It is not necessary for spiritual teachers to be seated in Egypt, Hamadan, Isfahan, or Baghdad. It is possible that he is in a village. [A]bū 'l-Ḥasan Kharaqānī was from a village, yet he reached [such] a state of perfection that if a million seekers set out on the path to God, not one of them will reach that rank."[100]

Without directly mentioning the regimes by name, it is safe to assume that Egypt refers to the Ismāʿīlīs, Baghdad to the ʿAbbāsid Caliphate, Isfahan to one of the Saljūq seats of power, and significantly, Hamadān to ʿAyn al-Quḍāt's own "station." It is perhaps this last element that separates ʿAyn al-Quḍāt from others: he does not privilege his own claim over others. The long letter ends the way many of his letters do, with an exhortation to follow love. Rather than seeking the teaching of the Ismāʿīlīs, ʿAyn al-Quḍāt states, "One must be the pupil of love, that is sufficient as a teacher and master (*shāgird-i ʿishq bāsh, tū rā ū bas ūstād*)."[101] If there is a privileging, it is not one of ʿAyn al-Quḍāt himself but of the path of love he follows and preaches.

The above example illustrates how the mere presence of the Ismāʿīlīs had forced all the intellectual discourses to account for them and offer clear demarcations between their own teachings and that of the Ismāʿīlīs. This was particularly the case for Sufis, who also held that they had access to an esoteric level of knowledge which was passed on to their initiates through a transmission. Given the overlapping discourses of esoteric knowledge, initiation, and transmission, it was particularly important for Sufis to demonstrate *how* the premise of their teachings differed from the Ismāʿīlīs.

ʿAyn al-Quḍāt's Complex Relationship with Philosophy and Sufism

Abū Hāmid Ghazālī offered a thorough critique of philosophy (*falsafa*) and classified many philosophers (in particular Ibn Sīnā and Fārābī) as heretics. While this did not lead to the complete exile of philosophy from Islamic intellectual discourse as some scholars have held, it is clear that philosophy would henceforth occupy an uneasy place in mainstream Sunni Muslim discourse. Philosophy was not usually taught as part of the official curriculum of any madrasa.

Given that ʿAyn al-Quḍāt matured less than a generation after Abū Ḥāmid Ghazālī, it is all the more surprising to find that at times he occasionally supported the arch-philosopher, Ibn Sīnā, against familiar Saljūq-friendly figures such as Abū Saʿīd-i Abī ʾl-Khayr and al-Ghazālī. In one instance, ʿAyn al-Quḍāt sides with Ibn Sīnā against the perspective of the famed Khurāsānī Sufi, Abū Saʿīd-i Abī ʾl-Khayr. Abū Saʿīd had written to Ibn Sīnā, asking, "Point me to a proof (of God)." Ibn Sīnā reponded in a treatise which ʿAyn al-Quḍāt identifies as *Aḍḥawī*: "It is entering into Real Infidelity (*al-kufr al-ḥaqīqī*) and leaving behind metaphorical Islam (*al-islām al-majāzī*). It is that you do not orient yourself towards anything except that which is beyond the 'Three Persons,'[102] until you become one who submits to God and is an infidel. If you are beneath this [rank], then you are a Muslim who is still associating partners with God (*mushrikun muslimun*). If you are still ignorant of this, then do not consider yourself among the beings."[103]

In response, Abū Saʿīd stated, "I have received more benefit from these words than I would have from a hundred thousand years of worship." Here ʿAyn al-Quḍāt steps into the narrative, stating, "But I state that Shaykh Abū Saʿīd had not yet tasted these words. If he had, he too would have been like [A]bū ʿAlī [Ibn Sīnā] and others who are reviled by the strangers: he too would have been reviled and stoned by people."[104]

Some contemporary scholars have attempted to offer alternative explanations for how a Sufi such as ʿAyn al-Quḍāt could be siding with a philosopher (Ibn Sīnā) against another Sufi (Abū Saʿīd). The most important and eloquent of these has been the contemporary Iranian scholar, Muḥammad-Riḍā Shafīʿī-Kadkanī. He admits that there might have been correspondences between Abū ʿAlī Sīnā and Abū Saʿīd. However, he prefers alternate readings of the above which suggest that ʿAyn al-Quḍāt had confused Abū Saʿīd with another individual (Abū Saʿd Hamadānī) and that the conversation had been in fact between a certain Abū ʾl-Qāsim Kirmānī and Ibn Sīnā.[105] The above objection is intriguing from the perspective of establishing the "authenticity" of this alleged correspondence between the famed philosopher and mystic. However, even if its historicity is to be questioned, from our perspective it is important to document that ʿAyn al-Quḍāt accepted it. It is more the meaning that this correspondence has to ʿAyn al-Quḍāt that concerns us, not its validity from a positivistic perspective. In formulating his audacious discourse on the sacred, ʿAyn al-Quḍāt would not confine himself to a wholehearted alliance with any of the established intellectual discourses. While he is primarily a mystical thinker, at times he would depart from their rank to incorporate philosophical perspectives that certain jurists might have deemed heretical. We recall again Hodgson's statement that the "best thinkers" of this time period, among whom ʿAyn al-Quḍāt must surely be counted, came to incorporate "the best insights" of various traditions.

Not only does ʿAyn al-Quḍāt side with Ibn Sīnā against Abū Saʿīd, he also supports the arch-philosopher against Abū Ḥāmid Ghazālī. He does so by offering a defense of Ibn Sīnā's controversial position on the pre-eternity of the world. ʿAyn al-Quḍāt states, "You have to excuse Shaykh Abū ʿAlī Sīnā when he said: 'The four elements are ancient.' The elements that he was calling ancient are the Real elements (*ʿanāṣir-i ḥaqīqī*) and the pillars of heaven. He did not mean the elements of [this realm of] being (*kawn*) and corruption (*fasād*), the elements of this world."[106] This defense is quite significant because Abū Ḥāmid Ghazālī had identified the philosophers' assertion that the world is eternal as one of the conditions by which they might legitimately be considered heretics.[107] More specifically, he had stated, "We must therefore reckon as unbelievers both these philosophers themselves and their followers among the Islamic philosophers, such as Ibn Sīnā, al-Fārābī and others."[108] In offering the above apologetic explanation, ʿAyn al-Quḍāt was coming to the rescue of an allegedly heretical Ibn Sīnā against the foremost theologian of the Saljūq regime. This was surely a dangerous position for one to take.

These are not the only occasions that ʿAyn al-Quḍāt praises Ibn Sīnā. In another instance, he favorably cites Ibn Sīnā's esoteric interpretation of eschatological realities. This narrative is featured in the lengthy last chapter of the *Tamhīdāt* in which ʿAyn al-Quḍāt elucidates the "principle and reality of the Heaven and the Earth as the Light of Muḥammad and Iblīs." After having stated that the "path to God," "everything that is in the Heaven and on Earth," and "the events of the grave" have to be sought inside the very being of humanity, ʿAyn al-Quḍāt moves on to discuss the inquisition each soul will receive in the grave from two angels, *Nakīr* and *Munkar*. It is at this point that he returns again to Ibn Sīnā, who is further praised by the added phrase "May God have mercy on him."

> The questioning done by *Munkar* and *Nakīr* are also inside the self. All those who are veiled from spiritual realities today raise this objection: how can the same two angels go to and examine a thousand different people in an instant? One must have faith in this!
>
> But Abū ʿAlī Sīnā, May God's mercy be upon him, has elucidated this meaning in two words when he said: "The *Munkar* is evil deed; the *Nakīr*, righteous action." Alas! What to do with this statement! How well has he expressed all this! This means that the carnal soul is the mirror of blameworthy vices; whereas the intellect and the heart are the mirror of praiseworthy virtues. If a man were to look within himself, he would see his own character traits, and how these correspond to his state: his own being becomes his torment. He thinks that the torment is other than him; it is him, and from him. If you wish, hear it also from Muṣṭafā [Prophet Muḥammad] when he explained the torment of the grave: *He said: "indeed it is your own deeds that will be returned to you."*[109]

It might be tempting to conclude from all of the above examples that ʿAyn al-Quḍāt had somehow abandoned Sufism in favor of philosophy. However, that would be a misreading of his complex discourse. In a typical ʿAyn al-Quḍātian fashion, he is not willing to allow his own multivalent interpretation to become collapsed into that of the philosophers, or any one intellectual community. Whereas previously he had demarcated his own reading from that of Sufis, here he also distinguishes his perspective from the majority of the philosophers: "Do you hear well what is being said? O you, the philosophical one, what do you say in response to this? Are these words not the words of philosophy? Everything from the philosophical discourse that is not like these words of philosophy [such as the Avicennan position of "exiting Metaphorical Islam and entering Real Infidelity"] is altogether weak and false."[110]

Elsewhere, he chastises the philosophers and theologians who fancy themselves "folk who know God; i.e., mystics (*ʿārif*)."[111] In other passages, he clearly privileges the understanding of the *ahl-i maʿrifat* (the people who know God intimately) over that of the philosophers and theologians: "O friend, I am writing these words through great difficulty. He is greater in the heart of the people who know God intimately than that which the philosophers and theologians imagine. They state: He is not accident, not substance, and not a body. They then imagine that saying what God is not is the same thing as comprehending real transcendence (*tanzīh*)."[112]

In surveying ʿAyn al-Quḍāt's attitude toward philosophy and philosophers, one can see why later authors of philosophical biographical dictionaries have often included ʿAyn al-Quḍāt, counting him as one of their own. Bayhaqī's *Tatimma ṣiwān al-ḥikma* includes an entry on ʿAyn al-Quḍāt in which it is asserted that he was a student of both ʿUmar Khayyām and al-Ghazālī. Furthermore, Bayhaqī states that in his *Zubdat al-ḥaqāʾiq*, ʿAyn al-Quḍāt "mixed together the discourse of the Sufis with that of the philosophical sages."[113] An almost identical phrase is found in Shams al-Dīn Shahrazūrī's *Nuzhat al-arwāḥ wa rawḍat al-afrāḥ*.[114] While from a historical perspective we can dismiss the link between ʿAyn al-Quḍāt and ʿUmar Khayyām, it is interesting to note that ʿAyn al-Quḍāt's own refusal to align himself squarely with Sufis against philosophers allowed both Sufis and philosophers to claim him as one of their own. Even more interestingly, biographers like Bayhaqī and Shahrazūrī could claim that he had "mixed" together the discourse of *falsafa* and *taṣawwuf*, in a sense anticipating Hodgson's remarks about the "best thinkers" of this time period. This trait did characterize many such thinkers, but few were willing to follow ʿAyn al-Quḍāt to the radical extent of critiquing theologians, philosophers, politicians, and even Sufis. It is in these aspects that he may well be said to have carved out a personal discourse on the sacred. While recalling our earlier cautionary points regarding ʿAyn al-Quḍāt's own privileged position as a judge, a scholar, and a Sufi, it is in this regard that one may, with some justification, use the phrase "intellectual maverick" in referring to ʿAyn al-Quḍāt.

ʿAyn al-Quḍāt, the Saljūqs, and Saljūq-Serving Scholars

We have seen that one of the key components of the Great Saljūq Myth was the patronage of religious scholars and institutions. Saljūq Sultans from Ṭughril to Sanjar sought legitimization by portraying themselves as patrons of the ʿulamāʾ and institutions of religious learning (both madrasa and khānaqāh). While there were individual scholars who criticized specific rulers,[115] there is not a great deal of evidence of the ʿulamāʾ critiquing the whole system of cooperating with rulers or the totality of the Saljūq regime. One previous evidence had been that of al-Ghazālī (if we are to accept the second part of the *Naṣīḥat al-mulūk* as authentic), who warned the sultan to stay away from the "religious scholars who anxiously yearn after the material world" (*ʿulamāʾ-yi ḥarīṣ bar dunyā*), those who praise the king and lust after him, so that they can gain some of the "corpse" (i.e., worldly possessions) that the sultan holds.[116] While al-Ghazālī's argument was stated for the benefit of the sultan himself, ʿAyn al-Quḍāt goes after the scholars' own integrity—or lack thereof. He states, "In the past ages, the caliphs of Islam would seek after the scholars of faith, and the scholars would run the other way. Now, for the sake of a hundred pissy (*idrār*) gold coins and fifty forbidden ones, they associate day and night with scoundrel emperors (*pādshāhān-i fāsiq*). The scholars go to greet them ten times, and each time become drunk, becoming so excited, as if discharging semen (*junub*) in sleep."[117]

This critique is twofold. On one hand the Saljūq Sultans are called "scoundrel emperors." In choosing the term *fāsiq* to characterize the Saljūq rulers, ʿAyn al-Quḍāt is formulating an antithesis to the Saljūqs' depictions of themselves as "orthodox" and righteous. By labeling the sultan *fāsiq*, a term which has strong ethical and moral connotations, ʿAyn al-Quḍāt had positioned himself as *the* anti-Saljūq intellectual. Not only are the Saljūqs not portrayed as being orthodox defenders of Islam, they are called morally corrupt figures who stand as the very antithesis of spiritual teachings. The second part of his critique concerns the scholars who work with the Saljūq regime. Continuing his critique in the paragraph after the one quoted above, ʿAyn al-Quḍāt states that the worst torment handed to humanity in the Day of Resurrection will be to the scholars whose knowledge has not earned them any spiritual merit. The above statement is a radical and unprecedented one in Saljūq discourse. Scholars would often seek the patronage of one vizier or another, often depending on the theological or legal preferences of the specific rulers. We have no evidence of any other figure who dismissed in toto the legitimacy of the Saljūqs themselves and also the merit of cooperating with the Saljūq regime.

There are a number of primary traits that characterize ʿAyn al-Quḍāt's critique: the worldliness of the scholars, their neglect of the inner levels of the Islamic tradition, the economic underpinnings of the whole Saljūq state, and the moral behavior of the Saljūqs themselves. I will analyze each component here.

ʿAyn al-Quḍāt and the Saljūq State

ʿAyn al-Quḍāt vehemently rejects the myth of the Saljūqs as the champions of normative Islam. We have already encountered his famous dismissal of the Saljūq rulers as *pādshāhān-i fāsiq*, "scoundrel emperors." In other passages, he returns to the same theme:

> You poor thing! You have spent your precious life in the service of sultan Maḥmūd. When will you get to the serving of the sandals of the spiritual teachers? The lovers on God's path are one group, the servants of Sultan Maḥmūd another. What do you say? This Sultan Maḥmūd: is he not a creature of God, like you, who is created *from an impure drop of water*.[118] With all of this lowliness, if someone desires to be one of his elite ones, can he attain to his wish immediately? Alas! What do you have to say now? If it is so difficult to attain to the rank of being one of the elite ones of the Sultan, you think it is an easy matter to be an elite of the Eternal Sultan? God forbid![119]

ʿAyn al-Quḍāt sets up a number of dichotomies in the above paragraph. In a theme he will expand on later, he contrasts service to the Sultan to that directed to spiritual teachers. The lovers of God are demarcated from the servants of Sultan Maḥmūd. Maḥmūd himself is contrasted with the "Eternal Sultan," that is, the Divine. No other intellectual in the Saljūq era so freely critiques and dismisses Saljūq rulers. Rather than portraying them as the "shadow of God on Earth,"[120] he depicts them as leading people away from God.

The second important critique that ʿAyn al-Quḍāt makes of the Saljūqs regards the iqṭāʿ system, which we have identified as one of the key components of the Saljūq economic model. In the following passage, he critiques ʿAzīz al-Dīn Mustawfī, the "financial officer," one of his followers who dealt with the iqṭāʿ administration. ʿAzīz al-Dīn had previously complained to ʿAyn al-Quḍāt that while he recognized the injustice of the iqṭāʿ, he had no choice in the matter. Furthermore, ʿAzīz al-Dīn seems to have stated that if he did not participate in the system, some other administrator would simply take his place. ʿAyn al-Quḍāt remained unconvinced:

> If you say, "if I do not do it, somebody else will," this excuse will not be accepted! If one attacks a caravan, and says: "if I do not do it, there are other highway robbers on the path who will do this," this is not an excuse! . . .
>
> You are dividing up the whole earth through the iqṭāʿ.
> If it has a specific owner, is this not the very essence of plunder?
> If it does not have a specific owner, it is for the use of all dervishes!
>
> You are plundering that which belongs to the dervishes.[121]

The above critique is a subtle and radical one. Iqṭāʿ, which the Saljūqs relied upon to pay their soldiers and administrators, was branded by the judge ʿAyn al-Quḍāt ("essence/spring/eye of judges") as none other than plunder. Furthermore, if the land did not specifically belong to anyone, it was said to be under the care of the *darwīshān* (dervishes, the poor). Here ʿAyn al-Quḍāt claims a social and economic role for the Sufi dervishes, as the real possessors of the land. If ʿAyn al-Quḍāt's critique had become a matter of public knowledge, it would have made for a highly contested challenge of the economic basis of the Saljūq regime.

Nor was ʿAyn al-Quḍāt's critique of the iqṭāʿ system purely an abstract one. He pointed out and criticized specific military commanders who had received land grants: "For example, in the Sultan's regime, there is an Amīr Qazal, who lacks any merit, but still who has many thousand gold coins' worth of land grants (iqṭāʿ). When the spread of justice was spread, and everyone was paired with the limit of his sustenance, how is one to know who was Qazal, who is Kāmil, and who ʿAzīz?[122] The condition today is the same as it was during the Age of Ignorance (*jāhilīyat*)."[123]

Once again, rather than representing the Saljūqs as instituting an idealized, normative Islam, ʿAyn al-Quḍāt rhetorically pulls the rug from under them by comparing the Saljūq era to the pre-Islamic *Jāhilīya*. As severe as his critiques of the Saljūq rulers are, they pale in comparison to his vehement dismissal of the religious scholars who have affiliated themselves with the Saljūqs.

ʿAyn al-Quḍāt and Saljūq-Serving "Externalist" ʿUlamāʾ

ʿAyn al-Quḍāt reserves some of his most severe critiques for the religious scholars who combine in them two traits the martyred mystic despised: service to the Saljūqs and a worldview that acknowledged the exteriors of Islam to the detriment of the interior elements. These Saljūq-serving "externalist scholars" bear the brunt of ʿAyn al-Quḍāt's sharp sarcasm and wit: "There is another religion nowadays. These scoundrels [call themselves ridiculous and unworthy titles such as] 'Perfection of the Faith' (*kamāl al-Dīn*), the 'Pillar of the Faith' (*ʿImād al-Dīn*), the 'Crown of the Faith' (*Tāj al-Dīn*), the 'Supporter of the Faith' (*Ẓahīr al-Dīn*), and the 'Beauty of the Faith' (*Jamāl al-Dīn*). Such a religion is the religion of Satans (*dīn-i shayāṭīn*). As for these scholars, their religion is the religion of Satans, and their path is the path of Satans (*rāh-i shayāṭīn*). Yet they claim to be following God's path . . ."[124]

A generation before, Niẓām al-Mulk had also lamented the cheapening of what might be termed the "currency of honorific titles." However, whereas Niẓām al-Mulk had been primarily concerned with administrators, ʿAyn al-Quḍāt here directs the same critique to members of the ʿulamāʾ. In other passages, he further scorned those who offered their services to the Saljūqs:

> What virtue is there in being proud of serving a scoundrel administrator, a Satan from the Satans of humanity, an enemy from the enemies of God and the Prophet? Dust be on the heads of the server and the served! *Verily God is sufficient for all the worlds.*[125] What pleasure do you derive from that service? What are you lacking in terms of sustenance or clothing?
>
> You have enough to suffice yourself and your children even if they live for a hundred years. Why do you not devote yourself to the service of the spiritual teacher's sandals? Perhaps that service can bring you out of the abyss of destruction. Shame on you for this occupation of yours! I advise you in accordance with the level of your intellect, or rather, of your lack of intellect! If you heed my advice, I know what you should do.[126]

The above paragraph combines ʿAyn al-Quḍāt's two weightiest insults: the administrators, like the Saljūq rulers themselves, are also described as "scoundrels." Both the scholars and the administrators are called "satans," and even further "enemies of God and the Prophet." In the premodern world of Islam, these are some of the nastiest (though not uncommon) words thrown around. What was new here was not the insult itself but rather the target. Scholars readily accused each other of being heretical and being "enemies of God." It was unheard of, however, for a prominent intellectual to call the Saljūq regime by the same title.

It is clear that in ʿAyn al-Quḍāt's perspective, service to the Saljūqs was a sign of worldly attachment. He impresses on his disciples that they have more than enough to provide for their families for a hundred years. Yet the real target of the charge of worldliness in his eyes were the ʿulamāʾ. ʿAyn al-Quḍāt stated that the original disciples of the Prophet and the previous messengers were ascetic beings who slept naked and went hungry in the daytime. However, ʿAyn al-Quḍāt recognizes that

> even while the companions of the Prophet, may God be pleased with them, were living that spiritual reality had become distorted. How is it to be today, after five hundreds years from the time of the Prophet . . . Nowadays the religious scholars are known through their mantles and wide sleeves. Were it the case that they would stop at that, but no! They wear gold rings, forbidden clothes, and unlawful steeds. Then they say: "We do this for the glory of Islam." If this is for the glory of Islam, then why did ʿUmar patch his robe? Was he seeking the abasement of Islam? Muʿāwīya had criticized him in precisely such a manner. ʿUmar responded: "We are a folk whom God has honored through Islam. So we don't seek honor in anything else."[127]

ʿAyn al-Quḍāt directly links service to the Saljūqs to materialism. He contrasts serving God to serving the Saljūq Sultan. This critique is one that comes up in many of the private letters written to his disciples. In one such letter, he states that in the day of judgment, it will become clear that these ʿulamāʾ were not really believers, because they feared not God but the sultan. Even their knowledge was said to be not through God but again through the sultan.[128]

ʿAyn al-Quḍāt's Advice to His Disciples in the Saljūq Court

Being convinced that serving the Saljūqs was spiritually deleterious, ʿAyn al-Quḍāt advised his disciples at the Saljūq court to leave the Saljūq regime:

> O ʿAzīz! If I tell you that day and night you are engaged in nothing other than sin, it will hurt your feelings! What do you say? Do you have any other task every day than dividing up to ten million gold coins through your calculations and assigning it to tyranny? If it is a reward for making peace, the Turks [i.e., the Saljūqs] do not deserve it!

> Whatever sin the Turks commit through spending the property that you have assigned and divided up through your own calculations, you also share in that sin! Have you not heard Muṣṭafā [Prophet Muḥammad], peace be upon him, said: "Whoever aids a tyrant, even if it is only through a word, has become a partner of that tyrant in his tyranny"?[129]

In addition to reminding his disciples that by serving the Saljūqs they were sharing in the iniquity and sin of the regime, ʿAyn al-Quḍāt fervently added another potent critique. He stated that it was not possible to serve two masters: the disciples would be able to serve either the spiritual master or the Saljūqs, but clearly not both.

> This affair that you are engaged in, serving the king and being in the army, this will never harmonize with acquiring knowledge. I swear this, by my life! Prepare yourself, so that in time you can devote yourself to the sandals of spiritual teachers. Then the prolonged companionship and service to them will give you true grandeur.
>
> You have not seen the faces of real Men . . . You have not made pain the source of your sustenance, instead of bread and water . . . You have not attended to the sandals of teachers, what are you to do with these discourses? What do those of high repute have to do with love?[130]

The above is one of the many passages where ʿAyn al-Quḍāt calls on the *khidmat-i kafsh*, "tending to the sandals," of the spiritual teacher. What sets the above passage apart is that *khidmat-i kafsh* is contrasted with *khidmat-i pādshāh*, "serving the king." In other passages, Hamadānī is even more emphatic: spiritual insight "can only be attained through attending to the sandals of (real) men (i.e., spiritual teachers). It is never to be attained through service to the Sultan. It is one thing to serve the servants of Satan (*banda-yi bandagān-i iblīs*) and to see one's own benefit and loss entire connected to them; it is entirely another matter to kick Satan's ass (*bar qafā-yi iblīs zadan*) with spiritual ambition and make one's own self lord. *Verily you will not have any authority* (sulṭān) *over my servants.*"[131]

The last sentence is vintage ʿAyn al-Quḍāt: combining earthy humor about "kicking Satan's ass" with a close reading of a familiar Qur'anic verse which states, literally, that there is to be no *sulṭān* over God's servants. We have previously documented that many Saljūq figures such as Ṭughril, Niẓām al-Mulk, and Sanjar had depicted themselves as the supporters, disciples, and patrons of Sufis. In doing so, they sought to legitimize their power. Here ʿAyn al-Quḍāt rejects that discourse of legitimization with the ultimate trump card, that of the Qurʾan.[132] The choice of the Qurʾanic verse is deliberate: it states that Satan is to have no *sulṭān* over God's servants. The discourse of God's servants (here taken to refer to Sufis) is thus completely demarcated from the "sultan discourse" of the Saljūqs. He used other Qurʾanic verses as well to critique cooperation with the Saljūqs. In asserting the importance of following the spiritual teacher instead of the Saljūqs, he offers the following paragraph, heavily impregnated with Qurʾanic quotations:

> The hypocrites are one group, and the lover another. Which one are you? *They are distracted in mind even in the midst of it—being sincerely for neither this group nor for that!*[133] O chivalrous youth! If you fear the sultan more than you fear the spiritual teacher, you are still a hypocrite. Hear it from the Qurʾan: *You are stronger because of the terror in their hearts sent by God. This is because they are a folk who will not understand.*[134] When you fear the spiritual teacher, you fear God: This is the meaning of *whosoever obeys the Messenger has obeyed God,*[135] and *the religious scholars are the inheritors of the prophets.*[136]

Nor did he restrict himself to Qurʾanic passages in critiquing the Saljūqs. In another passage, he offers an ingenious (and sarcastic) rewording of a well-known Prophetic tradition to remind his disciples of the master they are serving:

> What have you really seen? What do you really know? *Seeking knowledge is a religious obligation upon every Muslim male and female*. How many thousand *farsangs* (leagues) have you walked in the service of the Sultan? Then you say "I believe in the statement of Prophet Muḥammad, peace and blessing of God be upon him: *Seek knowledge even if it is to be found in China.*" Have some shame on the count of your faith! I am embarrassed to say this, but you are following one who says instead: *Seek the world, even if it is to be found in China!* Even if today the Sultan commands you to go to Marv, or do anything immediately, you do not have the gull to refuse, or offer any excuse.[137]

Not being content to utilize Prophetic traditions to chastise his disciples, ʿAyn al-Quḍāt even called on the very foundational statement of Islam (*lā ilāha illā Allāh*) to urge his disciples to choose between a spiritual life and the court:

> If a vegetable-seller says: "I am the Sultan," he is lying. However, if a Sultan says this, he is telling the truth. Likewise, when you say *lā ilāha illā Allāh* ("There is deity except God"), it is a lie from you, even though it would be a true statement if said by one who has achieved certainty in

faith. You say that you know nothing save God, see nothing save God, and worship nothing save God. Yet, you look for the good and the harm at the hands of the Sultan and the Vizier. It is to them that you express your obedience and opposition. This is a lie! So long as you worship your own self, there is no *lā ilāha illā Allāh*.[138]

Here is the ultimate judgment against the Saljūqs: so long as the Saljūq administrators continued to serve the regime, even their *lā ilāha illā Allāh* was a lie! In short, he was impressing on his disciples that service to the Saljūqs was incompatible with spiritual growth. Those who served the sultan are deemed more mindful of the sultan than of God. This he attributed directly to their lack of faith.[139] Even more harshly, he stated that by serving the Saljūqs, his disciples were directly sharing in the sins of the Saljūq regime. Here he reiterates that by serving "the Turks" (i.e., the Saljūqs), one was giving them resources to spend on "their forbidden clothes, forbidden food, steeds, gold, and silver," whereas it should have been given to the poor and the indigent.[140]

ʿAyn al-Quḍāt's Connections to the Saljūq Court: Disciples and Antagonists

Having explored the various challenges posed by ʿAyn al-Quḍāt to the intellectual disciplines of the times and his undermining of the Saljūq modes of legitimacy, we are now able to examine the people who are responsible for the actual martyrdom of ʿAyn al-Quḍāt. Most secondary sources that deal with ʿAyn al-Quḍāt have contented themselves with presenting him as a *fanā*-seeking Ḥallājian mystic and have explored a dehistoricized metaphysics of the theme of annihilation in ʿAyn al-Quḍāt's writings.[141] I will depart from this tendency by locating the events leading to ʿAyn al-Quḍāt's death in their historical context.

In the second chapter, I presented the competition between Niẓām al-Mulk, and ʿAmīd al-Mulk at an earlier date, and Tāj al-Mulk later on. I emphasized that these intervizier conflicts also had serious ramifications for the intellectuals who were patronized by the viziers (i.e., the exile and return of Ashʿarī scholars). The case of ʿAyn al-Quḍāt might well be seen as a further example of the consequences of such political fighting. It is my premise that the martyrdom of ʿAyn al-Quḍāt has to be contextualized in a larger historical setting that includes the competitive world of Saljūq courtly politics in which his disciples were immersed. It is a mistake to view ʿAyn al-Quḍāt's martyrdom as somehow arising out of his own "unorthodox" thought without taking into consideration the role of his disciples. In spite of ʿAyn al-Quḍāt's sustained critique of the Saljūq regime (and perhaps because of it), he had not stopped taking on prominent disciples from the Saljūq court. The immediate cause of the heresy trial leading to ʿAyn al-Quḍāt's martyrdom was the political downfall of one of his disciples, ʿAzīz al-Dīn. I will first go over his more prominent disciples in the Saljūq court.

The "Prince" (*pādshāh-zādah*) Jamāl al-Dīn Sharaf al-Dawla

Not much is known about him, apart from the fact that ʿAyn al-Quḍāt authored a text titled the *Risāla-yi jamālī* for the sake of this prince. He adds that it was specifically composed in Persian.[142] This text was composed of three chapters: the first chapter identified the prophets as physicians who heal humanity, using the treasure of the Qurʾan. The second chapter demonstrated that every patient required a different type of remedy. In the third chapter ʿAyn al-Quḍāt extended this motif to state that for some "patients" it would be necessary to use the science of kalām.[143]

Tāj al-Dīn ʿAlāʾ al-Dawla

Tāj al-Dīn was another of ʿAyn al-Quḍāt's highly placed disciples. In addressing this disciple, ʿAyn al-Quḍāt states that when the "folk who have gone astray" increased in number, he saw it fit to compose a treatise that would identify the path of the "righteous forefathers." In contrast to the *Risāla-yi jamālī* composed for Jamāl al-Dīn, the *Risāla-yi ʿalāʾī* was composed in Arabic. However, both works were named after their patron. This was a common premodern practice, which one can witness in many of ʿAyn al-Quḍāt's contemporaries such as Abū Ḥāmid al-Ghazālī[144] and al-Juwaynī.[145] It does, however, impress upon us the importance of not reading ʿAyn al-Quḍāt as a "rebel" who dismissed *all* modes of authority. Nor was he one to shun all politically significant personas. This is apparent in the above two figures and even more prominently in the next two disciples, Kāmil al-Dawla and ʿAzīz al-Dīn.

Kāmil al-Dawla [wa ʾl-Dīn]

In the extensive collection of letters composed by ʿAyn al-Quḍāt, Kāmil al-Dawla emerges as one of his two most important, or at least most frequently written to, disciples, the other one being ʿAzīz al-Dīn Mustawfī. Kāmil al-Dawla was situated in Baghdad and was the first to inform ʿAyn al-Quḍāt that there were juridical opinions (*fatwā*s) issued for his death.[146] ʿAyn al-Quḍāt identifies him elsewhere as one of the disciples to whom he had written voluminous letters.[147] On other occasions, he marks with great joy having received a letter from Kāmil al-Dawla.[148] Kāmil apparently served the same Amīr Qazal who was pointed out by ʿAyn al-Quḍāt as being unworthy of the many iqṭāʿs the Saljūqs had granted him. ʿAyn al-Quḍāt calls on Kāmil al-Dawla to abandon the service of Qazal and instead dedicate himself to serving God. In typically playful ʿAyn al-Quḍātian fashion, he seems to be playing on a pun, contrasting the name of Amīr Qazal with God's attribute of Azal, "the Eternal."[149] Rahim Farmanish correctly recognizes that many of the letters written to Kāmil al-Dawla deal with sophisticated nuances of Sufi teachings.[150]

ʿAzīz al-Dīn Mustawfī—and His Antagonist, the Vizier Dargazīnī[151]

We know more about ʿAzīz al-Dīn than all of ʿAyn al-Quḍāt's other disciples combined. This is not necessarily due to ʿAzīz al-Dīn's elevated spiritual rank but to what one might call a fortuitous historiographic occurrence: his familial relationship to one of the most well-known premodern Muslim historians, ʿImād al-Dīn al-Kātib al-Iṣfahānī.

The life of ʿAzīz al-Dīn is inextricably linked to that of the Saljūq vizier Qawwām al-Dīn Abū ʾl-Qāsim Ansābādhī Dargazīnī (d. 527/1133). ʿAyn al-Quḍāt's martyrdom was part of a larger set of events that involved the imprisonment and murder of ʿAzīz al-Dīn Mustawfī (d. 527/1133). After this, Dargazīnī moved against ʿAzīz al-Dīn's brothers, Ḍiyāʾ al-Dīn and Ṣafī al-Dīn. Ḍiyāʾ al-Dīn is also identified by ʿAyn al-Quḍāt as the recepient of many his correspondences.[152] Ṣafī al-Dīn is not particularly a noteworthy character except for the fact that his son is one of the more noted medieval chroniclers, ʿImād al-Dīn al-Kātib al-Iṣfahānī.[153] ʿImād al-Dīn is one of our more reliable sources for the history of the Saljūqs, and we have already made extensive use of him in documenting the rise of the Saljūqs and Niẓām al-Mulk. He is most well-known, of course, for having been the personal scribe and historian of the famed Saladin, the Muslim hero of the Crusades. However, when ʿImād al-Dīn gets to the events dealing with the life of Dargazīnī, he drops all pretence of objectivity and unleashes a sustained and highly charged polemic against the vizier. It is clear that as ʿAzīz al-Dīn's nephew, ʿImād al-Dīn holds Dargazīnī personally responsible for the murder of his two uncles—not to say anything of his own father. This polemic deploys all the expected polemical charges commonly found in Saljūq politics: Dargazīnī's lowly origin, his lack of refinement, his lack of loyalty, embezzlement of funds, Ismā'īlī leaning, and unimaginable cruelty. Among other insults, 'Imād al-Dīn calls Dargazīnī a "peasant who has given up working with cows" and has sought political power. Furthermore, he accuses him of shedding blood and attacking defenseless people.[154] In a typical display of Saljūq polemics, 'Imād al-Dīn accuses Dargazīnī of supporting the Bāṭinīs and squandering away the *niẓām* of the land.[155] As is characteristic of the Saljūq era, this polemical charge links together social disorder (*niẓām*) with the following of heretical Ismā'īlī teaching (*bāṭinīya*). 'Imād al-Dīn even states that the reason the Ismā'īlīs were favorably disposed toward Dargazīnī was that the vizier had called off Amīr Shīrgīr as the military commander was close to conquering the Alamūt castle.[156] 'Imād al-Dīn's polemic has shaped most of the later sources and certainly the contemporary sources. Two of the more prominent scholars who have studied Saljūq politics (Karla Klausner and Ann K. S. Lambton) have both depicted Dargazīnī in highly unfavorable terms. Klausner regards him as "one of the most corrupt, oppressive, and harmful of all Seljuk Vezirs."[157] Lambton is no more kind, stating that Dargazīnī "appears to have been one of the most corrupt of the Saljuq officials, making large sums of money from confiscation and fines."[158]

There is a further historiographic issue that complicates our reading of 'Imād al-Dīn al-Kātib al-Iṣfahānī's *Nuṣrat al-fatra* (available only through al-Bundārī's abridgement, *Zubdat al-nuṣra*) and the polemic against Dargazīnī. It is clear that in composing this source, the author had relied to a great extent upon Anūshirwān ibn Khālid's memoirs.[159] Anūshirwān was one of Dargazīnī's political enemies:[160] Anūshirwān served as Sultan Maḥmūd b. Muḥammad b. Malik-Shāh's vizier from 512 to 522/1118 to 1128, only to be replaced by Dargazīnī from 522 to 525.[161] They had been competing politically from an earlier time when Anūshirwān had been the *'arīḍ* of the Vizier Kamāl al-Mulk al-Sumayramī and Dargazīnī in charge of the *ṭughrā'*.[162] Anūshirwān's personal dislike of Dargazīnī is perhaps clearest in using insults such as "rabid dog and quarrelsome mule" (*al-kalb al-kalib wa 'l-baghl al-shaghb*) in referring to his competitor.[163] Given the bitter rivalry between the two, one must naturally view with some caution the material in the *Zubdat al-nuṣra* dealing with Dargazīnī's character which comes from Anūshirwān.

However, there is new textual evidence that suggests that Dargazīnī was not the evil-incarnate character that 'Imād al-Dīn and later sources have made him out to be. We now possess two new sources that can be used to arrive at a different characterization of Dargazīnī. These sources are Najm al-Dīn

Abū Rajā' Qummī's *Tārīkh al-wuzarā'* (*History of Viziers*) and the various letters and poems of the famed Ḥakīm Sanā'ī. The *Tārīkh al-wuzarā'* was composed no later than 584/1188, Qummī's death date. It is significant for our purposes here to note that this source, which is completely independent of ʿImād al-Dīn al-Kātib al-Iṣfahānī and his own personal polemic against Dargazīnī, was composed less than two generations after ʿAyn al-Quḍāt's (and ʿAzīz al-Dīn's) death. It is a rare opportunity for us to verify the persona attributed to Dargazīnī by ʿImād al-Dīn. Qummī offers a mixed assessment of Dargazīnī. On one hand Qummī states that Dargazīnī could demonstrate immense generosity, so that his compassion to those in need could be greater than that shown by a mother to her own child.[164] In particular, Qummī states that Dargazīnī was especially generous to people of his own countryside.[165] On a less positive note, Qummī also states that Dargazīnī had a terrible temper, likening it to a dark cloud that with every thunder would offer a lightening.[166] In perhaps the most fair assessment of this doubtless difficult and complex character, the author of *Tārīkh al-wuzarā'* states that Dargazīnī was like "a lightning in which there is both the possibility of merciful rain, and the fear of the fire caused by lightning. In him there was both loss and benefit."[167]

An interesting passage mentioned in the *Tārīkh al-wuzarā'* links Dargazīnī to Sufis, in particular to the famed Sufi poet Ḥakīm Sanā'ī (d. 1131). According to Qummī, it was Ḥakīm Sanā'ī's habit to not offer praise (*madḥ*) for anyone, in particular for no vizier or sultan, except for a few great scholars of religion.[168] Qummī states that when Dargazīnī sent honorific robes and some gold to the poet-saint, Sanā'ī responded by bestowing the robes to the messenger and the gold to the messenger's servants. He stated that he only accepted Dargazīnī's favor. In return, nonetheless, he composed the following poem in honor of Dargazīnī: "The firmament, sun, and the moon that traverse the universe kiss the dust of your alleyway."[169]

That Qummī would have known about Sanā'ī's panegyric for Dargazīnī is significant because Sanā'ī passed away on the eleventh of Shaʿbān 525 (9 July 1131 C.E.). Less than sixty years after his passing (i.e., by 584/1188, the latest possible date for Qummī's authorship of his text), a relationship between him and Dargazīnī was a matter of public knowledge and was recorded in sources such as the *Tārīkh al-wuzarā'*. For our purposes here, being concerned with perceptions and social constructions, it is significant to note how quickly this relationship became known and documented publicly.

We can offer independent verification of the above relationship from Sanā'ī's own corpus of works. There are a number of references in Sanā'ī's works to Dargazīnī: Mudarris Raḍawī, who edited the *Dīvān* of Sanā'ī, identifies two *qaṣīdas* in praise of Dargazīnī.[170] In addition, there are three letters written from Sanā'ī to the vizier which are reproduced in the present printing of the *Dīvān*.[171] It is the second letter which contains the lines quoted by Qummī in his *Tārīkh al-wuzarā'*: "The firmament, sun, and moon that traverse the world . . ."[172] Therefore, it was not only Sanā'ī's relationship with Dargazīnī which was known about in administrative circles but even the precise poems used by the poetic saint in praise of the vizier. Other poems in Sanā'ī's *Dīvān* offer further praise of Dargazīnī as well.[173] Contemporary scholarship on Sanā'ī has also noted this relationship.[174]

What makes the relationship between Dargazīnī and Sanā'ī particularly relevant for our purposes is that Sanā'ī emerges out of the same Khurāsānī Sufi milieu that shapes the discourse of 'Ayn al-Quḍāt (through his master, Aḥmad Ghazālī, and others). In fact, 'Ayn al-Quḍāt was also fond of quoting Sanā'ī in his writings. One place where he cites Sanā'ī by name is in a letter to his disciples in which he elucidates how it is possible for one to know the Qur'an even without having a mastery of Arabic.[175] There are many other poems in the *Tamhīdāt* and the *Nāma-hā* where Sanā'ī's poems are cited anonymously.[176] This is significant because it demonstrates a literary and spiritual affinity between Sanā'ī and 'Ayn al-Quḍāt, who, by his own reckoning, was not fond of "transmitting the sayings of others." The same vizier who is held responsible for 'Ayn al-Quḍāt's martyrdom is depicted as having been very favorable towards Sanā'ī. This is another proof that 'Ayn al-Quḍāt's martyrdom should not be read as a Saljūq vendetta against Sufis in general or even intellectuals who offer outlandish and bold discourses on the sacred. Our best explanation seems to be in contextualizing 'Ayn al-Quḍāt as an oppositional intellectual who was caught up in interpolitical intrigues of the Saljūq court. When Dargazīnī sought to bring about the demise of 'Azīz al-Dīn, it made political sense to also direct an attack against 'Azīz al-Dīn's spiritual master, 'Ayn al-Quḍāt. Doing so had a double effect: by accusing 'Ayn al-Quḍāt of heretical ideas, he was able to further discredit 'Azīz al-Dīn. Also, by imprisoning the popular and vocal Qāḍī of Hamadan, he was removing one further source of protection for 'Azīz al-Dīn.

Apart from 'Ayn al-Quḍāt's personal association with 'Azīz al-Dīn, and the latter's antagonistic relationship with Dargazīnī, was there a more direct case of animosity between 'Ayn al-Quḍāt and Dargazīnī? Several sources allude to precisely such a possibility. Bayhaqī's *Tatimma ṣiwān al-ḥikma* reports that 'Ayn al-Quḍāt was "hung on the account of an enmity between him and the Vizier Abū 'l-Qāsim al-Ansābādhī (*fa-ṣaliba bi-sababi 'idāwatan kānat baynihi wa bayn al-wazīr abī 'l-qāsim al-ansābādhī*)."[177] Given that Bayhaqī died in 565/1169, this shows that within approximately one generation of ʿAyn al-Quḍāt's passing, the cruel circumstances surrounding his death were directly blamed on Dargazīnī. Another philosophical biographical dictionary, Shahrazūrī's *Nuzhat al-arwāḥ*, confirms Bayhaqīs narrative, in particular the animosity (*dushmanī*) between ʿAyn al-Quḍāt and the vizier.[178] Both of these sources are significant in documenting the perceptions regarding the event more than its final causes.

Having documented the disciples of ʿAyn al-Quḍāt at the Saljūq court and the political infighting between them and a powerful vizier, we are now positioned to move to a closer examination of the persecution and martyrdom of ʿAyn al-Quḍāt.

The Persecution of ʿAyn al-Quḍāt

In the *Shakwa ʾl-gharīb*, ʿAyn al-Quḍāt states that the main reason he was being targeted for persecution was that many scholars who were inferior to him were jealous of his accomplishments. I have already cited his charmingly boastful claim, "It is no wonder that I am envied, . . . seeing that I composed as a mere youth . . . books which baffle the men of fifty and sixty to understand, much less to compile and compose."[179] That might well have been one factor. Indeed some of the historical sources, in particular ʿImād al-Dīn al-Kātib al-Iṣfahānī, point to precisely this fact. While he does attribute ʿAyn al-Quḍāt's death directly to Dargazīnī, he also states that "the ignorant ones of the age (*juhhāl al-zamān*), who were masquerading as scholars were invoked by the Vizier against ʿAyn al-Quḍāt (*wa waḍaʿahum al-wazīr ʿalayhi*) to harm him. In the end, the Vizier who feared neither God nor faith, had him hung in Hamadān (*ṣalabahu al-wazīr bi hamadhān wa lam yurāqabu Allāh fīhi wa lā īmān*)."[180]

It is intriguing to note that the events surrounding the deaths of ʿAzīz al-Dīn and ʿAyn al-Quḍat vexed ʿImād al-Dīn Kātib to the point that he returned to this polemic in another of his texts, the *Kharīdat al-qaṣr*, where he stated:

> There were those who made their name as the "people of knowledge," [but were in fact ignorant]. They became jealous of ʿAyn al-Quḍāt, who was one of the eminent scholars and saints, and had performed many wondrous deeds. They used phrases from his compositions that they did not even understand as an excuse to accuse him of infidelity. Abū ʾl-Qāsim Dargazīnī captured him, and sent him in chains to Baghdad, looking for an excuse to find a legally permissible way to shed his blood.

> He then returned him to Hamadan, and hung him on the gallows the night of Wednesday the sixth of Jamādī II, in the year 525 [/1131].[181]

ʿAyn al-Quḍāt's own prison memoirs, the *Shakwa ʾl-gharīb,* also provide us with a listing of the charges that he defends himself against. The charges cast against him might well have been different from the ones he so deftly dismisses. At the same time, it is worth remembering that the *Shakwa* is doubtlessly an apologetic text in which ʿAyn al-Quḍāt backs away from many of his more radical propositions: time and again he situates himself fully along the lines of the classical Sufi tradition and in particular appeals to the legacy of Abū Ḥāmid Ghazālī.[182] There is no mention here, naturally, of the more controversial aspects of his teachings in his Persian writings, such as the *Tamhīdāt* and the *Nāma-hā*. Nor is there, naturally, any mention of the severe critiques he makes of Ghazālī, which we have covered.

Nonetheless, it is still intriguing to note that in the *Shakwa*, ʿAyn al-Quḍāt identifies a number of charges his critics had cast against him. First, that he had allegedly stated that there is a stage of faith beyond reason, which would presumably "bar the way of the common people to faith in prophecy."[183] Second, that he had called God "the origin and source of being."[184] As a subset of this charge, he also states that he has been accused of claiming that the world was eternal, and also of claiming that God lacks knowledge of particulars.[185] Third, that he had stated that every spiritual novice needs a guide.[186] And lastly, that he claimed to be a prophet.[187]

What is intriguing about the above charges is that they require ʿAyn al-Quḍāt to demarcate his own discourse from the allegedly heretical philosophers and the Ismāʿīlīs. In identifying a stage of faith beyond reason, he has to directly engage the philosophical discussion of the relationship between reason and prophethood. In answering the charge that he had required every disciple to have a shaykh, he is fully aware of the fact that his own discourse is being accused of being in line with that of the Ismāʿīlīs.[188] Again we see an occasion when the mere presence of the Ismāʿīlīs required all the intellectual discourses of the time to demonstrate how their own discourses did not overlap with that of the allegedly heretical Bāṭinīs.

Lastly, it must be noted that at least some of the charges cast against ʿAyn al-Quḍāt (or rather, those that he defends himself against) do overlap with the criterion for distinguishing heresy that Abū Ḥāmid Ghazālī had identified a generation ago. In the *Munqidh*, Ghazālī had identified three claims of philosophers as constituting heresy: first, denying bodily resurrection; second, holding that God knows universals but not particulars; and third, stating that the world is eternal.[189] He had elaborated on all of these charges, bringing the total number to twenty dismissals of philosophy in his celebrated *Tahāfut al-falāsifa*.[190] ʿAyn al-Quḍāt's engagement of the criteria of heresy defined by Ghazālī is a great testimony both to the immediate impact of Ghazālī and also a final dismissal of attempts to read both ʿAyn al-Qūḍat and Ghazālī as "maverick intellectuals." ʿAyn al-Quḍāt's persecution is at the hands of jealous theologians (provoked by Dargazīnī) who have brought charges against him based on Ghazālī's criteria. One figure is clearly an outsider to the regime, the other its most vocal and recognizable voice.

The Martyrdom of ʿAyn al-Quḍāt

As it has already been mentioned, the martyrdom of ʿAyn al-Quḍat is wrapped up in many fantastic hagiographic accounts, culminating in the well-known poem attributed to him: "We have prayed for death, through martyrdom . . ." It is not my intention here to recapitulate the hagiographic narratives and certainly not to offer a modern-day addition to these accounts. Rather, I intend to examine some of the details of the events leading to ʿAyn al-Quḍāt's murder.

The public murder of a highly ranked religious scholar in the Saljūq era was not a common occurrence. While the charge of heresy was indeed a common one that many intellectuals cast against their rival schools, it was much more rare for an *ʿālim* to actually be killed on the charge of heresy. ʿAyn al-Quḍāt's case, for this reason as for so many others, deserves special mention.

ʿAyn al-Quḍāt himself states in the *Tamhīdāt* that some jurists in Baghdad had issued a fatwā calling for his death.[191] In a typically sarcastic, humorous, and undeterred ʿAyn al-Quḍātian fashion, he adds, "O friend, if they ask you for a fatwā, you issue one as well!"[192] In our own time period, the idea of a death-sentence fatwā resonates very closely, recalling Ayatollah Khomeini's Valentine's Day fatwā against Salman Rushdie. It is perhaps worth recalling that under the rubric of Islamic law, a fatwā is simply a juridical opinion and legally carries no force of law. Furthermore, a jurist cannot simply issue a fatwā by fiat, but can only do so in response to a petition or a specific case. While it is safe to assume that from a legal perspective the Baghdad jurists had overstepped their boundaries, one has to wonder whether an agent there (perhaps Dargazīnī?) had not petitioned them for a fatwā against ʿAyn al-Quḍāt. Many of our historical sources also confirm that a fatwā calling for ʿAyn al-

Quḍāt's death had been issued, perhaps at the instigation of Dargazīnī, by jealous and petty theologians.[193]

The second important aspect to keep in mind is that the actual court session that convicted ʿAyn al-Quḍāt was not a sharīʿa court. It has been a tendency of many scholars who have written on ʿAyn al-Quḍāt to identify elements in his teachings that are held to be "unorthodox."[194] It is then expected that the "unorthodoxy" of his teachings somehow resulted in his death. There are a number of problematic points with the above framework. There is no indication that those who charged ʿAyn al-Quḍāt had known about his more radical, Persian writings such as the *Tamhīdāt* and the *Nāma-hā*.[195] Even leaving aside for the moment the problematic of projecting a language of "orthodox"/"unorthodox" back onto the Saljūq intellectual discourses, it is important to recall that the court which convicted ʿAyn al-Quḍāt was not a sharīʿa court and was therefore not designed to decide matters of theology or law. The only source referring to the nature of this hastily assembled trial is al-Subkī's *Ṭabaqāt al-shāfiʿīya*, which calls it a *maḥḍar* organized by the Vizier Dargazīnī.[196] The nature of this *maḥḍar* is not clarified there, but it seems safe to assume that it is none other than the infamous para-sharīʿa *naẓar al-maẓālim* that was controlled by the viziers at this time.[197] We still lack thorough studies of this form of "secular justice" in the Saljūq period: the most detailed study of the *maẓālim* system dates from a later period, that of the Baḥrī Mamlūks.[198] However, the historical evidence does suggest that by Saljūq times, the dispensation of the *maẓālim* system was under the control of the viziers, although Niẓām al-Mulk considered it a duty of the sultan.[199] H. F. Amedroz's frequently cited study of the operation of the *maẓālim* under the ʿAbbāsids also confirms that in practice this power was gradually shifted from the caliphs to their viziers.[200] Furthermore, Lambton also confirms that in this time period of Saljūq history, the majority of sultans delegated their function of presiding over *maẓālim* to their viziers.[201] There was also the clear factor of financial corruption. It seems clear that the system had become open to much abuse, even prompting Ibn al-Athīr to comment that it was not the sense of duty but that of material gain alone which led viziers to concern themselves with the *maẓālim*.[202] Niẓām al-Mulk's *Siyāsat-nāma* is certainly full of corrupt officials who abuse their juridical positions to take possessions away from commoners. It seems that Dargazīnī's charges brought against ʿAzīz al-Dīn (and by extension ʿAyn al-Quḍāt) were at least partially motivated by the same desire. According to al-Kātib al-Iṣfahānī's account—which should be viewed with some skepticism—Dargazīnī bribed Sultan Maḥmūd 300,000 dinārs to permit him to imprison ʿAzīz al-Dīn. Dargazīnī seems to have recovered this sum by aquiring all of the Mustawfī's possessions.[203] Thus the motivation behind the whole fiasco was none other than a competition for political power and financial resources between ʿAzīz al-Dīn and Dargazīnī.

The political nature of ʿAyn al-Quḍāt's martrydom can be assessed through another historical reference. Again, according to al-Kātib al-Iṣfahānī, Dargazīnī tricked Sultan Sanjar by having the latter give him some blank *farmān*s (regal orders), allegedly so that the vizier could use them to take care of some administrative details in the sultan's absence. If we are to believe al-Kātib al-Iṣfahānī's polemical account, Dargazīnī used the very first of these signed farmāns to initiate the imprisonment of ʿAzīz al-Dīn and ʿAyn al-Quḍāt.[204] This again underscores the fact that the full context leading to the persecution and martyrdom of ʿAyn al-Quḍāt was as much political as intellectual. In fact, it would be impossible to make sense of the complex set of events that led to his tragic death without keeping in mind such realpolitik events such as a vizier obtaining through trickery what amounted to political carte blanche. Attempts to identify allegedly "unorthodox" elements in ʿAyn al-Quḍāt's writings that are held to have led to his death miss the nuance of the above political situation.

Discourses do not kill people. "Counterdiscourses" and "counternarrative" do not kill people. "Orthodoxy" and "unorthodoxy" do not kill people. Accusations of heresy do not kill people. People kill people. People are motivated through a whole host of means, including of course ideological deployment of various discourses of orthodoxy and blasphemy. Saljūq times offer a dizzying and complex set of rhetorical discourses, using the language of blasphemy, orthodoxy, and heresy. Without dismissing the power of those discourses, or the sincerity of many of those who deployed them, it is worthwhile to keep in mind the full historical, political, and social realities of the time. ʿAyn al-Quḍāt provides us with another example of an intellectual whose interaction with the Saljūq regime is often through his own disciples (like ʿAzīz al-Dīn and Kāmil al-Dawla), and viziers. The Saljūq political-intellectual world was a vast network of caliphs and sultans, viziers and ʿulamāʾ, soldiers and Sufis. Often what led to politically symbiotic relationships (such as with Abū Saʿīd-i Abī ʾl-Khayr) or antagonistic confrontations (such as with ʿAyn al-Quḍāt) was as much dependent on the relations between the saints' disciples and the viziers as on the saintly figures themselves. In other words, the context of ʿAyn al-Quḍāt's downfall has as much to do with the political downfall of his disciples as it does with his own existence. The case of ʿAyn al-Quḍāt provides with us with a tragic example of a brilliant voice of oppositional dissent whose life was cut short by being caught in these political intrigues.

In conclusion, it is useful to contrast the life and legacy of Sufis like Abū Saʿīd-i Abī ʾl-Khayr and ʿAyn al-Quḍāt: both might legitimately be called "ecstatic Sufis" who participated in *samāʿ* and the *khānaqāh* scene. Yet their baraka was negotiated in vastly different ways: Abū Saʿīd's descendants and disciples used the sacralized memory of the Shaykh to negotiate with the Saljūqs. They lent legitimacy to a regime that just generations before had been migrant pagans in Central Asia but had since attained power in the most cosmopolitan society in the Nile-to-Oxus region, and perhaps beyond, at the time. In exchange, they received the financial support of many Saljūq figures (and other Turkish invaders later on) who were more than eager to connect their own names to the venerable institutions that bore Abū Saʿīd's name. ʿAyn al-Quḍāt's case presents us with a stark contrast: he has almost no genealogical descendants to speak of, no disciples who form a silsila after him, no shrine complex, no record of rulers who came to pay homage to him after his death. Clearly it would be a mistake to view the Saljūqs as somehow being inimical to Sufism. Even the ecstatic variety of Sufism lived by masters such as Abū Saʿīd did not seem to pose a problem for the Saljūq rulers. However, it might also be said that more than Sufism, the Saljūqs were interested in saints—and the baraka they were seen as embodying. What sets ʿAyn al-Quḍāt apart is that in his own lifetime he deliberately refused to align himself with the Saljūqs, instead using his position of influence to critique them, the scholars who would work for them, and the administrators who served them. His calling was not that of legitimizing the Saljūqs but of challenging them and undermining the basis of their authority. This was one oppositional Sufi and social critic whose baraka was not up for bargaining.

Conclusion

It has not been my aim in this project to find shelter in the cool shade of positivist historicism. I do not suggest that we have somehow uncovered the *real* Saljūqs. While in chapter 1 I made some moves toward that, my aim consisted not of depicting the Saljūqs as they were, but rather to scrutinize how they came to be represented. Following Bruce Lincoln's lead, the aim of even that segment was to make their ideology visible. The focus of much of this project has been on the politics of depiction and representation, rather contemporary words about a not so contemporary world.

I have not attempted to write the history of the Saljūqs here. Nor will that be my aim in a future project. My historical concern is much more wide ranging: how do we come to read historical narratives in ways that let us recognize them as ideological in nature? I do not mean to state that we have to throw up our hands and retreat into a corner, lamenting that we cannot know anything with any level of certainty. Rather, I suggest that we ask different questions of the historical material than we thus far have. The age of positivism has passed; let us move on as well. We need not go on asking forever, "Did these events *really* take place?" We can, and should, instead ponder the following: given that there is a claim that such an event took place, how is the narrative constructed? What symbols of authority are appealed to? To whom is the narrative addressed? What does it conceal? Whom does it privilege? How does it legitimize the parties involved, while dismissing alternate ideologies, other possibilities, other modes of relating to God, humanity, and knowledge?

In the case of the Saljūqs, these questions are particularly important. Much of what we have come to know about the Nile-to-Oxus Islamicate society, in realms of politics and religion, literature and institutions, has had precedents in the formative era of the Great Saljūqs in the fifth/eleventh century. I suggest that we reapproach our studies of dominant political and intellectual institutions with such a perspective in mind, asking not merely what has happened but rather investigating how the narratives that tell us what happened legitimize some claimants while marginalizing others.

It is time perhaps for me to bring into light my debt to Edward Said, who like Foucault has lurked in the shadows of this project. More so than antipositivism, I have seen my own project here as following in Said's notion of a humanistic model of "secular criticism." By "secular" Said meant (it is strange to speak of such giants in the past tense) not antireligious but rather an oppositional quality of being in the world while holding on to "suspicion of totalizing concepts . . . discontent with reified objects . . . impatience with guilds, special interests, imperialized fiefdoms, and orthodox habits of mind . . . ."[1] I have sought to avoid reified and totalizing subjects such as "Islam," "Islamdom," "Orthodoxy," etc. I don't mean to suggest, naturally, that there is no Islam, or that the Islamic articulations of all are equally valid, equally profound, etc., but rather that Islam is always Islam to somebody, that those somebodies have differences as well as commonalities, and that there are always contested and negotiated definitions and practices.[2] To recall Rumi's lovely story, borrowed from ancient Indian sources, the reality of humanity and faith and community is like the elephant in the city of blind men, and we are all privileged and limited to experience a small part of these larger realities.

Myth of the "Three Schoolboy Friends"

Perhaps the best example to demonstrate the above is through a popular narrative told about a number of Saljūq-era figures. The story is the common myth of "three schoolboy friends."[3] This narrative has shaped the imagination of both later Muslim as well as early Western scholars' understanding of premodern Islam, particularly with respect to the Saljūq period. According to this narrative, Niẓām al-Mulk, ʿUmar Khayyām (the famous philosopher-mathematician, poet, and would-be Victorian muse), and Ḥasan-i Ṣabbāḥ (the leader of the Ismāʿīlīs in Alamūt) were classmates under Imām Muwaffaq in Nīshāpūr. We are told that they had allegedly made a pact that any of them who attained to a position of power would also appoint the other two to prestigious posts. Niẓām al-Mulk was the first to achieve to his position of prominence. When he approached ʿUmar Khayyām to fulfill their pact by appointing him as the governor of Nīshāpūr, the philosopher-mathematician said that he would be simply content with receiving a stipend.[4] The interaction with Ḥasan Ṣabbāḥ was considerably more complicated. The *Khwāja* at first had appointed him to the rule of Hamadān and Dīnvar. Yet (according to this account) Ḥasan Ṣabbāḥ was not satisfied, wishing to share in all of the vizierate with Niẓām al-Mulk. This gradually led to a rift between them, which resulted in Ḥasan Ṣabbāḥ fleeing the Saljūqs, capturing Alamūt, and "spreading the schools of heresy (*zandaqa*), licentiousness (*ibāḥa*), and irreligion (*ilḥād*)."[5]

This narrative would show up repeatedly in many of the later sources of Islamic literature, including *Dastūr al-wuzarāʾ* and *Tadhkirat al-shuʿarāʾ*.[6] It has also been met with skepticism. While E. G. Browne rightly casts doubt on this narrative,[7] he does point out that this narrative was quoted by the usually reliable Rashīd al-Dīn Faḍl Allāḥ.[8] Given the dubious sources upon which this narrative is based, it is perhaps surprising to note that this myth continues to be transmitted in certain recent academic works on Niẓām al-Mulk.[9] There is no reason to doubt that Niẓām al-Mulk might have studied with the named Imām Muwaffaq. However, the historicity of the narrative can safely be rejected: the late death dates for Ḥasan Ṣabbāḥ (d. 518/1123) and ʿUmar al-Khayyām (d. 517/1124) would have made it impossible for them to have been schoolboys at the same time as Niẓām al-Mulk.

Lost in all the controversy over the historicity of this alleged meeting is the *meaning* associated with this myth. This myth, like all myths, signifies something to the communities who told and retold this narrative. There is something particular about the choice of the three individuals who are brought together in childhood. These three, far more than merely individuals, represent three domains of knowledge, three discourses on the sacred in premodern Islam. Niẓām al-Mulk is the embodiment of right-knowledge (orthodoxy) perfectly wedded to right-politics. He is the personification of Saljūq religious ideology. ʿUmar Khayyām represents the Other within the fold. He is the philosopher, astronomer, mathematician—suspect, yet acceptable; outside the main strands which compose the orthodox construction, yet still capable of being appropriated by it. This is why in this narrative, he and Niẓām al-Mulk reach a mutually satisfactory agreement: ʿUmar would not be directly part of the system, yet he would be acknowledged b*y* it: no less than Malik-Shāh had called on ʿUmar Khayyām in the latter's capacity as an astronomer to establish an observatory in the year 467/1074.[10] As for Ḥasan Ṣabbāḥ, he is clearly the Other outside of the fold. It is he who is deluded away by selfishness and falls prey to heresy and licentiousness—all great words right out of the discourse of Saljūq ideology. His reasoning for abandoning Niẓām al-Mulk doubtless represents a polemic against all Ismāʿīlīs. Ḥasan represents both the religious heretic and the political traitor. Once again religious orthodoxy and political fidelity are linked, both in adherence and in rejection. While the myth of the "three schoolboy fellows" might not be verifiable when held to positivist historicist standards, it does provide us with invaluable insight into the overlapping discourses of political fidelity and religious inquiry in the Saljūq era.

One of the aims of this project has been to open up all (or at least many more) narratives of premodern Islamicate history to such analysis. The narratives of Bābā Ṭāhir and Ṭughril, Abū Saʿīd and Niẓām al-Mulk, and al-Ghazālī's allegedly spiritual quest are all about much more than the meetings of random individual human beings. They are legitimizing narratives, ideological myths. The multiple meanings of these narratives ultimately must take precedence over their singular historicity. Doing so makes the narratives relevant, not just to the would-be scholar of Saljūq history, but to all students of premodern Islamicate society and beyond.

Heresy and the Charges of Heresy

As one whose childhood was spent in Iran during the turbulent days of the 1979 revolution, I recall how easily the charges of heresy and treason (again, in an overlapping discourse of religious thought and political fidelity) were bandied about. My research has brought me back to the contemporary period—ironically not to Iran, but to the Western world. Living now in the United States, where we are told to measure all of reality in pre-9/11 and post-9/11 terms, I am daily reminded of how being branded "un-American" also implies both political treason as well as a violation of allegedly clear, unanimous, and universal morals. The linking of *dīn* and *dawla* is still with us . . .

I wish to return to the disturbing ease with which charges of heresy continue to be handed out—this time by contemporary Western scholars of Islamic thought. One expects the charge of heresy as part of premodern intra-Islamic polemics. More unexpected, perhaps, is the ease with which contemporary scholars accuse their premodern counterparts of heresy. How ironic that many Sufis of the Saljūq era are facing another inquisition of sorts, this time from Western scholars writing from the comfort of our/their privileged situation. Not infrequently, I have encountered some of the more established scholars of Sufi studies categorizing particular facets of some Sufi teachings as heretical and against "orthodox theologians."[11] Who are these orthodox theologians? The Ashʿarīs? The Ḥanbalīs? The ḥadīth transmitters? Which groups of theologians are thus privileged as the upholders of Islamic orthodoxy? Why them? On what authority has the contemporary scholar accorded that place of prominence to those theologians? How is the contemporary scholar's authority accounted for? Is it even acknowledged? What proof is there that those particular teachings were in fact deemed heretical?

A perfect example is the case of Shaykh Aḥmad Ghazālī (d. 520/1126), the younger brother of the much-discussed Abū Ḥāmid al-Ghazālī. The elder al-Ghazālī in fact appointed Aḥmad as his replacement (*nā'ib*) in the Baghdād Niẓāmīya when he abandoned his post. Recognized as a great scholar, Aḥmad was also a celebrated Sufi and the spiritual teacher of ʿAyn al-Quḍāt. Part of Aḥmad's teachings revolved around the concept of passionate and extreme love (*ʿishq*). His public discourses on this topic, particularly as related to Iblīs's refusal to prostrate himself before humanity at the dawn of creation, earned the wrath of some of his more strict coreligionists. Abū Saʿd al-Samʿānī is recorded in Sibṭ ibn al-Jawzī's *Mir'āt al-zamān* as having lamented, "Is there no one is this age from the great saints who will shed the blood of this sinner in order to get closer to God?"[12]

Apparently, no one from al-Samʿānī's age wanted to get closer to God, not if it meant shedding the blood of Aḥmad Ghazālī. Not only did Aḥmad live undisturbed, he was even taken up by hagiographic traditions that connected him to Saljūq figures such as Sultan Malik-Shāh.[13] To put the matter in another way, it was not such an easy task to get oneself killed as a Sufi in the Saljūq era. Aḥmad is said to have engaged in *samāʿ*, sung passionate poetry in love of God and/or earthly beloveds, given ecstatic sermons, and even engaged in the controversial practice of *shāhid-bāzī*, gazing upon unbearded youths, young males to be more precise, as embodiments of *jamāl*, "beauty."[14] In his public sermons, he is said to have offered highly original interpretations of Iblīs as the perfect chivalrous being who was the true monotheist, the perfect lover of God.[15] None of this is said to have brought upon him the charge of heresy in his own lifetime. The accusation of heresy, it surely must be recognized, is as much a construction of the time period. That which in one age would be considered perfectly plausible might be scandalous in another.

As for my beloved ʿAyn al-Quḍāt, there is absolutely no indication that those who brought the charge of heresy against him knew about his more unconventional teachings on the complementary natures of Iblīs and Muḥammad (Ṣ) or of his theory of the mystical interpretation of *kufr*. What he was killed for had to do with the politics of the Saljūq court and the challenge he represented to the dominant Saljūq religious ideology.

Shockingly, it seems that the premodern Islamic discourse on the sacred at times was capable of allowing for a much wider spectrum of interpretation than much modern scholarship. Our readings of the intellectual thought of this period are based on our own notions of what was orthodox and heterodox at that time. Surely it must be acknowledged that our own constructions deserve, at the least, closer scrutiny and, quite possibly, a radical re-envisioning.

So, where do we go after ʿAyn al-Quḍāt?

Ramifications of This Project

Like so many other scholarly projects, this one has grown from the seeds of a dissertation. By this point I have spent some twelve years of my life researching, writing, and revising the present study. In the introduction, I indulged a bit in the therapeutic, autohagiographical role of introductions. The genre of "conclusion" chapters is perhaps not all that different. Many of the most astute dissertations in this field are read by less than ten people. Now with the blessing of a resurrected life as a published monograph, it might have the chance of being—as one humorous English professor has said—"skimmed by literally dozens and dozens of people."

In light of that sad reality, it does seem more than a bit pompous to talk about how any one project will change the face of scholarship in a particular field. That is all the more the case when the work engages and challenges a number of disciplines, as this one does. Yet, after the twelve years of research and writing that this project has entailed, I will allow myself a bit of leisurely imagination. What follows is my ideal vision of how this work will challenge the disciplines to which it is so deeply indebted.

This project, not unlike its author-father who has given birth to it, is one that is simultaneously without an established home and at home in different places. I have deliberately sought to bring together insights from religious studies, critical theory, Islamic studies, and Middle Eastern studies. The findings of this project, I propose, have ramifications for each of those fields.

In terms of religious studies, the most important contribution is the need to historicize and problematize claims of orthodoxy and accusations of heresy. Clearly, one cannot naively take Saljūq claims of orthodoxy at face value without examining how such claims function to legitimize the Saljūqs and their religious ideology. Likewise, one must recognize that the boundary between orthodoxy and heresy was not a given but a perpetually negotiated and contested one.

I have also sought to problematize late nineteenth- and early twentieth-century notions of mysticism as a personal experience of the divine, particularly when the emphasis on the personal precludes the social and political significance of the same figures. This study serves as a reminder that one cannot simply abstract categories from one worldview and apply them to another without a perpetual search to see what gets left out, what gets included, and what gets blown out of proportion.

This project also makes a number of contributions and correctives to the present state of Islamic studies. It serves to underscore the importance of conceiving of premodern Islamdom, not as a reified entity, but as a diverse society of competing groups who nonetheless were brought together under a whole host of ideological and institutional apparatuses. This project aims to affirm and document the multiethnic, multilinguistic, and intellectually pluralistic nature of premodern Islam. While Arabic continued to be the preferred language of Qur'anic studies and *fiqh*, Persian was fully emerged in a number of other disciplines including *tārīkh* and Sufi writings. Any reconstruction of Muslim social history from this region would have to incorporate all the relevant texts, not just the Arabic ones. No reconstruction of the social history of this time period can be deemed valid if it relies on only Persian or only Arabic sources.

I have also argued here for the importance of Sufis in the social and political spheres. As recipients of a post-Enlightenment conception of religion, we all too often tend to think of Sufis as Muslim "mystics," that is, Muslims who seek after a private, emotional, nonrational experience of God in their hearts. I have attempted to problematize both the pietistic readings of hagiographies and the positivist approaches that dismiss the genre as a whole. The hagiographies were not written for superstitious and stupid masses but were carefully crafted narratives designed to connect two elite communities, one whose power was based on politics and another on *wilāya*.

In terms of critical theory, I have sought to problematize some of our privileged readings of modernity. I have attempted to point out premodern antecedents for some, allegedly, uniquely modern systems such as that of surveillance and reconnaissance. In this case, the line separating the modern and premodern is made less sharp and more fuzzy. As with Hodgson, I prefer to think of the transition to modernity, not as an abrupt break, but through the framework of "the Great Western Transmutation," a coming together of global factors that happened first in Europe and *to* Europe, and which is now happening in myriad forms all over this planet.[16]

Lastly, I hope that friends and colleagues from Middle Eastern studies seriously engage the findings of this study. The contemporary academic scene for the study of the Nile-to-Oxus region is heavily geared toward the modern study of political and economic systems. Once one gets beyond the contemporary obsession with the Palestine/Israel conflicts and a suddenly resurgent

Ottoman studies, the rest of Middle Eastern history lags far behind. The fact that we still possess no complete histories of the Saljūqs is but one indication. This project has sought to engage a wide range of primary sources which have for the most part remained underexplored. That the most essential sources of the time period have not been read beyond the same passages cited over and over again is an indication of a still maturing field.

This project, emphatically multidisciplinary, bears all the weaknesses and perhaps a few of the strengths of any multidisciplinary approach. Surely the historians might have wanted more discussion of conventional historical matters. Likewise, already more than a few scholars of Sufism have expressed their disappointment that I have—for some reason inexplicable to them—been more interested in the political and social function of these saintly beings than in their metaphysical teachings.

I am deeply interested in the study of Sufis, and in other projects I have and will continue to undertake studies of their profound teachings and luminous writings. On the other hand, the greatest gift that I can bring to them is to see their beauty, not in spite of their social function, but rather through it. It would be easy enough to be a saintly being in an isolated cave, but to be so in the very midst of the turbulent world of the Saljūqs, or our own, takes great beings. It is my sincere hope that the scholars of Sufism continue to move toward reading the rich heritage of Sufi writings not in an ethereal, timeless fashion but contextualized both within and against the social and intellectual milieu that formed the world of the Sufis in the first place. To recall the wise words of Shaykh Abū Saʿīd b. Abī ʾl-Khayr which were cited in the beginning of chapter 5, may it be that we recognize Sufis as those who remain perpetually mindful of God *while* remaining in the very midst of society.

wa mā tawfīqī illā bi ʾl-lāh

Appendix

Niẓām al-Mulk's Descendants in Saljūq Administration

One of the most important and tangible ways in which Niẓām al-Mulk established his legacy throughout the Saljūq realm was by appointing his many sons to important governmental posts. Rāwandī reports that the Khwāja had twelve sons, each of whom had been appointed to an important post and a position of authority (*wilāyat*).[1] Another important source for documenting Niẓām al-Mulk's legacy is Bayhaqī, particularly given that he derived his data from Niẓām al-Mulk's family members. Bayhaqī stated that the Khwāja had nine sons and four daughters and that "all of these children achieved the pinnacle of vizierate, and attained the power to issue commands and prohibitions."[2] According to Qazwīnī, Niẓām al-Mulk and his twelve sons held the control of all of "Iran and Tūrān."[3] All these estimates are far more impressive than Ann Lambton's estimate that "five of his sons, two of his grandsons, and one great-grandson held the office of vizier."[4] What follows is a list of Niẓām al-Mulk's children, as can be determined from the sources:

1. Mu'ayyid al-Mulk Abū Bakr ʿUbayd Allāh ibn Niẓām al-Mulk (d. 494/1100): He was probably the greatest statesmen among the children of Niẓām al-Mulk. According to both Ibn Athīr and al-Kātib al-Iṣfahānī, he was present during the *bayʿa* of the Caliph al-Muqtadī in 467/1074.[5]
2. Fakhr al-Mulk, Abū 'l-Fatḥ Muẓaffar ibn Niẓām al-Mulk (d. 500/1106): He was the eldest son of Niẓām al-Mulk. He served Malik-Shāh, replaced his brother ʿIzz al-Mulk as Bark-yāruq's vizier, and ultimately served Sultan Sanjar in Khurāsān for ten years.[6] He, like his father, is said to have been killed by an Ismāʿīlī assassin (*fidā'ī*) in the ʿĀshūrā of 500/1106.[7] To demonstrate gratitude for his service, Sanjar then appointed Fakhr al-Mulk's son, Nāṣir al-Dīn Ṭāhir ibn Fakhr al-Mulk ibn Niẓām al-Mulk, to the vizierate. Nāṣir al-Dīn remained Sanjar's vizier from 528/1133 to 548/1153: in doing so, his vizierate was second only to that of his grandfather, Niẓām al-Mulk, in

longevity.[8] After Nāṣir al-Dīn, his son Niẓām al-Mulk Abū ʿAlī Qawwām al-Dīn Ḥasan was chosen by a later Saljūq Sultan Sulaymān Shāh as his vizier, a post he continued during the reign of Sultan Maḥmūd.[9] In choosing the honorifics of Niẓām al-Mulk and Qawwām al-Dīn, the descendants were already reaching back (after three generations) to the enormous legacy of the prestige of the Khwāja. These examples are also illustrative of how Niẓām al-Mulk's legacy extended beyond his own children and in reality created a multigenerational pool of trained viziers that the various Saljūq rulers could (and frequently did) tap into. This last vizier already represented the fourth generation of viziers from the descendants of Niẓām al-Mulk.

3. ʿIzz al-Mulk, Abū ʿAbd Allāh Ḥusayn ibn Niẓām al-Mulk (d. 487/1094): He was younger than both Fakhr al-Mulk and Muʾayyid al-Mulk and was allegedly a drunkard who lacked in administrative skill (*tadbīr*).[10] He temporarily became Bark-yāruq's vizier, which is not surprising given that Niẓām al-Mulk had favored Bark-yāruq all along over Maḥmūd as the heir-apparent to Malik-Shāh. He died accompanying Bark-yāruq in a battle to fight Tutush and was buried in the Niẓāmīya madrasa in Baghdad.[11]
4. ʿImād al-Mulk Abū ʾl-Qāsim ibn Niẓām al-Mulk (died 490/1096–7): He was a vizier of Bark-yāruq's uncle (Arslān Arghūn ibn Alb Arslān) and ultimately he too was killed. His possessions were also confiscated.[12]
5. Jamāl al-Mulk, Manṣūr ibn Niẓām al-Mulk (died 475/1082): It was this son of Niẓām al-Mulk who killed Malik-Shāh's favorite clown, Jaʿfarak, who mocked Niẓām al-Mulk. In revenge, Malik-Shāh arranged to have Jamāl al-Mulk killed.[13]
6. Shams al-Mulk ʿUthmān ibn Niẓām al-Mulk (died 517/1123): He became Sultan Maḥmūd's vizier. He was killed on the instigation of Abū Ṭāhir Qummī, who was opposed to all of Niẓām al-Mulk's descendants.[14] This is another indication of the competition for the vizierate between the *niẓāmī* viziers and those outside of that lineage.
7. Bahāʾ al-Mulk Abū ʾl-Fatḥ Ibrāhīm ibn Niẓām al-Mulk: He worked in the *Ṭughrā* divān, and attended the *bayʿat* of al-Mustaẓhir.[15]
8. Ḍiyāʾ al-Mulk Qawwām al-Dīn Abū Naṣr Aḥmad ibn Niẓām al-Mulk (died 544/1149): He was known as the second Niẓām al-Mulk (*Niẓām al-Mulk-i thānī*). Sultan Muḥammad bestowed upon him the title of Niẓām al-Mulk as well as Qawwām al-Dīn and Ṣadr al-Islām. He also served the Caliph al-Mustarshid as his vizier. After being deposed from this post, he retired to a life of piety in a *zāwiya* that was located in the Niẓāmīya madrasa of

Baghdad.[16] He actually followed through with the "threat" of retiring into a *zāwiya* that Niẓām al-Mulk had repeatedly requested/threatened to do.

9. Amīr Manṣūr ibn Niẓām al-Mulk, regarding whom little information is available.

To the above list of descendants, one could add an impressive number of influential sons-in-law, whom Niẓām al-Mulk was able to use as political allies: Sayyid al-Ruʾasāʾ Abū ʾl-Maḥāsin, Shibl al-Dawla Abū ʾl-Hijāʾ Muqātil ibn ʿAṭīya al-Bakrī al-Ḥijāzī, Thiqqat al-Islām Abū Muslim Sarūshiyārī, and ʿAmīd al-Dawla ibn Fakhr al-Dawla ibn Juhayr.

Notes

Introduction

1. Lincoln, "Theses on Method," 397 [emphasis mine].

2. See, for example, Lawrence, "Religion, Ideology and Revolution."

3. Said, "Intellectual Exile," 368–81.

4. Lincoln, "Theses on Method," 397.

5. I am indebted to Matthew Gordon who called my attention to his superb study, *Breaking of a Thousand Swords*. Gordon's work remains among the best sources for the impact of the Turkish military elite in the ʿAbbāsid period.

6. The most exhaustive treatment of Ismāʿīlī remains Daftary's masterful *Ismāʿīlīs*.

7. Althusser, "Ideology and Ideological State Apparatuses," 100–140.

8. Ibid., 106–7.

9. Ibid., 110–11.

10. Ibid., 112.

11. Lease, "Ideology," 444.

12. Lincoln, "Theses on Method," 397.

13. Meier, "Aḥmad-i D̲jām," 284.

14. For one documentation of this impact, see Bosworth, *New Islamic Dynasties*, where he traces hereditary lines through the Būrids, Zangids, Eldigūzids, Salghurids, and others. All of these dynasties had their start through atabegs appointed by the Saljūqs.

15. Cahen, "Turkish Invasion," 135.

16. Humphreys, *Islamic History*, 159.

17. For a recent example of such tendency that treats the intellectual developments of the ʿAbbāsid era, see Ephrat, *Sunni ʿUlamaʾ of 11th-Century Baghdad*. This work, based on a dissertation completed at Harvard in 1992 titled "The Sunni ʿUlamaʾ of 11th-Century Baghdad and the Transmission of Knowledge: A Social History," includes a wide range of the relevant Arabic historical and biographical sources, while neglecting to include even a single relevant Persian and Turkish source. The fact that many of the ʿulamāʾ Ephrat studies are Persians themselves and have written in both Arabic and Persian makes this omission all the more inexcusable.

18. One example is the troubling lack of attention given to al-Ghazālī's Persian

texts by scholars who have compiled his writings, such as Maurice Bouyges and Michel Allard, ʿAbd al-Raḥmān Badawī, and even W. M. Watt.

19. For a particularly chauvinist example, see Homayouni, *Origins of Persian Gnosis*. The following passage is typical of such attitude: "*Tasavvof* . . . played an important role in preserving national identity and culture and defending the independence of Iran . . . Secret national organizations contesting the supremacy of the Arabs appeared . . ." Homayouni, *Origins of Persian Gnosis*, 11.

20. See, for example, Leiser, *History of the Seljuks*, 21.

21. Humphreys, *Islamic History*, 187–208.

Key Figures and Primary Sources

1. Bosworth, "Political and Dynastic History," 1–202.

2. Lambton, "Internal Structure of the Saljuq Empire," 203–82.

3. Bausani, "Religion in the Saljuq Period," 283–302.

4. Shils, "Ideology," 69.

5. For characteristic examples of this genre, see Watt, *Muslim Intellectual* and Nasrollah Pourjavady's superb work, *Sulṭān-i ṭarīqat*.

6. A noteworthy example is Lambton, *Landlord and Peasant in Persia*.

7. Rāwandī, *Rāḥat al-ṣudūr*, 98–99.

8. Massé, "ʿImād al-Dīn Muḥammad b. Muḥammad al-Kātib al-Iṣfahānī."

9. ʿImād al-Dīn al-Kātib al-Iṣfahānī, *Nuṣrat al-fatra* [Abr. by al-Bundārī as *Zubdat al-nuṣra*]. Edited by M. Th. Houtsma, *Recueil de Textes relatifs a l-histoire des Seldjoucides*, ii. [Henceforth, al-Bundārī, *Zubdat al-nuṣra*] Also, Cf. M. Th. Houtsma-[Cl. Cahen], "al-Bundārī, al-Fatḥ b. ʿAlī b. Muḥammad al-Iṣfahānī."

10. Laoust, "Ibn Kathīr."

11. Hillenbrand, "Rāwandī, Muḥammad b. ʿAlī."

12. Spuler, "Ḥamd Allāh b. Abī Bakr b. Aḥmad b. Naṣr al-Mustawfī al-Ḳazwīnī."

13. The second edition of this text, undertaken by Muḥammad Nūr al-Dīn, records that Ṣadr al-Dīn Ḥusaynī must have died after 622/1225.

14. Barthold, "Dj̲uwaynī, ʿAlāʾ al-Dīn ʿAṭā Malik b. Muḥammad"; see also Boyle's introduction in Juwaynī, *History of the World-Conqueror*.

15. Morgan, "Rashīd al-Dīn Ṭabīb."

16. Fück, "Ibn Khallikān."

17. For al-Subkī's life, see Schact, "al-Subkī" and Makdisi, "Ashʿarī and the Ashʿarites."

18. Makdisi, "Ibn Radjab." For Makdisi's demonstration that Hanbali scholars of this period were not inimical to Sufism, see his "Hanbali School and Sufism."

19. Al-Ghazālī, *Tibr al-masbūk fī naṣīḥat al-mulūk*.

20. See Jalāl al-Dīn Humaʾī, "muqaddima" to al-Ghazālī, *Tibr al-masbūk fī naṣīḥat al-mulūk*, 127.

21. Al-Ghazālī, *Tuḥfat al-mulūk*, 251, 258.

22. Hodgson, *Venture of Islam: Conscience and History in a World Civilization*, 2:48.

23. Muḥammad Riḍā Shafīʿī-Kadkanī, "muqaddima-yi muṣaḥḥiḥ" to Ibn Munawwar, *Asrār al-tawḥīd*, 1:169.

24. Muḥammad Riḍā Shafīʿī-Kadkanī, "muqaddima-yi muṣaḥḥiḥ," to Jamāl al-Dīn Rūḥ-i Luṭf Allāh ibn Abī Saʿīd ibn Abī Saʿd, *Ḥālāt wa sukhanān-i Abū Saʿīd-i Abū ʾl-Khayr,* 16.

25. Lory, "al-Shahrazūrī."

Chapter One

1. In Persian, *musalmānī* has a wider connotation than *Islām*: whereas Islām might be characterized as a body of beliefs and practices, *musalmānī* would encompass the entire Muslim way and manners. The caliph is asking Ṭughril to save not merely "Islamic beliefs" but the total socioreligious structure that supports Islamic ways of life.

2. *Qarmaṭī* is a term used polemically by Sunni authors and does not distinguish between the various groups of early Ismāʿīlīs. The relationship between the Fāṭimī imamate and the group of Qarmaṭīs who removed the Black Stone (*al-ḥajar al-aswad*) from the Kaʿba in 317/930 under the leadership of Abū Ṭāhir cannot be clearly established. Some scholars (De Goeje, Massignon) have posited a close relationship between the two, while more recent (Ismāʿīlī) scholarship, no doubt wishing to locate the Ismāʿīlīs within the wider fold of Islamdom, has attempted to distance the Fāṭimī imamate from the controversial actions of the Qarmaṭīs. For a review of this controversy, refer to Daftary, *Ismāʿīlīs*, 164–65. What is relevant to us here is not the actual connection between the Qarmaṭīs and the Fāṭimīs, but the implications of the alleged connection in this letter: the Fāṭimīd-backed coup led by Basāsīrī, which the caliph warned about, was believed by the Sunni authors to be related to the same forces that had (from a Sunni perspective) shown their blatant disregard for Islamic symbols. It is not so much the "fact" of the letter that we are concerned with here but the various layers of "meaning" ascribed to it.

3. Ẓahīr al-Dīn Nīshāpūrī, *Saljūq-nāma*, 20; Muḥammad Rāwandī, *Rāḥatuʾṣ-ṣudūr* [henceforth, *Rāḥat al-ṣudūr*], 108; Rashīd al-Dīn Faḍl Allāh Ṭabīb, *Jāmiʿ al-tawārīkh*, 2:269. Cf. Khwānd-Mīr, *Tārīkh-i ḥabīb al-siyar*, 2:311, who adds the following line: *Bināʾ-yi islām ruy bi inhidām dārad, va agar tavānī bī-taʾannī bidīnjā shitāb* (The edifice of Islam is being demolished. If it is within your power, hasten hither!)

4. For details regarding the transfer of Ismāʿīlī power from Tunis to Cairo, see Daftary, *Ismāʿīlīs*, 144–64.

5. Rāwandī, *Rāḥat al-ṣudūr*, 108, n. 1. The editor of *Rāḥat al-ṣudūr*, Muḥammad Iqbāl, identifies the person mentioned in the text simply as *"raʾīs al-ruʾasāʾ"* as this vizier.

6. Al-Bundārī, *Zubdat al-nuṣra*, 15–16.

7. Qurʾan 27:37.

8. Rāwandī, *Rāḥat al-ṣudūr*,107–8; Ibn al-Athīr, *al-Kāmil fī ʾl-tārīkh,* 9:639–52; Al-Bundārī, *Zubdat al-nuṣra*, 15–18; Khwānd-Mīr, *Ḥabīb al-siyar*, 2:312, 2:485–86. For an overview of the Basāsīrī episode, see also Makdisi, *Ibn ʿAqīl et la Résurgence*, 90–102; Daftary, *Ismāʿīlīs*, 205–6.

9. Bosworth "Political and Dynastic History," 45.

10. Robinson, *Historical Atlas of the Islamic World*, 26.

11. Leiser, *History of the Seljuks*, 3–4.

12. Meisami, *Persian Historiography*, 3.

13. For a brief overview of methodological issues in propaganda and ideology in the context of Islamic history, see Humphreys, *Islamic History*, 148–68. Humphreys's chapter includes ample references to theoretical works dealing with ideology.

14. In the introduction to the present work, I have identified a number of significant studies that discuss the ramifications of ideology for religious studies. Many studies of ideology have tended to dismiss or downplay religion as a serious category of analysis. Among the ones that do foreground religion and include extensive discussions of religious ideology are the works of Bruce Lincoln, Gary Lease, and most significantly, Louis Althusser. See Lincoln, "Theses on Method," 395–98. Similarly important is Lease's review article, "Ideology," 438–47. Most useful for the present project is the work of Althusser and the distinctions he makes between repressive state ideology and ideological state apparatuses. In one essay, Althusser has extended the ramifications of ideology far beyond material interest. He is particularly concerned with the projection of the material interests of ruling class ideology through a wide range of institutions, including specifically religious ones. See Althusser, "Ideology and Ideological State Apparatuses," 100–140.

15. As Claude Cahen and others have pointed out, we still lack a single reputable monograph in European languages devoted to Saljūq history. This remains one of the more significant gaps in the scholarship on premodern Islamic history.

16. That is, Baghdad.

17. Al-Bundārī, *Zubdat al-nuṣra*, 16.

18. Niẓām al-Mulk, *Siyar al-Mulūk (Siyāsat-nāma)*, 80 [henceforth, *Siyāsat-nāma*]. The translation appears in Darke's translation of the *Siyāsat-nāma*, published as *The Book of Government or Rules for Kings*, 60 [henceforth, Niẓām al-Mulk–Darke] .

19. A pun on the vizier's honorific, *Niẓām al-Mulk*.

20. Al-Bundārī, *Zubdat al-nuṣra*, 67.

21. For the description of the Saljūqs as the *mawālī-yi amīr al-mu'minīn* (clients of the Commander of the believers [i.e. ʿAbbāsid Caliph]), see Bayhaqī, *Tārīkh-i Bayhaqī*, 2:583.

22. This letter, quoted in Ibn al-Jawzī, *al-Muntaẓam*, 8:223, is translated in Bosworth, "Political and Dynastic History," 48.

23. To support his point, Qazwīnī states that the Banū Umayya were beset by *zandaqa* and Muʿtazili thinking, the Banū ʿAbbās with Muʿtazilis, the Buwayhids with Rāfiḍīs, and the Ghaznavids and Khwārazm-shāhis with accusations of being of lowly origins (*ḥiqārat-i gawhar*).

24. Ḥamd Allāh Qazwīnī, *Tārīkh-i guzīda*, 1:434. (Volume 1 contains the Persian text, henceforth referred to as Qazwīnī; volume 2 contains Browne's abridged translation, henceforth referred to as Qazwīnī-Browne.)

25. Rashīd al-Dīn Faḍl Allāh, *Jāmiʿ al-tawārīkh*, 2:264.

26. Rāwandī, *Rāḥat al-ṣudūr*, 103.

27. Nīshāpūrī, *Saljūq-nāma*, 17.

28. Rāwandī, *Rāḥat al-ṣudūr*, 29.

29. That is, the Persian Jabal region and the Arab Iraq.

30. Rāwandī, *Rāḥat al-ṣudūr*, 29–30.

31. There are suggestions that in realpolitik terms the Saljūqs (in particular Barkyāriq) may have used Ismāʿīlī troops to accomplish their goals. Ibn al-Athīr even hints at this. See Hillenbrand, "Power Struggle," 206–8. Again, our concern here is not merely with a historicist determination of what actually happened but also with determining the construction of meaning through Saljūq chronicles and other sources that continue to depict them as "orthodox."

32. For a treatment of myth from the perspective of history of religions, see Paden, *Religious Worlds*, 69–92. Paden's discussion builds on (even as it updates) Eliade's discussion of myth as a paradigmatic model in *Sacred and the Profane*, 95–99.

33. I am here indebted to invaluable discussions with Dr. Julie Meisami, who generously shared with me insights from her monograph, *Persian Historiography*, prior to its publication. Meisami documents Iṣfahānī-Bundārī's description of the "ten causes" of decline after the Saljūqid Sulṭān Muḥammad, and Rāwandī's attempt to inculcate the need for order and orthodoxy in the late Saljūq rulers Ṭughril and Kay-Khusrau.

34. Al-Bundārī, *Zubdat al-nuṣra*, 55, calls the reign of Malik-Shāh the "highlight" of the Saljūq era (*Ayyāmahu fī ayyām āl–i saljūq ka ʾl-wāsiṭa fī ʾl-ʿiqd*). Contemporary scholarship has tended to reflect this assessment: Bosworth calls the reign of Malik-Shāh (and Niẓām al-Mulk) the "Zenith of the Great Saljuq Empire." See Bosworth, "Political and Dynastic History," 66.

35. Bosworth, *Ghaznavids*, 211.

36. Ibn al-Athīr, *al-Kāmil fī ʾl-tārīkh*, 9:178.

37. "Saldjūkids," 938.

38. Bosworth, "Political and Dynastic History," 16–17.

39. Ibid. For example, Ṭughril's half-brother is called Ibrāhīm *Īnāl*, while his uncle is called Mūsā *Yabghū*. Several sources describe Ṭughril's grandfather, Saljūq ibn Duqāq, as having been the *Sū-bāshī* for the Turkish *pādshāh*s.

40. Bosworth, *Ghaznavids*, 211. This fact, among others, challenges the assertion of certain Turkish nationalist intellectuals who have read this migration as a "Turkish manifest destiny." For a particularly unproblematized acceptance (and even propagation) of these assertions, see Turan, "Ideal of World Domination," 77–90. Humphreys, *Islamic History*, 166, characterized this attitude as "chauvinistic." It would be good to document such ideologies of world domination and manifest destiny in a future project.

41. Kāshgharī, *Diwān lughāt al-turk*, 1:101. [Henceforth referred to as Kāshgharī-Dankoff] For a later confirmation of this assertion, see Rashīd al-Dīn Faḍl Allāh, *Jāmiʿ al-tawārīkh*, 2:251. See also Bosworth, "Political and Dynastic History," 17.

42. Kāshgharī-Dankoff, *Diwān lughāt al-turk*, 1:102.

43. It is this model of interaction that was presented in a most succinct fashion four centuries after the Saljūqs by the great Maghribi theoretician Ibn Khaldūn. For a summary of the theoretical issues of nomadic/sedentary cultures in premodern Iran, refer to Cahen, "Nomades et sèdentaires," 93–102.

44. Bosworth, *Ghaznavids*, 268.

45. Kāshgharī-Dankoff, *Diwān lughāt al-turk*, 1:83.

46. These two categories should not be collapsed; it is important to recall that not

all Persian culture was sedentary and, perhaps more importantly, that the Turks had their own cities (Jand, etc.) prior to their contact with Persians. For a thoughtful reflection on these issues, refer to Smith, "Turanian Nomadism and Iranian Politics."

47. Kāshgharī-Dankoff, *Diwān lughāt al-turk*, 1:84. In a rare display of nativist chauvinism, Kāshgharī proceeds to identify the Turkish spoken in the main cities of his hometown, Kāshghar, as the "Khāqānī" Turkish, hailed as the "most elegant" dialect of Turkish.

48. Kāshgharī-Dankoff, *Diwān lughāt al-turk*, 1:273.

49. There are, naturally, many intriguing questions that we can and should ask regarding these essentializing dichotomies. If it can be shown that these categories did not directly reflect existing social realities, one can still investigate how reality was being constructed through their very usage.

50. Ibn al-Athīr, *al-Kāmil fī 'l-tārīkh*, 9:520.

51. *Ḥudūd al-ʿālam* [published as *Ḥudūd al-ʿĀlam*].

52. The *Ḥudūd al-ʿālam* account pertains to the Eastern Oghuz, while the Saljūqs rose from the western Oghuz. Nonetheless, the account is still of relevance in offering a [counter-]depiction of the social conditions of the Oghuz prior to their glorification in later sources.

53. The Turkish name of this confederation is *Oghuz* and is clearly marked as such in Kāshgharī, *Diwān lughāt al-turk*, 1:56–58. In Persian sources the name is often written as *Ghūz* and in Arabic accounts, *Ghuzz*. See Minorsky's commentary on the *Ḥudūd al-ʿālam*, 311.

54. The geographer later contradicts himself where (p. 122) he mentions *dih-i nau* (The new town) on the Chāch river.

55. *Ḥudūd al-ʿālam*, 100–101.

56. I will point out later how these "inroads" (*ghazw*) became reinterpreted in Saljūq-legitimizing sources as *ghazwa*, i.e., religiously-motivated battles. Here one sees how tribal elements of raiding are recast in narratives that depict the Saljūqs as warriors for the faith.

57. *Pace* Al-Bundārī, *Zubdat al-nuṣra*, 5, where it is claimed: "The Saljūqs did not approach cities." Jand, Khuvār, and Yengi-Kent were all Turkish towns at this time.

58. Bosworth, *Ghaznavids*, 212.

59. Bosworth, *Ghaznavids*, 213.

60. Given the later negotiations of the Saljūq military commanders with Persian *aʿyān*, one can already see foreshadowing of the system of social order that Marshall Hodgson referred to as the "Aʿyān-Amīr" System. See Hodgson, *Venture of Islam*, 2:91–135. Hodgson's exhaustive discussion evokes themes such as importance of the role of villages, revenue assessment, the sharīʿa, and the social organization of the towns in the Earlier Middle Periods (950–1250 C.E.). On the importance of the *aʿyān* in constructing a social history of premodern Islamdom (particularly in urban centers), see Hourani's, article in *Islamic City*, 9–24. The whole volume contains many insightful articles addressing urban Islamic culture from different perspectives. Another useful discussion on the Aʿyān system is that of Mottahedeh, *Loyalty and Leadership*, 123–29.

61. Bosworth, *Ghaznavids*, 214. For one example where the Türkmen are cited as causing problems in regions near Khwārazm, see Bayhaqī, *Tārīkh-i Bayhaqī*, 2:583.

62. Niẓām al-Mulk, *Siyāsat-nāma*, 139.

63. The early biographer of the Prophet (Ṣ) Ibn Isḥāq identified *Dhū 'l-qarnayn* with Alexander the Great. For a discussion, see Newby, *Making of the Last Prophet*, 193–200.

64. Kāshgharī-Dankoff, *Diwān lughāt al-turk*, 2:362–63. Presumably *Turk-mānand* eventually became transformed to *Türkmen*.

65. Ibid.

66. Barthold, *Turkestan*, 257 n. 1. Kāshgharī's notation can be found in 1:397 of the Arabic original, edited by Kilisli Rif'at Bey, or in the Turkish translation by Besim Atalay (Ankara: TDK, 1939–41), 1:428.

67. Barthold, *Histoire des Turcs d'Asie centrale* (Paris: 1945), 80; cited in "Saldjūkids," 938.

68. Bosworth, *Ghaznavids*, 298–99 n. 44.

69. Sir Gerard Clauson, *An Etymological Dictionary of Pre-Thirteenth-Century Turkish*, 824.

70. In Qazwīnī, *Tārīkh-i guzīda*, 1:434, this name is recorded as Abū 'l-'Alā'[-i, i.e., ibn] Aḥūl. Following Qazwīnī, Khwānd-Mīr, *Ḥabīb al-siyar*, 2:479, concurs with this reading.

71. The Turkish encyclopedist, Maḥmūd Kāshgharī, brings up the legendary Tūrānī ruler, Afrāsiyāb, in the following poem but does not in any way associate him with the Saljūqs or the Oghuz: "Has King Afrāsiyāb died? Does the wicked world remain (empty of him)? Has Time exacted its revenge upon him? Now the heart burst (out of grief for his kingdom and out of rage against Time)." Kāshgharī-Dankoff, *Diwān lughāt al-turk*, 1:92.

72. Nīshāpūrī, *Saljūq-nāma*, 14; Rashīd al-Dīn Faḍl Allāh, *Jāmi' al-tawārīkh*, 2:259.

73. See the account in Al-Bundārī, *Zubdat al-nuṣra*, 17, which shows 'Amīd al-Mulk Kundurī acting as the translator for the meeting between Ṭughril and the caliph (*yufassiru lahumā wa yutarjimu wa yu'ribu wa yu'ājimu*). It is not without significance that the language shared between the vizier and the sultan was not Turkish but Persian. On one hand, this should be taken as a rebuttal to the attempts of certain Turkish scholars to document a "Turko-Islamic" culture brought forth by the Saljūqs without acknowledging the role of the Persian elements. On the other hand, it is a literal example of the vizier translating the institutions of Islamdom for the sultan. It is this task that was continued and expanded upon (though at times not to the extent he would have desired) by the able vizier of Alp Arslān and Malik-Shāh, Niẓām al-Mulk.

74. Nīshāpūrī, *Saljūq-nāma*, 10; Rashīd al-Dīn Faḍl Allāh, *Jāmi' al-tawārīkh*, 2:251.

75. Leiser, *History of the Seljuks*, 22–23, calls this account "groundless" and attempts to portray it as being based on a sixteenth-century author quoting a "baseless story" in Rashīd al-Dīn Faḍl Allāh's *Jāmi' al-tawārīkh*. Far from being a late account, the Saljūqs' early occupation is unproblematically (if not even proudly) described in Nīshāpūrī (see above, note 74). Given that in *Ḥudūd al-'ālam* the Oghuz were described as possessing many felt-huts, the makers of tent poles would be necessary contributors to the nomadic culture. The class anxieties manifested by these contemporary Turkish scholars seem to have more to do with the scholars themselves and their social milieu than with the Saljūq nomads and their social realities.

76. Khwānd-Mīr, *Ḥabīb al-siyar*, 2:479; Khwānd-Mīr, *Dastūr al-wuzarā'*, 147. Bos-

worth dismisses this assertion as being reflective of earlier Oghuz-Khazar connections. See Bosworth, "Political and Dynastic History," 17–18.

77. Cahen, "Le Malik-Nameh," 31–65; Cahen, *Pre-Ottoman Turkey*, 19–21.

78. See Khwānd-Mīr, *Dastūr al-wuzarā'*, 147, where he quotes from the editor or organizer (*nāẓim*) of the *Malik-nāma*. In another work of his, *Ḥabīb al-siyar*, 2:479, Khwānd-Mīr again refers to the *nāẓim* of the *Malik-nāma*.

79. Cahen, "Le Malik-Nameh," 32.

80. Gregory Abū 'l-Faraj, known as Bar Hebraeus, *Chronography*. [Henceforth, Bar Hebraeus]

81. Cahen, "Historiography of the Seljuqid Period," 78.

82. Khwānd-Mīr, *Dastūr al-wuzarā'*, 147. It is this spelling (*Dokāk*) which is also favored by Cahen, *Pre-Ottoman Turkey*, 19.

83. Khwānd-Mīr, *Ḥabīb al-siyar*, 2:479.

84. Bar Hebraeus, *Chronography*, 1:195.

85. His name is listed alternatively as Tuqāq in Ibn al-Athīr, Duqāq in Ibn Khallikān, and Luqmān in Rāwandī.

86. Bar Hebraeus, *Chronography*, 1:195. The various manuscripts of Khwānd-Mīr's *Dastūr al-wuzarā'* record the name alternatively as *Timur-bālīgh, Timur-mālīgh*, or *Timur-tālīgh*. [Khwānd-Mīr, *Dastūr al-wuzarā'*, 147] An etymological examination would tend to favor *yalığ*, meaning "saddle-bow" to *ba:lığ*, which means "wounded." Refer to Clauson, *An Etymological Dictionary of Pre-Thirteenth Century Turkish*, 924, 335. Some of the later sources (ignorant of Turkish), such as Nāṣir ibn 'Alī al-Ḥusaynī, *Akhbār al-dawlat al-saljūqīya*, 1, mistakenly believe that "iron-bow" is the literal meaning of Yiqāq ("Yiqāq bi al-lugha al-turkīya al-qaws min al-ḥadīd").

87. Khwānd-Mīr, *Dastūr al-wuzarā'*, 147.

88. al-Ḥusaynī, *Akhbār al-dawla al-saljūqīya*, 2.

89. Ibn al-Athīr, *al-Kāmil fī 'l-tārīkh*, 9:473–75.

90. Ibid. This conversion took place ca. 382/992.

91. Al-Ḥusaynī, *al-akhbār al-dawla al-saljūqīya*, 2.

92. Khwānd-Mīr, *Ḥabīb al-siyar*, 2:479–80.

93. The historian Abū Dulaf mentions that the Oghuz tribe had a "house of prayer" that was void of any stone idols. (Cited in Bosworth, *Ghaznavids*, 216). There has also been some inconclusive speculation among scholars over the Jewish presence in the Khazar plains, especially given the Biblical names of Saljūq's sons. We can only state with certainty that the Turks had been subjected to successive waves of missionary evangelism by Buddhists, Nestorian Christians, and Muslims, while also having had some contact with Judaism.

94. Bar Hebraeus, *Chronography*, 1:195. The fact that Saljūq and his followers had already lived for thirty years in this setting before embracing Islam further lends credibility to this factor rather than to a simple act of piety uninformed by larger political considerations.

95. Bar Hebraeus, *Chronography*, 1:196. Cf. Ibn al-'Ibrī, *Tārīkh mukhtaṣar al-duwal*, (Beirut, 1985), 1:292, which is cited in the more recent edition of *Akhbār al-dawla al-saljūqīya*, published as *Zubdat al-tawārīkh: Akhbār al-umarā' wa 'l-mulūk al-saljūqīya*, 24, n. 4.

96. Al-Ḥusaynī, *Akhbār al-dawla al-saljūqīya*, 2. Cf. Ibn al-Athīr, *al-Kāmil fī ʾl-tārīkh*, 9:474, where it is explicitly claimed: "fa-sāra bi-jamāʿatihi kullihim wa man yuṭīʿuhu min dār al-ḥarb ilā diyār al-islām."

97. *Ḥudūd al-ʿālam*, 122.

98. Al-Ḥusaynī, *Akhbār al-dawla al-saljūqīya*, 2; Ibn al-Athīr, *al-Kāmil fī ʾl-tārīkh*, 9:474.

99. Kāshgharī-Dankoff, *Diwān lughāt al-turk*, 1:356.

100. Khwānd-Mīr, *Ḥabīb al-siyar*, 2:479.

101. Bar Hebraeus, *Chronography*, 1:195; al-Ḥusaynī, *Akhbār al-dawla al-saljūqīya*, 2; Ibn al-Athīr, *al-Kāmil fī ʾl-tārīkh*, 9:474; Khwānd-Mīr, *Dastūr al-wuzarāʾ*, 147; Khwānd-Mīr, *Ḥabīb al-siyar*, 2:479.

102. See Masud, "Obligation to Migrate," 29–49.

103. Khwānd-Mīr, *Ḥabīb al-siyar*, 2:479.

104. Leiser, *History of the Seljuks*, 24.

105. For the classic treatment of this issue in an earlier period of Islamic history, see Fred Donner's invaluable study, *Early Islamic Conquests*.

106. Ibn al-Athīr, *al-Kāmil fī ʾl-tārīkh*, 9:474.

107. Al-Ḥusaynī, *al-Akhbār al-dawla al-saljūqīya*, published as *Zubdat al-tawārīkh*, 25 n. 1.

108. Khwānd-Mīr, *Ḥabīb al-siyar*, 2:480.

109. Ibn al-Athīr, *al-Kāmil fī ʾl-tārīkh*, 9:474.

110. Bayhaqī, *Tārīkh-i Bayhaqī*, 2:856.

111. Ibid., 2:867. For a more thorough discussion of this inter-Qïnïq rivalry, see Cahen, "Le Malik-Nameh," 41–44.

112. A clear example of this is the Saljūq appropriation of the title *Yabghū* for Mūsā Yabghū, Ṭughril's uncle. This would be a challenge to the other *Yabghū*s of the Oghuz tribe, situated in Jand and Yengi-Kent.

113. Al-Ḥusaynī, *Akhbār al-dawla al-saljūqīya*, 2.

114. Bosworth, *Ghaznavids*, 220.

115. I am here indebted to my colleague John C. Lamoreaux, who has completed a dissertation titled *Dream Interpretation in the Early Medieval Near East* (1999) at Duke University. That dissertation was subsequently published as *Early Muslim Tradition of Dream Interpretation*.

116. Ibn al-Athīr, *al-Kāmil fī ʾl-tārīkh*, 9:474. The name Mīkāʾīl might indicate a Jewish or Christian background.

117. Rāwandī, *Rāḥat al-ṣudūr*, 86, 99.

118. Qazwīnī, *Tārīkh-i guzīda*, 1:434

119. Āqsarāʾī, *Musāmarat al-akhbār wa musāyarat al-akhyār*, 10.

120. McDonough, "Orthodoxy and Heterodoxy," 124–25.

121. Bosworth, "Political and Dynastic History," 18–19.

122. The sources (e.g., Rashīd al-Dīn Faḍl Allāh, *Jāmiʿ al-tawārīkh*, 2:259) allude to this splitting up when they mention that upon every major battle, the Saljūqs gathered "from every corner."

123. Nīshāpūrī, *Saljūq-nāma*, 11; Rashīd al-Dīn Faḍl Allāh, *Jāmiʿ al-tawārīkh*, 2:252–53.

124. It is intriguing to note that Āqsarāʾī, *Musāmarat al-akhbār wa musāyarat al-akhyār*,

11 (written in 723/1323 under Anatolian Saljūq patronage) adds the following spurious section to the letter sent from the Īlik-Khān ruler to Maḥmūd: "*Even though these Turkmen have a beautiful religion, and even though no one has seen the slightest of vices from them yet*, one is still concerned that should the times change, they might have a hard time providing for themselves, and some harm might come to our realm because of them" (emphasis mine). The depiction of the Türkmen as possessing "beautiful religion," absent from earlier sources, is again an indication of the ideological process to legitimize the Saljūqs.

125. Meisami, *Persian Historiography*, 281.

126. Nīshāpūrī, *Saljūq-nāma*, 11. Bosworth, "Political and Dynastic History," 40, offers the date ca. 418/1027 for this event, while Muḥammad Iqbāl, the editor of Rāwandī's *Rāḥat al-ṣudūr*, 93 n. 3, prefers 416/1025.

127. Nīshāpūrī, *Saljūq-nāma*, 11; Rashīd al-Dīn Faḍl Allāh, *Jāmiʿ al-tawārīkh*, 2:254. Nīshāpūrī's numbers do not exactly match Rāwandī's: thirty thousand men for the bow. Rashīd al-Dīn also suggests a slightly different set of numbers. Obviously the numbers are meant to be suggestive rather than exact and need not concern us in a positivist sense here.

128. Nīshāpūrī, *Saljūq-nāma*, 12, adds that this fortress was located in Mūltān (India).

129. Rāwandī, *Rāḥat al-ṣudūr*, 90; Qazwīnī, *Tārīkh-i guzīda*, 1:434–35.

130. Rāwandī, *Rāḥat al-ṣudūr*, 93 n. 4, reports this event from Gardīzī's *Zayn al-akhbār*. Allegedly, four thousand Türkmen were killed in this battle.

131. Bosworth, "Political and Dynastic History," 19.

132. Rashīd al-Dīn Faḍl Allāh, *Jāmiʿ al-tawārīkh*, 2:257, uses the term *banda-zāda* to imply the same origin for Sulṭān Maḥmūd. Mawlā was a term more in usage in the earlier centuries, when the concept of non-Arab converts of Islam becoming a client [*Mawlā*, pl. *Mawālī*] of Arab tribes was more common.

133. Qazwīnī, *Tārīkh-i guzīda*, 1:435; Nīshāpūrī, *Saljūq-nāma*, 13; Rāwandī, *Rāḥat al-ṣudūr*, 91.

134. Nīshāpūrī, *Saljūq-nāma*, 13, records his name as Arslān the Jādhib, the *wālī* of Ṭūs.

135. Nīshāpūrī, *Saljūq-nāma*, 13–14; Qazwīnī, *Tārīkh-i guzīda*, 1:435; Rashīd al-Dīn Faḍl Allāh, *Jāmiʿ al-tawārīkh*, 2:258. Al-Bundārī, *Zubdat al-nuṣra*, 5, records Arslān as offering the ingenious solution of cutting off the thumbs of all the Saljūqs. Presumably, this was to keep them from wielding swords and drawing arrow-strings. Maḥmūd rejected the Ḥājib's advice, adding (perhaps humorously): "Aren't you a cold-hearted man!"

136. Al-Bundārī, *Zubdat al-nuṣra*, 5.

137. Rāwandī, *Rāḥat al-ṣudūr*, 93.

138. Nīshāpūrī, *Saljūq-nāma*, 14; Rashīd al-Dīn Faḍl Allāh, *Jāmiʿ al-tawārīkh*, 2:258.

139. In some sources, he is also called Mūsā, yet another "Biblical" name.

140. Bayhaqī, *Tārīkh-i Bayhaqī*, 2:583.

141. I am here in disagreement with Dr. Julie Meisami, with whom I have had the pleasure of an extensive discussion over e-mail. Her reading of the same narratives tends to view the articulation of the modes of justification of Saljūq rule as being the product of a later chronicle tradition, which retrospectively projected these

legitimizations back onto the Saljūqs themselves. While I do recognize this retrospective tendency (which I have already alluded to in my discussion), evidence such as Bayhaqī's *Tārīkh* which was written before the rise of Saljūqs to power (and are independent from that process) suggests that the Saljūqs themselves had initiated this process, which was subsequently expressed more fully by their administrators, especially Niẓām al-Mulk, and even later by chroniclers such as Nīshāpūrī, Rāwandī, Faḍl Allāh Ṭabīb, etc.

142. Qazwīnī, *Tārīkh-i guzīda*, 1:435.

143. This report, mentioned in Gardīzī's *Zayn al-akhbār*, is cited by Muḥammad Iqbāl in a footnote to Rāwandī's *Rāḥat al-ṣudūr*, 93 n. 4.

144. Al-Bundārī, *Zubdat al-nuṣra*, 6. This sentence, like so many others, is a testimony to al-Iṣfahānī's mastery of Arabic prose.

145. Bar Hebraeus, *Chronography*, 1:196.

146. Ibid.

147. Āqsarā'ī, *Musāmarat al-akhbār wa musāyarat al-akhyār*, 14.

148. Bar Hebraeus, *Chronography*, 1:196.

149. See Claude Cahen, "Chaghrī Beg." It is hard to ascertain Chaghrī Beg's exact actions in these expeditions, as the historiography of these wanderings has been wrapped up in a retrospective attempt to portray the Saljūqs as having initiated a campaign against the Byzantines. That is obviously not warranted at such an early age. What concerns us here is not the presence of "proto-Crusade" tendencies but the disturbance of urban culture, which violates one of the foundations of Saljūq ideology.

150. Rashīd al-Dīn Faḍl Allāh, *Jāmiʿ al-tawārīkh*, 2:215.

151. On this matter, as with other matters dealing with the Ghaznavids, the most insightful comments are that of Bosworth, *Ghaznavids*, 240–68.

152. Qazwīnī, *Tārīkh-i guzīda*, 1:436; Rāwandī, *Rāḥat al-ṣudūr*, 96–97.

153. There is some controversy over the spelling of this site: Qazwīnī's manuscript records *Dandaqān*, but Browne translates it as *Dandānaqān*. Le Strange, *The Lands of the Eastern Caliphate*, 400, prefers Dandankān [i.e., Dandanqān].

154. Rāwandī, *Rāḥat al-ṣudūr*, 100 n. 6; Qazwīnī, *Tārīkh-i guzīda*, 1:436; Qazwīnī-Browne, *Tārīkh-i guzīda*, 2:94 n. 1. The date 431 A.H. is taken from Abū 'l-Faḍl Bayhaqī, who was a participant in the battle. Qazwīnī offers the date 432 A.H. Nīshāpūrī reports this date as 429 A.H.; whereas Barthold, *Turkestan*, 24, gives the date as May 1040.

155. Qazwīnī, *Tārīkh-i guzīda*, 1:436; Qazwīnī-Browne, *Tārīkh-i guzīda*, 2:94.

156. Bregel, "Turko-Mongol Influences," 58 n. 10.

157. Bayhaqī, *Tārīkh-i Bayhaqī*, 2:788.

158. Ibid. Cf. Barthold, *Turkestan*, 303. Bayhaqī mentions some of the individuals to whom the letters were sent: "the *khān*s of Turkistān, the sons of ʿAlī-Tegīn and Pūr-Tegīn, ʿAyn al-Dawla, and all the notables of Turkistān."

159. According to Rāwandī, *Rāḥat al-ṣudūr*, 102, this consisted of Ṭughril, Chaghrī, their uncle Mūsā (who was called the Great Yabghū), their cousins, the elders of the family, and the (presumably prominent) warriors of the army.

160. Rāwandī, *Rāḥat al-ṣudūr*, 102.

161. Rashīd al-Dīn Faḍl Allāh, *Jāmiʿ al-tawārīkh*, 2:263–64.

162. The transition from a Turkish confederation to an imperial Perso-Islamic empire took generations to complete and was far from a smooth process. One evidence of

this was the gradual disappearance of the ubiquitous "bow and arrow" symbols from the coins issued under Alp Arslān and Malik-Shāh, whereas they were almost never absent from Ṭughril's coins. See Bulliet, "Numismatic Evidence," 291–92.

163. Bar Hebraeus, *Chronography*, 1:199.

164. Rashīd al-Dīn Faḍl Allāh, *Jāmiʿ al-tawārīkh*, 2:216.

165. Āqsarāʾī, *Musāmarat al-akhbār wa musāyarat al-akhyār*, 14. See also Bosworth, *Ghaznavids*, particularly chapter 9, "The Struggle with the Turkmens and the Downfall of Ghaznavid Power in Khurasan," 241–68.

166. Nīshāpūrī, *Saljūq-nāma*, 15.

167. Al-Bundārī, *Zubdat al-nuṣra*, 6.

168. Bar Hebraeus, *Chronography*, 1:198.

169. Qazwīnī, *Tārīkh-i guzīda*, 1:436.

170. Ibn al-Athīr, *al-Kāmil fī ʾl-tārīkh*, 9:481.

171. Rashīd al-Dīn Faḍl Allāh, *Jāmiʿ al-tawārīkh*, 2:261; Nīshāpūrī, *Saljūq-nāma*, 15; Rāwandī, *Rāḥat al-ṣudūr*, 97; Bar Hebraeus, *Chronography*, 1:198.

172. Ibn al-Athīr, *al-Kāmil fī ʾl-tārīkh*, 9:457.

173. Surprisingly, even a late Saljūq source like Āqsarāʾī, *Musāmarat al-akhbār wa musāyarat al-akhyār*, 14, preserves this account. While this account again focuses on Ṭughril's magnanimity, it still betrays the savagery of the nomadic Oghuz as a whole and offers a further confirmation of the accounts we have in Bar Hebraeus and Khwānd-Mīr.

174. Al-Bundārī, *Zubdat al-nuṣra*, 7.

175. Āqsarāʾī, *Musāmarat al-akhbār wa musāyarat al-akhyār*, 14.

176. Al-Bundārī, *Zubdat al-nuṣra*, 7.

177. Rashīd al-Dīn Faḍl Allāh, *Jāmiʿ al-tawārīkh*, 2:266.

178. Bar Hebraeus, *Chronography*, 1:203–4. [Translation slightly updated by author.]

179. Ibid.

180. Al-Bundārī, *Zubdat al-nuṣra*, 7; Nīshāpūrī, *Saljūq-nāma*, 18; Rashīd al-Dīn Faḍl Allāh, *Jāmiʿ al-tawārīkh*, 2:267. Given that Chaghrī is left out of all later political mythology of the Saljūqs [e.g., *Siyāsat-nāma*], one cannot entirely dismiss the idea that this is meant to show Ṭughril's magnanimity and his brother's uncontrollable desire for pillage. It is worth noting that in Bar Hebraeus, *Chronography*, 1:198 and Ibn al-Athīr, *al-Kāmil fī ʾl-tārīkh*, 9:458, it is Ṭughril who threatens to kill *himself* if Chaghrī proceeds with the looting.

181. Nīshāpūrī, *Saljūq-nāma*, 18; Rashīd al-Dīn Faḍl Allāh, *Jāmiʿ al-tawārīkh*, 2:267.

182. Al-Bundārī, *Zubdat al-nuṣra*, 7. Translation is modified from Bosworth, "Political and Dynastic History," 23.

183. *Lawzinaj* usually contains sugar, rose water, starch, almond, and cardamom.

184. Ibn al-Athīr, *al-Kāmil fī ʾl-tārīkh*, 9:483.

185. It is possible that the allusion to eating *kāfūr* (camphor) contains a hidden pun, alleging not only the Oghuz's shortcomings in refinement, but also their lack of virility. Refer to Steingass, *Comprehensive Persian-English Dictionary*, 1007.

186. Ibn al-Athīr, *al-Kāmil fī ʾl-tārīkh*, 9:483.

187. The translation here is based on Rāwandī, *Rāḥat al-ṣudūr*, 103–4. Rāwandī's account is clearly an elaboration on Nīshāpūrī's.

188. This phrase is from Nīshāpūrī, *Saljūq-nāma*, 17. Rashīd al-Dīn Faḍl Allāh, *Jāmiʿ al-tawārīkh*, 2:264, has a very similar phrase: "supporters of the ʿAbbāsid state, and obedient and submissive (*miṭwāʿ wa munqād*) with respect to religious obligations and traditions (*farāʾiḍ wa sunan*)."

189. This important line, again making a connection between *bidʿa* [Persian: *bidʿat*] and *fasād*, is in the earlier source, Nīshāpūrī, *Saljūq-nāma*, 17, as well as the later source, Rashīd al-Dīn Faḍl Allāh, *Jāmiʿ al-tawārīkh*, 2:265.

190. Literally, "flock" (*raʿīyat*).

191. A pun in Arabic: *raʿīyat* contrasted with *ruʾyat*, here meaning vision, insight, or judgment.

192. Another Arabic pun: *malaka* vs. *halaka*.

193. I have here gone by the Arabic original, rather than the Persian translation also provided by Rāwandī, which has the sense of "whoever *seeks* kingship for the sake of religion . . ."

194. Much of the subsequent information is derived from Rāwandī, *Rāḥat al-ṣudūr*, 104.

195. See also Qazwīnī, *Tārīkh-i guzīda*, 1:437. ʿAbbās Iqbāl, *Tārīkh-i mufaṣṣal-i īrān*, 310, provides more detail, stating that Chaghrī controlled areas from Nīshāpūr to the coast of Jayḥūn and Transoxiana. Chaghrī Beg would shortly add Bukhārā, Balkh, and Khwārazm to his realm.

196. Ibn al-Athīr, *al-Kāmil fī ʾl-tārīkh*, 9:480.

197. Bar Hebraeus, *Chronography*, 1:198.

198. Bulliet, "Numismatic Evidence," 289–96.

199. Qazwīnī-Browne, *Tārīkh-i guzīda*, 2:94, reads this as *Payghú*, clearly a corruption of Yabghū.

200. See also Qazwīnī, *Tārīkh-i guzīda*, 1:437, where it specifies Ghazna, Harat, and India.

201. Ibid.

202. Qazwīnī, *Tārīkh-i guzīda*, is more specific, identifying this as *ʿIrāq-i ʿajam*.

203. While the text reads Yināl, Houtsma prefers Īnāl, which I have also adopted. Iqbāl, *Tārīkh-i mufaṣṣal*, 310, states that the regions of Quhistān and Jurjān were given to Ibrāhīm Īnāl.

204. I am here indebted to Humphreys, *Islamic History*, 166. See also Barthold, *Turkestan*, 268.

205. Nīshāpūrī, *Saljūq-nāma*, 15–18.

206. Qazwīnī, *Tārīkh-i guzīda*, 1:436–39.

207. Rāwandī, *Rāḥat al-ṣudūr*, 97–113.

208. For a thorough discussion of the various Saljūq chronicles and their relationship, see Cahen, "Historiography of the Seljuqid Period," 37–64.

209. Qazwīnī, *Tārīkh-i guzīda*, 1:436.

210. The passage from Mīr-Khwānd's *Rawḍat al-ṣafā*, 4:102, is translated by Bosworth in "Political and Dynastic History," 20.

211. Al-Bundārī, *Zubdat al-nuṣra*, 8.

212. Qazwīnī *Tārīkh-i guzīda*, 1:437; Qazwīnī-Browne, *Tārīkh-i guzīda*, 2:94–95.

213. Ibn al-Athīr, *al-Kāmil fī ʾl-tārīkh*, 9:504–6

214. Ibid., 9:508.

215. The assertion of Rice, *History of Seljuks*, 30, that Ṭughril penetrated into India is completely false. The conquest in the eastern half of the Iranian plateau was left to Chaghrī Beg, and northern India remained under Ghaznavid control.

216. Bar Hebraeus, *Chronography*, 1:204.

217. Ibn al-Athīr, *al-Kāmil fī 'l-tārīkh*, 9:602–3.

218. Al-Bundārī, *Zubdat al-nuṣra*, 9.

219. Ibid.

220. Bar Hebraeus, *Chronography*, 1:202.

221. Ibn al-Athīr, *al-Kāmil fī 'l-tārīkh*, 9:609.

222. Ibid.

223. Ibn al-Athīr, *al-Kāmil fī 'l-tārīkh*, 9:610.

224. Bar Hebraeus, *Chronography*, 1:208.

225. Ibid.

226. Ibn al-Athīr, *al-Kāmil fī 'l-tārīkh*, 9:613.

227. Bar Hebraeus, *Chronography*, 1:208. [Slightly modified by author]

228. Ibn al-Athīr, *al-Kāmil fī 'l-tārīkh*, 9:612.

229. Bar Hebraeus, *Chronography*, 1:208. [Slightly modified] See also Ibn al-Athīr, *al-Kāmil fī 'l-tārīkh*, 9:611–14.

230. Bar Hebraeus, *Chronography*, 1:208.

231. Esposito, *Islam*, 58.

232. Al-Bundārī, *Zubdat al-nuṣra*, 22–23. Ṭughril went on to state that even though Ibn Dārist was well-endowed in material possessions, he was lacking in capability and skills.

233. Al-Bundārī, *Zubdat al-nuṣra*, 44.

234. Bar Hebraeus, *Chronography*, 1:207.

235. Rāwandī states 437, but this must be an error as all other sources agree on 447. *Rāḥat al-ṣudūr*, 105.

236. Rāwandī, *Rāḥat al-ṣudūr*, 105; Rashīd al-Dīn Faḍl Allāh, *Jāmiʿ al-tawārīkh*, 2:267; Nīshāpūrī, *Saljūq-nāma*, 18–19.

237. Qazwīnī, *Tārīkh-i guzīda*, 1:437; Qazwīnī-Browne, *Tārīkh-i guzīda*, 2:95.

238. Rāwandī, *Rāḥat al-ṣudūr*, 110; Rashīd al-Dīn Faḍl Allāh, *Jāmiʿ al-tawārīkh*, 2:271; Nīshāpūrī, *Saljūq-nāma*, 20. Qazwīnī, *Tārīkh-i guzīda*, 1:438, contains a brief version of the above events, mentioning that the Caliph had been captured by Basāsīrī and that the Sultan rescued the Caliph. Al-Kātib al-Iṣfahānī [through Al-Bundārī, *Zubdat al-nuṣra*] contains the fullest description.

239. Quoted by Makdisi, *Ibn ʿAqīl*, 87 n. 3.

240. Bar Hebraeus, *Chronography*, 1:206.

241. Qazwīnī, *Tārīkh-i guzīda*, 1:438, records the name as ʿAbd al-Mulk, no doubt a mistake. All the sources agree on the honorific of the vizier being ʿAmīd al-Mulk.

242. Qazwīnī, *Tārīkh-i guzīda*, 1:438.

243. Al-Bundārī, *Zubdat al-nuṣra*, 12. See also Bar Hebraeus, *Chronography*, 1:209.

244. Al-Bundārī, *Zubdat al-nuṣra*, 12.

245. Much of the subsequent section is based on Rāwandī, *Rāḥat al-ṣudūr*, 111.

246. While Rashīd al-Dīn Faḍl Allāh, *Jāmiʿ al-tawārīkh*, 2:272, clearly states that this

woman was the sister of the caliph, Qazwīnī identifies her as the Caliph's daughter, Sayyida Khātūn. Al-Kātib al-Iṣfahānī [through Al-Bundārī, *Zubdat al-nuṣra*] simply identifies her as the caliph's daughter without providing a name. He does go on to say that the custom of caliphs giving their daughters to sultans for marriage had not been established. The reverse, on the other hand, seems to have been customary; consider, for example, the marriage of the same caliph to Chaghrī Beg's daughter.

247. This is a reference to Ṭughril having killed his cousin, Ibrāhīm Īnāl. To honor the Central Asian injunction prohibiting the shedding of the blood of one's kin, Ṭughril used his bow-string to kill Ibrāhīm. For the background, see Al-Bundārī, *Zubdat al-nuṣra*, 16.

248. Ibid, 21.

249. See Bar Hebraeus, *Chronography*, 1:201.

250. Al-Bundārī, *Zubdat al-nuṣra*, 21; al-Ḥusaynī, *al-Akhbār al-dawla al-saljūqīya*, 17–18; Bar Hebraeus, *Chronography*, 1:209.

251. Rashīd al-Dīn Faḍl Allāh, *Jāmiʿ al-tawārīkh*, 2:272.

252. Al-Bundārī, *Zubdat al-nuṣra*, 25.

253. According to the sources, this mahr was patterned after the dowry of the Prophet's daughter, Fāṭima Zahrā, in her marriage to Ḥaḍrat ʿAlī.

254. Al-Bundārī, *Zubdat al-nuṣra*, 26.

255. Qazwīnī, *Tārīkh-i guzīda*, 1:438–39.

256. Rāwandī, *Rāḥat al-ṣudūr*, 111; Qazwīnī, *Tārīkh-i guzīda*, 1:438–39; Qazwīnī-Browne, *Tārīkh-i guzīda*, 2:95.

257. Rashīd al-Dīn Faḍl Allāh, *Jāmiʿ al-tawārīkh*, 2:273.

258. Makdisi, *Ibn ʿAqīl*, 90–120, offers a thorough discussion of the relationship between the caliph and Ṭughril.

259. Al-Bundārī, *Zubdat al-nuṣra*, 70.

260. Niẓām al-Mulk, *Siyāsat-nāma*, 255.

261. Poole, *Coins of the Turkumán Houses*, 31.

262. Ibid, 32. The date is obliterated on these coins; it seems that they were minted either in 485 or 475.

263. Ibid, 33–34.

264. Ibid, 34–36. The title in these cases again is the familiar *al-sulṭān al-muʿaẓẓam*.

265. Barthold, "Caliph and Sultan," 132.

266. Ibn al-Athīr, *al-Kāmil fī ʾl-tārikh*, 10:676. See also Siddiqi, "Caliphate and Kingship," 399.

267. Barthold, *Turkestan down to the Mongol Invasion*, 347. Barthold is following a Turkish translation of Rāwandī's text. The Persian original, more conciliatory, is from Rāwandī, *Rāḥat al-ṣudūr*, 334.

Chapter Two

1. A classic study remains Sourdel, *Vizirat ʿAbbasside*.

2. Lapidus, *History of Islamic Societies*, 72–73.

3. Muʿizzī was among the most notable of court poets at the Saljūq court, along with Anvarī (d. 1189–90). See Rypka, *History of Iranian Literature*, 195.

4. Āshtiyānī, *Vizārat dar ʿahd-i salāṭīn-i buzurg-i saljūqī*, 46.

5. Al-Subkī, *Ṭabaqāt al-shāfiʿīya*, 3:317.

6. Ibn Kathīr, *al-Bidāya wa ʾl-nihāya*, 12:141, includes an account of the people of Baghdad mourning his passing and poetry that was composed on this occasion, including one by Muqātil ibn ʿAṭiya: "The Vizier Niẓām al-Mulk was a unique pearl . . ."

7. Hindū-Shāh Nakhjawānī, *Tajārib al-salaf*, 281.

8. Bosworth, "Niẓām al-Mulk," 69.

9. Ibn al-Athīr, *al-Kāmil*, 9:526, states: "*wa awwalu man luqqiba niẓām al-mulk*."

10. Steingass, *Comprehensive Persian-English Dictionary*, 1410.

11. Schimmel, *Two-Colored Brocade*, 1–2.

12. See Arberry, "Orient Pearls at Random Strung," 688–712.

13. Steingass, *Comprehensive Persian-English Dictionary*, 1049.

14. Khwānd-Mīr, *Dastūr al-wuzarāʾ*, 153.

15. See Goitein, "Origin of the Vizierate," see also Sourdel, *Vizirat ʿAbbasside*.

16. ʿAqīlī, *Āthār al-wuzarāʾ*.

17. Qummī, *Tārīkh al-wuzarāʾ*.

18. Klausner, *Seljuk Vizierate*.

19. Āshtiyānī, *Vizārat*.

20. Āshtiyānī, *Vizārat*, 22–23. In the following section (*Vizārat*, 25–32), Āshtiyānī provides a more extensive discussion of each *dīvān*.

21. Ibn al-Athīr, *al-Kāmil fī ʾl-tārīkh*, 10:33.

22. I have been informed of a recent Ph.D. dissertation undertaken at McGill University by Erol Suleyman Gunduz, titled "Niẓām al-Mulk and Islamic Political Theory."

23. Ibn Kathīr, *al-Bidāya wa ʾl-nihāya*, 12:140; Ibn al-Athīr, *al-Kāmil fī ʾl-tārīkh,* 10:207: *fa kāna min abnāʾ al-dahāqīn bi Ṭūs* (he was descended from the dihqāns of Ṭūs).

24. Ibn al-Athīr, *al-Kāmil fī ʾl-tārīkh*, 10:207.

25. Ibn Khallikān, *Wafāyat*, 1:397; Ibn Khallikān–De Slane, *Ibn Khallikān's Biographical Dictionary*, 1:414; Ibn Kathīr, *al-Bidāya wa ʾl-nihāya*, 12:140. On the other hand, Bayhaqī, *Tārīkh-i bayhaqī* records his birth as 410/1020. See Āshtiyānī, *Vizārat*, 47; Bowen, "Niẓām al-Mulk," 69.

26. Ibn Kathīr, *al-Bidāya wa ʾl-nihāya*, 12:140.

27. Ibn al-Athīr, *al-Kāmil fī ʾl-tārīkh*, 10:207.

28. Al-Subkī, *Ṭabaqāt al-shāfiʿīya*, 4:312; Ibn Kathīr, *al-Bidāya wa ʾl-nihāya*, 12:140. According to Khwānd-Mīr, *Dastūr al-wuzarāʾ*, 150, he attained "perfect mastery" of this school of jurisprudence.

29. Khwānd-Mīr, *Dastūr al-wuzarāʾ*, 150.

30. Abū ʾl-Qāsim al-Qushayrī was the author of the famous systematic treatise on Sufism known as the *Risāla*. He was another member of the Sufi ʿulama in Nīshāpūr who sought to reconcile Sufism with Ashʿarī kalām and the Shāfiʿī madhhab. Following in his footsteps, al-Juwaynī and al-Ghazālī continued this same trend. Qushayrī's text was widely read and commented upon by later Sufis. In fact, a Persian translation of this text is one of the oldest extant Sufi sources in Persian, along with Hujwīrī's *Kashf al-Mahjūb*. For the full citations of the Arabic, Persian, and English versions of this work, see the bibliography.

31. Al-Subkī, *Ṭabaqāt al-shāfiʿīya*, 4:318.

32. Shams al-Dīn Dhahabī, *Tadhkirat al-ḥuffāẓ*, 3:343–44, cited in Kasā'ī, *Madāris-i niẓāmīya*, 58.

33. Al-Subkī, *Ṭabaqāt al-shāfiʿīya*, 4:318.

34. Ibn Khallikān–De Slane, *Ibn Khallikān's Biographical Dictionary*, 1:414; Ibn Kathīr, *al-Bidāya wa 'l-nihāya*, 12:141.

35. Al-Subkī, *Ṭabaqāt al-shāfiʿīya*, 4:318.

36. Ibn Munawwar, *Asrār al-tawḥīd*, 1:58–59, recalls Niẓām al-Mulk as a young child with Abū Saʿīd; ibid., 1:366 identifies Niẓām al-Mulk as a disciple of the Shaykh and the Shaykh's descendants.

37. Ibn Khallikān–De Slane, *Ibn Khallikān's Biographical Dictionary*, 1:413.

38. Ibid., 1:413–14. [Translation slightly modified by author.] The account can also be verified through Ibn Kathīr, *al-Bidāya wa 'l-nihāya*, 12:140.

39. Interestingly enough, Ibn Kathīr's account identifies the person who enjoins Niẓām al-Mulk to devote himself to the service of those who benefit him not as a Sufi, but merely as an *"insān."* The overall context of Ibn Kathīr's account is still one of explaining the connection of Niẓām al-Mulk to Sufis. However, the identification of the individual as a "human being" rather than specifically as a "Sufi," as in Ibn Khallikān's account, underscores even more that the point of the narrative was not to connect the Vizier to any particular Sufi genealogy.

40. Ibn Kathīr, *al-Bidāya wa 'l-nihāya*, 12:140.

41. ʿAqīlī, *Āthār al-wuzarā'*, 207.

42. Niẓāmī, *Chahār maqāla*; translated by Browne, *Chahâr Maqâla* ("Four Discourses"), 46.

43. Ibn Munawwar, *Asrār al-Tawḥīd*, 1:365.

44. The tendency to construct Sufism as a hierarchical, heterodox, and rural movement in contrast to an egalitarian, orthodox, and urban Islam has characterized many works on "Maraboutism," particularly in the North African context. The French historian Alfred Bel utilized the figure of the "Marabout" (interpreted as "human fetish") to describe popular Sufism. The contrast between the "doctor" (urban jurist) and the "saint" (rural marabout) continues to have resonance through the works of Ernst Gellner, etc. For a critique of this framework (and the political agenda behind it), see Cornell, *Realm of the Saint*, xxvi–xxvii.

45. Al-Subkī, *Ṭabaqāt al-shāfiʿīya*, 4:313.

46. Thābitī, *Asnād wa nāma-hā-yi tārīkhī*, 26.

47. Browne, *Literary History of Persia*, 3:214.

48. Al-Subkī, *Ṭabaqāt al-shāfiʿīya*, 4:312.

49. Niẓām al-Mulk-Darke, *Book of Government*, 100.

50. Ibid, 91.

51. Khwānd-Mīr, *Dastūr al-wuzarā'*, 150.

52. This quotation from Ibn al-Athīr is cited in Kasā'ī, *Madāris-i niẓāmīya*, 25.

53. Khwānd-Mīr, *Dastūr al-wuzarā'*, 148–49.

54. In the typically exaggerated style of Khwānd-Mīr, he refers to Kundurī as having possessed a Moses-like "White hand" for composition. The reference is to Qur'an 7:108, 20:22, 27:12, 28:32.

55. Ibn Khallikān–De Slane, *Ibn Khallikān's Biographical Dictionary*, 3:291.

56. Rāwandī, *Rāḥat al-ṣudūr*, 111; Rashīd al-Dīn Faḍl Allāh, *Jāmiʿ al-tawārīkh*, 2:272; Al-Bundārī, *Zubdat al-nuṣra*, 20; Nīshāpūrī, *Saljūq-nāma*, 21. According to Ibn Khallikān–De Slane, *Ibn Khallikān's Biographical Dictionary*, 3:293, in an earlier episode Ṭughril had also sent him to the Khwārazm-Shāh prince to demand the hand of the latter's daughter in marriage.

57. Al-Bundārī, *Zubdat al-nuṣra*, 10.

58. Rāwandī, *Rāḥat al-ṣudūr*, 98–99.

59. Al-Bundārī, *Zubdat al-nuṣra*, 14.

60. Kāshgharī-Dankoff, 1:92.

61. Ibid., 2:361.

62. Khwānd-Mīr, *Dastūr al-wuzarāʾ*, 149.

63. Al-Bundārī, *Zubdat al-nuṣra*, 26.

64. Ibn al-Athīr, *al-Kāmil fī ʾl-tārīkh*, 10:33.

65. Ibid.

66. For a background to the *fitna* in Nīshāpūr, the best source remains Bulliet, *Patricians of Nishapur*. See also Ibn al-Athīr, *al-Kāmil*, 10:33.

67. In addition to Bulliet's work, also see Madelung, "Two Factions of Sunnism," 26–38.

68. Al-Bundārī, *Zubdat al-nuṣra*, 30.

69. Ibn Khallikān–De Slane, *Ibn Khallikān's Biographical Dictionary*, 3:291.

70. Bulliet, *Patricians of Nishapur*, 71–74.

71. Ibid., 72.

72. Madelung, "Spread of Māturīdism."

73. Niẓām al-Mulk–Darke, *Book of Government*, 96.

74. My understanding of Niẓām al-Mulk's policy toward factions in Nīshāpūr is indebted to Bulliet, *Patricians of Nishapur*, 74.

75. ʿAqīlī, *Athār al-wuzarāʾ*, 204. However, one cannot entirely dismiss the possibility that the sources are holding Kundurī responsible for the confiscation to deflect blame away from Ṭughril. This would seem to be a stronger possibility, especially as Al-Bundārī, *Zubdat al-nuṣra*, 21, states that Kundurī was merely following Ṭughril's command.

76. Al-Subkī, *Ṭabaqāt al-shāfiʿīya*, 4:322. Of course one has to remember Subkī's partisan support of the ultimate Shāfiʿī patron, Niẓām al-Mulk.

77. Al-Bundārī, *Zubdat al-nuṣra*, 55; Khwānd-Mīr, *Tarīkh ḥabīb al-siyar*, 2:496.

78. Al-Subkī, *Ṭabaqāt al-shāfiʿīya*, 4:322.

79. Niẓām al-Mulk–Darke, *Book of Government*, 188.

80. Ibn Khallikan–De Slane, *Ibn Khallikān's Biographical Dictionary*, 3:294–95. Ibn al-Athīr, *al-Kāmil*, 10:32, likewise calls it one of the *ʿajāʾib* (strange events) that Kundurī's sexual organ was buried in Khwārazm, his blood shed in Marv, his torso buried in Kundur, his head "minus the skull" buried in Nīshāpūr, and his skull taken to Niẓām al-Mulk in Kirmān. The historian adds in a grim note, *fa aʿtabirū yā ūli ʾl-abṣār*, "O you who possess insight, learn [from this]!"

81. Ibn al-Athīr, *al-Kāmil fī ʾl-tārīkh*, 10:32.

82. Ibid., 10:33.

83. *Mujmal al-tawārīkh wa ʾl-qiṣaṣ*, 407; Ibn al-Athīr, *al-Kāmil fī ʾl-tārīkh,* 10:33–34.

84. Rāwandī, *Rāḥat al-ṣudur*, 118.

85. Nīshāpūrī, *Saljūq-nāma*, 24

86. Rashīd al-Dīn Faḍl Allāh, *Jāmiʿ al-tawārīkh*, 2:277; Khwānd-Mīr, *Dastūr al-wuzarāʾ*, 149; Nīshāpūrī, *Saljūq-nāma*, 23–24.

87. Niẓām al-Mulk, *Siyāsat-nāma*, 217.

88. ʿAqīlī, *Āthār al-wuzarāʾ*, 208; Rashīd al-Dīn also relates this account in *Jāmiʿ al-tawārīkh*, 2:277–78, while adding that this bestowal was also a result of the sultan "not desiring" the Christian princess. On the other hand, al-Kātib al-Iṣfahānī [through al-Bundārī, *Zubdat al-nuṣra*, 38] states that upon marrying the daughter of Buqrāṭ ibn George, the sultan divorced another of his own wives, named Malaka Karjī, who was then given over to Niẓām al-Mulk.

89. Kasāʾī, *Madāris-i Niẓāmīya*, 5.

90. Al-Bundārī, *Zubdat al-nuṣra*, 45.

91. Ibn Kathīr, *al-Bidāya wa ʾl-nihāya*, 12:105.

92. For one example, see Al-Bundārī, *Zubdat al-nuṣra*, 44.

93. This is one evidence of a surveillance and espionage system under the Saljūqs that operated independent of Niẓām al-Mulk.

94. Ibn Kathīr, *al-Bidāya wa ʾl-nihāya*, 12:107; Ibn al-Athīr, *al-Kāmil fī ʾl-tārīkh*, 10:75.

95. Rashīd al-Dīn Faḍl Allāh, *Jāmiʿ al-tawārīkh*, 2:278–79.

96. Ibn al-Athīr, *al-Kāmil fī ʾl-tārīkh*, 10:71–72.

97. As we shall see later on during Malik-Shāh's reign, this was the first time that a vizier was bestowed the military title of *Atabeg*.

98. For Niẓām al-Mulk's role during the crucial battle between Alp Arslān and Qutulmish in the year 456/1063, refer to Ibn al-Athīr, *al-Kāmil fī ʾl-tārīkh*, 10:36. He also demonstrated his bravery during the campaign against the Christians in Ānī, in Ādharbāījān. See Ibn al-Athīr, *al-Kāmil fī ʾl-tārīkh*, 10:38–41.

99. Ibn al-Athīr, *al-Kāmil fī ʾl-tārīkh*, 10:78.

100. Al-Subkī, *Ṭabaqāt al-shāfiʿīya*, 4:313.

101. Rāwandī, *Rāḥat al-ṣudūr*, 120.

102. Al-Bundārī, *Zubdat al-nuṣra*, 46.

103. Rashīd al-Dīn Faḍl Allāh, *Jāmiʿ al-tawārīkh*, 2:286–7. Al-Bundārī, *Zubdat al-nuṣra*, 46, provides an account of Yūsūf having struck the Sultan at his *khāṣiratihi*.

104. Al-Bundārī, *Zubdat al-nuṣra*, 46–47.

105. Ibid., 58.

106. Niẓām al-Mulk–Darke, *Book of Government*, 60.

107. Rāwandī, *Rāḥat al-ṣudūr*, 127.

108. Ibn al-Athīr, *al-Kāmil fī ʾl-tārīkh*, 10:80.

109. On the *atabeg* system, see Lambton, "Internal Structure of the Saljuq Empire," 5:239–44, and Cahen, "Atabak."

110. Thābitī, *Asnād wa nāma-hā-yi tārīkhī*, 23.

111. Ibn al-Athīr, *al-Kāmil fī ʾl-tārīkh*, 10:80.

112. Al-Bundārī, *Zubdat al-nuṣra*, 55.

113. Al-Subkī, *Ṭabaqāt* 4:316–17.

114. Ibn Khallikhān–De Slane, *Ibn Khallikān's Biographical Dictionary*, 3:441. In attempting to put the best face on this lifestyle, many of the sources do state that Malik-

Shāh would donate a gold coin to "a dervish" for every animal that he would hunt. The total number of creatures hunted by the Sultan is said to have been over 10,000.

115. Where applied to Divine, this word can have the connotation of "One who exerts his will without being deterred, i.e., Almighty." Here the connotation seems to suggest an oppressive tyrant. The two connotations were of course not separated for the Saljūqs, whose primary justification was their sheer power.

116. Rāwandī, *Rāḥat al-ṣudūr*, 125.

117. Ibid., 126.

118. Rashīd al-Dīn Faḍl Allāh, *Jāmiʿ al-tawārīkh*, 2:295. This was no accident, since as we shall see it was precisely Tarkān Khātūn who was ultimately responsible for the downfall of the aging yet powerful vizier.

119. Al-Bundārī, *Zubdat al-nuṣra*, 55.

120. This term is a testimony to the close relationship between the two and also to age difference.

121. Rāwandī, *Rāḥat al-ṣudūr*, 128; Rashīd al-Dīn Faḍl Allāh, *Jāmiʿ al-tawārīkh*, 2:291–92.

122. Ibn al-Athīr, *al-Kāmil fī ʾl-tārīkh*, 10:160–61.

123. Al-Bundārī, *Zubdat al-nuṣra*, 72–73; Ibn al-Athīr, *al-Kāmil fī ʾl-tārīkh*, 10:123–24.

124. Ibn Kathīr, *al-Bidāya wa ʾl-nihāya*, 12:124.

125. Ibn al-Athīr, *al-Kāmil fī ʾl-tārīkh*, 10:131; al-Subkī, *Ṭabaqāt*, 4:325.

126. Thābitī, *Asnād wa nāma-hā-yi tārīkhī*, 27–28.

127. Ibid, 28.

128. I am deeply grateful to Ḥāmid Algar, who generously shared with me the correct pronunciation of Tarkān Khātūn's name. Even the usually reliable E. G. Browne and R. A. Nicholson have rendered her name as "Turkān Khātūn" in their abridgment and translation of Qazwīnī-Browne, *Tārīkh-i guzīda*, 2:96.

129. Khātūn was an honorific given to women, meaning lady or matron. Fāṭima, the Prophet Muḥammad's daughter, is known as *Khātūn-i jannat*, "Lady (queen) of Paradise."

130. According to Muḥammad Iqbal, the editor of Rāwandī's *Rāḥat al-ṣudūr*, Ṭamghāj Khan was none other than ʿImād al-Dawla Ibrāhīm Ṭafqāj ibn Naṣr, who was one of the Transoxiana rulers from 440 to 460/1048 to 1068. Rashīd al-Dīn Faḍl Allāh, *Jāmiʿ al-tawārīkh*, 2:295, verifies this lineage. The lineage given by Qazwīnī, *Tārīkh-i guzīda*, 1:444, is even more complete: Tarkān Khātūn, daughter of Ṭamghāj Khān, ibn Bughrā Khān ibn Ibrāhīm ibn Naṣr. (Ṭamghāj=Ṭafqāj ?)

131. Nīshāpūrī, *Saljūq-nāma*, 32.

132. Ibn al-Athīr, *al-Kāmil fī ʾl-tārīkh*, 10:240.

133. Kāshgharī-Dankoff, 1:92.

134. Louis Massignon seems to have confused the names of the first two wives in *Passion of al-Hallāj*, 2:162.

135. Āshtiyānī, *Vizārat*, 343, records his full name as Tāj al-Mulk Abū ʾl-Ghanāʾim Marzbān ibn Khusraw Fīrūz Shīrāzī. Qazwīnī, *Tārīkh-i guzīda*, 1:448, records his name as Tāj *al-Dīn*, an understandable mistake.

136. Rāwandī, *Rāḥat al-ṣudūr*, 133.

137. Al-Bundārī, *Zubdat al-nuṣra*, 82

138. Nīshāpūrī, *Saljūq-nāma*, 32.

139. Rashīd al-Dīn Faḍl Allāh, *Jāmiʿ al-tawārīkh*, 2:259

140. Qazwīnī, *Tārīkh-i guzīda*, 1:447–48; Rāwandī, *Rāḥat al-ṣudūr*, 134–36.

141. Rāwandī, *Rāḥat al-ṣudūr*, 134.

142. Ibn al-Athīr, *al-Kāmil fī ʾl-tārīkh*, 10:169. This source also includes an account of massive mourning of the passing away of this young prince.

143. Rashīd al-Dīn Faḍl Allāh, *Jāmiʿ al-tawārīkh*, 2:299.

144. Qazwīnī, *Tārīkh-i guzīda*, 1:447; Qazwīnī-Browne, *Tārīkh-i guzīda*, 2:97; Rashīd al-Dīn Faḍl Allāh, *Jāmiʿ al-tawārīkh*, 2:296.

145. It would seem that Zabīda Khātūn was thus the first cousin of Sultan Malik-Shāh, a common marriage choice for citizens of premodern (and occasionally modern) Nile-to-Oxus. Zabīda Khātūn's father, Amīr Yāqūtī, was also a son of Chagrī Beg, and thus the brother of Sultan Alp Arslān, Malik-shāh's father.

146. Niẓām al-Mulk–Darke, *Book of Government*, 178–9.

147. Ibid., 178 n. 21.

148. Rāwandī, *Rāḥat al-ṣudūr*, 133; Nīshāpūrī, *Saljūq-nāma*, 33.

149. Rashīd al-Dīn Faḍl Allāh, *Jāmiʿ al-tawārīkh*, 2:259; Rāwandī, *Rāḥat al-ṣudūr*, 133.

150. Ibn al-Athīr, *al-Kāmil fī ʾl-tārīkh*, 10:216.

151. Al-Bundārī, *Zubdat al-nuṣra*, 61.

152. Niẓām al-Mulk-Darke, *Book of Government*, 158.

153. Ibid., 158 n. 11: "This is probably a reference to Nizam al-Mulk's rival Taj al-Mulk, who was patronized by Tarkan Khatun, wife of Malikshah."

154. Ibid., 165.

155. Ibid.

156. Grabar, *Great Mosque of Isfahan*. For more images and discussion, see MIT's digital archive of Islamic architecture, ARCHNET, "Friday Mosque of Isfahan," <http://archnet.org/library/sites/one-site.tcl'site_id=2305> (January 17, 2005).

157. Niẓām al-Mulk–Darke, *Book of Government*, 179–80.

158. Ibid., 180–81.

159. Ibid., 181.

160. Ibid., 182.

161. Ibid.

162. Ibid.

163. Ibid.

164. Cornell, *Early Sufi Women*, esp. 17–20 and 54–63. Also see Spellberg, *Politics, Gender, and the Islamic Past*.

165. Niẓām al-Mulk–Darke, *Book of Government*, 185.

166. Ibid., 158–79.

167. Ibid., 187–89.

168. Ibid., 188.

169. Ibid., 188–89.

170. Ibid., 189.

171. See Holt, Lambton, and Lewis in the bibliography.

172. Spuler, "Disintegration of the Caliphate in the East," 151.

173. Lewis, *Assassins*, 47.

174. Thābitī, *Asnād wa nāma-hā-yi tārīkhī*, 23.
175. Rāwandī, *Rāḥat al-ṣudūr*, 125.
176. Al-Bundārī, *Zubdat al-nuṣra*, 70.
177. It was rivaled by Nīshāpūr, Bukhārā, Samarqand, Isfahan, Cordoba, Cairo, Fez, etc.
178. Ibn Kathīr, *al-Bidāya wa ʾl-nihāya*, 12:139.
179. Niẓām al-Mulk–Darke, *Book of Government*, 188.
180. Al-Subkī, *Ṭabaqāt al-shāfiʿīya*, 4:323–26.
181. Al-Bundārī, *Zubdat al-nuṣra*, 63.
182. Al-Subkī, *Ṭabaqāt al-shāfiʿīya*, 4:324.
183. Ibid.
184. Ibid.
185. Rāwandī, *Rāḥat al-ṣudūr*, 135.
186. "Heretics" was a code word for followers of Ḥaṣan-i Ṣabbāḥ operating out of the Alamūt castle.
187. Rāwandī, *Rāḥat al-ṣudūr*, 135.
188. Nīshāpūrī, *Saljūq-nāma*, 33.
189. Rashīd al-Dīn Faḍl Allāh, *Jāmiʿ al-tawārīkh*, 2:296
190. Ibn Khallikān–De Slane, 1:415.
191. Ibid.
192. Qazwīnī, *Tārīkh-i guzīda*, 1:448. Qazwīnī adds that Niẓām al-Mulk was the first assassination victim of the Alamūt-based Assassins. This becomes a commonly accepted and frequently repeated allegation. There is some discrepancy in the sources over the exact date of this assassination: Rashīḍ al-Dīn Faḍl Allāh, *Jāmiʿ al-tawārīkh* 2:300, mentions "Saturday, the tenth of Ramaḍān of 485" instead of the twelfth of Ramaḍān, as Qazwīnī and other sources suggest.
193. Rāwandī, *Rāḥat al-ṣudūr*, 134; Rashīd al-Dīn Faḍl Allāh, *Jāmiʿ al-tawārīkh*, 2:296.
194. Qazwīnī, *Tārīkh-i guzīda*, 1:447.
195. A sash that is wrapped around a turban.
196. Rāwandī, *Rāḥat al-ṣudūr*, 134; also see Qazwīnī, *Tārīkh-i guzīda*, 1:447.
197. Nīshāpūrī, *Saljūq-nāma*, 33.
198. Al-Subkī, *Ṭabaqāt*, 4:325.
199. Al-Bundārī, *Zubdat al-nuṣra*, 63.
200. Ibid.
201. Ibn al-Athīr, *al-Kāmil fī ʾl-tārīkh*, 10:204–6.
202. Rāwandī, *Rāḥat al-ṣudūr*, 134.
203. Qazwīnī, *Tārīkh-i guzīda*, 1:447.
204. Al-Bundārī, *Zubdat al-nuṣra*, 63.
205. Subkī, *Ṭabaqāt al-shāfiʿīya*, 4:326; Ibn Khallikān-De Slane, *Ibn Khallikan's Biographical Dictionary*, 3:444–45 provides extensive details of this narrative as well.
206. Ibn Khallikān-De Slane, *Ibn Khallikan's Biographical Dictionary*, 3:444.
207. Rāwandī, *Rāḥat al-ṣudūr*, 135–36.
208. Ibid., 136.
209. Charming Victorian translation is from Browne, *Literary History of Persia*, 2:190.
210. Rāwandī, *Rāḥat al-ṣudūr*, 135–36; Qazwīnī, *Tārīkh-i guzīda*, 1:448.

211. Rāwandī, *Rāḥat al-ṣudūr*, 135.

212. He offers that Malik-Shāh died on the sixteenth of Shawwāl, 485 A.H.

213. Ibn Khallikān–De Slane, *Ibn Khallikan's Biographical Dictionary*, 1:415.

214. Qazwīnī, *Tārīkh-i guzīda*, 1:448; Hindū-Shāh Nakhjawānī, *Tajārib al-salaf*, 281.

215. Nīshāpūrī, *Saljūq-nāma*, 33; Rāwandī, *Rāḥat al-ṣudūr*, 135.

216. Āshtiyānī, *Vizārat*, 51.

217. *Mujmal al-tawārīkh wa 'l-qiṣaṣ*, 408.

218. The most significant of these was Malik Ismāʿīl, Bark-yāruq's uncle. Rāwandī, *Rāḥat al-ṣudūr*, 141–42, holds that Tarkān Khātūn had promised her own hand in marriage to Malik Ismāʿīl if he would defeat Bark-yarūq.

219. Nīshāpūrī, *Saljūq-nāma*, 35. Rāwandī, *Rāḥat al-ṣudūr*, 139, asserts that the *Amīr al-mu'minīn* refused, stating: "Your son is a mere child (*ṭifl*), and is not suited for *pādshāhī*."

220. Nīshāpūrī, *Saljūq-nāma*, 36; Rāwandī, *Rāḥat al-ṣudūr*, 142; Ibn al-Athīr, *al-Kāmil fī 'l-tārīkh*, 10:240.

221. Hindū-Shāh Nakhjawānī, *Tajārib al-salaf*, 281.

222. Ibn al-Athīr, *al-Kāmil*, 10:206. The translation is modified from Browne, *Literary History of Persia*, 2:188.

223. Āshtiyānī, *Vizārat*, 51; *Mujmal al-tawārīkh wa 'l-qiṣaṣ*, 409; Al-Bundārī, *Zubdat al-nuṣra*, 93.

224. Hindū-Shāh Nakhjawānī, *Tajārib al-salaf*, 280–81. The Karān neighborhood is today known as Aḥmadīya in Isfahan.

Chapter Three

1. Lambton, "Internal Structure of the Saljūq Empire," 203.

2. Althusser, "Ideology and Ideological State Apparatuses," 100–140.

3. Al-Bundārī, *Zubdat al-nuṣra*, 58.

4. Ibid., 56–59.

5. Among his other works, also see Foucault, *Discipline and Punish*.

6. Foucault, *Power/Knowledge*, 146–65.

7. Niẓām al-Mulk, *Siyāsat-nāma*, 101.

8. Ibid.

9. Ibn al-Athīr, *al-Kāmil fī 'l-tārīkh*, 10:75.

10. Niẓām al-Mulk, *Siyāsat-nāma*, 96.

11. Ibid., 31.

12. Ibid., 85

13. Ibid., 56.

14. Ibid., 59.

15. It is intriguing to note that ʿAyn al-Quḍāt himself was fully aware of the discourse of surveillance and espionage, even casting himself in such a role. In this case he depicts himself as the espionage agent who is bringing secrets back from the divine realm. See his *Tamhīdāt*, 269, where he states, "Look at how much *nammāmī* (calumination) and *jāsūsī* (espionage, spying) I have done!" This is no less than a mockery and parody of the whole system of reconnaissance and surveillance. In this case he

is not reporting the bringing of news from the judges to the king, but acting as a judge, he is bringing the news of the King (God) back to the world. The system is turned on its head. Nor can one dismiss here an allusion to his own honorific, ʿAyn al-Quḍāt, which while having the primary meaning of "essence" or "spring" of judges can also mean "eye of the judges."

16. Niẓām al-Mulk, *Siyāsat-nāma*, 63.

17. Tilly, "War Making and State Making," 170.

18. Ibid., 181.

19. Hodgson, *Venture of Islam*, 2:45.

20. Muḥammad b. Ibrāhīm, *Tārīkh-i saljūqīyān-i kirmān*, 29–30, cited in "Saljdūḳids," 945.

21. Cahen, "L'évolution sociale du monde musulman." Also see his thought-provoking article, "Evolution de ʾl-Iqṭāʿ," 25–52.

22. Cahen, "*Iḳṭāʿ*."

23. Hodgson, *Venture of Islam*, 2:49.

24. Ibid.

25. Al-Bundārī, *Zubdat al-nuṣra*, 58. Cahen, "*Iḳṭāʿ*," points out the way that this account has been misread.

26. Niẓām al-Mulk, *Siyāsat-nāma*, 134.

27. Lambton, "Reflections on the *iqṭāʿ*," 369.

28. Ibid., 373.

29. Niẓām al-Mulk, *Siyāsat-nāma*, 134.

30. Ibid.

31. Ibn Khallikān–De Slane, *Ibn Khallikān's Biographical Dictionary*, 3:297.

32. Thābitī, *Asnād wa nāma-hā-yi tārīkhī*, 22–23.

33. Niẓām al-Mulk, *Siyāsat-nāma*, 43.

34. Ibid.

35. Al-Bundārī, *Zubdat al-nuṣra*, 58.

36. Niẓām al-Mulk, *Siyāsat-nāma*, 139.

37. Niẓām al-Mulk–Darke, *Book of Government*, 102. The context of this aversion to settled life is Niẓām al-Mulk's recommendation that the sultan employ Türkmen as pages in the court.

38. Niẓām al-Mulk, *Siyāsat-nāma*, 177.

39. Al-Bundārī, *Zubdat al-nuṣra*, 57.

40. Hodgson, *Venture of Islam*, 2:51–52.

41. Ibid., 2:48.

42. Lapidus, "Ayyubid Religious Policy," 281.

43. Rāwandī, *Rāḥat al-ṣudūr*, 29.

44. I will explore notions of reciprocity in Sufi hagiographies and historical works of the Saljūq period (connections between legitimization and patronage) in greater depth in chapter 5.

45. Ḥāfiẓ Abrū, *Zubdat al-tawārīkh*, 177, quoted in Kasāʾī, *Madāris-i Niẓāmīya*, 69.

46. Meisami, *Persian Historiography*, 270, n. 6: "There is little in the archealogical record to substantiate these claims." While Meisami's point is valid to a certain extent, it is important to point out she uses as part of her criteria "Friday mosques built entirely

in the Saljūq period." We know that Niẓām al-Mulk and Tāj al-Mulk, among others, made additions to existing mosque structures in Isfahan, thus not qualifying as being built entirely in the Saljūq period.

47. See Nāṣir Khusraw, *Safar-nāma*, translated by Thackston as *Nāṣer-e Khosraw's Book of Travels*, 2.

48. Ibn Kathīr, *al-Bidāya wa 'l-nihāya*, 12:142.

49. ʿAqīlī, *Āthār al-wuzarāʾ*, 207.

50. Al-Bundārī, *Zubdat al-nuṣra*, 57.

51. The starting place for any study of the madrasa system in this period remains the many writings of George Makdisi, such as *Rise of Colleges; Religion, Law, and Learning in Classical Islam*; and *History and Politics in Eleventh-Century Baghdad.*

52. Ibn al-Athīr, *al-Kāmil fī 'l-tārīkh*, 10:49.

53. Ibid., 10:54.

54. Al-Subkī, *Ṭabaqāt al-shāfiʿīya*, 4:318.

55. Al-Bundārī, *Zubdat al-nuṣra*, 80.

56. Bulliet, *Patricians of Nishapur*, 73 n. 37.

57. For example, Ibn Khallikān-De Slane, *Ibn Khallikān's Biographical Dictionary*, 1: 414, states that Niẓām al-Mulk was the first to have founded a madrasa.

58. Al-Subkī, *Ṭabaqāt al-shāfiʿīya*, 4:314.

59. According to the *Tārīkh-i bayhaqī*, Niẓām al-Mulk was born in 410/1019–20.

60. For a history of this madrasa, see Bulliet, *Patricians of Nishapur*, 250–51. Bulliet specifically recognizes that this madrasa might have served as the model of the later Niẓāmīya madrasas.

61. Al-Subkī, *Ṭabaqāt al-shāfiʿīya*, 4:314.

62. See Madelung, "Spread of Māturīdism," 109–168.

63. Madelung, *Religious Trends*, 30.

64. Ibid., 32.

65. Ibid., 33.

66. For example, al-Bundārī, *Zubdat al-nuṣra*, 41, records that Sultan Alp Arslān was accompanied by "his own *faqīh*, his own *imām*, Abū Naṣr Muḥammad b. ʿAbd al-Malik al-Bukhārī al-Ḥanafī," in his battles against the Byzantine ruler.

67. Makdisi, "Muslim Institutions of Learning," 19.

68. Niẓām al-Mulk, *Siyāsat-nāma*, 129.

69. Ibn Kathīr, *al-Bidāya wa 'l-nihāya*, 12:142.

70. Ibid.

71. Beaurecueil, *Khawādja ʿAbdullāh Anṣārī*. Persian translation by Ravān-Farhādī as *Sargudhasht-i pīr-i harāt, Khwāja ʿAbd Allāh Anṣārī Harawī*, 149–150.

72. For his most detailed critique, see Anṣārī, *Dhamm al-kalām*.

73. Ibn Jawzī, *al-Muntaẓam*, 8:312, cited in Kasāʾī, *Madāris-i Niẓāmīya*, 67.

74. Bulliet, *Patricians of Nishapur*, 74.

75. Kasāʾī, *Madāris-i Niẓāmīya*, 14.

76. Daftary, *Ismāʿīlīs*, 189; Lambton, "Internal Structure of the Saljūq Empire," 215.

77. One of the earliest scholars to have argued for the teaching of Ashʿarī kalām in the Niẓāmīya was Ignaz Goldziher, who held that Niẓām al-Mulk had created "public chairs" in the Niẓāmīyas. Goldziher held that these madrasas could be used as a

post through which "Ashʿarite dogmatic theology could be taught officially and was admitted into the system of orthodox theology." Goldziher's discussion in the *Vorlesungen über den Islam* is translated and critiqued in Makdisi, "Muslim Institutions," 3.

78. Makdisi, "Muslim Institutions," 37. Makdisi does recognize that some Shāfiʿī teachers may have introduced Ashʿarī principles, but he holds that this is far from the madrasa having been set up to teach Ashʿarī kalām.

79. Ibid., 47.

80. Makdisi cites Shīrāzī's treatise *Kitāb al-lumaʿ fī uṣūl al-fiqh* and Ibn Rajab's *Ṭabaqāt al-ḥanābila* where Shīrāzī is cited as stating that he was anti-Ashʿarī in terms of his legal theory: *wa hādhihi kutubī fī ūṣūli 'l-fiqhi aqūlu fīhā khilāfan li 'l-ashʿarīya*. See Makdisi, "Ashʿarī and the Ashʿarites," reprinted in *Religion, Law and Learning in Classical Islam*, 74 n. 1.

81. I am here much indebted to Vincent Cornell for his clear articulation of *uṣūlization*.

82. Gibb, "Interpretation of Islamic History," 24.

83. Lambton, "Internal Structure of the Saljūq Empire," 214–15.

84. Hodgson, *Venture of Islam*, 2:47–48.

85. Lambton, "Internal Structure of the Saljūq Empire," 215.

86. Mottahedeh, *Loyalty and Leadership*, 140.

87. Makdisi, "Muslim Institutions," 10–12.

88. Bulliet, *Patricians of Nishapur*, 41–42. Bulliet provides a chart that provides the following information: between the years 405/1014 and 525/1130, the proportion of epithets that refer to the Sufis rose from 35 to 68 percent. Conversely, the proportion of the *zāhid* category declined from 42 to 21 percent. Clearly, this points to the gradual dominance of the designation Sufi at the expense of other pietistic labels.

89. For a discussion of the various usages of these terms, refer to Kiyānī, *Tārīkh-i khānaqāh dar īrān*, 65–122.

90. Badīʿ al-Zamān Furūzanfar, "muqaddama-yi muṣaḥḥiḥ," to *Tarjuma-yi risāla-yi qushayrīya*, 21. (See under Qushayrī, *Risāla*.)

91. Zakarīya Qazwīnī, *Āthār al-bilād*, 361–62, cited in Kiyānī, *Tārīkh-i khānaqāh dar īrān*, 187.

92. For example, see Ibn Munawwar, *Asrār al-tawḥīd*, 1:207, where it is said that Abu ʿAbd Allāh Bākū was in the khānaqāh of Abū ʿAbd al-Raḥmān al-Sulamī. Qushayrī's own khānaqāh is mentioned in 1:83.

93. One example is the individual that Ibn Munawwar, *Asrār al-tawḥīd*, 1:105, identifies as [A]Bū ʿUthmān Ḥīrī. Ibn Munawwar's translator, John O'Kane, *Secrets of God's Mystical Oneness*, 608 n. 112, persuasively argues that Ibn Munawwar is confusing this individual with Abū ʿUthmān Bāḥirī, since Ḥīrī lived a full century before Abū Saʿīd, passing away in the year 298/910.

94. This approach characterizes the framework of Hamid Dabashi, "Historical Conditions of Persian Sufism," 150.

95. Al-Subkī, *Ṭabaqāt al-shāfiʿīya*, 4:293–94.

96. Ibid., 3:369. The account of his khānaqāh can also be verified through Ibn Munawwar, *Asrār al-tawḥīd*, 1:83.

97. Jāmī, *Nafaḥāt al-uns*, 295.

98. *Tarjuma-yi risāla-yi qushayrīya*, 2–3. [See under qushayrī, *Risāla*.]

99. Bulliet, *Patricians of Nishapur*, 151.

100. Al-Bundārī, *Zubdat al-nuṣra*, 52.

101. Jāmī, *Nafaḥāt al-uns*, 376.

102. Ibn Kathīr, *al-bidāya wa 'l-nihāya*, 12:149.

103. Ibn Munawwar, *Asrār al-tawḥīd*, 1:119. This narrative is quoted virtually verbatim by Jāmī, *Nafaḥāt al-uns*, 373–74.

104. See Jāmī, *Nafaḥāt al-uns*, 376.

105. Another example is that of Khwāja Imām [A]bū Naṣr ʿIyāḍī, who had studied *fiqh* with Imām al-Ḥaramayn Juwaynī. See Ibn Munawwar, *Asrār al-tawḥīd*, 1:120–21.

106. Al-Ghazālī, "dar bāra-yi amwāl–i khānaqāh." Published in Pourjavady, *Du Mujaddid*, 79–100. Section on avoiding the sultan's *ḥarām* finances in on p. 90.

107. Niẓām al-Mulk, *Siyāsat-nāma*, 95.

108. Al-Bundārī, *Zubdat al-nuṣra*, 67, also reiterates Alp Arslān's dislike for the *ṣāḥib khabar*, and goes so far to state that the Sultan sought to put an end to this practice of surveillance and espionage. In ominous terms, the historian ʿImād al-Dīn adds that the value of having spies and surveillance agents would become known with the rise of the Ismāʿīlīs.

109. Lambton, "Reflections on the *Iqṭāʿ*," 358.

110. ʿAyn al-Quḍāt, *Nāma-hā*, 1:166–67.

111. See Al-Bundārī, *Zubdat al-nuṣra*, 89, where the vizier of Bark-yāruq, a certain Ustād ʿAbd al-Jalīl Dahistānī (d. 495/1101–2), is held to have taken people's possessions as his own iqṭāʿ.

112. Ibn Khallikān–De Slane, *Ibn Khallikān's Biographical Dictionary*, 1:414.

113. Sibṭ ibn al-Jawzī *Mirʾāt al-zamān* 8:246–47, cited in Makdisi, "Muslim Institutions," 31–33.

114. "Prayer on unjustly appropriated grounds is not permitted" (*lā taḥillu 'l-ṣalātu fī arḍin maghṣūba*). Cited in Makdisi, "Muslim Institutions," 34 n. 3.

115. Ibn al-Athīr, *al-Kāmil fī 'l-tārīkh*, 10:55.

116. Hindū-Shāh Nakhjawānī, *Tajārib al-salaf*, 277.

Chapter Four

1. Among other sources, one can point to Watt, *Muslim Intellectual* and Jalāl al-Dīn Humāʾī, *Ghazzālī-nāmah*.

2. Watt, "al-Ghazālī, Abū Ḥāmid," 1038.

3. This important detail is provided in Ghazālī's collections of letters, *Faḍāʾil al-anām*, 4.

4. There is a good translation of this text in R. J. McCarthy, *Al-Ghazali*.

5. This edition has been available to me through the reprint in *Zamīna-yi īrān-shināsī* (1364/1985), 91–118. I am deeply grateful to Dr. Nasrollah Pourjavady for having provided me with a copy of this edition.

6. Al-Ghazāli, *Ḥimāqa ahl al-ibāḥa*, 95–96. For an insightful discussion of libertine attitudes (*ibāḥa*) see Ernst, *Words of Ecstasy*, 120.

7. The best edition of this text is the bilingual edition *Incoherence of the Philosophers*.

8. Al-Ghazālī, *Incoherence of the Philosophers*, 12–46.

9. Ibid., 137–46.

10. Ibid., 212–29.

11. Ibid., 230.

12. Al-Ghazālī, *Munqidh min al-ḍalāl*, trans. by Watt as *Faith and Practice of al-Ghazālī*, 37–38.

13. Ibid., 32.

14. Ibid., 27–29. He returns to the same discussion in the *Kitāb al-ʿilm* of the *Iḥyāʾ*.

15. Hodgson, *Venture of Islam*, 2:181. Hodgson's whole assessment of al-Ghazālī (2:180–92) is worth repeated readings.

16. Ibid., 2:180.

17. Ibid., 2:188.

18. Al-Bundārī, *Zubdat al-nuṣra*, 80.

19. See for example Watt's discussion of the difficulty in ascertaining the length of al-Ghazālī's sojourn in Damascus in *Muslim Intellectual*, 145.

20. Al-Ghazālī, *Faith and Practice of al-Ghazālī*, 57.

21. Ibid., 58.

22. Ibn Kathīr, *al-Bidāya wa ʾl-nihāya*, 12:149.

23. MacDonald, "Life of al-Ghazzālī," 71–132.

24. Jabre, "La biographie et l'oeuvre de Ghazālī reconsidérées," 73–102. However, see Hodgson, *Venture of Islam*, 2:189 n. 19, where he critiques Jabre's tendency to make Ghazālī "unduly singleminded."

25. McCarthy, "Introduction" to *Al-Ghazali*, 26.

26. Watt, "al-Ghazālī."

27. Al-Ghazālī, *Faḍāʾil al-anām*, 45.

28. Ibid.

29. Watt, *Faith and Practice of al-Ghazali*, 76.

30. Laoust, *La Politique de Gazālī*. Laoust's text has only been available to me through Mozaffari's Persian translation, *Siyāsat wa Ghazālī*.

31. Binder, "Al-Ghazali and Islamic Government."

32. Lambton, "Theory of Kingship," 47–55.

33. Hillenbrand, "Islamic Orthodoxy or Realpolitik?," 81–94.

34. Ibid., 92.

35. Ibn Rushd, *Faṣl al-maqāl*, L. Gauthier, ed., (Algiers, 1948), 21, cited in Rosenthal, *Political Thought in Medieval Islam*, 239.

36. Al-Ghazālī, *Faḍāʾiḥ al-bāṭinīya wa faḍāʾil al-mustaẓhirīya*, 169. See also McCarthy, *Deliverance from Error*, 151–244.

37. Lane, *Arabic-English Lexicon*, 2:2768, defines *najda* as "courage and sharpness, or vigour and effectiveness, in those affairs which others lack the power or ability to accomplish."

38. It is unfortunate that McCarthy's otherwise wonderful translation of the *Faḍāʾiḥ* (*Deliverance from Error*, 238) eliminates this discussion from the Arabic text, simply substituting "Answer to an Objection."

39. Al-Ghazālī, *Faḍāʾiḥ al-bāṭinīya wa faḍāʾil al-mustaẓhirīya*, 182.

40. Ibid.

41. Niẓam al-Mulk, *Siyāsat-nāma*, 217.

42. Al-Ghazālī, *Faḍā'iḥ al-bātinīya wa faḍā'il al-mustaẓhirīya*, 183.

43. Al-Ghazālī, *al-Iqtiṣād fī 'l-i'tiqād.*

44. This can be ascertained through the reference in the *al-Iqtiṣād*, 259, to the *al-Mustaẓhirī.*

45. Hillenbrand, "Islamic Orthodoxy or Realpolitik?," 87.

46. I am reading *al-ma'qūlāt* for *al-muhimmāt* in this sentence, especially as the next item in the pair is *al-manqūlāt*. The juxtaposition of rational sciences and transmitted disciplines is a very common one in Islamic education. Hillenbrand, "Islamic Orthodoxy or Realpolitik?," 86 (and 94 n. 84) prefers *al-muhimmat.*

47. Hillenbrand, "Islamic Orthodoxy or Realpolitik?," 88.

48. Al-Ghazālī, *Iḥyā' 'ulūm al-dīn*, 2:155–67.

49. Ibid., 2:154.

50. Ibid.

51. Ibid. See also Hillenbrand, "Islamic Orthodoxy or Realpolitik?," 90–91.

52. Al-Ghazālī, *Iḥyā' 'ulūm al-dīn*, 2:154.

53. Bagley, "Introduction" to *Ghaẓālī's Book of Counsel for Kings* [see under Al-Ghazālī, *Naṣīḥat al-mulūk*], xix–xxiv.

54. For an overview of this debate, see Jalāl al-Dīn Humā'ī's "muqaddima" to Al-Ghazālī, *Naṣīḥat al-mulūk*, 119–127. Humā'ī himself, in line with most Persian scholars, prefers Sultan Sanjar as the king addressed in the *Naṣīḥat al-mulūk.*

55. Bagley, "introduction" to *Ghaẓali's Book of Counsel for Kings*, xvii.

56. Humā'ī, "muqaddima" to Al-Ghazālī, *Naṣīḥat al-mulūk*, 83.

57. Zarrīnkūb, *Farār az madrasa*, 260.

58. Pourjavady, *Du Mujaddid*, 413–24. My discussion here is entirely indebted to Nasrollah Pourjavady. Ustād Pourjavady has kindly demonstrated to me his case for the lack of authenticity of the *Naṣīḥat al-mulūk*, and it is perhaps a sign of my foolishness in not conceding the point to him.

59. Crone, "Did al-Ghazālī."

60. Ibid., 176.

61. Ibid., 180.

62. Ibid.

63. Humā'ī, "muqaddima" to Al-Ghazālī, *Naṣīḥat al-mulūk*, 93–102; Bagley, "Introduction" to *Ghaẓali's Book of Counsel for Kings*, lvi–lx.

64. Laoust, *La Politique de Gaẓālī*, 144. Cited in Crone, "Did Al-Ghazālī," 168 n. 5, translated to Persian by Mozaffari, *Siyāsat wa Ghaẓālī*, 202–214.

65. Lambton, *State and Government*, 117–26.

66. See Bagley, "introduction" to *Ghaẓali's Book of Counsel for Kings.*

67. Bouyges, *Essai de Chronologie*, 61, cited in Crone, "Did Al-Ghazālī," 168 n. 5.

68. 'Abd al-Raḥmān Badawī, *Mu'allafāt al-Ghaẓālī*, no. 47, cited in Crone, "Did Al-Ghazālī," 168 n. 5.

69. Ṭabāṭabā'ī, "Munḥanī-yi taḥawwul-i andīsha-yi siyāsī-yi Ghazālī"; Ṭabāṭabā'ī *Darāmadī falsafī bar tārīkh-i andīsha-yi siyāsī dar Iran*, 78.

70. Lambton, *State and Government*, 117.

71. Al-Ghazālī, *Naṣīḥat al-mulūk*, 16.

72. Ibid., 17.

73. Ibid., 19.

74. Ibid.

75. Ibid., 16. See also Al-Ghazālī–Bagley, *Ghazālī's Book of Counsel for Kings*, 14.

76. Al-Ghazālī, *Naṣīḥat al-mulūk*, 27.

77. Ibid., 106.

78. I am here indebted to Paden, *Religious World*, which includes a chapter on "systems of purity."

79. To see how closely al-Ghazālī's discourse on this matter mirrors Niẓām al-Mulk's position, see Niẓām al-Mulk, *Siyāsat-nāma*, 80.

80. For the political thought of these two important figures, see the relevant chapters in Lambton, *State and Government in Medieval Islam*, 69–82. I have not here focused on the political thought of these figures as their writing is focused primarily on the period prior to the rise of the Saljūqs.

81. Al-Ghazālī, *Naṣīḥat al-mulūk*, 131.

82. Ibid., 81.

83. Mu'ayyid al-Dawla Atābeg al-Juwaynī, *'Atabat al-kataba*, 9.

84. For a discussion of *farr/Xvarᵊnah*, see Yarshater, "Iranian Common Beliefs," 345–46. In Middle Persian this term became transformed to *Farrah*, and in modern Persian to *Farr*. It could be translated as "Divine Fortune, Grace, or Glory." In pre-Islamic Iran, no king could rule without it, and the rise (and fall) of various rulers was explained through the presence (or absence) of *Xvarᵊnah*.

85. Al-Ghazālī, *Naṣīḥat al-mulūk*, 81–82.

86. Qur'an 4:59.

87. Al-Ghazālī, *Naṣīḥat al-mulūk*, 82.

88. Ibid.

89. Ibid. Al-Ghazālī attributes this statement to the Prophet Muḥammad as well: *al-mulku yabqā ma'a 'l-kufr wa lā yabqā ma'a 'l-ẓulm*.

90. Ibid., 83.

91. Ibid., 149.

92. Badawī, *Mu'allafāt al-Ghazālī*. Badawī is in general weaker in dealing with the Persian works of al-Ghazālī. Sadly, this is somewhat typical of many Arab scholars of al-Ghazālī and other bilingual premodern Muslim figures. Very few contemporary Arab scholars explore the Persian writings of these figures, often resulting in a partial or incomplete understanding.

93. Bouyges, *Essai de Chronologie des*, 130. Cited in Pourjavady, *Du Mujaddid*, 329 n. 4.

94. Al-Ghazālī, *Tuḥfat al-mulūk*, 249–300.

95. Al-Ghazālī, *Tuḥfat al-mulūk*, re-edited by Nasrollah Pourjavady and published in Pourjavdy, *Du Mujaddid*, 345–412 (henceforth, *Tuḥfat2*).

96. Nasrollah Pourjavady offers a typically thorough and superb overview of these debates. In the end, he partially bases his reasoning on the observation that the writer of these texts offers his explanations based on the Ḥanafī madhhab, whereas al-Ghazālī

is decidedly Shāfiʿī. While it is true that some of the opinions, such as those dealing with whether the *zakāt* belongs to the sultan (*Tuḥfat2*, 372) and on hunting (*Tuḥfat2*, 375–476) are written according to the Ḥanafī school, others (dealing with *ṭahārat, ghusl* and *tayammum*) are given according to both the Ḥanafī and the Shāfiʿī perspectives (*Tuḥfat2*, 362, 366, 373). While in this matter, as indeed in all matters dealing with Persian Sufism, I gladly defer to the wisdom of Ustād Pourjavady, I do wonder whether it would be possible to read the author's reference to both madhhabs as conforming to the precedence that Niẓām al-Mulk had already set, respecting both the Shāfiʿī madhhab (which he himself and al-Ghazālī followed) and the Ḥanafī madhhab (which the Saljūqs followed). *Wa Allāhu aʿlam* . . .

97. For a review of these debates, see Pourjavady, *Du Mujaddid*, 327–36.

98. Al-Ghazālī, *Tuḥfat al-mulūk*, 295. The name of this figure is recorded as ʿAbd al-Razzāq Ṣanʿānī.

99. Ibid., 296.

100. Al-Ghazālī, *Tuḥfat al-mulūk*, 258.

101. Al-Ghazālī, *Tuḥfat2*, 355. See also Al-Ghazālī, *Tuḥfat al-mulūk*, 258.

102. Al-Ghazālī, *Tuḥfat2*, 356.

103. Ibid.

104. Al-Ghazālī, *Pand-nāma*, in Pourjavady, *Du Mujaddid*, 425–49.

105. Pourjavady, *Du Mujaddid*, 418–22.

106. Al-Ghazālī, *Pand-nāma*, in Pourjavady, *Du Mujaddid*, 426.

Chapter Five

1. For the appropriateness of "sainthood" in a discussion of premodern Sufism, see Cornell, *Realm of the Saint*, xvii–xliv.

2. For example, see Watt, *Muslim Intellectual.*

3. Watt's book on al-Ghazālī, cited above, devotes seven pages to the segment on "Political Background."

4. For a clear example, one could point to the studies of Saljūq Sufism whose only citation of Rāwandī's *Rāḥat al-ṣudūr* is the exchange between Ṭughril and Bābā Ṭāhir. See Rāwandī, *Rāḥat al-ṣudūr*, 98–99.

5. There are notable exceptions to this tendency, such as the works of Bruce Lawrence, Richard Eaton, Simon Digby, Devin DeWeese, Carl Ernst, Jo-Ann Gross, and Vincent Cornell. However, the above criticism still holds for many studies of Sufism.

6. One of the latest publications on Saljūq history and historiography only confirms this point: Julie Meisami's otherwise superb work, *Persian Historiography to the End of the Twelfth Century*, makes no attempt to utilize any hagiographies in reconstructing the process of writing history in the Saljūq period. Interestingly, one of the most important extant works dating to this period which provides us with a great deal of information about social life in Saljūq society, the *Asrār al-tawḥīd* (being the hagiography of Abū Saʿīd-i Abī ʾl-Khayr) is not analyzed in Meisami's work, probably because it falls outside the narrow genre of "tārīkh."

7. Ibn Munawwar, *Asrār al-tawḥīd fī maqāmāt al-shaykh abī saʿīd.*

8. Certain types of finches—dippers, or water ouzels (*Cinclus*)—are semiaquatic creatures and can in fact walk on water surfaces.

9. One variant reads *zaghanī*, implying a "black sparrow" according to Dehkhoda, *Lughat-nāma*, 9:12873. Another variant indicates *murghī*, simply a bird.

10. Ibn Munawwar, *Asrār al-tawḥīd*, 1:199.

11. Safi, "Bargaining with *Baraka*," 259–88.

12. For a recent and thorough critique of these tendencies, refer to King, *Orientalism and Religion*, 7–35. King's work builds on themes introduced by McCutcheon, *Manufacturing Religion*, and Jonathan Z. Smith, *Imagining Religion*.

13. Underhill, *Mysticism*, 81.

14. The oppositional presence of Saljūq era Sufis such as ʿAyn al-Quḍāt Hamadānī is the subject of the sixth chapter of the present study.

15. I am here indebted to Cornell, *Realm of the Saint*.

16. Eaton, *Sufis of Bijapur*.

17. Digby, "Sufi Shaykh and the Sultan," 71–81.

18. DeWeese, "Eclipse of the Kubraviyah," 45–83.

19. Ernst, *Eternal Garden*.

20. Gross, "Authority and Miraculous Behavior," 159–71.

21. Cornell, *Realm of the Saint*.

22. Examples could range from the classic work of Browne, *Literary History of Persia*, to Dabashi, "Historical Conditions of Persian Sufism," 137–74.

23. In other cases, such as the hagiography of Aḥmad-i Jām, the saint's firāsat could also be portrayed as literally saving the life of a political figure from assassination or treason.

24. For a brilliant discussion of issues of power and knowledge in premodern sainthood, see Cornell's *Realm of the Saint: Power and Authority in Moroccan Sufism*.

25. Ghaznavī, *Maqāmāt-i zhanda pīl*, 93.

26. Ibid., 95.

27. Ibid.,97.

28. Ibid., 99–100.

29. Ibid., 100–101.

30. Ibid., 153.

31. Ibid., 154.

32. Ibid.

33. Ibid., 88.

34. Doniger, "Other People's Lies," 27.

35. For a discussion of the role of myth as a paradigmatic force that shapes religious worlds, refer to Paden, *Religious Worlds*, 69–92.

36. Heffernan, *Sacred Biography*, 19.

37. Indeed both hearing and reading are important elements, as almost all of these hagiographic accounts started out as oral tales, often being transmitted for generations before they were written down.

38. These quatrains are not composed in the standard *rubāʿī* meter, but in a style known as the *hazaj*. See Storey–deBlois, *Persian Literature*, 5(1): 96. Bābā Ṭāhir's qua-

trains follow a different meter than the well-known *Rubāʿiyāt* of ʿUmar Khayyām. Elwell-Sutton has identified this meter as "*hazaj mosaddas maḥdūf*."

39. Rypka, *History of Iranian Literature*, 234, concludes: "[I]t is difficult to place him chronologically . . ."

40. Cited by Rashīd Yāsamī in his *"muqadimma"* to Bābā Ṭāhir, *Dīvān-i Kāmil-i Bābā Ṭāhir-i ʿUryān-i Hamadānī*, 14.

41. Elwell-Sutton, "Bābā Ṭāher," 296–97.

42. Ibid.

43. Heron-Allen, *Lament of Bábá Ṭáhir.*

44. Reprinted many times as *Dīvan-i Kāmil-i Bābā Ṭāhir-i ʿUryān-i Hamadānī.*

45. ʿAyn al-Quḍāt Hamadānī, *Nāma-hā-yi ʿAyn al-Quḍāt-i Hamadānī*, 2:258.

46. Nasrollah Pourjavady, *ʿAyn al-Quḍāt wa ustādān-i ū*, 102 n. 2, points to this possibility, without offering a definitive answer.

47. For example, the Russian scholar Valentin Zhukovski alludes to an alleged meeting between Bābā Ṭāhir and another Hamadānian resident, the famed philosopher Abū ʿAlī Sīnā (d. 1036). This Russian article appeared in vol. 13 of *Zapiski* of the Oriental Section of the Imperial Russian Archaeological Society (1901, 104–8). E. G. Browne referred to this article in *Literary History of Persia*, 2:259 n. 1, 2:261.

48. Possibly a corruption of Ḥamshād. Safa, *Tārīkh-i adabiyāt dar irān*, 2:383 n. 2, believes this name to be an abbreviation for Aḥmad-Shāh or Aḥmad-Shād.

49. Rāwandī, *Rāḥat al-ṣudūr*, 98–99. See also Browne, *Literary History of Persia*, 2:260.

50. For some examples, refer to Elwell-Sutton, "Bābā Ṭāher," 296–97; Safa, *Tārīkh-i adabiyāt dar irān*, 2:383; Browne, *Literary History of Persia*, 2:260; Storey-de Blois, *Persian Literature*, 5(1): 96. The lone exception is Julie Scott Meisami, who has also translated this narrative in *Persian Historiography*, 243. She calls it "clearly apocryphal" and correctly recognizes the narrative as one of a "virtual investiture of a pious *pīr*." She also points out that the narrative is not featured in Nīshāpūrī, to whom Rāwandī is much indebted.

51. Dabashi, "Historical Conditions of Persian Sufism," 155.

52. See, for example, Aḥmad Ghazālī's statement that "the beginning of love is when the seed of beauty is seen in the ground of the heart's solitude with the hand of witnessing. Then it is nurtured under the radiance of *naẓār*." Ghazālī, *Sawāniḥ*, 39. The above translation is modified from Pourjavady, *Sawānih*, 41.

53. Browne, *Literary History of Persia*, 2:261. He renders the phrase which I have translated as "Bābā Ṭāhir, the enthralled soul" in the following manner: "Bábá Ṭáhir, who was somewhat crazy in his manner . . ."

54. Niẓām al-Mulk-Darke, *Book of Government*, 161.

55. A memorable episode is that of Ruzbihān Baqlī appearing to a Turkish Atabeg in a dream, and saying (while grabbing the Atabeg's ears, nonetheless!): "Turk! You will not sit in Authority without getting your punishment!" See Ernst, *Ruzbihan Baqli*, 134.

56. The conclusion of the Qurʾanic verse 16:90.

57. For a thoughtful reflection on *iḥsān* through this ḥadīth, see Murata and Chittick, *Vision of Islam*, xxv–xxxix.

58. Rāwandī, *Rāḥat al-ṣudūr*, 99.

59. Other political figures included in the *Asrār al-tawḥīd* include the governor of

Khurāsān (*Asrār al-tawḥīd*, 1:89); the *shaḥna* (lieutenant or policeman) of Nīshāpūr (*Asrār al-tawḥīd*, 1:111); the heads of villages (*Asrār al-tawḥīd*, 1:181–82); and other early Saljūq figures such as Ibrāhīm Īnāl (*Asrār al-tawḥīd*, 1:116–17).

60. The best and most recent edition of this text is Jamāl al-Dīn Abū Rūḥ Luṭf Allāh ibn Abī Saʿīd ibn Abī Saʿd, *Ḥālāt wa sukhanān-i Abū Saʿīd-i Abū ʾl-Khayr,* edited by Muḥammad Riḍā Shafīʿī-Kadkanī.

61. Before Shafīʿī-Kadkanī's edition, the common edition of this text was the version edited by Zabihollah Safa. There are a number of translations available. (See the bibliography under Ibn Munawwar, Muḥammad.) Both the French and the Arabic translations rely on the older (and somewhat inferior) Safa edition. John O'Kane based his translation on Safa but also took the Shafīʿī-Kadkanī edition into consideration.

62. See the assessment of the great scholar of Persian literature Zabihollah Safa, who stated: "*Asrār al-tawḥīd* is one of the undeniable masterpieces of Persian prose." He went on to praise the work's clarity of composition, lack of artificially ornate style, usage of authentic Persian vocabulary, and charm of narrative. *Tārīkh-i adabiyāt dar irān*, 2:982.

63. Among the many turbulent events depicted at the time of the hagiographer's composition are the repeated raids of the Ghuzz tribes into Khurāsān, and their capture of Sultan Sanjar. See Ibn Munawwar, *Asrār al-tawḥīd*, 1:349–51, 378.

64. Ibn Munawwar, *Asrār al-tawḥīd*, 1:95.

65. Ibid., 1:96–98.

66. Ibid., 1:58–59.

67. Cornell, *Realm of the Saint*, 63.

68. For one more example, see Ibn Munawwar, *Asrār al-tawḥīd*, 1:89, where Muḥammad ibn Manṣūr is depicted as mentioning that he had been appointed by Shaykh Abu Saʿīd as the governor of Khurāsān, a post he held for fifty years.

69. In this context, ʿIrāq probably includes both the "Arab ʿIrāq" and the "ʿAjam ʿIrāq."

70. Ibn Munawwar, *Asrār al-tawḥīd*, 1:156.

71. Ibid., 1:157.

72. Ibid., 1:158.

73. For a particularly thoughtful analysis of the human-Divine relationship in Islam, refer to the work of the late Japanese scholar Toshihiko Izutsu, *God and Man in the Koran*, 138 and 231. Izutsu describes the way in which, in the Qurʾan, the concept of *shukr* ("thankfulness" or "gratitude") becomes a religious concept. A human being is intended to reflect on God's *āyāt* ("signs") using the faculty of the *ʿaql* ("reasoning," "intellect"). The proper response to God's overwhelming Goodness and Mercy, then, becomes that of *shukr*. Izutsu expanded on some of these themes in his equally thought-provoking work, *Ethico-Religious Concepts in the Qurʾan*.

74. It is a part of extra-Qurʾanic Islamic lore that upon death, every person will be met and questioned by two angels (*nakīr* and *munkar*). These angels will ask the person about the Prophet, before moving on to other interrogations. According to some accounts, the angels will assume beautiful or horrific forms during this questioning, with the forms corresponding to the beauty of the deeds "sent forth" by the recently deceased prior to his/her death.

75. Ibn Munawwar, *Asrār al-tawḥīd*, 1:115–16.

76. Ibid., 1:96–99, mentions that in one day the Shaykh sent his followers seven times to the businessman for various items needed in the feast.

77. The trope-laden nature of this narrative is evident by recalling that both numbers (4,000 and 400) are multiples of forty, a frequently encountered trope in hagiographies.

78. Ibn Munawwar, *Asrār al-tawḥīd*, 1:90.

79. Paden, *Religious Worlds*, 73: "[M]yth is not solely a matter of representation . . . It is always paradigmatic, authoritative, and applicable . . . Myth as world script not only explains the world but also constructs and governs it."

80. Ibn Munawwar, *Asrār al-tawḥīd*, 1:179.

81. Refer to the Qur'anic presentation of this covenant in 7:172, and the famous verse *alastu bi-rabbikum*, "Am I not your Cherishing Lord?"

82. In early Sufism, Sufis were often referred to as the "folk" (*al-qawm*) or the "party" (*ṭā'ifa*). The terminology of Sufi *ṭarīqa* was developed later.

83. Ibn Munawwar, *Asrār al-tawḥīd*, 1:365–66. Every Muslim would be required to memorize at least the *Fātiḥa* (opening chapter of the Qur'an) for the daily prayers. It is hard to believe that a person would memorize the obscure forty-eighth chapter without also having committed the *Fātiḥa* to memory. Obviously, the point of this narrative is not its historicity, but rather the insight of the saint in foreseeing an event that would take place decades after his own death.

84. Ibid., 1:365.

85. Ibid.

86. For some of the earliest Western studies on Aḥmad-i Jām, see Ivanow, "Biography of Shaykh Aḥmad-i Jām," 291–365, as well as Meier, "Zur Biographie Aḥmad-i Ǧām's und zur Quellenkunde von Ǧāmī's *Nafaḥātu 'l-uns*," 47–67.

87. The hagiography of Shāh ibn Shujā' Kirmānī (d. after 270/884) contains very similar narratives about Shāh Shujā''s son, who had been a drunkard before his conversion. See Farīd al-Dīn 'Aṭṭar, *Tadhkirat al-awliyā'*, 378. Also see Arberry's partial translation of 'Aṭṭār's work, *Muslim Saints and Mystics*, 182–83.

88. Ghaznavī, *Maqāmāt-i ẓhanda pīl*, 104. This account contains a charming record of some of the saint's old drinking fellows who found the repentant saint making life difficult for them.

89. Jāmī, *Nafaḥāt al-uns*, 363.

90. Ghaznavī, *Maqāmāt-i ẓhanda pīl*, 162–65.

91. Meier, "Aḥmad-i D̲jām," 283.

92. Jāmī, *Nafaḥāt al-uns*, 364. In Jāmī's account, Abū Ṭāhir is actually described as being Abū Sa'īd's own son. The mythical *khirqa* is said to have been passed on from Abū Bakr Ṣiddīq through twenty-two generations of saints.

93. This would appear to be a pun on Aḥmad-i Jām's own name, being the same as one of the names of the Prophet Muḥammad.

94. Aḥmad-i Jām, *Dīvān-i Shaykh Aḥmad-i Jām*, 317–18.

95. 'Alī Fāḍil, "muqaddama-yi muṣaḥḥiḥ [editor's introduction]" to *Miftāḥ al-najāt*, 17. Fāḍil acknowledges that Aḥmad-i Jām in all likelihood did compose poetry, but rejects the attribution of any of the various manuscripts of *Dīvān* to Aḥmad-i Jām himself.

96. Another example of this might be found in the incredible popularity of the *Munājāt* of Khwāja ʿAbd Allāh Anṣārī, which has little in common with many of the austere, and theologically polemical, writings of the Ḥanbalī mystic.

97. Meier, "Aḥmad-i D̲j̲ām," 283: "The sources speak also of a personal connection with Sultan Sand̲j̲ar."

98. The inclusion of this remark indicates a pious editor's addition.

99. Aḥmad-i Jām, *Rawḍat al-mudhnibīn*, 3.

100. Ibid., 3–4.

101. *Farr* is a term that goes back to pre-Islamic Iranian heritage. It was conceived of as a halo which surrounded the ancient Persian king-prophets. References to *farr* abounded in the literature of this period. For an example see Niẓām al-Mulk–Darke, *Book of Government*, 61. See also Yarshater, "Iranian Common Beliefs."

102. Aḥmad-i Jām, *Rawḍat al-mudhnibīn*, 4.

103. Ibid., 5.

104. Ibid., 8.

105. It is interesting to note that while much of the discourse of "doctrine" is concerned with identifying, labeling, and punishing "innovations" (*bidʿa*), in a real sense it is the very term "doctrine" that represents an innovation from the Qurʾanic emphasis on "faith" (*imān*). It is worth recalling here Wilfred Cantwell Smith's distinction between the terms "belief" and "faith" in *Faith and Belief*.

106. Ghaznavī, *Maqāmāt-i ẓhanda pīl*. For the English translation, see Moayyad and Lewis, *Colossal Elephant and His Spiritual Feats*.

107. Meier, "Aḥmad-i D̲j̲ām," 284.

108. In addition to the above, ʿAlī Fāḍil, the editor of the *Maqāmāt*, believes that Sultan Sanjar visited the *turbat* of Aḥmad-i Jām.

109. Ghaznavī, *Maqāmāt-i ẓhanda pīl*, 61.

110. Juwaynī [Juvaini], *Jahān-gushā-yi Juwaynī*, translated in Boyle, *The History of the World-Conqueror*, 2:681–82. [Henceforth Juvaini-Boyle] Heshmat Moayyad, the editor of the Persian edition of the *Maqāmāt*, also reports that the story is included in *Ḥabīb al-siyar*.

111. Juvaini-Boyle, *History of the World-Conqueror*, 2:682.

112. The lowly socioeconomic and knowledge status of the servant, of course, is underscored by the depiction of him as carrying shoes, the objects that one has to toss aside before entering sacred spaces. Shoes are also associated with feet, symbolically the lowest and basest parts of the human body that are in contact with filth and dirt.

113. Ghaznavī, *Maqāmāt-i ẓhanda pīl*, 62. (emphasis mine)

114. Ibid., 62–63.

115. Ibid., 46–47.

116. ʿAlī Fāḍil, *"muqaddama"* to Aḥmad-i Jām, *Miftāḥ al-najāt*, 31.

117. Ibid.

118. A cursory list of such descendants would include Shaykh Quṭb al-Dīn Muhammad, Ḥibbat al-Raḥmān, Khwāja Abū ʾl-Fatḥ, Khwāja Raḍī al-Dīn Aḥmad, and Khwāja Ḍiyāʾ al-Dīn Yūsuf Jāmī. See ʿAlī Fāḍil, *"muqaddama"* to Aḥmad-i Jām, *Anīs al-tāʾibīn*, 24–27.

119. ʿAlī Fāḍil, *"muqaddama"* to Aḥmad-i Jām, *Miftāḥ al-najāt*, 31.

120. ʿAlī Fāḍil, *"muqaddama"* to Aḥmad-i Jām, *Anīs al-tāʾibīn*, 29 n. 2. Humāyūn is said to have composed a heartfelt poem to the great saint after having suffered defeat at the hands of Shīr Shāh Afghānī:

> Your court (*dargāh*) and your door are the qibla of all humanity.
> Cast an amorous glance, through your grace, O protector of all . . .

121. ʿAlī Fāḍil informs us that Khwānd-Mīr, the author of *Ḥabīb al-siyar*, offers praises for this Muʿīn al-Dīn Jāmī.

122. While the clearest reference would seem to be that of being gathered under the banner of the Prophet Muḥammad, the pun on the name Aḥmad, being both a name of the Prophet as well as that of Aḥmad-i Jām, should also be noted.

123. Cited by ʿAlī Fāḍil, *"muqaddama"* to Aḥmad-i Jām, *Rawḍat al-mudhnibīn*, 34.

124. Ibid., 36.

125. Ibid. At least one reason the historicity of such an event may be legitimately questioned is that the very hagiography of Sadīd al-Dīn, the *Maqāmāt*, records an identical narrative in which not Sanjar but a certain ruler named Ḥalīm performs the exact same task. In the narrative Ḥalīm is identified as one who was "serving Sanjar." It seems that in subsequent hagiographies it was deemed more dramatic to have Sanjar himself fulfill such a role.

126. ʿAlī Fāḍil, *"muqaddama"* to Aḥmad-i Jām, *Rawḍat al-mudhnibīn*, 36. While even a superficial reading of Saljūq history would contradict the claim that "none harmed" Sanjar during his reign, the point of the hagiographic narrative is to make a connection between a prosperous reign and devotion to a Sufi spiritual master.

Chapter Six

1. Said, "Secular Criticism," 241.

2. The most insightful secondary source on the life of Khwāja ʿAbd Allāh Anṣārī remains the classic study of Beaurecueil, *Khawādja ʿAbdullāh Anṣārī (396–481 H./1006–1089), Mystique Ḥanbalite*. A. G. Ravān-Farhādī has translated the above work into Persian as *Sargudhasht-i Pīr-i Harāt, Khwāja ʿAbd Allāh Anṣārī Harawī*. Ravān-Farhādī has also published an English work based substantially on the above, titled *ʿAbdullah Ansari of Herat*.

3. Beaurecueil, "Al-Anṣārī al-Harawī."

4. Farmanish, *Aḥwāl wa āthār-i ʿAyn al-Quḍāt*, 64.

5. Bertels, *Taṣawwuf wa adabīyāt-i taṣawwuf*, 426.

6. See Arberry, *Sufi Martyr*, 9: "In the following pages an account is given of the life, works and death of a third Sufi martyr, comparable in spiritual insight and tragic end with al-Ḥallāj and al-Suhrawardī . . ."

7. This phrase is taken from Lewisohn's insightful essay on ʿAyn al-Quḍāt, "In Quest of Annihilation," 285–336.

8. Mīyāna, "the middle," seems to have been called so due to its location halfway between Tabrīz and Marāgha.

9. Ibn Samʿānī's account is recorded in al-Subkī, *Ṭabaqāt al-shāfiʿīya*, 5:256. As I will discuss further, this hagiographic trope only foreshadows many later ones in ʿAyn al-Quḍāt's own life, claiming that he was killed in front of his own *madrasa*.

10. ʿAyn al-Quḍāt, *Tamhīdāt*, 250.

11. Al-Subkī, *Ṭabaqāt al-shāfiʿīya*, 6:151. There must have been a close connection between ʿAyn al-Quḍāt's father and Shīrāzī, even the likelihood that they accompanied each other on a trip to Khurāsān.

12. Samʿānī, *al-Ansāb*, 5:426, cited in Najīb Māyil Haravī, *Khāṣṣīyat-i āyinagī*, 4; see also Al-Subkī, *Ṭabaqāt al-shāfiʿīya*, 6:151.

13. Arberry, *Sufi Martyr*, 70.

14. Gohlman, *Life of Ibn Sina*, 33–35. Ibn Sīnā asserts that he was confounded after reading Aristotle's *Metaphysics* until a salesman in the booksellers' quarter appeared out of nowhere, offering him Fārābī's text.

15. ʿAyn al-Quḍāt, *Zubdat al-ḥaqāʾiq*, 6.

16. Ibid.

17. Ibid.

18. Ibid., 7.

19. Farmanish, *Aḥwāl wa āthār*, 16.

20. ʿAyn al-Quḍāt, *Zubdat al-ḥaqāʾiq*, 6–7.

21. Jāmī, *Nafaḥāt al-uns*, 418.

22. Riḍā Qulī-Khān Hidāyat, *Majmaʿ al-fuṣaḥāʾ*, ed. Maẓāhir Muṣaffāʾ, 2 vols., (Tehran: Amīr Kabīr, 1339–1440/1960–61), 1:145; cited in Haravī, *Khāṣṣīyat-i āyinagī*, 11 n. 5.

23. Haravī, *Khāṣṣīyat-i āyinagī*, 11 n. 5.

24. Dabashi, "Historical Condition of Persian Sufism," 146, asserts that "the character and significance of Ghazālī's brother, Shaykh Aḥmad Ghazālī, are dwarfed next to his far superior brother . . ." This is unwarranted, particularly given Aḥmad's own accomplishments as a Sufi, a preacher, and also the vast set of hagiographic narratives that assert his spiritual superiority over his brother. For an extensive list of these, see Ghazālī, *Majmūʿa-yi āthār-i fārsī-yi Aḥmad-i Ghazālī*, 27–29. Dabashi's claim (*Truth and Narrative*, 213) that Aḥmad did not frequent Hamadān can easily be dismissed through a number of other accounts, independent of ʿAyn al-Quḍāt. Aḥmad must have visited Hamadān and held public sermons there. See, for example, al-Subkī, *Ṭabaqāt al-shāfiʿīya*, 6:60, where a certain al-Ḥāfiẓ al-Salafī recalls having attended one such *majlis waʿẓ* in Hamadān and having been in the same *ribāṭ* with Aḥmad. One can thus safely assume that Aḥmad had a Sufi hospice in Hamadān, which he frequented. This would be completely consistent with ʿAyn al-Quḍāt's own account in *Tamhīdāt*, 250, recalling his father in a khānaqāh with Aḥmad. All these accounts refute Dabashi's claim.

25. Nasr, *Three Muslim Sages*, 150 n. 15.

26. ʿAyn al-Quḍāt, *Zubdat al-ḥaqāʾiq*, English translation by Jah, *Zubdat al-ḥaqāʾiq of ʿAyn al-Quḍāh al-Hamadānī*.

27. For an example of sources confusing the two, see Mīrzā Muḥammad ʿAlī Mudarris, *Rayḥānat al-adab fī tarājim al-maʿrūfīn bi ʾl-kunya aw ʾl-laqab*, (Tabrīz, n.d.), cited in Afrāsīyābī, *Sulṭān al-ʿushshāq*, 29.

28. ʿAyn al-Quḍāt, *Tamhīdāt*, 193.

29. The first two volumes were edited by ʿAlī-naqī Munzawī and ʿAfīf ʿUsayrān, and published as *Nāma-hā-yi ʿAyn al-Quḍāt Hamadānī*. The third volume, edited by ʿAlī-naqī Munzawī, was published in 1377/1998. The third volume features a lengthy (274 pages!) introduction by Munzawī and is deeply flawed by categories used in classifying

ʿAyn al-Quḍāt as quite literally an "Ismāʿīlī gnostic" (*gnusīst-i bāṭinī*). Furthermore, the work displays a tendency that is all too common within contemporary Iranian scholarship: an anachronistic Iranian nationalism that (p. 58) retrospectively analyzes events of twelfth and thirteenth-centuries as a "nationalistic tension" (*kashākish-hā-yi millī*) between Iranians, Arabs, and Turks.

30. ʿAyn al-Quḍāt, *Shakwa ʾl-gharīb*. Translated by Arberry, *Sufi Martyr*.

31. *Risāla-yi lawāʾiḥ*, attributed to Abū ʾl-Maʿālī ʿAbd Allāh ibn Muḥammad ibn ʿAlī ibn al-Ḥasan ibn ʿAli al-Mīyānajī al-Hamadānī, known as ʿAyn al-Quḍāt.

32. See Böwering, "ʿAyn-al-Qożāt," 142.

33. Nāgawrī [attributed erroneously to ʿAyn al-Quḍāt], *Lawāʾiḥ*, 41.

34. Cited in Afrāsīyābī, *Sulṭān al-ʿushshāq*, 115.

35. Böwering, "ʿAyn-al-Qożāt," 143, considers the text "spurious." Seyyed Hossein Nasr attributes the text to Shaykh al-Ishrāq. See Nasr, "Muqaddama-yi muṣaḥḥiḥ," in Sohravardi, *Majmūʿa-yi muṣannafāt-i shaykh al-ishrāq*, 3:57–60.

36. For a complete list of these works, see Arberry, *Sufi Martyr*, 12–13.

37. Cited in Farmanish, *Aḥwāl wa āthār*, 60 n. 1. This treatise can be no other than the *Shakwa ʾl-gharīb*.

38. I.e., God. *Dūst* ("friend") in Persian Sufi writings is usually a code word for God.

39. Among other sources, this apocryphal poem is quoted by Amīn Aḥmad Rāzī, author of the *Haft Iqlīm*. Cited in Afrāsīyābī, *Sulṭān al-ʿushshāq*, 18. Also see the account in Farmanish, *Aḥwāl wa āthār*, 68, citing *Tadhkira-yi ʿurafāt*.

40. Muḥammad Maʿṣūm Shīrāzī, better known as Maʿṣūm ʿAlī Shāh, *Ṭarāʾiq al-ḥaqāʾiq*, 2:568–72.

41. The identity of this "Badīʿ al-Mutakallim" is something of a mystery; that is, if one is to even expect him to represent an actual historical personality. It is somewhat tempting to try and connect him to a Badīʿ (d. 535/1140), also from Hamadān, who was contemporary with ʿAyn al-Quḍāt. This Aḥmad ibn Saʿd ibn ʿAlī ibn al-Ḥasan ibn Qāsim, al-Hamadhānī, known as Badīʿ, is mentioned in al-Subkī's *Ṭabaqāt al-shāfiʿīya*, 6:17–18. However, since he is not specifically identified as a "theologian," it would be pure speculation to assert that he is in fact the character named in the above narrative. My reading of the narrative is that, apart from the historicity of the narrative, this myth represents three facets of ʿAyn al-Quḍāt's thought, all of which are in fact historically accurate: first, his dismissive attitude towards theologians; second, his willingness to incorporate what I (following Marshall Hodgson) will later present as "the best insights" of any school of thought into his own discourse; and third, his willing utilization of the language of love in referring to God as "the Beloved." This provides us with another opportunity to see the usefulness of not dismissing hagiographic narratives, but of reading them closely for other information apart from that of a positivistic historical nature.

42. In the text, Badīʿ actually calls the term a technical one used by the "sages" (*ḥukamāʾ*), a term that was also used for philosopher-physicians.

43. Farmanish, *Aḥwāl wa āthār*, 68.

44. For Nasafī's usage of this endearing title, see Nasafī, *Insān al-kāmil*, 403. Afrāsīyābī relied upon the same phrase in titling his monograph on ʿAyn al-Quḍāt.

45. Farmanish, *Aḥwāl wa āthār*.

46. See for example, Afrāsīyābī, *Sulṭān al-ʿushshāq*, 201–91, which reaches back to the early period of Islamic history. The discussion is tainted by a Shīʿī perspective which is compounded by Iranian *shuʿūbīsm*.

47. Pourjavady, *ʿAyn al-quḍāt wa ustādān-i ū*.

48. Ernst, *Words of Ecstasy*, 73–84.

49. Lewisohn, "In Quest of Annihilation."

50. Dabashi, *Truth and Narrative*, 3.

51. ʿAyn al-Quḍāt, *Nāma-hā*, 1:216.

52. Dabashi, "Historical Conditions of Persian Sufism," 150.

53. Dabashi, *Truth and Narrative*, 120–21.

54. Hodgson, *Venture of Islam*, 2:153.

55. Dabashi, *Truth and Narrative*, 36.

56. Safi, "Sufi Path of Love," 221–66.

57. Niẓām ad-Din Awliya, *Morals for the Heart*, 177.

58. Ḥamīd Qalandar, *Khayr al-majālis*, 97, 195.

59. I am grateful to Zia Inayat Khan for having brought this connection to my attention.

60. See Rukn al-Dīn's unique bibliography at the end of his *Shamāʾil al-atqiyāʾ*. This list has been translated and published as an appendix by Ernst, *Eternal Garden*, 251–63, entitled "A Sufi Bookshelf: The Bibliography of Rukn al-Dīn Dabīr Kāshānī." In looking through this extensive list of 257 Sufi sources, we find *Tamhīdāt, Zubdat al-ḥaqāʾiq*, and others from ʿAyn al-Quḍāt.

61. A selection of his *sharḥ*, "commentary," was published in Iran as an appendix (p. 355–417) to ʿAyn al-Quḍāt's *Tamhīdāt*. The full commentary has been published in India; see Gīsū Dirāz, *Sharḥ zubdat al-ḥaqāʾiq, al-maʿrūf bi sharḥ-i Tamhīdāt*.

62. Schimmel, *Mystical Dimensions of Islam*, 348.

63. Khwārazmī, *Jawāhir al-asrār*, 1:109. In this text, a *Masnavī* commentary, Khwārazmī identifies the *silsila* of Sufis who have come before him. He devotes a long section to Aḥmad Ghazālī, and follows this up with a hagiographic recollection of ʿAyn al-Quḍāt: "And one of the disciples of that manifestation of Divine graces is Imām ʿAyn al-Quḍāt Hamadānī. He had a Christ-like temperament (*ʿīsawī mashrab*). His perfection and wondrous deeds are clear. Through Divine Power, even those of giving life and taking it away became manifest in him."

64. Jāmī, *Nafaḥāt al-uns*, 418. Jāmī identifies ʿAyn al-Quḍāt as having had the spiritual company of Shaykh Muḥammad ibn Ḥamūya and Shaykh Imām Aḥmad Ghazālī. Praising ʿAyn al-Quḍāt, Jāmī states, "External and Spiritual perfection and graces are evident from his compositions in both Arabic and Persian. There are few people who have unveiled realities and explained subtleties the way that he has. Among extraordinary wondrous deeds performed by him is bringing people to life, and taking their life away. There were many letters and correspondences between him and His Holiness Shaykh Aḥmad [Ghazālī]." Jāmī also reports the well-known narrative of ʿAyn al-Quḍāt's spiritual crisis prior to meeting Aḥmad Ghazālī, and the *samāʿ* episode with Aḥmad Ghazālī in which a person allegedly was made to die and brought back to life. Jāmī clearly identifies ʿAyn al-Quḍāt as a Sufi, placing his entry immediately after that

of Shaykh Abū ʾl-Ḥasan Bustī and his disciples Shaykh Ḥasan Sakkāk Simnānī and Muḥammad ibn Hamuway al-Juwaynī, and immediately prior to two of ʿAyn al-Quḍāt's own masters, Shaykh Baraka of Hamadan and Shaykh Fatḥa. To a premodern Sufi like Jāmī, ʿAyn al-Quḍāt clearly belonged in such a silsila of Persian Sufis.

65. Nasr, *Sadr al-Din Shirazi*, 74. In an unpublished conference paper titled "Sufism and Philosophy in Mulla Sadra" at the World Congress on the Philosophy of Mulla Sadra in Tehran, May 23–27, 1999, Carl Ernst documented that Mullā Ṣadrā has ten separate references to ʿAyn al-Quḍāt.

66. Gölpınarlı, *Mevlânâ Müzesi*. ʿAyn al-Quḍāt's *Tamhīdāt* was read along with the *Jawāhir al-asrār* ("The Jewels of Secrets") of Ḥusayn-i Khwārazmī (d. 840/1436), an important commentary on Rumi's *Masnavi*. See Gölpınarlı, *Mevlânâ Müzesi*, 2:iv. Reference in the *majmūʿa*, "collection," itself is to page 52. In an even more direct example, Gölpınarlı refers to another *majmūʿa* where the Letters (*Nāma-hā*) of ʿAyn al-Quḍāt have been preserved next to the *Masnavi* of Rumi itself. See Gölpınarlı, *Mevlânâ Müzesi*, 3:xvi. Reference in this *majmūʿa* is to pages 362–364.

67. Arberry, *Sufi Martyr*, 9.

68. Böwering, "ʿAyn-al-Qożāt Hamadānī," 140.

69. Corbin, *History of Islamic Philosophy*, 202.

70. This tendency is characteristic of Dabashi's approach to ʿAyn al-Quḍāt.

71. Hodgson, *Venture of Islam*, 2:154.

72. This is indeed how al-Subkī introduces him, stating that he was "of the Khurāsānī folk." Among contemporary scholars, Nasrollah Pourjavady also connects ʿAyn al-Quḍāt to Khurāsānian Sufism, particularly that of Aḥmad Ghazālī.

73. ʿAyn al-Quḍāt, *Nāma-hā*, 2:204.

74. Dabashi, "Historical Conditions," 144.

75. ʿAyn al-Quḍāt, *Tamhīdāt*, 280–81.

76. Ibid., 255–56.

77. ʿAyn al-Quḍāt, *Nāma-hā*, 2:457 and 124.

78. For a thorough discussion, see Pourjavady, *ʿAyn al-Quḍāt wa ustādān-i ū*.

79. ʿAyn al-Quḍāt, *Nāma-hā*, 1:79.

80. Ibid., 2:311.

81. This title would seem to refer to Ghazālī's *al-Maqṣad al-asnā*.

82. ʿAyn al-Quḍāt, *Nāma-hā*, 2:314.

83. Ibid., 2:316.

84. Ibid., 2:319.

85. Ibid., 2:330.

86. Ibid., 2:316.

87. This is an important point given ʿAyn al-Quḍāt's emphasis that real insight can best be transmitted orally, from a living spiritual teacher.

88. ʿAyn al-Quḍāt, *Nāma-hā*, 2:488.

89. This "a firmly rooted scholar" (*ʿālimī rāsikh*) is the same term that ʿAyn al-Quḍāt had previously used in referring to ten people, including himself and the Ghazālī brothers. It would seem then that he has in mind a situation where a very small number of spiritually advanced scholars would master theology, to defend the tradition

against charges of heresy. However, theology would not be taught to common scholars or nonscholars.

90. ʿAyn al-Quḍāt, *Nāma-hā*, 2:487–88.

91. Ghazālī, "Kitāb al-ʿilm," in *Iḥyāʾ ʿulūm al-dīn*, translated in Faris, *Book of Knowledge*, 104.

92. ʿAyn al-Quḍāt, *Tamhīdāt*, 255.

93. Qurʾan 24:35.

94. ʿAyn al-Quḍāt, *Nāma-hā*, 2:113.

95. Ibid., 2:115.

96. It is worth mentioning that in the *Tamhīdāt*, 229, ʿAynal-Quḍāt offers a superbly ingenious explanation of the Prophet Muḥammad's "sin" as consisting of God's great love for him. He contrasted this with Iblīs' great sin, which was his great love for God.

97. Qurʾan 48:2.

98. Qurʾan 94:2–3

99. ʿAyn al-Quḍāt, *Nāma-hā*, 2:118.

100. Ibid., 2:119.

101. Ibid., 2:125.

102. The identity of these *shukūṣ-i thalātha* has proven utterly mysterious. The commentary of Gīsū Dirāz identifies them as the three realms of *malakūt, jabarūt*, and *lāhūt*. (See *Risāla-yi ʿishq-i ḥaqīqī*, 130). I would like to offer another reading. According to Dehkhoda's *Lughat-nāma* (new edition, 9:14183), the term *shakhṣ-i thālith* can refer to a third party in a dispute who offers a resolution without aligning himself totally with either side. It could well be the case that ʿAyn al-Quḍāt is calling on the reader to rise above the "first two parties" (being that of a *muslim* and a *kāfir*) and transcend to the "third perspective," that of one who is *both* "one who submits to God and is an infidel." In other words, he is recommending that the reader transcend the conventional dichotomies of faith and infidelity.

103. ʿAyn al-Quḍāt, *Tamhīdāt*, 350.

104. Ibid.

105. Shafīʿī-Kadkanī, "muqaddama" to *Asrār al-tawḥīd*, 1:43–46. Among other objections, Shafīʿī-Kadkanī points out that Abū Saʿīd is not known to have authored a text titled the *Maṣābiḥ*; that is it difficult to locate a time and place where Abū Saʿīd and Ibn Sīnā could have met; and that there is no report of this quotation in the current edition of the *Aḍḥawī*.

106. ʿAyn al-Quḍāt, *Tamhīdāt*, 167.

107. Ghazālī, *Munqidh min al-ḍalāl*, translated in Watt, *Faith and Practice of al-Ghazālī*, 37–38.

108. Ibid., 32.

109. ʿAyn al-Quḍāt, *Tamhīdāt*, 289.

110. Ibid., 350.

111. ʿAyn al-Quḍāt, *Nāma-hā*, 1:113.

112. Ibid., 1:105.

113. Bayhaqī, *Tatimma ṣiwān al-ḥikma*, 109; Bayhaqī, *Tārikh ḥukamāʾ al-islām*, 123.

114. Shahrazūrī, *Nuzhat al-arwāḥ wa rawḍat al-afrāḥ*, 397. This work, which is a *tadhkira* of philosophers culminating with Shaykh al-Ishrāq Suhrawardī, has only been avail-

able to me in print through the above Persian translation. Afrāsīyābi, *Sulṭān al-ʿushshāq*, 7 refers to a printing of the original Arabic, which I have not had access to.

115. A prominent example is Shaykh Abū Isḥāq Shīrāzī's critique of Niẓām al-Mulk in the context of the Niẓāmīya, which we encountered in chapter 3.

116. Al-Ghazālī, *Naṣīḥat al-mulūk*, 27.

117. ʿAyn al-Quḍāt, *Nāma-hā*, 1:244.

118. The phrase *min nutfa* occurs in nine places in the Qurʾan, such as 16:4. Contemporary modernist translations of the Qurʾan often interpret *nutfa* ("a little water") as "sperm."

119. ʿAyn al-Quḍāt, *Nāma-hā*, 2:339.

120. See for example, Rāwandī, *Rāḥat al-ṣudūr*, 125, where Malik-Shāh is described in these glowing terms.

121. ʿAyn al-Quḍāt, *Nāma-hā*, 2:166–67.

122. These last two names are references to two of ʿAyn al-Quḍāt's own disciples (ʿAzīz al-Dīn and Kāmil al-Dawla) at the Saljūq court.

123. ʿAyn al-Quḍāt, *Nāma-hā*, 2:427.

124. Ibid., 1:244.

125. Qurʾan 29:6.

126. ʿAyn al-Quḍāt, *Nāma-hā*, 2:375.

127. Ibid., 1:243.

128. Ibid., 1:34.

129. Ibid., 2:166.

130. Ibid., 2:57–58.

131. ʿAyn al-Quḍāt, *Nāma-hā*, 2:68. The last Qurʾanic citation is from 15:42.

132. We had noted a similar attempt to use the Qurʾan as a trump card in a narrative (albeit in the justification of the Saljūqs) in Rāwandī's account of Bābā Ṭāhir's meeting with Ṭughril. There the saint had commanded the Sultan to recall that "indeed God commands justice and virtue." (Qurʾan 16:90).

133. Qurʾan 4:143. The Qurʾanic passage is addressing the hypocrites (*munāfiqūn*), the same phrase ʿAyn al-Quḍāt uses in the beginning of this paragraph. Once again, he is demonstrating his own mastery of the Qurʾanic discourse.

134. Qurʾan 59:13.

135. Qurʾan 4:80.

136. ʿAyn al-Quḍāt, *Nāma-hā*, 1:46–47. The last citation is of course the famous Prophetic ḥadīth, except that again ʿAyn al-Quḍāt has reinterpreted the verse to imply that it is the spiritual teachers who are intended by the religious scholars to be the inheritors of the Prophet.

137. Ibid., 1:157.

138. Ibid., 1:234.

139. Ibid., 2:430.

140. Ibid., 2:430.

141. The most erudite example of this trend is Lewisohn, "In Quest of Annihilation."

142. Most Saljūq Turkish figures, at least in the early generations, were ignorant of Arabic.

143. ʿAyn al-Quḍāt, *Nāma-hā*, 2:483–88.

144. Ghazālī He authored the *al-Mustaẓhirī* treatise for the Caliph al-Mustaẓhir (ruled 1094–1118 C.E.). This text is better known as *Faḍāʾiḥ al-bāṭinīya*.

145. Juwaynī authored the *ʿAqīdat al-niẓāmīya*, in honor of Niẓām al-Mulk.

146. ʿAyn al-Quḍāt, *Tamhīdāt*, 251.

147. Ibid., 15.

148. ʿAyn al-Quḍāt, *Nāma-hā*, 2:432.

149. Ibid., 2:428.

150. Farmanish, *Ahwāl wa āthār*, 28.

151. There is some uncertainty about the correct transliteration of the powerful vizier's name. De Bruijn prefers Darguzīnī, while Dabashi renders the name as Daragazīnī. The correct form, according to Dehkhoda, *Lughat-nāma-yi Dehkhoda* (new edition, 7:10648), is Dargazīnī.

152. ʿAyn al-Quḍāt, *Tamhīdāt*, 15, makes mention of a certain "Imām Ḍiyāʾ al-Dīn."

153. Al-Bundārī, *Zubdat al-nuṣra*, 151, confirms this, calling Ṣafī al-Dīn "wālidī."

154. Ibid., 146–47.

155. Ibid., 144.

156. Ibid., 146.

157. Klausner, *Seljuk Vezirate*, 56.

158. Lambton, "Internal Structure of the Saljuq State," 251.

159. Al-Kātib al-Iṣfahānī himself confesses this in al-Bundārī, *Zubdat al-nuṣra*, 54: "This is the book that the vezir Anūshirwān had composed, and I have translated it into Arabic."

160. This point has also been recognized by Klausner, *Seljuk Vezirate*, 128 n. 100.

161. Ibid., 108.

162. Ibid.

163. Al-Bundārī, *Zubdat al-nuṣra*, 150.

164. Ibid., 19.

165. Ibid.

166. Ibid., 21.

167. Ibid., 22.

168. Ibid., 17.

169. Ibid., 18.

170. Mudarris Raḍawī, "Muqaddama-yi muṣaḥḥiḥ," *Dīvān-i Ḥakīm Abū ʾl-Majd Majdūd ibn Ādam Sanāʾī-yi Ghaznavī*, 97.

171. Sanāʾī, *Dīvān*, 119. The relationship between the two cannot be called one of straightforward patronage, as Sanāʾī did avoid face-to-face meetings with Dargazīnī, instead contenting himself to sending the latter poems. Mudarris Raḍawī records (Sanāʾī, *Dīvān*, 118–19) that in the Rabīʿ al-awwal of 518/1124, Dargazīnī came to Sarakhs to see the famed Sanāʾī, but the saintly poet apologetically refused.

172. Ibid., 122–23. The present printing of the *Dīvān* switches the second and fourth lines from the order in which they are presented in the Qummī text.

173. Ibid., 561–64.

174. Bruin, *Of Piety and Poetry*, 68–70.

175. ʿAyn al-Quḍāt, *Nāma-hā*, 2:50.

176. Farmanish, *Aḥwāl wa āthār*, 290–340, provides a detailed list of many of the poems cited by ʿAyn al-Quḍāt. Farmanish has traced a large number of these poems to Sanāʾī, and others to Aḥmad Ghazālī, Abū Saʿīd-i Abī ʾl-Khayr, Abū ʾl-Ḥasan Kharaqānī, etc.

177. Bayhaqī, *Tatimma ṣiwān al-ḥikma*, 117; Bayhaqī, *Tārīkh ḥukamāʾ al-islām*, 123. There is a Persian translation of the *Tatimma ṣiwān al-ḥikma*, which was completed by Nāṣir al-Dīn ibn ʿUmdat al-Mulk Muntajib al-Dīn Munshī Yazdī for the benefit of Ghiyāth al-Dīn Muḥammad, son of the famous vizier-scholar Rashīd al-Dīn Faḍl Allāh. Therefore, the translation in all likelihood dates from the period of Ghiyāth al-Dīn's vezirate, 725–36/1324–35. See pages 73–74 for ʿAyn al-Quḍāt's narrative in this Persian text.

178. It is perhaps indicative of the status and class consciousness of premodern Islamic sources that both Bayhaqī's *Tārīkh ḥukamāʾ al-islām* and Shahrazūrī's *Nuzhat al-arwāḥ* refer to the vizier as hailing not from the more respectable Dargazīn, but from the surrounding villages of Ansābādh or Astarābādh. Indeed, one can almost use the name the sources use in referring to the vizier (i.e., "Dargazīnī" or "Ansābādhī") as a measure of whether they are favorable towards him or not.

179. Arberry, *Sufi Martyr*, 70.

180. Al-Bundārī, *Zubdat al-nuṣra*, 151.

181. Al-Kātib al-Iṣfahānī, *Kharīdat al-qaṣr*, 58, cited in Farmanish, *Ahwāl wa āthār*, 65.

182. See for example, Arberry, *Sufi Martyr*, 33: "Yet the pronouncements of which they have disapproved in me are all to be found, in word and meaning, in the books of the Imam, the Proof of Islam, Abū Ḥāmid al-Ghazālī."

183. Ibid., 32.

184. Ibid., 33. ʿAyn al-Quḍāt explains this charge away by stating that he had merely intended by it that "he is the creator of all things."

185. Ibid., 34. Both of these charges are among the criteria for heresy that Ghazālī had identified.

186. Ibid. In defense of his own position, ʿAyn al-Quḍāt cites the Prophetic *ḥadīth* that "whoever dies without an imam, dies the death of a pagan."

187. Ibid., 38. In the *Tamhīdāt*, 251, he states that he has also been accused of claiming divinity, the next logical step in accusation once one has been charged with pretense to *nubuwwa*.

188. For ʿAyn al-Quḍāt's self-conscious reflection on this charge, see Arberry, *Sufi Martyr*, 34.

189. Ghazālī, *al-Munqidh*, translated in Watt, *Faith and Practice of Ghazālī*, 37.

190. For a wonderful bilingual edition and translation of this text, see al-Ghazālī, *Incoherence of the Philosophers*. For Ghazālī's thorough dismissal of the alleged pre-eternity of the world, see 12–46. On refuting the philosopher's statement that God does not know the particulars, see 137–146. On the philosopher's denial of bodily resurrection, see 212–29.

191. ʿAyn al-Quḍāt, *Tamhīdāt*, 251.

192. Ibid.

193. Among the sources are Amīn Aḥmad Rāzī's *Haft Iqlīm*, al-Subkī, *Ṭabaqāt al-shāfiʿīya*, and Imām Shihāb al-Dīn al-ʿAsqalānī, *Lisān al-mīzān*. See all of these citations in full in Afrāsīyābī, *Sulṭān al-ʿushshāq*, 15–16, 18.

194. See Böwering, "'Ayn al-Qożāt Hamadānī."

195. If they had known about it and those points had come up in the heresy trial, ʿAyn al-Quḍāt does not raise that point in the *Shakwā*.

196. See al-Subkī, *Ṭabaqāt al-shāfiʿīya*, cited in Afrāsīyābī, *Sulṭān al-ʿushshāq*, 11.

197. Ernst, *Words of Ecstasy*, 101, reports on the usage of the *naẓar al-maẓālim* in the trial of another Sufi, Nūrī (d. 295/907).

198. See Nielsen, *Secular Justice*.

199. Ibid., 7.

200. Amedroz, "Mazalim Jurisdiction," 656.

201. Lambton, "Internal Structure," 227.

202. Amedroz, "Mazalim Jurisdiction," 660.

203. Al-Bundārī, *Zubdat al-nuṣra*, 153–54, records Dargazīnī as "*istawla ʿala amlākinā wa amwālinā*." Al-Kātib al-Iṣfahānī's personal involvement is once again betrayed by his usage of the phrase "our possessions."

204. Ibid., 167.

Conclusion

1. Said, "Secular Criticism", 242.

2. For a more elaborate articulation of this modality of interpreting Islam, see the essays in Safi, *Progressive Muslims*.

3. Among many other sources, see Khwānd-Mīr, *Dastūr al-wuzarāʾ*, 170.

4. See Browne, *Literary History*, 2:252–54.

5. Samarqandī, *Tadhkirat al-shuʿarāʾ*, 108.

6. Ibid., 106–8.

7. He points correctly to the dubious nature of the *Waṣāya* attributed to Nizam al-Mulk, which contains this narrative. The *Waṣāya*, in its present form, dates from the fifteenth century. See Browne, *Literary History*, 2:191 n. 2.

8. Browne, "Yet More Light on ʿUmar Khayyám," 409–20; Browne, *A Literary History*, 2:192.

9. One example of such works is Rizvi, *Nizam al-Mulk Tusi*, 13–19.

10. Ibn al-Athīr, *al-Kāmil fī 'l-tārīkh*, 10:98.

11. See, for example, Böwering, "'Ayn-al-Qożāt."

12. Cited in Farmanish, *Aḥwāl wa āthār*, 23, 76. The narrative is brought up under the events of the year 520/1126, the same year that Aḥmad Ghazālī passed away.

13. Among other accounts, Qazwīnī, *Āthār al-bilād*, contains an account in which the son of Sultan Malik-Shāh went to see Aḥmad Ghazālī, and Aḥmad kissed him on one cheek. When the prince returned to Malik-Shāh, he told him about what had happened. Malik-Shāh is said to have replied, "You have attained to rule of half the world. Had he kissed your other cheek as well, you would have had rule over the whole world." The original of the above narrative is cited in Ghazālī, *Majmūʿa-yi āthār-i fārsī-yi Aḥmad-i Ghazzālī*, 100–101.

14. For a fuller discussion of Aḥmad Ghazālī and the "school of love", including the practice of *shāhid-bāzī*, see Safi, "Sufi Path of Love," 221–66.

15. Ghazālī, *Majālis*, 13–14.

16. Hodgson, *Venture of Islam*, 3:204. Particularly illuminating are Hodgson's chapters "The Impact of the Great Western Transmutation: The Generation of 1789" (176–222) and "European World Hegemony: The Nineteenth Century" (223–48).

Appendix

1. Rāwandī, *Rāḥat al-ṣudūr*, 132.
2. Bayhaqī, *Tārīkh-i bayhaq*, 147, cited in Kasā'ī, *Madāris-i Niẓamīya*, 49.
3. Qazwīnī, *Tārīkh-i guzīda*, 447.
4. Lambton, "Internal Structure," 264.
5. Al-Bundārī, *Zubdat al-nuṣra*, 51; Ibn al-Athīr, *al-Kāmil fī 'l-tārīkh*, 10:98. For a full discussion of his life, see Āshtiyānī, *Vizārat*, 124–47.
6. Āshtiyānī, *Vizārat*, 202–21.
7. Ibn al-Athīr, *al-Kāmil fī 'l-tārīkh*, 10:418–19.
8. Āshtiyānī, *Vizārat*, 275.
9. Kasā'ī, *Madāris-i niẓāmīya*, 52.
10. Al-Bundārī, *Zubdat al-nuṣra*, 83.
11. Ibn al-Athīr, *al-Kāmil fī 'l-tārīkh*, 10:234–35.
12. Ibid., 10:262–63.
13. Al-Bundārī, *Zubdat al-nuṣra*, 72–73; Ibn al-Athīr, *al-Kāmil fī 'l-tārīkh*, 10:123–24.
14. Ibn al-Athīr, *al-Kāmil fī 'l-tārīkh*, 10:614.
15. Kasā'ī, *Madāris-i niẓāmīya*, 53.
16. Ibid.

Bibliography

E.I.^{2} = *Encyclopaedia of Islam*. New edition. Leiden: E. J. Brill, 1954–2004.

Primary sources
(where available, European translations are provided)

Aḥmad-i Jām (Zhanda Pīl). *Anīs al-tā'ibīn*. Edited by ʿAlī Fāḍil. Tehran: Chāpkhāna-yi Haydarī, 1368/1989.

———. *Dīvān-i Shaykh Aḥmad-i Jām (Zhanda Pīl)*. Edited by Aḥmad Karamī. Tehran: Nashriyāt-i Mā, 1365/1985.

———. *Miftāḥ al-najāt*. Edited by ʿAlī Fāḍil. Tehran: Bunyād-i Farhang-i Irān, 1347/1968. Reprint, Tehran: Pazhūhishgāh-i ʿUlūm-i Insānī wa Muṭāliʿāti Farhangī, 1373/1994.

———. *Rawḍat al-mudhnibīn*. Edited by ʿAlī Fāḍil. Tehran: Bunyād-i Farhang-i Irān, 1355/1976.

Al-ʿAlawī, Abū 'l-Maʿālī Muḥammad al-Ḥusaynī. *Bayān al-adyān dar sharḥ-i adyān wa madhāhib-i jāhilī wa islāmī*. Edited by ʿAbbās Iqbāl. Tehran: Ibn Sīnā, 1976.

Anṣārī, Khwāja ʿAbd Allāh. *Dhamm al-kalām*. Edited by Samīḥ Daghīm. Beirut: Dār al-Fikr al-Lubnānī, 1994.

———. *Manāzil al-sā'irīn*. Beirut: Dār al-Kutub al-ʿIlmīya, 1988.

———. *Munājāt*. Tehran: Intishārāt-i ʿIlmīya-yi Islāmīya, n.d. Translated by Wheeler M. Thackston, in Victor Danner and Wheeler Thackston, *Ibn ʿAta'illah: The Book of Wisdom; Kwaja Abdullah Ansari: Intimate Conversations*. New York: Paulist Press, 1978.

ʿAqīlī, Sayf al-Dīn Ḥājī ibn Niẓām. *Āthār al-wuzarā'*. Edited by Mīr Jalāl al-Dīn Ḥusaynī Urmavī "Muḥaddith." Tehran: Intishārāt-i Dānishgāh-i Tehrān, 1337/1959.

Āqsarā'ī, Maḥmūd ibn Muḥammad. *[Tārīkh-i salājiqa] Musāmarat al-akhbār wa musāyarat al-akhyār*. Edited by Osman Turan. Tehran: Intishārāt-i Asāṭīr, 1362/1983.

ʿAṭṭar, Farīd al-Dīn. *Tadhkirat al-awliyā'*. Edited by Muḥammad Istiʿlāmī. Tehran: Intishārāt-i Zavvār, 1347/1968. Reprint, 1372/1993. Partial English translation by A. J. Arberry, *Muslim Saints and Mystics*. London: Arkana, 1966.

ʿAyn al-Quḍāt, Abū 'l-Maʿālī ʿAbd Allāh al-Miyānajī al-Hamadānī. *Lawā'iḥ*. [See under Nāgawrī, Qāḍī Ḥamīd al-Dīn]

———. *Nāma-hā-yi ʿAyn al-Quḍāt-i Hamadānī*. 3 vols. Vols. 1–2 edited by ʿAlī-naqī Munzawī and Afif Osseiran. Tehran: Bunyād-i Farhang-i Irān, 1363/1983. Vol. 3 edited by ʿAlī-naqī Munzawī. Tehran: Intishārāt-i Asāṭīr, 1377/1998.

———. *Shakwā al-gharīb*. Edited with an introduction by Mohammed Ben Abd el-Jalil. *Journal Asiatique* 216. (Janvier–Mars 1930). Re-edited by Afif Osseiran. Tehran: Intishārāt-i Dānishgāh-i Tehran, 1961. Translated by A. J. Arberry as *A Sufi Martyr: The Apologia of ʿAin al-Quḍāt al-Hamadhānī*. London: George Allen and Unwin, 1969.

———. *Tamhīdāt*. Edited by Afif Osseiran [ʿAfīf ʿUsayrān]. 4th ed. Tehran: Intishārāt-i Manūchihrī, 1994. French translation by Christiane Tortel as *Les Tentations Métaphysiques*. Paris, Deux Océans, 1992.

———. *Zubdat al-Ḥaqāʾiq*. Edited by Afif Osseiran. Tehran: Intishārāt-i Dānishgāh-i Tehran, 1961. Translated by Omar Jah as *The Zubdat al-ḥaqāʾiq of ʿAyn al-Quḍāh al-Hamadānī: An Annotated English Translation from the Arabic*. Kuala Lumpur: International Institute of Islamic Thought and Civilization, 2000.

Bābā Ṭāhir. *Dīvān-i Kāmil-i Bābā Ṭāhir-i ʿUryān-i Hamadānī*. Edited by Wahīd-i Dastgirdī. Tehran: Majalla-yi Armaghān, 1322/1943. Reprint, with an introduction by Rashīd Yāsamī, Tehran: Kitābfurūshī-yi Adab, 1331/1952.

Bahr al-fawāʾid. [Anonymous] Edited by Muḥammad Taqī Dānishpazhūh. Tehran: Bungāh-i Tarjuma wa Nashr-i Kitāb, 1345/1966.

Al-Bāqillānī, Abū Bakr Muḥammad ibn al-Ṭayyib. *Al-Tamhīd fī ʾl-radd ʿalā ʾl-mulḥida al-muʿaṭṭala wa ʾl-rāfiḍa wa ʾl-khawārij wa ʾl-muʿtazila*. Edited by Maḥmūd Muḥammad al-Khuḍayrī. Beirut: Dār al-Fikr al-ʿArabī, 1947.

Bar Hebraeus, Gregory Abū ʾl-Faraj. *Chronography*. Translated by Ernest A. Wallis Budge as *The Chronography of Gregory Abu ʾl-Faraj, the Son of Aaron, the Hebrew Physician Commonly Known as Bar Hebraeus, Being the First Part of His Political History of the World*. Vol. 1 of English translation from Syriac. London: Oxford University Press, 1932.

Bayhaqī, ʿAlī ibn Zayd. *Tārīkh ḥukamāʾ al-islām*. Edited by Muḥammad Kurd ʿAlī. Damascus: Maṭbaʿa al-Tarraqī, 1946. Reprint, 1976.

———. *Tatimma ṣiwān al-ḥikma*. Edited by Rafīq al-ʿAjam. Beirut: Dār al-Fikr al-Lubnānī, 1994. The fourteenth-century Persian translation by Nāṣir al-Dīn ibn ʿUmdat al-Mulk Muntajib al-Dīn Munshī Yazdī published as *Durrat al-akhbār wa lamaʿat al-anwār* in Tehran-based journal *Majalla-yi Mihr* (5), 1318/1939.

Bayhaqī, Muḥammad ibn Ḥusayn Abū ʾl-Faḍl. *Tārīkh-i Bayhaqī*. 2 vols. Edited by W. H. Morley. Calcutta: College Press, 1862. Reprinted, Osnabrück: Biblio Verlag, 1981.

Al-Bundārī, al-Fatḥ b. ʿAlī b. Muḥammad al-Iṣfahānī. *Zubdat al-nuṣra*. [Abridgment of ʿImād al-Dīn Iṣfahānī's *Nuṣrat al-fatra*] Edited by M. Th. Houtsma in *Recueil de Textes Relatifs à l'Histoire des Seldjoucides*. Vol. 2, *Histoire des Seldjoucides de l'Iraq*. Leiden: E. J. Brill, 1889.

Al-Ghazālī, Abū Ḥāmid. *Faḍāʾiḥ al-bāṭinīya wa faḍāʾil al-mustaẓhirīya*. Edited by ʿAbd al-Raḥmān Badawī. Cairo: al-Dar al-Qawmīya, 1964. Translated in Richard J. McCarthy, *Freedom and Fulfillment*. Boston: Twayne Publishers, 1980. Reprint, Louisville, Ky.: Fons Vitae, 1999.

———. *Faḍāʾil al-anām min rasāʾil ḥujjat al-islām*. Edited by ʿAbbās Iqbāl Āshtiyānī. Tehran: Kitābkhāna-yi Sanāʾī, 1363/1984.

———. *Fatwā-yi Ḥujjat al-Islām Abū Ḥāmid Ghazālī dar bāra-yi samāʿ*. Edited by Nasrollah Pourjavady and included in "Chahār athar-i kūtāh-i fārsī az Abū Ḥāmid-i Ghazālī," *Maʿārif* 7:1 (1369/1990).

———. *Fayṣal al-tafriqa bayn al-islām wa ʾl-zandaqa*. Translated in Richard J. McCarthy, *Freedom and Fulfillment*. Boston: Twayne Publishers, 1980. Reprinted as *Al-Ghazālī: Deliverance from Error; Five Key Texts including His Spiritual Autobiography, al-Munqidh min al-ḍalāl*. Louisville, Ky.: Fons Vitae, 1999.

———. *Ḥimāqa ahl al-ibāḥa*. Edited by Otto Pretzl in *Die Streitschrift des Gazālī gegen die Ibāḥīja*. Munich, 1933. Reprint in *Zamīna-yi īrān-shināsī* (1364/1985), 91–118. Re-edited in Nasrollah Pourjavady, *Du Mujaddid*, 153–209. [Under Pourjavady]

———. *Iḥyāʾ ʿulūm al-dīn*. Cairo: Dār al-Diyān li ʾl-Turāth, 1987. The chapter titled "Kitāb al-ʿilm" translated by Nabih Amin Faris as *The Book of Knowledge*. Lahore: Sh. Muhammad Ashraf, 1966.

———. *al-Iqtiṣād fī ʾl-iʿtiqād*. Edited by ʿAli Bū Mulḥīm. Beirut: Dār al-Hilāl, 1993.

———. *Kīmīyāʾ-yi saʿādat*. 2 vols. Edited by Aḥmad Ārām. Tehran: Intishārāt-i Ganjīna, 1376/1997. Translated by Claud Field as *The Alchemy of Happiness*. Lahore: Sh. Muhammad Ashraf, 1987. [Reprint of earlier edition]

———. *al-Maqṣad al-asnā*. Edited by Fadlou A. Shehadi. Beirut: Dar el-Machreq, 1971. Translated by David Burrell and Nazih Daher as *Al-Ghazālī: The Ninety-Nine Beautiful Names of God*. Cambridge: Islamic Texts Society, 1992.

———. *Mishkāt al-anwār*. Translated by W. H. T. Gairdner as *Al-Ghazzālī's Mishkat al-Anwar ("The Niche for Lights")*. Lahore: Sh. Muhammad Ashraf, 1952. [Reprint of Royal Asiatic Society, 1924]

———. *Al-Munqidh min al-ḍalāl*. Translated by W. M. Watt as *The Faith and Practice of al-Ghazali*. Chicago: Kazi Publication, 1982. Reprint of Allen and Unwin, 1952. See also R. J. McCarthy, *Al-Ghazālī: Deliverance from Error; Five Key Texts including His Spiritual Autobiography, al-Munqidh min al-ḍalāl*. Louisville, Ky: Fons Vitae, 1999. First published Boston: Twayne Publishers, 1980 as *Freedom and Fulfillment*.

———. *Al-Mustasfā min ʿilm al-uṣūl*. 2 vols. Edited by Muḥammad Sulaymān al-Ashqar. Beirut: Al-Resalah Publishing House, 1997.

———. *Pand-nāma*. Printed in Nasrollah Pourjavady, *Du Mujaddid*.

———. *Al-Qisṭās al-mustaqīm*. Translated by D. P. Brewster as *The Just Balance*. Lahore: Sh. Muhammad Ashraf, 1978. Retranslated in R. J. McCarthy, *Freedom and Fulfillment*. Boston: Twayne Publishers, 1980. Reprinted as *Al-Ghazālī: Deliverance from Error; Five Key Texts including His Spiritual Autobiography, al-Munqidh min al-ḍalāl*. Louisville, Ky.: Fons Vitae, 1999.

———. *Tahāfut al-falāsifa*. Edited by D. Jīrār Jahāmī. Beirut: Dār al-Fikr al-Lubnānī, 1993. Translated by Sabih A. Kamali as *Incoherence of the Philosophers*. Lahore: Pakistan Philosophical Society, 1958. New translation as *Incoherence of the Philosophers*. A parallel English-Arabic text translated, introduced, and annotated by Michael Marmura. Provo, Utah: Brigham Young University Press, 1997.

———. *Tibr al-masbūk fī naṣīḥat al-mulūk*. Edited and introduced by Jalāl al-Dīn Humāʾī. Tehran: Intishārāt-i Bābak, 1361/1982. Translated by F. R. C. Bagley as *Ghazali's Book of Counsel for Kings (Nasihat al-muluk)*. Oxford: Oxford University Press, 1964.

———. *Tuḥfat al-mulūk*. Edited by Muḥammad Taqī Dānishpazhūh. *Majalla-yi Dānishgāh-i Adabīyāt wa ʿUlūm-i Insānī-yi Mashhad* 1:2–3 (1344/1965). Re-edited by Nasrollah Pourjavady and published in Pourjavady, *Du Mujaddid*.

Ghazālī, Aḥmad. *Majālis*. Edited by Aḥmad Mujāhid. Tehran: Intishārāt-i Dānishgāh, 1376/1997.

———. *Majmūʿa-yi āthār-i fārsī-yi Aḥmad-i Ghazālī*. Edited with an introduction by Aḥmad Mujāhid. Tehran: Intishārāt-i Dānishgāh-i Tehran, 1979.

———. *Makātib-i Khwāja Aḥmad Ghazālī bi ʿAyn al-Quḍāt Hamadānī*. Edited by Nasrollah Pourjavady. Tehran: Khānaqāh-i Niʿmatullāhī, 1977.

———. "Maktūbī az Aḥmad-i Ghazzālī." Edited by Nasrollah Pourjavady. *Sophia Perennis* 3:1 (1977).

———. *Risāla-yi sawāniḥ wa risāla-yī dar mawʿiẓa*. Edited by Javad Nurbakhsh. Tehran: Intishārāt-i Khāniqāh-i Niʿmatullāhī, 1973.

———. *Sawāniḥ*. Edited by Hellmut Ritter. Reprint edition. Tehran: Markaz-i Nashr-i Dānishgāhī, 1368/1989. Translated by Nasrollah Pourjavady as *Sawānih: Inspirations from the World of Pure Spirits*. London: KPI, 1986.

———. *Sirr al-asrār fī kashf al-anwār*. Edited by ʿAbd al-Ḥāmid Ṣāliḥ Hamdān. Cairo: al-Dār al-Miṣrīya al-Lubnānīya, 1988.

Ghaznavī [Ghaznawī], Khwāja Sadīd al-Dīn Muḥammad. *Maqāmāt-i Zhanda-Pīl*. Edited by Heshmat[Allāh] Moayyad [Sanandajī]. Tehran: Bungāh-i Tarjuma wa Nashr-i Kitāb, 1961. Translated by Heshmat Moayyad and Franklin Lewis as *The Colossal Elephant and His Spiritual Feats: Shaykh Ahmad-e Jam: The Life and Legend of a Popular Sufi Saint of 12th-Century Iran*. Costa Mesa, Calif.: Mazda Publishers, 2004.

Gīsū Dirāz, Muḥammad Chishtī. *Sharḥ Zubdat al-ḥaqāʾiq, al-maʿrūf bi sharḥ-i Tamhīdāt*. Hyderabad: Kitābkhāna-yi Gulbarga Sharīf, 1364/1944.

Hamadānī, Khwāja Yūsuf. *Rutbat al-ḥayāt*. Edited by Muḥammad Amīn Riyāḥī. Tehran: Intishārāt-i Ṭūs, 1362/1993.

Ḥamīd Qalandar. *Khayr al-majālis (malfuẓāt-i Shaykh Naṣīr al-Dīn Maḥmūd Chirāgh)*. Edited by K. A. Nizami. Aligarh: Department of History, Aligarh Muslim University, 1959.

Hindū-Shāh Nakhjawānī. *Tajārib al-salaf*. Edited by ʿAbbās Iqbāl. Tehran: Ṭahūrī, 1965.

Ḥudūd al-ʿĀlam. Translated and commentary by V. Minorsky in *The Regions of the World, a Persian Geography 372–982 A.D.* E. J. W. Gibb Memorial, NS. 11. London: Luzac, 1937.

Ḥusaynī, Nāṣir ibn ʿAlī Ṣadr al-Dīn. *Akhbār al-dawla al-saljūqīya*. Edited by Muḥammad Iqbāl. Lahore: Punjab University, 1933. Reprinted as *Zubdat al-tawārīkh: Akhbār al-umarāʾ wa ʾl-mulūk al-saljūqīya*. Edited by Muḥammad Nūr al-Dīn. Beirut: Dār al-Iqrāʾ, 1985.

Ibn Abū Yaʿlāʾ, Qāḍī Abū ʾl-Ḥusayn Muḥammad. *Ṭabaqāt al-ḥanābila*. Edited by Muḥammad Ḥāmid al-Faqī. Cairo: Maṭbaʿat al-Sunna al-Muḥammadīya, 1952.

Ibn al-Athīr. *Al-Kāmil fī ʾl-tārīkh*. Edited by C. J. Tornberg. Leiden: E. J. Brill, 1864. Reprint, with corrections and new pagination. 13 vols. Beirut: Dār Ṣādir, 1966. Partial translation and annotation by D. S. Richards as *The Annals of the Saljuq Turks:*

Selections from al-Kāmil fī 'l-Ta'rīkh of 'Izz al-Dīn Ibn al-Athīr. Richmond, Surrey: RoutledgeCurzon, 2002.

Ibn al-Balkhī. *Fārs-nāma*. Edited by ʿAlī Naqī Bihrūzī. Shīrāz: Intishārāt-i Maṭbūʿātī-yi Fārs, 1343/1964.

Ibn Jubayr. *Riḥla*. Beirut: Dār Ṣādir, 1964.

Ibn Kathīr. *Al-Bidāya wa 'l-nihāya*. Beirut: Maktabat al-Maʿārif, 1966.

Ibn Khaldūn. *The Muqaddimah; an Introduction to History*. Translated by Franz Rosenthal. New York: Pantheon Books, 1958.

Ibn Khallikān. *Wafāyat al-aʿyān*. Edited by Iḥsān ʿAbbās. 8 vols. Beirut: Dar Assakafa, 1977. Translated by Baron MacGuckin de Slane as *Ibn Khallikān's Biographical Dictionary*. Paris: Oriental Translation Fund of Great Britain and Ireland, 1842–71.

Ibn Munawwar, Muḥammad. *Asrār al-tawḥīd fī maqāmāt al-shaykh Abū Saʿīd*. Edited by Zabihullah Safa. Tehran: Intishārāt-i Amīr Kabīr, 1348/1969. Re-edited by Muḥammad Riḍā' Shafīʿī-Kadkanī. 2 vols. Tehran: Intishārtāt-i Āgāh, 1376/1997. [Fourth reprint] Translated by John O'Kane as *The Secrets of God's Mystical Oneness*. Costa Mesa, Calif.: Mazda Publications in association with Bibliotheca Persica, 1992. Translated into French by Mohammad Achena [Muḥammad Āshnā] as *Les étapes mystiques du Shaykh Abu Saʿid: Mystères de la connaissance de l'Unique*. Paris: UNESCO, 1974. Translated into Arabic by Asʿād ʿAbd al-Hādī Qandīl. Cairo: Al-Dār al-Miṣriyya li 'l-Taʿlīf wa 'l-Tarjuma in Cairo, 1966.

Ibn Rajab, Zayn al-Dīn. *Kitāb al-dhayl ʿalā ṭabaqāt al-ḥanābila*. Edited by Muḥammad Ḥāmid al-Faqī. Cairo: Maṭbaʿat al-Sunna al-Muḥammadīya, 1952.

Jamāl al-Dīn Abū Rūḥ-i Luṭf Allāh ibn Abī Saʿīd ibn Abī Saʿd. *Ḥālāt wa sukhanān-i Abū Saʿīd-i Abū 'l-Khayr*. Edited by Muḥammad Riḍā' Shafīʿī-Kadkanī. Tehran: Intishārāt-i Āgāh, 1367/1998. [Reprint of earlier edition]

Jāmī, Mawlānā ʿAbd al-Raḥmān ibn Aḥmad. *Nafaḥāt al-uns min ḥaḍarāt al-quds*. Edited by Mahdī Tawḥīdī-pūr. Tehran: Intishārāt-i Saʿd, 1366/1987. [Reprint of earlier edition] Re-edited by Maḥmūd ʿĀbidī. Tehran: Iṭṭilāʿāt, 1370/1991.

Al-Juwaynī, Abū 'l-Maʿālī ʿAbd al-Malik [Imām al-ḥaramayn]. *ʿAqīda al-niẓāmīya fī arkān al-islāmīya*. Edited by Aḥmad Ḥijāzī al-Saqqa'. Cairo: Maktabat al-Kullīyāt al-Azharīya, 1978.

———. *Ghiyāth al-umam fī iltiyāth al-ẓulam*. Edited by ʿAbd al-ʿAẓīm al-Dīb. Cairo: Maṭbaʿa Nahḍat Miṣr, 1401/1981.

———. *Kitāb al-irshād*. Edited by Muḥammad Yūsuf Mūsā. Cairo: Khānijī, 1950. Re-edited by Asʿad Tamīm. Beirut: Mu'assasat al-Kutub al-Thaqāfīya, 1985.

———. *Lumaʿ al-adilla fī qawā'id ahl al-sunna wa 'l-jamāʿa*. Edited by Fawqīya Ḥusayn Maḥmūd. Cairo: Dār al-Misrīya, 1965.

———. *Textes Apologétiques De Ǧuwainī*. [Contains *Shifā' al-ghalīl fī bayān mā waqaʿa fī 'l-tawrāt wa 'l-injīl min al-tabdīl* and *Lumaʿ fī qawāʿid ahl al-sunna wa 'l-jamāʿa*] Edited by Michel Allard. Beirut: Dar El-Machreq [Dār al-Mashriq], 1968.

Juwaynī [Juvaini], ʿAlā' al-Dīn ʿAṭā-Malik. *Tārīkh-i jahān-gushāy*. Translated by John Andrew Boyle as *The History of the World-Conqueror by ʿAla-ad-Din ʿAta-Malik Juvaini*. 2 vols. Cambridge: Harvard University Press, 1958.

Kāshānī, Abū 'l-Qāsim. *Tārīkh-i Ismāʿīlīya* [A section of *Zubdat al-tawārīkh*]. Edited by Muḥammad Taqī Dānishpazhūh. Tabrīz: Nashrīya-yi Dānishgāh-i Adabīyāt-i Tabrīz, 1343/1961.

Kāshgharī, *Dīwān lughāt al-Turk*. Edited and translated by Robert Dankoff and James Kelly as *Compendium of the Turkish Dialects*. 3 vols. Duxbury, Mass.: Harvard University Press, 1982–84.

Khwānd-Mīr, Ghiyāth al-Dīn. *Dastūr al-wuzarā'*. Edited by Said Naficy (Sa'īd Nafīsī). Tehran: Iqbāl, 1317/1958.

———. *Tārīkh ḥabīb al-siyar*. 4 vols. Tehran: Khayyām, 1333/1954.

Khwārazmī, Kamāl al-Dīn Ḥusayn ibn Ḥasan. *Jawāhir al-asrār*. Edited by Muḥammad Jawād Sharī'at. Isfahan: Mu'assasa-yi Intishārāt-i Mash'al-i Iṣfahān, 1360/1981.

Ma'ṣūm 'Alī Shāh. [Muḥammad Ma'ṣūm Shīrāzī] *Ṭarā'iq al-ḥaqā'iq*. 3 vols. Edited by Muḥammad Ja'far Maḥjūb. Tehran: Kitābkhāna-yi Sanā'ī, 1970–79.

Al-Māwardī, 'Alī ibn Muḥammad. *Aḥkām al-sulṭānīya wa al-wilāyāt al-dīnīya*. Edited by Muḥammad Fahmī al-Sarjānī. Cairo: al-Maktabat al-tawfīqīya, 1978. Translated by Wafaa H. Wafaa as *The Ordinances of Governement of al-Ahkam al-Sultaniyya*. London: Garnet Publishing, 1996.

———. *Qawānīn al-wizāra*. Edited by Ṣalāḥ al-Dīn Aslān. Cairo: Maktaba Nahḍa al-Sharq, 1986.

Mu'ayyid al-Dawla Atabeg al-Juwaynī. *'Atabat al-kataba*. Edited by Muḥammad Qazwīnī and 'Abbās Iqbāl. Tehran: Shirkat-i Sahāmī Chāp, 1329/1950.

Mujmal al-tawārīkh wa 'l-qiṣaṣ. [Anonymous] Edited by Malik al-shu'arā'-yi Bahār, with further corrections by Muḥammad Ramaḍānī. Tehran: Khāvar, 1318/1939.

Nāgawrī, Qāḍī Ḥamīd al-Dīn. *Lawā'iḥ*. Published under its attribution to Abū 'l-Ma'ālī 'Abd Allāh ibn Muḥammad ibn 'Alī ibn al-Ḥasan ibn 'Ali al-Mīyānajī al-Hamadānī, known as 'Ayn al-Quḍāt. Edited by Rahim Farmanish. Tehran: Kitābkhāna-yi Manūchihrī, 1338/1958–59.

Nasafī, 'Aziz al-Dīn. *Insān al-kāmil*. Edited by M. Molé. Tehran: Kitābkhāna-yi Ṭahūrī, 1980.

Nāṣir-i Khusraw. *Dīvān*. Edited by Sayyid Naṣr Allāh Taqawī. Tehran: Mu'assasa-yi Intishārāt-i Amīr Kabīr, 1355/1978. Sections of *Dīvān* translated by Peter Lamborn Wilson and Gholam-Reza Aavani as *Nasir-i Khusraw: Forty Poems from the Divan*. Tehran: Imperial Iranian Academy of Philosophy, 1977.

———. *Rushanā'ī-nāma*. Edited by Tahsin Yacizi with further corrections by Bahman Ḥamīdī. Tehran: Intishārāt-i Ṭūs, 1373/1994.

———. *Safar-nāma*. Translated by W. M. Thackston Jr. as *Nāṣer-e Khosraw's Book of Travels (Safarnāma)*. New York: Bibliotheca Persica, 1986.

———. *Wajh-i Dīn*. Edited by Golam-Reza Aavani [Ghulām-Riḍā' A'wānī]. Tehran: Imperial Iranian Academy of Philosophy, 1977.

———. *Zād al-musāfirīn*. Edited by Muḥammad Badhl al-Raḥmān. Berlin: Kāvyānī, 1923.

Nīshāpūrī, Ẓahīr al-Dīn. *Saljūq-nāma*. Edited by Ismā'īl-khān Afshār. Tehran: Gulāla Khāvar, 1953. Also see *The History of the Seljuq Turks, from The Jāmi' al-Tawārīkh: An Ilkhanid Adaption of the Saljūq-nāma of Ẓahīr al-Dīn Nīshāpūrī*. Translated and annotated by Kenneth Allin Luther. Edited by C. Edmund Bosworth. Richmond, Surrey: Curzon, 2001.

Nizam ad-Din Awliya. *Morals for the Heart*. Translated by Bruce B. Lawrence. Mahwah, N.Y.: Paulist Press, 1992.

Niẓām al-Mulk. *Siyar al-Mulūk (Siyāsat-nāma)*. Edited by Hubert Darke. Tehran: Chāpkhāna-yi Shirkat-i Intishārāt-i ʿIlmī wa Farhangī, 1372/1993. [Reprint of 1340/1961]. Translated by Hubert Darke as *The Book of Government or Rules for Kings*. London: Routledge & Kegan Paul, 1960.

Niẓāmī, Aḥmad ʿArūḍī Samarqandī. *Chahār Maqāla*. Edited by Muḥammad Qazwīnī. Tehran: Kitābkhāna-yi Ṭaḥūrī, 1368/1989. Translated by E. G. Browne as *Chahâr Maqâla ("Four Discourses") of Niẓâmī-i-ʿArūḍī of Samarqand*. London: E. J. W. Gibb, 1921.

Qazwīnī, Ḥamd Allāh Mustawfī. *Tarīkh-i guzīda*. Vol. I, text, edited by E. G. Browne. Leiden: E. J. Brill, 1910. Vol. 2, abridged translation by E. G. Browne & R. A. Nicholson. Leiden: E. J. Brill, 1913.

Qummī, Najm al-Dīn Abū Rajāʾ. *Tarīkh al-wuzarāʾ*. Edited by Muḥammad Taqī Dānishpazhūh. Tehran: Ṭūs, 1984.

Qushayrī, Abū ʾl-Qāsim ʿAbd al-Karīm. *Risāla* Edited by ʿAbd al-Ḥalīm Maḥmūd and Maḥmūd ibn al-Sharīf. 2 vols. Cairo: Dār al-Kutub al-Ḥadītha, 1966. Persian translation, *Tarjuma-yi risāla-yi qushayrīya*. Edited, with an introduction, by Badīʿ al-Zamān Furūzanfar. Tehran: Markaz-i Intishārāt-i ʿIlmī wa Farhangī, 1361/1982. Partial English translation by B. R. Von Schlegell in *Principles of Sufism*. Berkeley, Calif.: Mizan Press, 1990.

Rashīd al-Dīn Faḍl Allāh (Ṭabīb). *Jāmiʿ al-tawārīkh*. Edited by Aḥmad Ātash. 2 vols. Tehran: Dunyā-yi Kitāb, 1983.

———. *Sargudhasht-i Ḥasan-i Ṣabbāḥ*. (A chapter of *Jāmiʿ al-tawārīkh*) Edited by Sayyid Muḥammad Dabīr Siyāqī. Tehran: Alburz, 1366/1987.

Rāwandī, Muḥammad b. ʿAlī. *Rāḥat al-ṣudūr*. Edited by Muḥammad Iqbāl. London: Luzac, 1921.

Rāzī, Naṣīr al-Dīn Abū ʾl-Rashīd ʿAbd al-Jalīl Qazwīnī. *Kitāb al-naqḍ, maʿrūf bi baʿḍ mathālib al-nawāṣib fī naqḍ "baʿḍ faḍāʾiḥ al-rawāfiḍ"*. 3 vols. (one volume of text, plus two volumes of editor's notes). Edited by Jalāl al-Dīn Urmavī Muḥaddith. Tehran: Intishārāt-i Anjuman-i Āthār-i Millī, 1358/1979.

Samarqandī, Amīr Dawlatshāh. *Tadhkira al-shuʿarāʾ*. Edited by Muḥammad Ramaḍānī. Tehran: Kulāla Khāvar, 1366/1987. [Reprint]

Sanāʾī, Ḥakīm. *Dīvān-i Sanāʾī*. Edited by Muddaris Raḍawī. Tehran: Intishārāt-i Sanāʾī, 1975.

———. *Maktūbāt-i ḥakīm Sanāʾī*. Edited by Nadhīr Aḥmad. Tehran: Kitāb-i Farzān, 1983.

Shahrazūrī, Shams al-Dīn. *Nuzhat al-arwāḥ wa rawḍat al-afraḥ*. Edited by Muḥammad Taqī Dānishpazhūh and Muḥammad Sarvar Mawlāʾī. Tehran: Shirkat-i Intishārāt-i ʿIlmī wa Farhangī, 1987.

Sohravardi [Suhrawardī], Shihaboddin Yahya. *Majmūʿa-yi muṣannafāt-i shaykh al-ishrāq shihāb al-dīn yaḥyā suhrawardī*. Edited by S. H. Nasr. 3 vols. Tehran: Intishārāt-i Shāhanshāhī-yi Falsafa-yi Iran, 1348/1969.

Al-Subkī, Tāj al-Dīn. *Ṭabaqāt al-shāfiʿīya al-kubra*. Cairo: ʿIsa al-Bābī al-Ḥalabī, 1964.

Thābitī, Sayyid ʿAli Muʾayyid. *Asnād wa nāma-hā-yi tārīkhī: Az Avāʾil–i daura-hā-yi islāmī tā avākhir-i ʿahd-i shāh ismāʿīl–i ṣafavī.* Tehran: Ṭahūrī, 1346/1969.

Secondary Sources

Abul Quasem, Muhammad. "Al-Ghazali's Theory of Qurʾan Exegesis According to one's Personal Opinion." In *International Congress for the Study of the Qurʾan: Series 1.* Edited by A. H. Johns. Canberra: Australian National University, 1980.

Abu-Sway, Mustafa Mahmoud. "Al-Ghazali's 'Spiritual Crisis' Reconsidered." *Al-Shajarah: Journal of the International Institute of Islamic Thought and Civilization* 1, no. 1 (1996).

Adhkāʾī, Parvīz, ed. *Bābā-Ṭāhir-nāma.* Tehran: Intishārāt-i Ṭūs, 1375/1996.

Afrāsiyābī, Ghulām Riḍāʾ. *Sulṭān al-ʿushshāq.* Shirāz: Dānishgāh-i Shirāz, 1372/1993.

Algar, Hamid. "Eblīs." *Encyclopaedia Iranica.* Edited by Ehsan Yarshater. Boston: Routledge & Kegan Paul, 1982–.

Althusser, Louis. "Ideology and Ideological State Apparatuses (Notes towards an Investigation)." In *Mapping Ideology*, edited by Slavo Žižek. London: Verso, 1994.

Amedroz, H.F. "The Mazalim Jurisdiction in the Ahkam Sultaniyya of Mawardi." *Journal of the Royal Asiatic Society* (1911).

Aminrazavi, Mehdi. *Suhrawardi and the School of Illumination.* Richmond, Surrey: Curzon Press, 1997.

Anvarī [Anwarī], Ḥasan. *Iṣṭlāḥāt-i Dīvānī Dawra-yi Ghaznavī wa Saljūqī.* Tehran: Ṭahūrī, 1976.

Arberry, A. J. *Classical Persian Literature.* Richmond, Surrey: Curzon Press, 1994. [Reprint of 1958 edition]

———. "Orient Pearls at Random Strung." *BSOAS* 11 (1943–46).

Āshtiyānī, ʿAbbās Iqbāl. *Vizārat dar ʿahd-i salāṭīn-i buzurg-i saljūqī.* Tehran: Intishārāt-i Dānishgāh-i Tehran, 1338/1959.

Awn, Peter J. *Satan's Tragedy and Redemption: Iblīs in Sufi Psychology.* Leiden: E. J. Brill, 1983.

Ayoub, Mahmoud. "The Speaking Qurʾan and the Silent Qurʾan: A Study of The Principles and Development of Imami Shiʿi Tafsir." In *Approaches to the History of the Interpretation of the Qurʾan*, edited by Andrew Rippin. Oxford: Clarendon press, 1988.

Badawī, ʿAbd al-Raḥmān. *Muʾallafāt al-Ghazālī.* Cairo: al-Maṭbaʿa al-Majlis al-Aʿlāʾ li-Riʿāyat al-Fann wa ʾl-Adab wa ʾl-ʿUlūm al-Ijtimāʿīya, 1961.

Barthold, W. *An Historical Geography of Iran.* Translated by Svat Soucek. Edited with an Introduction by C. E. Bosworth. Princeton: Princeton University Press, 1984.

———. *Turkestan down to the Mongol Invasion.* London: Luzac, 1928. E. J. Gibb Memorial Series, New Series. Reprinted and revised by author and H. A. R. Gibb. London: Luzac, 1968.

Barthold, W. [Under V. V. Bartold] "Caliph and Sultan." Translated by N. S. Doniach. *Islamic Quarterly* 7 (1963).

Barthold, W. [J. A. Boyle], "Djuwaynī, ʿAlāʾ al-Dīn ʿAṭā Malik b. Muḥammad." *E.I.*^{2}

Bausani, A. "Religion in the Saljuq Period." In *The Saljuq and Mongol Periods.* Vol. 5,

The Cambridge History of Iran, edited by J. A. Boyle. Cambridge: Cambridge University Press, 1968.

Bayḏāʾī, Partau. "Ashʿār-i Rāwandī, muʾallif-i *Rahat al-ṣudūr*." *Yādgār* 2:6 (1946).

Bayoumi, Moustafa, and Andrew Rubin, eds., *The Edward Said Reader*. New York: Vintage, 2000.

Beaurecueil, S. de Laugier de. "Al-Anṣārī, al-Harawī." *E.I.²*

———. *Khawādja ʿAbdullāh Anṣārī (396–481 A.H./1006–1089), Mystique Ḥanbalite*. Beirut: Recherches d'Institut de lettres orientales de Beyrouth, 1965. Persian translation by A. G. Ravān-Farhādī as *Sargudhasht-i pīr-i harāt, Khwāja ʿAbd Allāh Anṣārī Harawī*. Thaur: Bayhaqī Kitāb Khapar-lū Muʾassasa, 1355/1976.

Berkey, Jonathan. *The Transmission of Knowledge in Medieval Cairo: A Social History of Islamic Education*. Princeton: Princeton University Press, 1992.

Bertels, Y. *Taṣawwuf wa adabīyāt-i taṣawwuf*. Persian translation from the original Russian by Sīrūs Īzadī. Tehran: Amīr Kabīr, 1356/1977.

Binder, Leonard. "Al-Ghazali and Islamic Government." *Muslim World* 45 (1955).

Bin Ismail, Mohd. Zaidi. "Logic in al-Ghazālī's Theory of Certitude." *Al-Shajarah: Journal of the International Institute of Islamic Thought and Civilization* 1:1–2 (1996).

Bosworth, C. E. "Barbarian Incursions: The Coming of the Turks into the Islamic World." In *Islamic Civilisation, 950–1150*, edited by D. S. Richards. Oxford: Bruno Cassirer, 1973.

———. "An Early Persian Sufi: Shaykh Abu Saʿid of Mayhanah." Reprinted in C. E. Bosworth, *The Arabs, Byzantium and Iran: Studies in Early Islamic History and Culture*. Brookfield, Mass.: Variorum, 1996.

———. *The Ghaznavids: Their Empire in Afghanistan and Eastern Iran*. Edinburgh: Edinburgh University Press, 1963.

———. "The Heritage of Rulership in Early Islamic Iran and the Search for Dynastic Connections with the Past." *Iran* 11 (1973).

———. *The New Islamic Dynasties: A Chronological and Genealogical Manual*. New York: Columbia University Press, 1996.

———. "Niẓām al-Mulk." *E.I.²*

———. "The Political and Dynastic History of the Iranian World (A.D. 1000–1217)." In *The Saljuq and Mongol Periods*. Vol. 5, *The Cambridge History of Iran*, edited by J. A. Boyle. Cambridge: Cambridge University Press, 1968.

———. "The Rise of the Karamiyyah in Khurasan." *Muslim World* 50 (1960).

Bouyges, Maurice. *Essai de Chronologie des oeuvres de al-Ghazali (algazal)*. Edited by Michel Allard. Beirut: Imprimerie catholique, 1959.

Bowen, Harold. "Notes on Some Early Seljuqid Viziers." *BSOAS* 20 (1977).

———. [Revised by C. E. Bosworth] "Niẓām al-Mulk." *E.I.²*

Böwering, Gerhard. "Abū Saʿīd Abi'l-Kayr." *Encyclopaedia Iranica*. Edited by Ehsan Yarshater. Boston: Routledge & Kegan Paul, 1982-.

———. "ʿAyn-al-Qożāt Hamadānī," *Encyclopaedia Iranica*. Edited by Ehsan Yarshater. Boston: Routledge & Kegan Paul, 1982–.

Bregel, Yuri. "Turko-Mongol Influences in Central Asia." In *Turko-Persia in Historical Perspective*, edited by R. L. Canfield. Cambridge: Cambridge University Press, 1991.

Brockelmann, Carl. [Revised by L. Gardet] "Djuwaynī, Abū ʾl-Maʿālī ʿAbd al-Malik." *E.I.*²

Browne, Edward G. *A Literary History of Persia.* 4 vols. Cambridge: Cambridge University Press, 1902. Reprint, 1964.

———. "Yet More Light on ʿUmar Khayyám," *Journal of Royal Asiatic Society* (April 1899).

Bruijn, J. T. P. de. *Of Piety and Poetry: The Interaction of Religion and Literature in the Life and Works of Ḥakīm Sanāʾī of Ghazna.* Leiden: E. J. Brill, 1983.

Bulliet, Richard. "Numismatic Evidence for the Relationship between Ṭughril Beg and Chaghrī Beg." In *Near Eastern Numismatics, Iconography, Epigraphy and History: Studies in Honor of George C. Miles*, edited by Dickran K. Kouymijian. Beirut: American University of Beirut, 1974.

———. *The Patricians of Nishapur.* Cambridge: Harvard University Press, 1972.

Cahen, Claude. "Atabak." *E.I.*²

———. "Chaghrī Beg." *E.I.*²

———. "Evolution de ʾl-Iqṭâʿ." *Annales: Economies, Sociétés, Civilisations* 8 (1953).

———. "L'évolution sociale du monde musulman jusqu'au XIIe siècle face à celle du monde chrétien," *Cahiers de civilisation médiévale: Xe–XIIe siècles* 1 (1958) and 2 (1959).

———. "The Historiography of the Seljuqid Period." In *Historians of the Middle East*, edited by Bernard Lewis and P. M. Holt. London: Oxford University Press, 1962.

———. "*Iḳṭāʿ*." *E.I.*².

———. *Introduction à l'histoire du monde musulman médiéval: VIIe–XVe siècle.* Paris: Librairie d'Amérique et d'Orient, 1982.

———. "Le Malik-Nameh et l'Histoire des Origines Seljukides." *Oriens* 2:1 (1949).

———. "Nomades et sèdentaires dans le monde musulman du milieu du Moyen Âge." In *Islamic Civilisation, 950–1150*, edited by D. S. Richards. Oxford: Bruno Cassirer, 1973.

———. *Pre-Ottoman Turkey.* Translated by J. Jones-Williams. New York: Taplinger, 1968.

———. "Tribes, Cities, and Social Organization." In vol. 4 of *Cambridge History of Iran*, edited by R. N. Frye et al. Cambridge: Cambridge University Press, 1968.

———. "The Turkish Invasion: The Selchukids." In *A History of the Crusades*, edited by K. M. Setton. Madison: University of Wisconsin Press, 1969–89.

The Cambridge History of Iran. 7 vols. Cambridge: Cambridge University Press, 1968–91. Reprint 1993.

Clauson, Sir Gerard. *An Etymological Dictionary of Pre-Thirteenth-Century Turkish.* Oxford: Clarendon Press, 1972.

Corbin, Henry. *History of Islamic Philosophy.* Translated by Laidain Sherrard. London: Kegan Paul International, 1993.

———. "The Ismāʿīlī Response to the Polemic of Ghazali." In *Ismāʿīlī Contributions to Islamic Culture*, edited by Seyyed Hossein Nasr. Tehran: Imperial Academy of Iranian Philosophy, 1977.

———. "Nāṣir-i Khusrau and Iranian Ismāʿīlīsm." In vol. 4 of *Cambridge History of Iran*, edited by R. N. Frye et al. Cambridge: Cambridge University Press, 1968.

Cornell, Rkia E. *Early Sufi Women: Dhikr an-niswa al-muta'abbidāt aṣ-Ṣūfiyyāt by Abū 'Abd ar-Raḥmān as-Sulamī*. Louisville, Ky.: Fons Vitae, 1999.

Cornell, Vincent J. *Realm of the Saint: Power and Authority in Moroccan Sufism*. Austin: University of Texas Press, 1998.

Crone, Patricia. "Did al-Ghazālī Write a Mirror for Princes? On the Authorship of *Naṣīḥat al-mulūk*." *Jerusalem Studies in Arabic and Islam* 10 (1987).

Dabashi, Hamid. "'Ayn al-Quḍāt Hamadānī wa Risāla-yi *Shakwā 'l-gharīb-i* ū." *Iran Nameh* 11:1 (1993).

———. "Historical Conditions of Persian Sufism during the Seljuk Period." In *Classical Persian Sufism: From Its Origins to Rumi*, edited by Leonard Lewisohn. London: KNP, 1993.

———. *Truth and Narrative: The Untimely Thoughts of 'Ayn al-Qudat al-Hamadhani*. Richmond, Surrey: Curzon, 1999.

Daftary, Farhad. "Ḥasan-i Ṣabbāḥ and the Origins of the Nizārī Isma'ili Movement." In *Mediaeval Isma'ili History and Thought*, edited by Farhad Daftary. Cambridge: Cambridge University Press, 1996.

———. *The Ismā'īlīs: Their History and Doctrines*. Cambridge: Cambridge University Press, 1990.

Dehkhoda [Dihkhudā], 'Alī Akbar. *Lughat-nāma*. 15 vols. Edited by Mohammad Mo'in and Ja'far Shahihi. Tehran: Tehran University Publications, 1998.

DeWeese, Devin. "The Eclipse of the Kubraviyah in Central Asia." *Iranian Studies* 21 nos. 1–2 (1988).

Digby, Simon. "The Sufi Shaykh and the Sultan: A Conflict of Claims to Authority in Medieval India." *Iran: Journal of the British Institute of Persian Studies* 28 (1990).

Doniger, Wendy [O'Flaherty]. "Other Peoples' Lies." In *Other Peoples' Myths*. New York: Macmillan, 1988.

Donner, Fred. *The Early Islamic Conquests*. Princeton: Princeton University Press, 1981.

Eaton, Richard. *The Sufis of Bijapur (1300–1700): Social Roles of Sufis in Medieval India*. Princeton: Princeton University Press, 1978.

Eliade, Mircea. *The Sacred and the Profane: The Nature of Religion*. Translated by William R. Trask. San Diego: HBJ, 1959, 1987.

Elwell-Sutton, L. P. "Bābā-Ṭāher." *Encyclopaedia Iranica*. Edited by Ehsan Yarshater. Boston: Routledge & Kegan Paul, 1982-

Encyclopaedia Iranica. Edited by Ehsan Yarshater. Boston: Routledge & Kegan Paul, 1982–.

Encyclopaedia of Islam. New ed. [E.I.²] Leiden: E. J. Brill, 1954–2004.

Ephrat, Daphna. *The Sunni 'Ulama' of 11th-Century Baghdad*. Albany, N.Y.: SUNY Press, 2000.

———. "The Sunni 'Ulama' of 11th-Century Baghdad and the Transmission of Knowledge: A Social History." Ph.D. diss., Harvard University, 1992.

Ernst, Carl W. "Blasphemy: Islamic Concept." *Encyclopedia of Religion*. Edited by Mircea Eliade. New York: Macmillan, 1987

———. *Eternal Garden: Mysticism, History, and Politics at a South Asian Sufi Center*. Albany, N.Y.: SUNY Press, 1992.

———. *Ruzbihan Baqli: Mysticism and the Rhetoric of Sainthood in Persian Sufism.* Richmond, Surrey: Curzon Press, 1996.

———. *Words of Ecstasy in Sufism.* Albany, N.Y.: SUNY Press, 1985.

Esposito, John. *Islam: The Straight Path.* Oxford: Oxford University Press, 1991.

Farmanish, Rahim. *Aḥwāl wa āthār-i ʿAyn al-Quḍāt.* Tehran: Chāp-i Āftāb, 1338/1959.

Foucault, Michel. *Discipline and Punish.* Translated by Alan Sheridan. New York: Vintage Books, 1995.

———. *Power/Knowledge: Selected Interviews and Other Writings, 1972–1977.* Edited by Colin Gordon. New York: Pantheon Books, 1980.

Frank, R. M. "Knowledge and *Taqlīd*: The Foundations of Religious Belief in Classical Ashʿarism." *Journal of the American Oriental Society* 109:1 (1989).

———. "Two Short Dogmatic Works of Abū ʾl-Qāsim al-Qushayrī." *MIDEO* 15 (1982).

Frye, Richard N. "The Iranianization of Islam." In *Islamic Iran and Central Asia (7th–12th centuries).* Richmond, Surrey: Variorum Reprints, 1979.

———. "The New Persian Renaissance in Western Iran." In *Arabic and Islamic Studies in Honor of Hamilton A. R. Gibb*, edited by George Makdisi. Leiden: E. J. Brill, 1965.

———. "A Note on Bureaucracy and School in Early Islamic Iran." In *Arabic and Islamic Garland: Historical, Educational and Literary Papers Presented to Abdul-latif Tibawi*, edited by Adel Awa et al. London: Islamic Cultural Center, 1977.

———. "Notes on the Renaissance of the 10th and 11th Centuries in Eastern Iran." In *Islamic Iran and Central Asia (7th–12th Centuries).* Richmond, Surrey: Variorum Reprints, 1979.

———. "The Turks in Khurasan and Transoxania at the Time of the Arab Conquest." *Muslim World* 35 (1945).

Fück, J. W. "Ibn Khallikān," *E.I.*²

Furūzānfar, Badīʿ al-Zamān. *Sukhan wa sukhanwarān.* Tehran: Khwārazmī, 1369/1990. [Reprint]

Gibb, H. A. R. "An Interpretation of Islamic History." *Journal of World History* 1, no. 1 (1953): 39–62. Reprinted in his *Studies on the Civilization of Islam.* Edited by Stanford J. Shaw and William R. Polk. Boston: Beacon Press, 1962.

———. "The Reasons for the Composition of al-Ahkam as-Sultaniyah." In his *Studies on the Civilization of Islam.* Edited by Stanford J. Shaw and William R. Polk. Boston: Beacon Press, 1962.

———. "The Significance of the 'Amirate by Seizure'." In his *Studies on the Civilization of Islam.* Edited by Stanford J. Shaw and William R. Polk. Boston: Beacon Press, 1962.

———. *Studies on the Civilization of Islam.* Edited by Stanford J. Shaw and William R. Polk. Boston: Beacon Press, 1962.

Gohlman, William E. *The Life of Ibn Sina; a Critical Edition and Annotated Translation.* Albany, N.Y.: SUNY Press, 1974.

Gölpınarlı, Abdülbaki, ed. *Mevlânâ Müzesi: Yazmalar Kataloğu.* Ankara: Türk Tarih Kurumu, 1967–72.

Goitein, S. D. "The Origin of the Vizierate and Its True Character." In *Studies in Islamic History and Institutions.* Leiden: E. J. Brill, 1966.

Goodman, L. E. *Avicenna*. New York: Routledge, 1992.
Gordon, Matthew. *The Breaking of a Thousand Swords: A History of the Turkish Military of Samarra A.H. 200–275/815–889 C.E.* Albany, N.Y.: SUNY Press, 2001.
Grabar, Oleg. *The Great Mosque of Isfahan*. New York: New York University Press, 1990.
Gross, Jo-Ann. "Authority and Miraculous Behavior: Reflections on *Karāmāt* Stories of Khwāja ʿUbaydullāh Aḥrār." In *The Legacy of Mediaeval Persian Sufism*, edited by L. Lewisohn. New York: KNP, 1992.
Gutas, Dimitri. *Avicenna and the Aristotelian Tradition*. New York: E. J. Brill, 1988.
Ḥākimī, Ismāʿīl. *Samāʿ dar taṣawwuf*. Tehran: Intishārāt-i Dānishgāh-i Tehran, 1367/1988.
Hallaq, Wael. "Caliphs, Jurists and the Saljuqs in the Political Thought of Juwaynī." *Muslim World* 74, no. 1 (1984).
Haravī [Harawī], Najīb Māyil. *Khāṣṣīyat-i āyinagī*. Tehran: Nashr-i Ney, 1995.
Ḥātam, Ghulām-ʿAlī. "Barrisī wa shinākht-i gūsha-hā-yī az tamaddun-i islāmī-yi īrān-i saljūqī-hā." *Dānesh-kadeh* 3:9 (1356/1977).
Havemann, Axel. "The Vizier and the Raʾis in Saljuq Syria: The Struggle for Urban Self-Representation." *International Journal of Middle East Studies* 21 (1989).
Heath, Peter. "Ibn Sīnā's Journey of the Soul." *Journal of Turkish Studies* 18 (1994).
Heffening, W. "Murtaḍḍ." *Shorter Encyclopedia of Islam*. Edited by H. A. R. Gibb and J. H. Kramers. Leiden: E. J. Brill, 1953.
Heffernan, Thomas J. *Sacred Biography*. New York: Oxford University Press, 1988.
Heron-Allen, Edward. *Lament of Bábá Ṭáhir*. London: B. Quaritch, 1902. Reprinted as *A Fool of God: The Mystical Verse of Baba Tahir*. London: Octagon Press, 1976.
Hillenbrand, Carole. "Islamic Orthodoxy or Realpolitik? Al-Ghazali's Views on Government." *Iran: Journal of the British Institute of Persian Studies* 26 (1988).
———. "The Power Struggle between the Saljuqs and the Ismaʿilis of Alamūt, 487–518/1094–1124: The Saljuq Perspective." In *Mediaeval Ismaʿili History and Thought*, edited by Farhad Daftary. Cambridge: Cambridge University Press, 1996.
———. "Rāwandī, Muḥammad b. ʿAlī," *E.I.*²
Hodgson, Marshall G. S. "Ḥasan-i Ṣabbāḥ." *E.I.*²
———. "The Ismaili State." In vol. 4 of *Cambridge History of Iran*, edited by J. A. Boyle. Cambridge: Cambridge University Press, 1968.
———. *The Order of Assassins*. The Hague: Mouton, 1955.
———. *The Venture of Islam: Conscience and History in a World Civilization*. 3 vols. Chicago: University of Chicago Press, 1974.
Hogga, Mustapha. *Orthodoxie, subversion et réforme en Islam: Gazali et les Seljuqides*. Paris: J. Vrin, 1993.
Holt, P. M., Ann K. S. Lambton, and Bernard Lewis, eds. *The Cambridge History of Islam, 1A: The Central Islamic Lands from Pre-Islamic Times to the First World War*. Cambridge: Cambridge University Press, 1970.
Homayouni, Massoud. *The Origins of Persian Gnosis*. Translated by F. J. Stone. London: Mawlana Centre, 1992.
Hostler, Charles Warren. *The Turks of Central Asia*. Westport, Conn.: Praeger, 1993.
Hourani, A. H., and S. M. Stern, eds. *The Islamic City: A Colloquium*. Oxford: Bruno Cassirer, 1970.

Hourani, George F. "A Revised Chronology of Ghazālī's Writings." *Journal of the American Oriental Society* 104:2 (1984).

Houtsma, M. Th. "Al-Bundārī." *E.I.*²

———. "Some Remarks on the History of the Saljuks." *Acta Orientalia* 3 (1924).

Humā'ī, Jalāl al-Dīn. *Ghazzālī-nāma.* 2nd ed. Tehran: Kitābfurūshī-yi Furūqī, 1342/1963.

Humphreys, R. Stephen. *Islamic History: A Framework for Inquiry*. Princeton: Princeton University Press, 1992.

"Ideology and Religion." In *The HarperCollins Dictionary of Religion*, edited by Jonathan Z. Smith. San Francisco: HarperSanFrancisco, 1995.

Iqbāl, ʿAbbās [Āshtiyānī]. "Rājiʿ bi-zindagī-yi Imām Ghazālī." In *Majmūʿa-yi maqālāt-i ʿAbbās Iqbāl Āshtiyānī*, edited by Muḥammad Dabīr Siyāqī. Tehran: Khayyām, 1350/1971.

———. *Tārīkh-i mufaṣṣal-i Irān*. Tehran: Khayyām, 1968.

———. *Vizārat [wizārat] dar ʿahd-i salāṭīn-i buzurg-i saljūqī*. Tehran: Intishārāt-i Dānishgāh-i Tehran, 1338/1959.

Ivanow, W. "A Biography of Shaykh Aḥmad-i Jām." *Journal of the Royal Asiatic Society* (1917).

Izutsu, Toshihiko. "Creation and the Timeless Order of Things: A Study in the Mystical Philosopy of Ayn al-Qudat Hamadani." *Philosophical Forum* 4:1 (1972): 124–40. Reprinted in *Creation and the Timeless Order of Things: Essays in Islamic Mystical Philosophy*. Ashland: White Cloud Press, 1994. [no editor listed]

———. *Ethico-Religious Concepts in the Qur'an*. Montreal: McGill-Queens' University Press, 2002. Reprint of *The Structure of Ethical Terms in the Koran*. Tokyo: Keio Institute of Philosophical Studies, 1959.

———. *God and Man in the Koran*. Tokyo: Keio Institute of Cultural and Linguistic Studies, 1964.

———. "Mysticism and the Linguistic Problem of Equivocation in the Thought of Ayn al-Qudat Hamadani." *Studia Islamica* 30 (1970): 153–70. Reprinted in *Creation and the Timeless Order of Things: Essays in Islamic Mystical Philosophy*. Ashland: White Cloud Press, 1994. [no editor listed]

Jabre, F. "La biographie et l'oeuvre de Ghazālī reconsidérées à la lumière des Ṭabaqāt de Sobki." *MIDEO* 1 (1954).

Kasā'ī, Nūr Allāh. *Madāris-i Niẓāmīya wa ta'thīrāt-i ʿilmī wa ijtimāʿī-yi ān*. Tehran: Amīr Kabīr, 1363/1984.

King, Richard. *Orientalism and Religion: Postcolonial Theory, India, and the "Mystic East."* London: Routledge, 1999.

Kiyānī, Muḥsin. *Tārīkh-i khānaqāh dar īrān*. Tehran: Kitābkhāna-yi Ṭahūrī, 1369/1990.

Klausner, Carla. *The Seljuq Vezirate: A Study of Civil Administration: 1055–1194*. Cambridge: Harvard University Press, 1973.

Knysh, Alexander. "'Orthodoxy' and 'Heresy' in Medieval Islam: An Essay in Reassessment." *Muslim World* 83 (1993).

Lambton, A. K. S. "The Administration of Sanjar's Empire as Illustrated in the *ʿAtabat al-kataba*." *BSOAS* 20 (1957).

———. "Aspects of Saljuq-Ghuzz Settlement in Persia." In *Islamic Civilisation, 950–1150*, edited by D. S. Richards. Oxford: Bruno Cassirer, 1973.

———. "Concept of Authority in Persia: Eleventh to Nineteenth Centuries A.D." *Iran* 26 (1988).

———. *Continuity and Change in Medieval Persia: Aspects of Administrative, Economic and Social History, 11th–14th Century*. Albany, N.Y.: SUNY Press, 1988.

———. "The Dilemma of Government in Islamic Persia: The *Siyasat-nameh* of Nizam al-Mulk." *Iran* 22 (1984).

———. "Internal Structure of the Saljuq Empire." In vol. 5 of *Cambridge History of Iran*, edited by J. A. Boyle. Cambridge: Cambridge University Press, 1968.

———. "Justice in the Medieval Persian Theory of Kingship." *Studia Islamica* 17 (1962).

———. *Landlord and Peasant in Persia*. London: Oxford University Press, 1953.

———. "Quis Custodiet Custodes: Some Reflections on the Persian Theory of Government." *Studia Islamica* 5 (1956).

———. "Reflections on the *iqṭāʿ*." In *Arabic and Islamic Studies in Honor of Hamilton A. R. Gibb*, edited by George Makdisi. Leiden: Brill, 1965.

———. *State and Government in Medieval Islam*. New York: Oxford University Press, 1981.

———. *Theory and Practice in Medieval Persian Government*. London: Variorum Reprints, 1980.

———. "The Theory of Kingship in the *Naṣīḥat ul-mulūk* of Ghazālī." *Islamic Quarterly* 10, no. 1 (1954).

Lamoreaux, John C. *The Early Muslim Tradition of Dream Interpretation*. Albany: SUNY Press, 2002.

Landolt, Hermann. "Ghazālī and *Religionswissenschaft*." *Asiatische Studien-Etudes Asiatiques* 45, no. 1 (1991).

———. "Two Types of Mystical Thought in Muslim Iran: An Essay on Suhrawardi Shaykh al-Ishraq and Aynulquzat Hamadani." *Muslim World* 68 (1978).

Lane, E. W. *An Arabic-English Lexicon*. 1877. Reprint in two volumes, Cambridge: Islamic Texts Society, 1984.

Laoust, Henri. "Ibn Kathīr." *E.I.*[2]

———. *La Politique de Gazālī*. Paris: Paul Geuthner, 1970. Translated to Persian by Mehdi Mozaffari as *Siyāsat wa Ghazālī*. Tehran: Intishārāt-i Bunyād-i Farhang-i Iran, 1354/1975.

Lapidus, Ira. *A History of Islamic Societies*. Cambridge: Cambridge University Press, 1988.

———. "Ayyubid Religious Policy and the Development of the Schools of Law in Cairo." In *Colloque international sur l'histoire du Caire*. Cairo: Wizārat al-thaqāfa, 1974.

Lawrence, Bruce. "Religion, Ideology and Revolution: The Problematical Case of Post-1979 Iran." In *The Terrible Meek: Religion and Revolution in Cross-Cultural Perspective*, edited by Lonnie D. Kliever. New York: Paragon House, 1987.

Lease, Gary. "Ideology." In *Guide to the Study of Religion*, edited by Willi Braun and Russell T. McCutcheon. London: Cassell, 2000.

Leiser, Gary, ed. and trans. *A History of the Seljuks: Ibrahim Kafesoğlu's Interpretation and the Resulting Controversy*. Carbondale: Southern Illinois University Press, 1988.

Le Strange, Guy. *The Lands of the Eastern Caliphate: Mesopotamia, Persia, and Central Asia from the Moslem Conquest to the Time of Timur*. Cambridge: Cambridge University Press, 1905.

Levy, Reuben. "The Account of the Isma'ili Doctrines in the *Jami' al-Tawarikh* of Rashid al-Din Fadlallah." *JRAS* (1930).

Lewis, Bernard. *The Assassins*. London: Weidenfeld and Nicolson, 1967; reprint, New York: Oxford University Press, 1987.

Lewis, Bernard and P. M. Holt, eds. *Historians of the Middle East*. London: Oxford University Press, 1962.

Lewisohn, Leonard. "In Quest of Annihilation: Imaginalization and Mystical Death in the *Tamhīdāt* of 'Ayn al-Quḍāt Hamadhānī." In *Classical Persian Sufism: From Its Origins to Rumi*, edited by Leonard Lewisohn. London: KNP, 1993.

———, ed. *Classical Persian Sufism: From Its Origins to Rumi*. London: KNP, 1993.

———, ed. *The Legacy of Medieval Persian Sufism*. London: KNP, 1992.

Lincoln, Bruce. "Theses on Method." *Method and Theory in the Study of Religion* 8:3 (1996): 225–27. Reprinted in *The Insider/Outsider Problem in the Study of Religion*, edited by Russell T. McCutcheon. London: Cassell, 1999.

Lory, P. "al-Shahrazūrī," *E.I.*[2]

Lowick, Nicholas. "A Gold Coin of Rasūltegīn, Seljūk Ruler in Fārs." Reprinted in *Coinage and History of the Islamic World*, edited by Joe Cribb. Aldershot, Eng.: Variorum, 1990.

———. "Seljuq Coins." *Numismatic Chronicle* 10 (1970).

Luther, Kenneth A. "A New Source for the History of the Iraq Seljuqs: The *Tārīkh al-Vuzarā'*." *Der Islam* 45 no. 1–2 (1969).

———. "The Political Transformation of the Seljuq Sultanate of Iraq and Western Iran (1152–1187)." Ph.D. diss., Princeton University, 1964.

MacDonald, D. B. "Bid'a." *Shorter Encyclopedia of Islam*, edited by H. A. R. Gibb and J. H. Kramers. Leiden: E. J. Brill, 1953.

———. "The Life of al-Ghazzālī." *Journal of the American Oriental Society* 20 (1899).

Madelung, Wilferd. *Religious Schools and Sects in Medieval Islam*. London: Variorum, 1985.

———. *Religious Trends in Early Islamic Iran*. Albany, N.Y.: Bibliotheca Persica, 1988.

———. "The Spread of Māturīdism and the Turks." In *Actas do IV Congresso de Estudios Ârabes e Islâmicos, Coimbra-Lisboa*, 109–168. Leiden, 1971. Reprinted in W. Madelung, *Religious Schools and Sects in Medieval Islam*. London: Variorum, 1985.

———. "The Two Factions of Sunnism: Ḥanafism and Shāfi'ism." In his *Religious Trends in Early Islamic Iran*. Albany, N.Y.: Bibliotheca Persica, 1988.

Makdisi, George. *Arabic and Islamic Studies in Honor of Hamilton A. R. Gibb*. Leiden: Brill, 1965.

———. "Ash'ari and the Ash'arites in Islamic Religious History." *Studia Islamica* 17–18 (1962–63). Reprinted in *Religion, Law and Learning in Classical Islam*. Brookfield, Mass.: Variorum, 1991.

———. "Authority in the Islamic Community." In *La notion d'autorté au Moyen Age: Islam, Byzance, Occident*, edited by George Makdisi et al. Paris: Presses Universitaires de France, 1982. Reprinted in Makdisi, *History and Politics in Eleventh-Century Baghdad*. Brookfield, Mass.: Variorum, 1990.

———. "The Hanbali School and Sufism." In *Religion, Law and Learning in Classical Islam*. Brookfield, Mass.: Variorum, 1991.

———. *History and Politics in Eleventh-Century Baghdad*. Brookfield, Mass.: Variorum, 1990.

———. *Ibn ʿAqīl et la Résurgence de l'Islam Traditionaliste au XIe Siècle*. Damascus: Institut Français de Damas, 1963.

———. *Ibn ʿAqil: Religion and Culture in Classical Islam*. Edinburgh: Edinburgh University Press, 1997.

———. "Ibn Radjab." *E.I.*[2]

———. "The Marriage of Tughril Beg." *International Journal of Middle East Studies* 1 (1970).

———. "Muslim Institutions of Learning in Eleventh-Century Baghdad." In *Religion, Law and Learning in Classical Islam*. Brookfield, Mass.: Variorum, 1991.

———. "Les Rapports entre Calife et Sultan à l'Epoque Saljuqide." *International Journal of Middle East Studies* 6 (1975)

———. *Religion, Law and Learning in Classical Islam*. Brookfield, Mass.: Variorum, 1991.

———. *The Rise of Colleges*. Edinburgh: Edinburgh University Press, 1981.

———. "The Sunni Revival." In *Islamic Civilisation, 950–1150*, edited by D. S. Richards. Oxford: Bruno Cassirer, 1973.

Malamud, Margaret Irene. *The Development of Organized Sufism in Nishapur and Baghdad from the Eleventh to the Thirteenth Century*. Ph.d. diss., University of California at Berkeley, 1990.

Massé, H. "Kātib al-Iṣfahānī." *E.I.*[2]

Massignon, Louis. *The Passion of al-Hallāj: Mystic and Martyr of Islam*. 4 vols. Bolinger Series 98. Translated by Herbert Mason. Princeton: Princeton University Press, 1982.

———. "Zindīḳ." *Shorter Encyclopaedia of Islam*, edited by H. A. R. Gibb and J. H. Kramers. Leiden: E. J. Brill, 1953.

Masud, Muhammad Khalid. "The Obligation to Migrate: the Doctrine of *Hijra* in Islamic Law." In *Muslim Travelers: Pilgrimage, Migration, and the Religious Imagination*, edited by Dale F. Eickelman and James Piscatori. Berkeley: University of California Press, 1990.

McCarthy, Richard J. *Al-Ghazali: Deliverance from Error; Five Key Texts including His Spiritual Autobiography, al-Munqidh min al-ḍalāl*. Louisville, Ky.: Fons Vitae, 1999. First published Boston: Twayne Publishers, 1980, as *Freedom and Fulfillment*.

———. *Freedom and Fulfillment*. Boston: Twayne Publishers, 1980.

McCutcheon, Russell. *Manufacturing Religion: The Discourse on Sui Generis and the Politics of Nostalgia*. New York: Oxford University Press, 1997.

———, ed. *The Insider/Outsider Problem in the Study of Religion*. London: Cassell, 1999.

McDonough, Sheila. "Orthodoxy and Heterodoxy." *Encyclopedia of Religion*, edited by Mircea Eliade. New York: Macmillan, 1987.

Meier, Fritz. *Abū Saʿīd-i Abūl-Ḥayr, Wirklichkeit und Legende*. Leiden: E. J. Brill, 1976.

Sections translated into Persian by Mihr Āfāq Bāybivardī as "Abū Saʿīd Abū ʾl-Khayr wa Ṣāḥibān-i qudrat: taʿqīb wa ādhār-i ṣūfiyān." *Maʿārif* 10:2–3 (1372/1993). Complete Persian translation by Bāybivardī as *Abū Saʿīd[-i] Abū ʾl-Khayr: Ḥaqīqat wa afsāna*. Tehran: Markaz-i Nashr-i Dānishgāhī, 1378/1999.

———. "Aḥmad-i D̲j̲ām." *E.I.*²

———. *Essays in Islamic Piety and Mysticism*. Translated by John O'Kane with editorial assistance from Bernd Radtke. Leiden: Brill, 1999.

———. "Zur Biographie Aḥmad-i Ǧām's und zur Quellenkunde von Ǧāmī's *Nafaḥātu ʾl-uns*." *ZMDG* 97 (1943).

Meisami, Julie. *Medieval Persian Court Poetry*. Princeton: Princeton University Press, 1987.

———. *Persian Historiography to the End of the Twelfth Century*. Edinburgh: Edinburgh University Press, 1999.

Minorski, V. "Bābā-Ṭāhir." *E.I.*².

Minuvi [Mīnuwī], Mujtabāʾ. "Nāṣir-i Khusraw." *Majalla-yi Dānishgāh-i Adabīyāt wa ʿUlūm-i Insānī-yi Mashhad* 8:2 (1351/1972).

Mitha, Farouk. *Al-Ghazālī and the Ismailis: A Debate on Reason and Authority in Medieval Islam*. London: I. B. Tauris, 2001.

Morgan, D. O. "Rashīd al-Dīn Ṭabīb." *E.I.*²

Morris, James W. "The Philosopher-Prophet in Avicenna's Political Philosophy." In *Political Aspects of Islamic Philosophy*, edited by C. E. Butterworth. Cambridge: Harvard University Press, 1992.

Mottahedeh, Roy P. *Loyalty and Leadership in an Early Islamic Society*. Princeton: Princeton University Press, 1980.

Murata, Sachiko and William Chittick. *Vision of Islam*. New York: Paragon House, 1994.

Nanji, Azim. "Nāṣir-i Khusraw." *E.I.*²

———. "Shīʿī Ismāʿīlī Interpretations of the Qurʾan." In *International Congress for the Study of the Qurʾan: Series 1*, edited by A. H. Johns. Canberra: Australian National University, 1980.

Nasr, Seyyed Hossein. *Sadr al-Din Shirazi and His Transcendent Theosophy*. Tehran: Imperial Iranian Academy of Philosophy, 1978.

———. *Three Muslim Sages*. Cambridge: Harvard University Press, 1964.

Nawāʾī, ʿAbd al-Ḥusayn. "Farmān-i tadrīs-i Niẓāmīya-yi Nīshāpūr." *Yādgār* 1:6 (1945).

Newby, Gordon. *The Making of the Last Prophet*. Columbia: University of South Carolina, 1989.

Nielsen, Jørgen S. *Secular Justice in an Islamic State: Maẓālim under the Baḥrī Mamlūks, 662/1264–789/1387*. Istanbul: Nederlands Historisch–Archaeologisch Instituut, 1985.

Paden, William E. *Religious Worlds: The Comparative Study of Religion*. Boston: Beacon Press, 1988.

Pearson, M. N. "Premodern Muslim Political Systems." *Journal of the American Oriental Society* 102:1 (1982).

Poole, Stanley Lane. *The Coins of the Turkumán Houses of Seljooḳ, Urtuḳ, Zengee, etc. in the British Museum*. Vol. 3, *Catalogue of Oriental Coins in the British Museum*. London, 1877. Reprint, Bologna: Forni Editore, 1967.

Pourjavady, Nasrollah. *ʿAyn al-Quḍāt wa ustādān-i ū*. Tehran: Intishārāt-i Asāṭīr, 1995.
———. *Bū-yi jān*. Tehran: Markaz-i Nashr-i Dānishgāhī, 1372/1993.
———. *Du Mujaddid: Pazhuhish-hāyī dar bāra-yi Muḥammad Ghazālī wa Fakhr Rāzī*. Tehran: Markaz Nashr-i Dānishgāhī, 1381/2002.
———. "Iblīs-i du-rū." *Maʿārif* 2:1 (1364/1985).
———. *Sulṭān-i ṭarīqat*. Tehran: Āgāh, 1358/1979.
Qafas-ūghlū [Kafesoğlu], Ibrāhīm. "The Sons of Saljūq." *Majalla-yi Dānishgāh-i Adabīyāt wa ʿUlūm-i Insānī-yi Mashhad* 26 (1974).
Ravān-Farhādī, A. G. *ʿAbdullah Ansari of Herat (1006–1089 C.E.): An Early Sufi Master*. Richmond, Surrey: Curzon Press, 1996.
Rice, T. T. *The History of Seljuks in Asia Minor*. New York: Praeger, 1961.
Richards, D. S. "Ebn al-Aṯīr." [Ibn al-Athīr] *Encyclopaedia Iranica*. Edited by Ehsan Yarshater. Boston: Routledge & Kegan Paul, 1982–.
———, ed. *Islamic Civilisation, 950–1150*. Oxford: Bruno Cassirer, 1973.
Ritter, H. "Abū Saʿīd Faḍl Allāh b. Abī ʾl-Khayr." *E.I.*[2]
———. "Al-Ghazālī, Aḥmad." *E.I.*[2]
Riyāḍī, Ḥishmat Allāh. *Ayāt-i ḥusn wa ʿishq*. 2 vols. Tehran: Ṣāliḥ, 1369/1990.
Rizvi, S. Rizwan Ali. *Nizam al-Mulk Tusi*. Lahore: Sh. Muhammad Ashraf, 1978.
Robinson, Francis. *A Historical Atlas of the Islamic World Since 1500*. New York: Facts On File, 1982.
Rosenthal, E. I. J. *Political Thought in Medieval Islam*. Cambridge: Cambridge University Press, 1962.
Rudolph, Kurt. "Heresy: An Overview." *Encyclopedia of Religion*, edited by Mircea Eliade. New York: Macmillan, 1987.
Rypka, Jan. *History of Iranian Literature*. Edited by Karl Jahn. Dordrecht: D. Reidel, 1968.
Safa, Zabihollah [Ṣafā, Dhabīḥ Allāh]. *Tārīkh-i adabīyāt dar Irān*. 5 vols. Tehran: Intishārāt-i Dānishgāh-i Tehran, 1335–64/1956–85.
Safi, Omid. "Abū Saʿīd b. Abi ʾl-Khayr." *Encyclopaedia of Islam*. 3rd ed. Leiden: E. J. Brill, forthcoming.
———. "Aḥmad-i Jām." *Encyclopaedia of Islam*. 3rd ed. Leiden: E. J. Brill, forthcoming.
———. "ʿAyn al-Quḍāt al-Hamadānī." *Encyclopaedia of Islam*. 3rd ed. Leiden: E. J. Brill, forthcoming.
———. "Bargaining with *Baraka*: Persian Sufism, 'Mysticism,' and Politics." *Muslim World* 90:3–4 (2001).
———. "The Sufi Path of Love in Iran and India." In *A Pearl in Wine*, edited by Zia Inayat Khan. New Lebanon, N.Y.: Omega Press, 2001.
———, ed. *Progressive Muslims: On Justice, Gender, and Pluralism*. Oxford: Oneworld Publications, 2003.
Said, Edward. *The Edward Said Reader*. Edited by Moustafa Bayoumi and Andrew Rubin. New York: Vintage, 2000.
———. "Intellectual Exile: Expatriates and Marginals", from *Representations of the Intellectual*. Reprinted in Moustafa Bayoumi and Andrew Rubin, *The Edward Said Reader*.

———. "Secular Criticism," from *The World, The Text, and the Critic*. Reprinted in Bayoumi and Rubin, *The Edward Said Reader*.

"Saldjukids." *E.I.*²

Sanaullah, Mawlawi Fadil. *The Decline of the Saljuqid Empire*. Calcutta: University of Calcutta, 1938.

Sauvaget, Jean. *Quatre Décrets Seldjoukides*. Beirut: Institut Français de Damas, 1947.

Sayar, I. M. "The Empire of the Salčuqids of Asia Minor." *Journal of Near Eastern Studies* 10 (1951): 268–80.

Schact, J. [Revised by C. E. Bosworth] "al-Subkī." *E.I.*²

Schimmel, Annemarie. *Mystical Dimensions of Islam*. Chapel Hill: University of North Carolina Press, 1975.

———. *A Two-Colored Brocade: The Imagery of Persian Poetry*. Chapel Hill: University of North Carolina Press, 1992.

Shils, Edward. "Ideology: The Concept and Function of Ideology." In vol. 7 of *International Encyclopedia of the Social Sciences*, edited by David Sills. New York: Macmillan, 1968–.

Siddiqi, A. H. "Caliphate and Kingship in Medieval Persia." *Islamic Culture* 10 (1936) and 11 (1937).

Smith, John Masson, Jr. "Turanian Nomadism and Iranian Politics." *Iranian Studies* 11 (1978).

Smith, Jonathan Z. *Imagining Religion: From Babylon to Jonestown*. Chicago: Chicago University Press, 1982.

Smith, Wilfred Cantwell. *Faith and Belief*. Princeton: Princeton University Press, 1979.

Sourdel, Dominique. *Le Vizirat ʿAbbasside de 749 à 936 (132 à 324 de l'hégire)*. 2 vols. Damascus: Institut Français de Damas, 1959–60.

Spellberg, Denise. *Politics, Gender, and the Islamic Past*. New York: Columbia University Press, 1996.

Spuler, Bertold. "Disintegration of the Caliphate in the East." In *The Cambridge History of Islam, 1A*. Edited by P. M. Holt, Ann K. S. Lambton, and Bernard Lewis. Cambridge: Cambridge University Press, 1970.

———. "The Evolution of Persian Historiography." In *Historians of the Middle East*, edited by Bernard Lewis and P. M. Holt. London: Oxford University Press, 1962.

———. "Ḥamd Allāh b. Abī Bakr b. Aḥmad b. Naṣr al-Mustawfī al-Ḳazwīnī." *E.I.*²

Steingass, F. *A Comprehensive Persian-English Dictionary*. 1892. Reprint, Beirut: Librairie Du Liban, 1975.

Storey, C. A. [Continued by Francois de Blois]. *Persian Literature: A Bio-Bibliographical Survey*. Vol. 5, part 1 *Poetry to Ca. A.D. 1100*. London: Royal Asiatic Society of Great Britain and Ireland, 1992.

Ṭabāṭabā'ī, Sayyid Jawād. *Darāmadī falsafī bar tārīkh-i andīsha-yi sīyāsī dar Iran*. Tehran: Daftar-i Muṭāliʿāt-i Sīyāsī wa Bayn al-Milalī, 1367/1988.

———. "Munḥanī-yi taḥawwul-i andīsha-yi siyāsī-yi Ghazālī." *Maʿārif* 3:3 (1365/1996).

Teubner, J. K. "ʿAyn al-Ḳuḍāt al-Hamadhānī." *E.I.*²

Thābitī, Sayyid ʿAlī Mu'ayyid. *Tārīkh-i Nīshāpūr*. Tehran: Intishārāt-i Anjuman-i Millī, 1355/1976.

Tibawi, A. L. "Origin and Character of *al-Madrasah*." *BSOAS* 25:2 (1962).

Tilly, Charles. "War Making and State Making as Organized Crime." In *Bringing the State Back In*, edited by Peter Evans, Dietrich Rueschemeyer, and Theda Skopcol. Cambridge: Cambridge University Press, 1985.

Turan, Osman. "The Ideal of World Domination among the Medieval Turks." *Studia Islamica* 4 (1955).

Umar-ud-Din, Muhammad. *The Ethical Philosophy of al-Ghazzali*. Lahore: Sh. Muhammad Ashraf, 1991. [Reprint of earlier edition, n.d.]

Underhill, Evelyn. *Mysticism: A Study in the Nature and Development of Man's Spiritual Consciousness*. London: Methuen, 1911. Reprint, New York: Image Books, 1990.

Watt, W. Montgomery. "Al-Ghazālī, Abū Ḥāmid." *E.I.*[2]

———. "The Authenticity of the Works Attributed to al-Ghazālī." *JRAS* (April 1952).

———. *Muslim Intellectual: A Study of al-Ghazali*. Edinburgh: Edinburgh University Press, 1963.

Yakānī, Ismāʿīl. *Ḥakīm ʿUmar Khayyām: Nādira-yi ayyām*. Tehran: Bahman, 1963.

Yarshater, Ehsan. "Iranian Common Beliefs and World-View." In *The Cambridge History of Iran*. Vol. 3, part 1, *The Seleucid, Parthian and Sasanian Periods*, edited by Ehsan Yarshater. Cambridge: Cambridge University Press, 1983. Reprint, 1996.

Yūsufī, Ghulām-Ḥusayn. "Pīr-i Siyāsat." *Majalla-yi Dānishgāh-i Adabīyāt wa ʿUlūm-i Insānī-yi Mashhad* 4:1–2 (1347/1968).

Zarrīnkūb, ʿAbdul Ḥusayn. *Farār az madrasa*. Tehran: Amīr Kabīr, 1974.

———. *Justjū dar taṣawwuf-i Irān*. Tehran: Intishārāt-i Amīr Kabīr, 1367/1988.

Žižek, Slavoj, ed. *Mapping Ideology*. London: Verso, 1994.

Index

ʿAbbāsid Caliphate: rescue from Ismāʿīlī revolt, xxix; and Niẓām al-Mulk, xxx; and Saljūq politics, xxxi, xl; and Ṭughril Beg, 1–2, 34, 35, 36, 37–39; and Saljūq legitimization, 2, 56, 79, 114; religious legitimization of, 3, 5; and Saljūq military presence, 5; and Buwayhids, 30, 128; on women, 73; and Malik-Shāh's death, 80; and Tarkān Khātūn, 80, 235 (n. 219); and al-Ghazālī, 107, 108–9, 110, 111, 112, 122, 124; and ʿAyn al-Quḍāt Hamadānī, 177; and *maẓālim* system, 198. *See also* Saljūq Sultanate/ʿAbbāsid Caliphate relationship

Abode of Islam (*Dār al-islām*), 11, 15, 16, 17, 75

Abode of the government (*Dār al-Mulk*), 30, 31, 38–39

Abū ʿAlī Ḥasan ibn ʿAlī ibn Isḥāq al-Ṭūsī. *See* Niẓām al-Mulk

Abū Jaʿfar Bāzargān Nīshāpūrī, 138

Abū ʾl-Faraj, Gregory. *See* Bar Hebraeus

Abū ʾl-Futūḥ ʿAbbās, Khwāja Imām, 142, 143

Abū ʾl-Maḥāsin, Sayyid al-Ruʾasāʾ, 66, 211

Abū Muḥammad al-Ḥasan ibn Manṣūr al-Samʿānī, 48

Abū Nuʿaym al-Iṣfahānī, xxv

Abū Saʿīd-i Abī ʾl-Khayr: and Saljūq ideology, xxv, li; and Niẓām al-Mulk, xxvii, xxxii, xli, xliii, 48–49, 50, 131, 137, 138, 139, 141–44, 204, 229 (n. 36); and Ṭughril Beg and Chaghrī Beg, xxvii, xl, xlii–xliii, 137, 139–40; and hagiographies, xxxii, lii, 126–27, 130–31, 137–44, 243 (n. 6), 247 (n. 83); and khānaqāh, xlii, 87, 98, 99, 100; and Sufis' social role, 127, 208; and Saljūq dynasty, 128; and Saljūq legitimization, 131, 137, 139–40, 158; and Bābā Ṭāhir, 132; and *aʿyān*, 137, 245–46 (n. 59); feasts of, 141, 247 (n. 76); and Aḥmad-i Jām, 145; and Saljūq politics, 146, 199; sociohistorical context of, 157; and ʿAyn al-Quḍāt Hamadānī, 170, 178–79, 200, 254 (n. 105)

Abū Ṭāhir (grandson of Abū Saʿīd), 139, 215 (n. 2)

Abū ʿUmarū Ḥaskū, 138, 141

Ādharbāijān, 23, 33

Afrāsiyāb (Tūrānī king), 13, 219 (n. 71)

Aḥmad-i Jām: and Saljūq ideology, xxv, li; and Sanjar, xxvii, xxxii, xl, xliv, li, lii, 131, 137, 144, 145, 146, 147–53, 155–56, 249 (nn. 125, 126); and hagiographies, xxxii, lii, 129–30, 144–45, 149–53, 244 (n. 23), 247 (n. 88); and Saljūq politics, xliii–xliv, 146, 149, 244 (n. 23); and Saljūq legitimization, li, 131, 146, 148, 158; and Saljūq dynasty, 128; writings of, 145–49, 247 (n. 95); and Saljūq orthodoxy, 146, 148–49, 156, 248 (n. 105); shrine of, 153, 155, 249 (n. 120); sociohistorical context of, 157

Alamūt, 74, 203

Alexander the Great, 12, 72

ʿAlī b. Abī Ṭalib (A), 121

Alp Arslān, Sultan: and Niẓām al-Mulk, xl, 44, 45, 51, 52, 53, 56, 57–60, 61, 88, 94; Saljūq Sultanate/ʿAbbāsid Caliphate relationship, 35, 58; and coins, 41; and ʿAmīd al-Mulk Kundurī, 57; death of, 60–61; Malik-Shāh compared to, 63; and surveillance and reconnaissance, 84, 101, 239 (n. 108); and land-grant system, 88; and

Islamic Civilization and Muslim Networks

Omid Safi, *The Politics of Knowledge in Premodern Islam: Negotiating Ideology and Religious Inquiry* (2006).

Ebrahim Moosa, *Ghazālī and the Poetics of Imagination* (2005).

miriam cooke and Bruce B. Lawrence, eds., *Muslim Networks from Hajj to Hip Hop* (2005).

Carl W. Ernst, *Following Muhammad: Rethinking Islam in the Contemporary World* (2003).